ALSO BY TED STEINBERG

DOWN TO EARTH
NATURE'S ROLE IN AMERICAN HISTORY

Fourth Edition

TED STEINBERG
Case Western Reserve University

NEW YORK   OXFORD
OXFORD UNIVERSITY PRESS

Oxford University Press is a department of the University of Oxford.
It furthers the University's objective of excellence in research, scholarship,
and education by publishing worldwide. Oxford is a registered trade mark of
Oxford University Press in the UK and certain other countries.

Published in the United States of America by Oxford University Press
198 Madison Avenue, New York, NY 10016, United States of America.

Library of Congress Cataloging-in-Publication Data
Names: Steinberg, Theodore, 1961- author.
Title: Down to earth : nature's role in American history / Ted Steinberg,
    Case Western Reserve University.
Description: Fourth Edition. | New York : Oxford University Press, [2018] |
    Previous edition: 2013. | Includes bibliographical references and index.
Identifiers: LCCN 2018006201| ISBN 9780190864422 (Paperback) | ISBN
    9780190864439 (E-Book)
Subjects: LCSH: Human ecology—United States—History. | Philosophy of
    nature—United States—History. | Human beings—Effect of environment
    of—United States—History. | United States—Environmental conditions.
Classification: LCC GF27 .S85 2018 | DDC 304.20973—dc23 LC record available
at https://lccn.loc.gov/2018006201

9 8 7 6 5 4 3 2
Printed by LSC Communications, Inc., United States of America

TO DONALD WORSTER

CONTENTS

ACKNOWLEDGMENTS

I would like to thank the following people who devoted time to improving this fourth edition of the book: Maria Del Monaco, Allen Dieterich-Ward, Shippensburg University; Andrew Dorchak, Case Western Reserve University School of Law; Greg O'Brien, University of North Carolina–Greensboro; and Jesse Tarbert. Jim O'Brien is my indispensable critic and comrade in the quest for a better world. I can't imagine working on any writing project, no matter how minor, without him. At Oxford University Press, I have had the good fortune to work with Charles Cavaliere and Rowan Wixted. Jana MacIsaac oversaw the production of the book with patience from her base in Lewiston, Maine, a place I have grown fond of recently. Finally, my gratitude to Sarah Vogelsong for straightening out the English.

PREFACE

This book will try to change the way you think about American history. It deals with some familiar topics, such as colonization, the industrial revolution, slavery, the Civil War, and the growth of cities, and some not-so-well-known topics, such as the Little Ice Age, horse manure, pigsties, fast food, lawns, SUVs, electronics, and garbage. I will argue that the natural world—defined here as plants and animals, climate and weather, soil and water—has profoundly shaped the American past.

Historians, of course, have not completely overlooked nature. Virtually every U.S. history textbook has an obligatory section on Theodore Roosevelt and the conservation movement, as well as a brief discussion of the environmental reforms that began in the 1960s. Nature as politics has long been the main concern. You are unlikely to learn anything about the role of climate or soil fertility in history. Little about how Americans and Indians before them went about the task of feeding themselves. Virtually nothing about pigs, chickens, cows, and corn—or hamburgers, despite the important role that McDonald's plays in the lives of so many people. Nothing about global warming or cooling. Not a word about volcanic eruptions across the world that led to hunger in America.

For most members of the profession and, almost by definition, for most Americans, history unfolds against a stable environmental backdrop. Nature is taken for granted and passed over in the rush to discuss wars, elections, and the other mainstays of political and intellectual history. Social history, pioneered during the 1960s and centered on exploring the lives of ordinary people, has proved no more receptive to the idea of nature as a dynamic force. Practicing history "from the bottom up," as some social historians once put it, meant digging down into the nitty-gritty of everyday existence, into work, family life, sexual orientation, gender relations, and race. But the social historians retired their shovels when they reached the land and soil itself.

For the last century, most historians have written books as if natural forces did not affect the events the books describe. The stories that unfold across these pages, however, demonstrate that the natural world is hardly an unchanging backdrop to the past. The industrial revolution, for example, did not take place in a setting from which nature was somehow magically excluded. New England factories never would have developed in the way that they did were the region not blessed with the ample precipitation and rivers required to power the cotton mills. Even a world-shattering political and military event like the Civil War was shaped by ecological factors. Soldiers and horses needed to be fed, and for that to happen, both the Union and the Confederacy had to turn to the land. Robert E. Lee may have been a brilliant military strategist, but between battles, he found himself scouring the land for forage for his army's horses. Likewise, the growth of modern auto-centered suburbs hardly liberated people from nature. Natural forces impinged on suburban life, at times dramatically, as homeowners confronted landslides, floods, fires, and outbreaks of insects and weeds. Nature has not been nearly as passive and unchanging as historians have led us to believe.

Writing history "from the ground up" means rethinking the time periods that have thus far defined the American past. Three turning points, corresponding to the parts of this book, are worth our attention. First, the European arrival in North America produced ecological tumult galore as the populations of two long-isolated landmasses suddenly came into contact with one another. European colonizers introduced a new approach to the earth, transforming it with complex legal instruments into pieces of "land" that could be bought and sold. Never before in North America had the earth been viewed in such a way. Even so, this still remained a world in which natural forces—climate especially—played an outsized role in determining the course of history.[1]

A second turning point was becoming evident by the end of the eighteenth century. Both Indians and many ordinary Euro-Americans found themselves losing their direct connection with the land and forced to rely for their survival on more indirect interactions with nature. These dealings were mediated by a market economy organized to advance the interests of capitalists, that is, those seeking to profit from combining the labor of others and the riches found on the earth. Everything from water and birds to trees and even buffalo bones eventually came under the thumb of economic institutions bent on the accumulation of wealth.

Turning point number three came with the rise of consumerism in the late nineteenth century, with its automobiles, brand-name foods, and other innovative products. The modern corporation was the primary architect of this new economic order. Once a relatively insignificant institution chartered by the state to perform some public service—such as building a bridge or canal—and often harnessed to the public good by legal restrictions, the corporation had by the Gilded Age lost its public soul. Changes in the law soon legally bound the corporation to act solely on behalf of its shareholders, regardless of the impact on the natural world or the public welfare. In the name of shareholder profits, companies selling everything from waterpower to, eventually, cars and computers transferred the costs of business to the environment and the public, profoundly affecting not just the American landscape but the entire planet as capitalism evolved to dominate the earth's physical, chemical, and biological processes.[2]

* * *

My argument in this book is that the transformation of nature—land, water, trees, animals, minerals—into a commodity (a thing that can be traded for profit) was the most important single force behind environmental change. It was not the only factor, of course, but it has been and remains the most important one.

Putting a price tag on the natural world and forcing it to do service in the interests of economic growth constitute the material foundation of the capitalist system. *Capitalism* is a difficult word to define. I think of it as a socioecological system in which large numbers of people lose their connection with the earth and are thus left with little choice but to make money selling their labor in order to survive, lest they go bankrupt and starve. Its roots go back to fifteenth-century England, where landlords, in a quest for more rent, first began compelling tenants to push the land harder to increase output and sell what they grew on the market or risk being thrown off the land. Everyone—whether a tenant, a landlord, or a landless person—was soon subjected to market forces to buy and sell labor, a development precipitated by the "enclosure movement." This was the process whereby wealthier farmers accumulated plots of land, wiped out customs of shared use that peasants depended on to survive, and instead specialized in, for example, raising sheep in order to produce wool for profit. People began to compete with one another to produce more cost-effectively and eventually turned to accumulating and maximizing profits because there was no other choice in a world in which everyone was dependent on the market for survival. A system founded on competition and maximizing imperatives is, of course, one prone to expansion, and that, it turned out, is precisely what happened when, under the stewardship of the United States, capitalism evolved in the latter part of the twentieth century to conquer virtually the entire planet.[3]

Capitalism has long been understood as a system that exploits wage laborers, paying them less than the value that they produce, say, on the factory floor. It is also, however, a system that creates wealth by extracting value from the natural world. And the chief means for organizing the earth into the raw materials necessary for the production of wealth is the commodity.

Commodities have a kind of magical quality about them. When people think of an orange or a piece of lumber, they tend to view its very essence as bound up in its price. Monetary value, in other words, is seen as being intrinsic to the commodity in question, ingrained within the object itself. Commodities thus often obscure from view the human labor that produced them in the first place. Karl Marx called attention to this phenomenon back in the nineteenth century. In this book I will show that more than simply social relationships between workers and owners became masked in the process of commodification. Human relations with nature—the logging of forests, damming of rivers, plowing of grasslands, and other attempts to significantly transform ecosystems—suffered a similar fate. The benefits of modern living, from fast food to flush toilets to cell phones, for all their virtues, have come at the price of ecological amnesia.

Environmental history centers on the examination of various relationships—how natural forces shaped history, how humankind impacted nature, and how

those ecological changes then turned around to influence human life in a re-
ciprocating pattern. The field's practitioners are thus well equipped to examine
the ramifying effects and hidden costs of development, bringing previously obscure relationships into sharp relief. Investigating the California Gold Rush, for
example, we discover how this event helped to trigger an ecological crisis far
away on the Great Plains. Exploring the conservation of tourist-friendly animals
in national parks reveals this policy's damaging effects on the survival strategies of poor whites and Indians. Examining an activity as mundane as eating a
steak brings to light meat production's drain on the West's underground water
supply. Even something as seemingly immaterial as an Internet search requires
the cooperation of some of North America's mightiest rivers to power the vast,
electricity-intensive data centers operated by Google and other companies. Environmental history is full of many such surprises.

We must acknowledge the unpredictability and, indeed, the limits involved
in incorporating nature into human designs. As Marx wrote, people "make their
own history, but they do not make it just as they please."[4] He had economic
forces in mind, but his statement applies as well to the world of nature, to the
far-reaching climatic, biological, and geological processes that have determined
the possibilities open to human beings on this planet. When it comes to human
control of nature, beware: the wind shifts, the earth moves, and a flock of birds
swoops in for a meal.

NEW TO THE FOURTH EDITION

This fourth edition of *Down to Earth* includes:
- A revised preface that articulates more clearly the major turning points in
  the environmental history of America
- A revised Part One that offers a treatment of the separation of Indians and
  ordinary Euro-Americans from the earth as the eighteenth century came
  to a close
- Changes to all chapters that explain nature's role in the rise of the United
  States as the world's paramount power
- A substantial revision of Chapter 16 that takes account of recent work in
  the history and theory of capitalism to explain more precisely the global
  ecological changes that have occurred since World War II and the United
  States' role in bringing them about
- An updated bibliography

DOWN TO EARTH

PROLOGUE

ROCKS AND HISTORY

Open a U.S. history textbook and glued inside the cover will likely be a familiar map of the nation, as if the place were simply a given. But land is a much less settled issue than those maps suggest. While historians have spent a great deal of time examining how various immigrant groups came to America, they have spent almost no time considering how America itself—the land—came to be where it is on the globe. In this sense, U.S. history began not in 1607 with Jamestown, in 1492 with Columbus, or even thousands of years before then whenever the first Paleoindians came here. Rather, American history got underway 180 million years ago when the earth's only continent, a huge landmass known as Pangaea, began to break apart.

At first, Pangaea split into two parts. Then, as the Atlantic Ocean expanded, North America separated from Africa and later from South America. Slowly, the continents began to take their present positions on the globe. By about 60 million years ago, North America—the discrete and contiguous landmass we know today—had been born.

From this one momentous geological occurrence, a host of profound consequences followed. Separated from the so-called Old World of Eurasia, life forms in North and South America developed in isolation, explaining why Europeans who ventured to the New World for the first time were so struck, at times even horrified, by the continent's strange new plants and animals, especially its bison, moose, cougars, alligators, and rattlesnakes. Continental drift also explains why the Americas, severed from Eurasia by water, were the last of the habitable continents to be settled by humankind. When the Paleoindians did reach these places, they lived in isolation from Europeans and their diseases, a fact that would have a stunning impact in post-Columbian times. Indeed, without the breakup of Pangaea, the entire rationale for Columbus's voyage simply would not have existed. The year 1492 would be of no particular importance, the national holiday honoring Columbus just another ordinary autumn day.

Nowhere is it written that U.S. history must begin with the breakup of Pangaea. Beginnings are in themselves quite arbitrary. One could just as easily start the story with the emergence of life 4 billion years ago or even the development of the earth itself 500 million years before that. But beginnings do tell us a great deal about an author's underlying assumptions. When historians open their narrative of the American republic with Columbus or, as is more common today, with Paleoindians trekking across the Bering Strait, they put forth a very anthropocentric view of the past, one in which history begins when people come onto the scene. But by dwelling, as most U.S. historians do, on such a relatively short expanse of time—1492 or even 12,000 B.C. to the present—it is easy to lose sight of the powerful natural forces that have played such a formative role in the history of this country. It becomes easy to forget that the earth's climate, geology, and ecology are not simply a backdrop to, but an active, shaping force in, the historical process.

History is structured by a vast array of natural factors: geological forces that determine if minerals will be available for mining, if the soil will be fertile enough for planting crops, and if sufficient water and level land exist to grow those crops; ecological forces that determine which forms of plant and animal life will be available for domestication, and if there will be adequate forests to supply timber; and climatic forces that determine if enough frost-free days will occur to permit an ample harvest. Such natural factors—largely beyond the control of human beings—have had enormous impacts on how the past has unfolded.

Thus America's place on the globe, while often glossed over and forgotten, needs to be taken seriously. The land area of the United States is uniquely positioned to capture a relatively large amount of solar energy—the key ingredient for transforming inorganic matter and water into food through the process known as photosynthesis. Food crops such as wheat, corn, soybeans, and oranges, among others, flourish in the nation's temperate climate, rich soils, and abundant sunlight, explaining why California and the central part of the nation are in the front ranks of world food production.[1] Imagine how severely curtailed the food supply would be were the present continental United States rotated 90 degrees. Such a move would make the nation's north–south dimension three times its distance from east to west, instead of the other way around. Spanning many more degrees of latitude and with much of its landmass now lying outside the temperate zone, America would be far less suitable for agriculture.

Continental drift is hardly the only geological episode to have far-reaching consequences for American history. Consider the birth of the Rocky Mountains and its effect on the biogeography of the world's breadbasket, the Great Plains. Before the creation of the mountains, a process geologists refer to as the Laramide Orogeny, beginning 80 million years ago, the Great Plains were a tremendous inland sea. The emergence of the Rockies, however, plugged water's entry from the Pacific and Arctic oceans, creating conditions favorable to the eventual emergence of forest cover on the plains. The mountains also dried out the land by

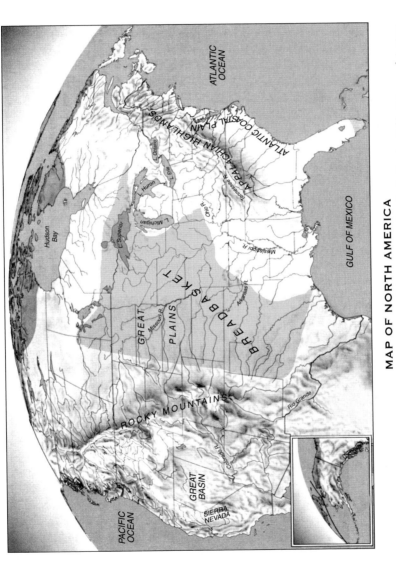

MAP OF NORTH AMERICA

(Adapted from *Out of Many*, vol. 2, Brief 3ʳᵈ ed., *A History of the American People*, by Faragher, Buhle, Czitron, and Armitage, © 2001, by permission of Pearson Education, Inc., Upper Saddle River, NJ.)

capturing the moisture of clouds on their windward side, creating a huge rain shadow that left the leeward plains in an even more arid state, an environment suitable for the growth of grass. Meanwhile, the rain that did fall in the mountains washed away sediments and deposited them farther east with each passing year, covering the old seabed with a layer of loose silt that was hundreds of feet thick and producing in the process one of the most level stretches of land on earth. The Rockies, by drying out the landscape of the plains, forced plant life to adapt accordingly. Grasses have complicated root systems that can exploit even the smallest amount of moisture; they flourish in such an environment. Into these grasslands the American pioneer eventually forged, prepared to break the sod and replace it with another grass: the wheat that was also so fabulously adapted to life in an arid locale.

That was not all the Laramide mountain-building episode did to contribute to America's rise to world economic dominance. It also broke up granite and metamorphic rocks, allowing metallic minerals to insinuate themselves into the faults left behind. Gold, silver, zinc, lead, and copper settled that much nearer the earth's surface, where they could be mined with relative ease. Without this geological episode there would have been no mineral belt running through the state and no Colorado gold rush in the 1850s. Nor would the United States be the so-called Saudi Arabia of coal—possessor of more than one-fourth of the world's supply—had the uplift of the Rocky Mountains not helped create the super-rich coal lands of Wyoming and Montana. The Laramide revolution was but one geological event on the nation's road to wealth. The combined effect of the region's geological history accounts for North America's near-total self-sufficiency in minerals. As one geologist has exclaimed, "No other continent has it so good!"[2]

One other event from the distant past is also worth our attention: the Pleistocene epoch that began 1.6 million years ago, the period commonly referred to as the Ice Age. During this time, huge glaciers, as much as one to two miles thick, covered the northern reaches of the continent (as well as Europe and Asia). Tundra stretched out over what is now Manhattan. The ice expanded south and then retreated on 18 to 20 different occasions. The switches between these glacial and interglacial periods are not completely understood, but many attribute them to the Milankovitch cycle, named after the Yugoslav geophysicist who discovered this phenomenon back in the 1920s. From time to time, he observed, the earth's orbit around the sun changes, sometimes placing the planet closer where it can receive more heat, and sometimes placing it farther away, making the climate colder and producing a glaciation. Altogether, glacial conditions have prevailed for 90 percent of the last few million years. Beginning about 10,000 years ago, however, the climate shifted and the ice sheet that covered much of Canada and the northern United States withdrew. It is no coincidence that American history has taken place during an interglacial period. Indeed, it is difficult to imagine the course U.S. history might have taken—or whether there would even be a United States—had the earth's orbit not changed and the ice not retreated.

It is also sobering to note that although there is much concern today with global warming, in the long run it may be cold—that is, the return of another ice age—that will turn out to be our true nemesis.

Like continental drift and mountain building, glaciation too has had tremendous consequences for life on this continent. U.S. agriculture, in particular, has benefited greatly. When the glaciers retreated on several occasions from the Great Plains, they left behind a fine soil deposit called loess. The loess was eventually driven east by the prevailing westerly winds, finding its way to Kansas, Nebraska, Iowa, Wisconsin, and Indiana and providing the basis for rich, fertile soil—in some places 20 feet thick. Likewise, the soils of eastern Canada were scraped up and dumped by the glacier in the Midwest, again bolstering the fertility of U.S. farms. It was not for nothing that the nineteenth-century geologist Louis Agassiz dubbed the glaciers "God's great plough."[3]

Without these soils, without the requisite sunlight and the right climate, America would not be the world's breadbasket. John Deere with his "singing plow" and Cyrus McCormick with his famed reaper would have been obscure tinkerers with projects of little practical importance, instead of icons discussed in virtually every American history textbook. Such are the implications of the really long view of the past. Suddenly the earth itself becomes an actor, a force to be reckoned with, instead of a simple line drawing inside a book's cover.

PART ONE

ALIENATION IN THE LAND

WILDERNESS UNDER FIRE

If only we really knew who the first human being was to stumble into the New World! As it turns out, the peopling of North America remains clouded in considerable mystery.

For some time archeologists held that human beings trekked out of Siberia no earlier than 18,000 years ago and ventured across the Bering land bridge headed for Alaska. Within less than a millennium, they traveled the length of the continents, venturing to the Great Plains and the American Southwest—where their stone points were first discovered in Clovis, New Mexico—eventually ending up at the tip of South America. More recent evidence discovered in Chile, however, suggests that human beings arrived long before the Clovis people, as early as 23,000 years ago. Perhaps these early settlers came by sea. What we can be certain of is that two formerly uninhabited continents were quite suddenly—in geologic time at least—brought into the orbit of *Homo sapiens*. This was a discovery on a scale that can never be repeated on this planet.[1]

Did these early settlers walk lightly on the earth, extracting a living ever so gently from nature, leaving behind a pristine wilderness? The short answer is no. Human presence always brings with it environmental impacts, which is to say that these people were not without a history. Whether these impacts rose to the level of what might today be called significant ecological degradation is, according to paleo-ecologists at least, doubtful. Nearly all of human history, save for the last 150 years, unfolded in a world in which climate, especially drought and cold, overshadowed any possibility of human domination of the earth.[2]

OVERKILL

When the Paleoindians arrived on the Great Plains, they found a great variety of large mammals. Some were of almost grotesque stature: mammoths weighing between eight and nine tons (50 percent more than an African elephant), three-ton ground sloths, beavers the size of bears, 500-pound tapirs, creatures known as pampatheres that were akin to armadillos but with the size of a rhinoceros. Other large animals on a more familiar scale included camels, saber-toothed cats, cheetahs, lions, antelopes, and horses. All roamed the American West, and all went extinct sometime before 10,000 years ago, near the end of the Pleistocene epoch.

CRYING INDIAN

This advertisement, which became an American icon in the 1970s, helped popularize the erroneous idea of Indians as conservationists. (Keep America Beautiful, Inc.)

Much scientific evidence points to changes in global climatic conditions as the cause of these extinctions. Temperatures increased dramatically and the climate became more arid near the end of the Pleistocene. Even worse from the standpoint of living organisms was the onset of large swings in seasonal temperatures that resulted in much colder winters and hotter summers. Plant and insect communities sensitive to such shifts confronted a new and far less hospitable physical reality. The creation of radically different habitats, goes the theory, had dire consequences for the megafauna, as the animals found less food to eat. It is even possible that the growth of new toxic species of grass poisoned the mastodons and other large creatures.[3]

Not all scientists agree that climate keyed the mass extinctions. Some researchers hold the Paleoindians themselves to blame. Waging the equivalent of a prehistoric "blitzkrieg," they argue, the Paleoindians exterminated animals unprepared to deal with being attacked by human beings, who might kill a mammoth one day, a ground sloth the next, as they expanded south down through the continents. Little in the way of archeological or other evidence, however, supports the view that human beings played the central role in the Pleistocene extinctions. A variant of this theory holds that large predators had kept the populations of megafauna in check and that when the "super-predator" Paleoindians arrived, their hunting destabilized the prevailing ecosystem and caused it to crash, leading to the eradication of the megafauna. According to both versions of this theory, the continent's first settlers were hardly the low-impact stewards of the land that they are often made out to be. Nevertheless, over the course of the last 10 million years North America has experienced several other such episodes of extinction, and in none of these events was humankind the culprit. That would seem to leave the changing climate as the likely suspect, although no available scientific evidence definitively proves that the megafauna starved to death.[4]

Perhaps more important than precisely what caused the extinctions is the legacy left by this catastrophic annihilation. It is not too much to say that the Pleistocene extinctions altered the course of modern history, depriving America of valuable animal wealth. Although the exact number of species exterminated remains unclear, unquestionably the vast bulk of North America's large mammals disappeared in the event. That left the continent in a state of biological impoverishment. It is no accident that of the 14 species of big domesticated animals relied on by cultures around the world for food, clothing, and transportation (the cow, pig, horse, sheep, and goat being the most important), only one, the llama, was domesticated in the Americas. The remaining 13 all came from Eurasia. The New World originally had a single species of horse, and unfortunately it was exterminated during the Pleistocene. History might indeed have unfolded differently if the European explorers of the sixteenth century had ventured to the Americas to face a mounted cavalry.[5]

HIGH AND LOW COUNTERS

Although a great deal of ink has been spilled on the subject, we still have only a vague idea of North America's Indian populations at the time of European contact. The native peoples kept no records, and with no direct demographic evidence available, researchers have had to devise various methods for estimating the continent-wide population from European observations recorded in diaries and other written sources. Early estimates done in the mid-nineteenth century— one by artist George Catlin, the other by missionary Emmanuel Domenech— concluded that the aboriginal peoples numbered roughly 16 to 17 million at the time of European arrival. When bona fide researchers got out their pencils and pads, however, the numbers plummeted. In 1928, the disciples of ethnologist James Mooney, the first scholar to study the problem, put forth a figure that was only slightly over a million.

How did Mooney and his colleagues arrive at such a small number? Employing what some have labeled a "bottom-up" approach, Mooney calculated a total population for each nation in North America based on historical evidence provided by European missionaries and soldiers—only he chose to lower the figures given by these white observers. He reasoned that soldiers may have felt compelled to overestimate indigenous peoples as a way to enhance the magnitude of their own accomplishments. Victory over 10,000 Indians certainly looked better on paper than a triumph over half as many. After discounting the historical record, Mooney then simply added together the numbers he had deduced for the various nations. His million-person estimate endured for several decades and is still sometimes cited by conservative pundits eager to show that North America was largely virgin land populated by small communities of hunters before the Europeans arrived on the scene to pave the way for civilization. Today, however, most researchers reject this extremely low number.[6]

In 1966, anthropologist Henry Dobyns created a huge stir when he proposed a figure in the 10 to 12 million–person range, revising that number upward in 1983 to 18 million. Employing a "top-down" approach, Dobyns used "depopulation ratios" based on his assessment of how various epidemic diseases—the most significant factor in the decline of Native American populations—affected the various Indian groups. He then broke up the continent into regions and multiplied the lowest figure for each area by the ratio, yielding a far higher population estimate than Mooney's. Predictably, Dobyns and the so-called high counters have been accused of being pro-Indian. The dispute over the size of the indigenous population rages on, as scholars debate the role in the Indians' demographic collapse played not only by disease but by the disruption of trade routes, warfare, and mass murder.[7]

If the population in 1492 was indeed much closer to 18 million than to 1 million, then the rationale behind European conquest begins to unravel. The Europeans justified wresting the land from its indigenous inhabitants on the grounds that scattered settlements of native peoples—practicing a mobile existence, no less—failed to make good use of it. Increase the size of the indigenous population, however, and the Europeans can begin to look more like thieves bent on genocide than "settlers" of virgin land.

MANY EGG BASKETS

To survive in North America, the Indians exploited the seasonal diversity of the continent's various landscapes. This was especially true in the far northern reaches of New England, where cold and frost, in addition to the stony soil deposited by the glaciers, made agriculture a risky and difficult venture. Compelled to adopt hunting and gathering as strategies for survival, Native American peoples found that in temperate climates, the spring and summer months offered a plentiful supply of food. From March through May, Indian nations in the northern part of what is today the United States used nets, weirs, and canoes to catch fish on their way to spawn upstream, while migrating birds such as Canada geese and mourning doves further bolstered the food supply. In the summer months, they also gathered various kinds of nuts and berries. In the fall, as the temperature turned colder and the region's plants began storing energy in their roots, the Indians ventured inland to find other sources of food. Eventually breaking up into small hunting groups, men set off after beaver, moose, deer, and bear, tracking the animals through the snow; women cleaned and prepared the meat while tending to the campsites. In contrast to the summer, when food was in abundance, February and March often spelled privation, especially if a lack of snow made it more difficult to follow the animals. The Indians in this region thus exploited various habitats, migrating across the landscape depending on the season of the year. As one European observer noted, "They move . . . from one place to another according to the richness of the site and the season."[8]

In the South, a warmer climate more conducive to agriculture allowed indigenous peoples to combine farming with hunting and gathering to produce an even more secure subsistence diet. With the onset of warmer weather, late in February or early in March, men built fires to clear trees and ready the ground for planting. Women then formed the soil into small hills, on which they sowed corn and beans, while planting squash and pumpkins in trenches between the mounds. Mixing such crops together had a number of important benefits that typically led to bumper agricultural yields. As the different plants competed for sunlight and moisture, the seed stock eventually became hardier. The crop mix may also have cut down on pests, as insects lost sight of their favorite crop in the tangled mass of stalks. Meanwhile, bacteria found on the roots of the beans helped to replace the nitrogen that the corn sucked out of the soil, enhancing the field's fertility. But the so-called nitrogen-fixing bacteria were never able to add back all of the nitrogen lost, and fertility eventually declined, spurring the Indians to move on to find another area of trees to burn.[9]

Southern Indians scheduled hunting and gathering around their shifting agricultural pursuits. In the spring, after burning the trees, men set off to catch fish. In the summer, the Indians along the coast moved inland to hunt turkeys and squirrels and gather berries, returning back downstream in time to harvest crops in the fall. These Indians were so attuned to the seasonal variation that characterized the forest that they often gave the months such names as "herring month" (March) or "strawberry month" (June) to describe the food they had come to expect from the landscape. Meanwhile, as the weather turned colder, nuts and acorns proliferated, attracting deer and bears. As the animals fattened themselves on the food, their coats became thicker, making them inviting targets for Indians, who in the winter hunted them for meat and clothing.[10]

A similar seasonal subsistence cycle based on farming and hunting and collecting prevailed on the Great Plains. Apart from the climate, which despite its potential for drought favored agriculture, the soil of the midwestern prairies was as much as a full foot deeper than the two to four inches commonly found in New England.

In the valleys of the Platte, Loup, and Republican rivers in present-day Nebraska and Kansas, the Pawnee capitalized on the excellent soil and favorable weather conditions to develop their own system of subsistence. Areas were first burned during the early spring. Women then sowed corn, beans, and squash in small plots during April and May, hoeing them periodically. Women also spent the spring gathering Indian potatoes, an abundant root crop on which local populations often relied in periods of scarcity. In July and August the Pawnee packed up the dry foods—both wild and domesticated—that they had harvested in the river valleys and journeyed to the mixed-grass prairie west of the 98th meridian to hunt buffalo. (Buffalo thrive on the grasses of this region—blue grama, buffalo grass, and red three-awn—primarily because they are easy to digest.) In September, the Pawnee returned to the river valleys to harvest their crops, before leaving again in November for the plains to hunt buffalo. The primary goal of this system of hunting and horticulture—in existence for centuries before the coming of white settlers to the plains region—was to obtain a diversified set of food sources. It might be termed a "not-putting-all-your-eggs-in-one-basket" approach to deriving a living from the land.[11]

Obviously the indigenous peoples transformed the ecology of North America in order to survive. Two points about their particular relationship with the land are worth underscoring. First, ample evidence suggests that in many instances, Native American communities exploited the landscape in a way that maintained species population and diversity. In California, for instance, Indians pruned shrubs for the purpose of basket making but took care to do so during the dormant fall or winter period when the plant's future health would not be jeopardized. Similarly, shifting agriculture tended to mimic natural patterns, unlike modern agriculture with its emphasis on single-crop production. Second, dietary security, not the maximization of crop yields, was the most important focus of Native American subsistence. At times this decision not to stockpile food could hurt populations, even if it contributed to long-term ecological balance. It was common in northern New England for Indians to go hungry and even starve during February and March (when animal populations dipped) rather than to store more food during the summer for winter use. While this failure to maximize food sources may have jeopardized Indian lives, it also helped to keep population densities relatively low. The low density, in turn, may have contributed to the overall stability of these ecosystems, preserving the future prospects of indigenous modes of food production. North America suffered from a relative lack of biological resources when compared with Eurasia, but the Indian peoples managed to see in the land a vast expanse of possibilities for ensuring food security.[12]

PLEASE FORGIVE US

None of this is meant to suggest that the indigenous peoples viewed the land and its plant and animal life in only a practical light. In fact, Native Americans invested nature with a great deal of symbolic value, engaging in ritual behavior and telling stories that tended to complicate the relationship they had with the natural world.

Indian understandings of animals are a case in point. Among the Northern Algonquian, for example, the boundary between people and game animals appears to have been quite fluid and porous. Beavers were seen as participating in social relationships with human beings. One account of the killing of a bear from the 1760s observed that Ojibwe hunters took the animal's head "in their hands, stroking and kissing it several times; begging a thousand pardons for taking away her life; calling her their relation and grandmother."[13] Unlike the Europeans, who tended to uphold a clear and distinct difference between themselves and the animal world, some Indian groups seemed inclined to blur such boundaries.

The Cherokee Indians in the South believed that the deer they hunted experienced emotions just as human beings did. Were they to fail to treat deer with the proper respect, the animals, as the Indians saw it, would become angry and exact revenge on the hunters. According to one Cherokee teaching, if a hunter forgot to ask forgiveness for killing a deer, he might make the animal so vengeful that it would retaliate by inflicting disease. The emotional bond they had with animals, in combination with the fear of retaliation, may have led the Cherokee to refrain from killing more creatures than they needed to survive, creating, in the words of one anthropologist, a kind of "natural balance" based on the idea that "nature is capable of striking back."[14] In general, Native Americans had a far more symbolically rich understanding of nature than the Europeans, who generally embraced a utilitarian stance toward game.

FIRE AND FOREST

No Indian practice has done more to counter the view of precontact America as a wilderness than the indigenous peoples' use of fire. Ecological data indicate that fire commonly occurred in North America prior to European settlement. With scientific evidence revealing that it would have been impossible for lightning strikes alone to have caused these conflagrations, that leaves the Native Americans as the likely instigators. By the eve of European settlement, large parts of the continent had been radically transformed from forest into open ground—a point underlined by European observers. Of the area near Salem, Massachusetts, the Rev. Francis Higginson wrote in 1630, "I am told that about three miles from us a man may stand on a little hilly place and see diverse thousands of acres of ground as good as need to be, and not a Tree on the same." The Puritan Edward Johnson remarked that New England was "thin of Timber in many places, like our Parkes in England."[15]

Similar observations about the openness of the landscape were made farther south as well. One Andrew White, on a trip along the Potomac in 1633, remarked that the forest was "not choked up with an undergrowth of brambles and bushes, but as if laid out by hand in a manner so open, that you might freely drive a four horse chariot in the midst of the trees." After arriving in Florida in 1538, Hernando de Soto and his party of 600 men spent three years exploring a large section of the South, including parts of present-day Georgia, Alabama, Mississippi, Arkansas, and Louisiana. On their extensive travels they found the land—save for swamps—to be eminently unobstructed.[16]

Besides a source of ignition, it takes favorable weather in combination with fuels dry enough to burn for a wildland fire to start. Some parts of North America (Florida) are more conducive to fire than others (New England). But within these geographic parameters, the Indian nations seem to have burned the land for a number of different reasons. In the South especially, burning provided a frontline defense against fleas, biting flies, mosquitoes, and ticks. By thinning the forest, burning also facilitated travel and hunting and made it easier for Indians to avoid surprise attacks from human and animal enemies. On the Great Plains, they lit fires to signal the discovery of buffalo herds or the approach of whites.

Fire also played an important role in Indian subsistence strategies. It was especially useful in creating environments attractive to game animals such as deer, elk, turkey, and quail. In various parts of the East, burning the land fostered the so-called edge effect, creating an area of open meadowland on the border of a forest. A variety of wildlife flocked to such edge habitats, where Indian hunters easily dispatched them.[17]

Indigenous peoples also employed fire more directly to improve hunting prospects. Across the continent, they used fire to surround animals such as deer and buffalo, killing them as they passed through the one possible path left open (on purpose) for escape. The Sioux, for example, were known to set fire to the plains during buffalo hunts. According to one observer, the buffalo, "having a great dread of fire, retire towards the centre of the grasslands as they see it approach, and here being pressed together in great numbers, many are trampled under foot, and the Indians rushing in with their arrows and musketry, slaughter immense numbers in a short period."[18]

After nations such as the Pawnee adopted the horse, they too employed fire as a way to manage the grasslands of the plains to help feed the creatures. Burning the land removed ground mulch and allowed sunlight to penetrate the earth more directly, accelerating the growth of grass and, more importantly, increasing yields during the spring and summer when the horses needed food most. Whites traveling out to the plains, for their part, remained quite aware that venturing through unburned sections of the prairie risked the possibility of inadequate feed for their mounts.[19]

In California, fire had long played a vital role in the ecology of the region. Indeed, much of the state's plant life evolved in response to fire, incorporating the periodic burnings into their life cycles. Indigenous peoples such as the Wukchumni Yokut and Timbisha Shoshone set fire to freshwater marshes, thereby fostering the growth of forage for livestock, providing more space for waterfowl nesting, and increasing overall species diversity.[20] These groups thus harvested food that they themselves played a key role in creating. In this sense, many coastal California environments were human artifacts, the product of Indian burning,

PRAIRIE ON FIRE

Indigenous peoples set fire to the land, as shown here in Alfred Jacob Miller's 1836 painting, to shape it to meet their subsistence needs. Not all parts of the continent experienced such anthropogenic burning. (National Archives of Canada/c-000432)

and would have reverted to woody vegetation had the native peoples not intervened. The notion of a precontact "wilderness" certainly has no place here.

Although burning played an important positive role in Indian survival, it also had some negative effects. First, fires (especially those that raged out of control) destroyed trees, creating at times a shortage of timber in the grasslands, where such vegetation was scarce to begin with. Second, in upland areas of the South, repeated burning increased erosion and destroyed the mineral content of the soil. Finally, setting fire to some forests, notably oak ones, reduced the nuts and acorns available for human and animal consumption, again potentially undermining a subsistence regime.[21]

The Indian nations clearly left their mark on the North American landscape. Fire, generated by both lightning and deliberate Indian practice, produced the open, grassy expanses that dominated large sections of the continent. Such fires also simplified the forest cover. In the South, fire encouraged the growth of various species of pine trees at the expense of such hardwoods as hickory and oak.[22] To call North America on the eve of European arrival a pristine wilderness is to deny the very powerful role that indigenous communities, with fire as their principal tool, played in shaping the landscape.

CONCLUSION

To conjure up a wilderness is inaccurate, not only because of native peoples' use of fire but also in light of the stunning building achievements carried out before European colonization. The Hohokam living in the Salt River Valley in the ninth century built more than 1,300 miles of canals and channels for irrigating crops. The Anasazi of the San Juan Basin grew enough corn to support thousands of people by 1100. One of the pueblos they built had at least 600 rooms. Farther east, near today's St. Louis, Indians took advantage of a warming climate and increasing rainfall (a climatic trend between 900 and 1350 known as the Medieval Optimum) to farm on a scale productive enough to sustain Cahokia, the largest city ever built north of the Rio Grande until the expansion of Philadelphia and New York City late in the eighteenth century.[23]

The Hohokam might have overreached, engaging in so much irrigation that salinization destroyed the soil. The Anasazi seem to have been the victims, according to tree-ring analysis, of a 50-year drought in the twelfth century. And Cahokia, which may have rivaled medieval London at its peak in population, succumbed to enemy pressure and a shift toward a colder climate and shorter growing season in the fourteenth century. The travails of these peoples underscore the outsized role that climate played in cultures engaged in direct, largely unmediated interactions with the earth. In the end, deriving a living from a place is a complex process, and all cultures are capable of miscalculations, even the earliest ones organized around human needs and not the logic of capitalist markets.[24]

To see indigenous peoples as the continent's "first environmentalists," operating in a wilderness until the Europeans arrived, is not only anachronistic, but demeaning to such communities, because it creates a caricature of them as primitive users of the environment and thus unworthy of any rights to the land in the first place.[25]

2

A TRULY NEW WORLD

It ranks as perhaps the most ill-timed expedition in the history of exploration. In 1587, Sir Walter Raleigh, the English courtier and navigator, recruited 117 people to venture to the New World under the command of John White. Their destination: a spot of land roughly 10 miles long and 2 miles wide off the coast of North Carolina now named Roanoke Island. White put the settlers ashore and a few weeks later returned to England to find supplies and additional recruits for the venture. War with Spain, however, delayed his return. In 1590, when he finally managed to make his way back to Roanoke, he found not a bustling plantation, as he had hoped, but utter desolation. Not a trace of the colonists could be found.

No one can say definitively what happened to the "Lost Colony." Some suspect an Indian attack; others, that the settlers decided, on their own, to go off to live with the Indians. As it turns out, scientific analysis of tree rings has revealed that the colonists landed at Roanoke amid the island's worst drought in 800 years (1185 to 1984). Even the most foresighted and resourceful of explorers would have found the task of survival on the island a monumental challenge.[1] Raleigh could not have picked a worse time to launch his undertaking.

England had a problem in the sixteenth century that such colonization ventures—as fragile as they were—had the potential to solve. That problem revolved around the fate of the poor wandering about the country. Poverty reared its ugly head as people found themselves separated from the land on which they depended for survival. The driving force behind this separation was the emergence of capitalism, a system in which people had no choice but to rely on markets to sell their labor power and to buy food and the other necessities of life. In this system based on competition and maximizing profits, tremendous attention was lavished on making the land productive, on improving it for gain. Because people's customary access to common lands interfered with squeezing more money from the earth, a so-called enclosure movement developed that funneled that land into the hands of a minority of the population. Forest, meadow, and pasture once subject to local control and used for the benefit of entire communities declined as private ownership arrangements intervened to create a mass of landless laborers no longer able to count on common rights to the fruits of the earth. The process began as far back as the 1200s but reached a

peak in the fifteenth and sixteenth centuries, driving a wedge between the commoners and the sustenance provided by trees, game, and wild plants. What better
way to address this problem of a glut of people no longer able to survive on the
land—some driven to crime, some so desperate they indentured themselves—
than to ship them to North America?[2]

The problem was exacerbated by changing conditions in the European environment, especially its estuaries, rivers, and seas, which were in the throes of
depletion by the late Middle Ages. Across Western Europe, the shad, sturgeon,
and other migrating fish so crucial to the lives of ordinary people had been
brought to a state of exhaustion by 1500 as milldams, siltation, and overfishing
took their toll.[3]

Faced with an embattled environment and, in England at least, a growing
population of people whose bonds with the land had been severed, Europeans
headed across the Atlantic. The era of exploration opened sweeping expanses of
temperate biome—with massively abundant supplies of land, fish, minerals, and
water—that the newcomers in North America turned, in the words of one colonist, into "a second England." The discovery of the earth's Western Hemisphere,
argues historian Donald Worster, "ushered in an age of unprecedented material abundance."[4] That prosperity was based, of course, on the expropriation of
the indigenous peoples who preceded the colonists on the land, a slow, violent
process that in eastern North America had yet to be completed as late as the
American Revolution.[5]

Meanwhile, farther south, in the Caribbean, calculating European planters
cleared islands of forests and took advantage of the favorable climate and soil to
establish sugar plantations. The demand for labor power was so immense that
the planters eventually imported African slaves, who were packed aboard miserable ships and under threats of violence sent to work in the scorching sun cultivating a product that was becoming a staple of daily life in Europe. Commodity
production organized along agro-industrial lines and based on slave labor powered capital accumulation and became the model that would transform land and
lives across the American South in the eighteenth century.

CLIMATE SHOCK

One of the hardest problems the colonists confronted was the gap between their
preconceived ideas about the natural environment and the reality that faced
them on the ground. The colonists believed, mistakenly, that latitude determined
climate. They thus expected that Virginia, which has the same latitude as Spain,
would also have conditions suitable for growing oranges, lemons, sugarcane,
and grapes. European settlers persisted in this fantasy into the mid-seventeenth
century. A pamphlet promoting the virtues of settlement in Maryland from the
early 1630s assured newcomers of the likelihood "that the soil will prove to be
adapted to all the fruits of Italy, figs, pomegranates, oranges, olives, etc."[6]

It took the colonists until the late eighteenth century to learn that their ideas about climate in America bore little relationship to reality. South Carolina was positioned "in the same latitude with some of the most fertile countries on the globe," wrote historian Alexander Hewit in 1779. "Yet he is in danger of error who forms his judgement of its climate from the latitude in which it lies."[7] As Hewit correctly surmised, latitude, although a factor in determining climate, is not all there is to the story. How a landmass is oriented with respect to the ocean also figures prominently in a region's weather. Because weather comes from the west, the Atlantic Ocean plays a major role in determining the climate of Western Europe. By heating up and cooling down more slowly than the land it abuts, the Atlantic has had a moderating effect on the region's climate. Marked by relatively small variations in temperature and with adequate rainfall spread throughout the seasons, the humid environment found between 35 and 45 degrees north of the equator favors the production of citrus fruits and olives. In contrast, the eastern part of North America at that same latitude lacks such a tempering influence. Instead, a continental climate dominates, one subject to temperature extremes and with rainfall mainly concentrated in the summer, when the hot weather aids evaporation. Growing olives in Maryland is all but impossible.

Despite such misunderstandings, climate figured prominently in the thoughts of the Europeans, especially the British. Climate mattered to them not simply because of its connection to agricultural production and survival but also because the British identified it as a key element of character. The English thrived, it was believed, in a moderate climate. They feared tropical heat, holding that such an environment better suited the French and Spanish. Travel to the southern part of America was thus perceived as carrying a great risk to life and health.[8]

In this last respect at least, the perceptions of British colonists matched up well with reality. The hotter the climate, the higher, generally speaking, the death rate. The settlement of the American South is a case in point. Jamestown, Virginia, was the first area in North America to be permanently settled by the English, although all the attention devoted to the Pilgrims and Plymouth Rock might easily lead one to think otherwise. The colony of Jamestown is easily overlooked because its checkered history serves as a poor starting point for a great nation. Late in 1606, three ships carrying 144 people left Britain and by the following spring had entered Chesapeake Bay, establishing a colony on the James River roughly 50 miles from where it empties into the bay. This was a prime agricultural area, with a growing season roughly two months longer than New England's. Although the colony got off to a fine start, its prospects had turned sour by the summer, when, according to one observer, "our men were destroyed with cruell diseases, as swellings, Flixes, Burning Fevers, and by warres, and some departed suddenly, but for the most part they died of meere famine."[9]

By January of the following year, the colony was edging toward the brink of extinction, with only 35 of the original settlers still alive. Indeed, between 1607 and 1625, some 4,800 out of 6,000 colonists perished at Jamestown. "Meere

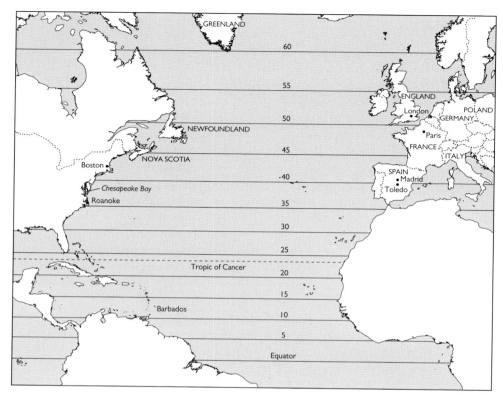

MAP OF COMPARATIVE LATITUDES

famine," however, does not do justice to the complex set of environmental factors that may have played a role in the staggering death toll. It seems, based again on tree-ring analysis, that like their predecessors on Roanoke Island, the colonists at Jamestown confronted extraordinary drought conditions. Drought stalked the Virginia landscape between 1606 and 1612, the worst seven-year dry spell in 770 years (from 1215 to 1984). Malnutrition may well have been the cause of the high death rate, but it would be remarkable if such a severe drought did not impact the food supply.[10]

Poor water quality—a situation made worse by the drought—also contributed to the settlers' woes. The colonists relied heavily on the James River, a supply that proved safe for most of the year but not in the summer, when the flow of the river lessened considerably. Pools of stagnant water contaminated with human waste created conditions favorable for the spread of typhoid fever and amoebic dysentery. Worse still, the decline in the flow of freshwater allowed saltwater from the bay to intrude farther upstream. As a result, the colonists found themselves drinking water laden with salt in concentrations five times the amount recommended for human consumption today. Salt poisoning was what

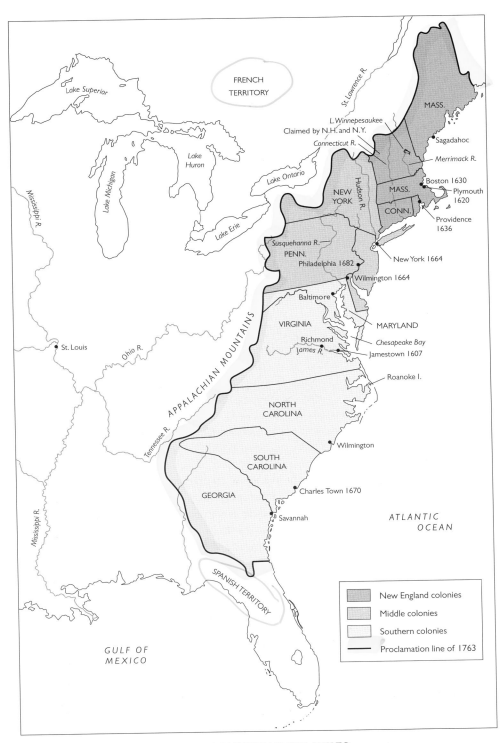

Lake Superior

FRENCH
TERRITORY

St. Lawrence R.

Lake Huron

Lake Michigan

Lake Ontario

Mississippi R.

Lake Erie

L. Winnepesaukee

Claimed by N.H. and N.Y.

Connecticut R.

MASS.

Sagadahoc

Merrimack R.

NEW
YORK

Hudson R.

MASS.

CONN.

Boston 1630

Plymouth
1620

Providence
1636

Susquehanna R.

PENN.

Philadelphia 1682

New York 1664

Wilmington 1664

Baltimore

Ohio R.

St. Louis

APPALACHIAN MOUNTAINS

Tennessee R.

VIRGINIA

MARYLAND

Chesapeake Bay

Richmond

James R.

Jamestown 1607

Roanoke I.

NORTH
CAROLINA

Wilmington

SOUTH
CAROLINA

GEORGIA

Charles Town 1670

Savannah

ATLANTIC
OCEAN

Mississippi R.

SPANISH TERRITORY

GULF OF
MEXICO

New England colonies

Middle colonies

Southern colonies

Proclamation line of 1763

MAP OF AMERICAN COLONIES

plagued them. By sticking close to the river's estuary (the zone where freshwater and saltwater meet) during the summer, the colonists were killing themselves, yet they continued this suicidal behavior until Captain John Smith intervened. Smith noticed that the Indians left the estuarine zone in July, heading for high ground where freshwater springs could be found. Mobility thus ensured the Indians' good health. In the spring of 1609, Smith urged his comrades to scatter into the countryside, and the summertime death toll declined. Unfortunately, Smith soon left the colony to return to Britain, and when he did so the colonists again congregated like sitting ducks in Jamestown.[11]

Malaria also flourished in the warmer southern climate. Once again, the colonists found themselves caught between their erroneous perception of the landscape and its tragic reality. Europeans first introduced malaria into North America; later a more lethal form of the disease arrived from Africa. High mortality rates plagued the South, but particularly the colony of South Carolina, where some parishes failed to see a natural increase in population until the American Revolution. A common proverb circulating in Britain in the revolutionary period went: "They who want to die quickly, go to Carolina."[12] It was an apt prophecy, in part because the colonists wrongly believed until well into the eighteenth century that swampy areas were relatively healthful. They preferred swamps to cities, where, they believed, arriving ships brought diseased passengers ashore. In fact, the swampy Low Country was precisely the best breeding ground for mosquitoes, a scientific reality that explains the recurrent summer and fall malaria problem.

While colonists in the South faced the problem of heat and its implications for disease, settlers in the North struggled with the reverse situation: persistent cold. If few remember Jamestown in the rush to glorify the success at Plymouth Rock, virtually no one recalls the colony of Sagadahoc in Maine, founded the very same year (1607) that Virginia Company ships landed in the Chesapeake. Bad management contributed to the settlement's demise within less than a year, but a bitterly cold winter also played a part. The prospects for settlement, wrote one observer some years later, were literally "frozen to death."[13] It would be more than a decade before the Pilgrims—perhaps discouraged by this miserable initial effort—again tried to establish a beachhead in the region. Focusing only on the successful efforts of the colonists has thus obscured the very real struggle the colonists faced in coming to terms with the environment in the northern reaches of this new world.

Larger climatic forces also may have contributed to some of the problems the New England colonists encountered. History in North America has thus far unfolded, as noted earlier, during an interglacial period. But the ice and cold have already made one major return visit. A Little Ice Age intervened from the mid-fifteenth century (or perhaps as early as 1300) to the mid-nineteenth century. Although dubbed an ice age, the period is best viewed as one made up of a series of intense climatic shifts—cold winters giving way to more mild ones and heavy rains in the spring and summer switching to droughts and summer heat waves. The exact cause of the schizophrenic climate is still not completely understood. A change in the relationship between the ocean and the atmosphere may have been to blame.[14] Nevertheless, there is little doubt that the most severe cold was felt in the northern hemisphere between 1550 and 1700. During the seventeenth century, the temperature of the water off the coast of New England rivaled that found in the Labrador Sea today.

During the most intense part of the Little Ice Age, the New England colonists experienced one of the most significant early challenges to their survival: severe food shortages in the years 1696, 1697, and 1698, precisely the years when the cold was at its worst. The winter of 1697–1698 was probably the coldest winter on record in the seventeenth century. Near winter's end, the Puritan Samuel Sewall lamented the consequences of the extreme cold:

> To Horses, Swine, Net-Cattell, Sheep and Deer
> Ninety and Seven prov'd a Mortal yeer.

By this time, New England's population—which may have increased as much as four times between 1640 and the end of the century—had already strained the available resource base, turning the region into a net importer of corn, wheat, rye, and other grains. The cold weather in the latter part of the 1690s raised the even worse possibility of famine. In 1696, prices for wheat and corn increased 50 to 100 percent. Reports circulated of people in Boston having to do without bread for weeks at a time.[15]

Focusing on the darker underside of early American history—the famine, disease, and failure that the colonists experienced—does much to challenge the view that the past has been one direct march onward and upward. But more than undermining the triumphalism that has so marred our understanding of this nation, these examples demonstrate that, like the Indians, the Europeans needed to figure out a way to survive in a literally new world that was as unforgiving as it was unfamiliar.

NO ACT OF GOD

Just as long-term climatic forces such as glaciations shaped agricultural prospects in the New World, so too did ecological changes. The Pleistocene extinctions 13,000 years ago might seem barely relevant to the European arrival. But without those extinctions the colonists probably never would have succeeded to the degree that they did in dominating North America.

In the first place, the Pleistocene mass death, by eliminating most of the big mammals, helped to remove a major source of disease from North America. Unlike Eurasia, the New World's lack of cows, pigs, horses, and other domesticated species capable of transmitting disease to human beings insulated it from epidemics. And if the first human settlers, the Paleoindians, did indeed journey

to the continent by passing across the Bering land bridge, the cold environment they encountered there would have filtered out diseases and killed off
the sick, preventing illness from being passed along to descendants. Prior to
the end of the fifteenth century, the Native Americans had acquired no immu-
nity from a variety of illnesses that Europeans had long lived with. Smallpox,
measles, whooping cough, chicken pox, malaria, typhoid fever, cholera, yellow
fever, influenza, and amoebic dysentery were all unknown to the Indian immune
system and would have remained foreign to them had not the European Age of
Discovery reunited what geological forces had rent asunder hundreds of millions of years before.

The epidemiological upheaval created by European contact with the New
World is difficult to measure. Precisely how many Indians lived on the continent
before the arrival of the colonists is, as has been mentioned, the point of some
contention. But whatever the exact figure, no one disputes that the indigenous
population loss by 1900 was truly monstrous. Even assuming that only a million
people inhabited the continent—an implausibly low number—their numbers
can be calculated to have been slashed by two-thirds after four centuries of
European contact. The higher initial population figures, which seem more likely,
yield a rate of attrition of between 95 and 99 percent, one of the most dramatic
population reductions in human history.[16]

Smallpox, a horrific disease once described by British historian Thomas
Macaulay as "the most terrible of all the ministers of death," was one of the
greatest killers. Merely breathing air contaminated by a smallpox victim who
had coughed or sneezed could result in infection. Since the virus often survived
in dried-up bodily secretions that clung to bedclothes or blankets, an activity
as mundane as sweeping the floor could cause contaminated particles to float
through the air and be inhaled. And with a 10- to 14-day incubation period,
smallpox spread easily, as seemingly healthy people exposed to the disease infected others.[17]

The Spanish first introduced the disease into Hispaniola in 1519. Eventually,
the deadly virus worked its way across Puerto Rico, Cuba, and Mexico before
landing in what is today the United States. The first recorded epidemic occurred
in the 1630s among the Algonquian of Massachusetts, with one account reading: "Whole towns of them were swept away, in some not so much as one
soul escaping Destruction." The disease wreaked havoc in New England and ultimately spread west to the St. Lawrence and Great Lakes region, devastating
the Huron and Iroquois of New York in the 1630s and 1640s. Mortality rates
ranged as high as 95 percent. When a sailor suffering from the disease set foot
in Northampton County, Virginia, in 1667, smallpox began its march through
the South. According to one report, Indians in Virginia "died by the hundred."[18]

Some colonists did not regret the demographic collapse, using it as a pretext
to assert claims of ownership over the land. John Winthrop, governor of the
Massachusetts Bay Colony, observed in 1634, "For the natives, they are neere all

dead of small Poxe, so as the Lord hathe cleared our title to what we possess."
Others, feeling dependent on the Indians and their knowledge of the land, extended help in times of sickness. When the Plymouth colonists learned of the
illness of Massasoit, the leader of the Wampanoag, they "sente him such comfortable things as gave him great contente, and was a means of his recovery."[19]

Seeing the enormous advantages that accrued from the decimation of the
Indians by disease, some colonists took matters into their own hands. During
Pontiac's Rebellion in 1763, a war for Indian autonomy, British soldiers under
the command of Gen. Jeffrey Amherst distributed smallpox-infected blankets
to the Indians. Whether Amherst ordered his subordinates to employ the virus
against the Indians surrounding Fort Pitt or not (and evidence suggests that he
was not the first person to dream up the plan), the move coincided with a major
epidemic in the spring and summer. Although the blanket affair has gone down
as one of the most notorious efforts to employ disease as a weapon, biological
warfare was by no means uncommon in the eighteenth century.[20]

Novel germs alone were not responsible for the decimation of the Indians.
The reality is that the slave-based Atlantic economy worked to spread disease. A
good example is the smallpox epidemic that struck the Southeast beginning in
1696. In the years before the epidemic, English colonists initiated a slave trade
with the Indians. Eager for slaves to work the land in Virginia and on the West
Indian sugar plantations, the colonists traded cloth, pots, firearms, and alcohol
for deerskins and Indian captives. The dislocation caused by Indians seeking to
flee slave raids brought malnutrition to indigenous peoples as they were forced
from familiar surroundings. Famine combined with constant contact with
Europeans trafficking in slaves caused widespread circulation of disease among
indigenous groups. Eventually, the Indian slave trade foundered as the supply of
captives dried up because of the appalling death rates.[21]

The Europeans imported far more than disease into America. They also
brought Old World plants and animals, species that had never before been introduced into the New World: wheat, rye, horses, sheep, pigs, and cattle. Old World
plants and animals experienced such amazing success in their new environment that historian Alfred Crosby has deemed this development a "biological
revolution." The Pleistocene is an excellent place to go looking for the roots of
this enormous biological success. Once again, the massive animal extinctions
13,000 years ago shaped the course of modern history. The elimination of the
bulk of the continent's large mammals may have created huge, empty eco-niches
into which European livestock entered with spectacular success. Meanwhile, the
introduction of Old World plants may have doubled or perhaps even tripled the
number of food crops available for cultivation in the Americas.[22]

More than just seeds came to the Americas. An entire knowledge base also
had to be imported. Rice is a case in point. Of the 20 or so species of rice found
on earth, only two ever became domesticated. One of those species originated
along the Niger River in Mali. Although it is commonly believed that Europeans

HOW HORSE WILL TRAVEL

Transporting large animals such as horses to North America necessitated special devices and extreme care. Despite such measures, many of the animals died en route. (Robert M. Denhardt, The Horse of the Americas *[Norman: University of Oklahoma Press, 1975])*

brought rice to the Americas, in truth, Africans played the key role in this particular intercontinental biological exchange. Only West Africans, enslaved and shipped across the Atlantic from the "Rice Coast" that extended from Senegal to Liberia, knew how to cultivate the crop productively. African women, in particular, understood the plant's optimal soil and water conditions and how to process and cook it. Racist notions seem to have kept scholars from recognizing the truly fundamental role played by Africans in the biological revolution that swept across the New World.[23]

On balance, the European settlers greatly benefited from the biological exchange that accompanied their journey to America. Perhaps the most important payoff came as New World plant foods such as maize, potatoes, beans, and squash crossed the Atlantic in the other direction, giving European farmers more options in adapting to local soil and weather conditions. The importance of maize alone, which can flourish in areas that are too dry for planting rice and too wet for planting wheat, cannot be overstated. The plant went on to become one of the world's premier food crops. "The Indian Corn, or Maiz," wrote one colonist in 1701, "proves the most useful Grain in the World." Maize could grow in a large number of different environmental settings. "It refuses no Grounds, unless the barren Sands, and when planted in good Ground, will repay the Planter seven

TO BE SOLD on board the Ship *Bance-Yland*, on tuefday the 6th of *May* next, at *Afhley-Ferry* ; a choice cargo of about 250 fine healthy NEGROES, juft arrived from the Windward & Rice Coaft. —The utmoft care has already been taken, and fhall be continued, to keep them free from the leaft danger of being infected with the SMALL-POX, no boat having been on board, and all other communication with people from *Charles-Town* prevented.

Auftin, Laurens, & Appleby.

N. B. Full one Half of the above Negroes have had the SMALL-POX in their own Country.

"TO BE SOLD"

Slaves from the west coast of Africa, where tidal rice cultivation had long been practiced, provided indispensable knowledge to southern planters. This late-eighteenth-century advertisement calls attention to the homeland of newly arrived slaves being auctioned outside of Charleston, South Carolina. (Library of Congress)

or eight hundred fold."[24] It is unlikely that the population of Europe could have surged as it did in the two and a half centuries after Columbus without the New World crops. Nor, for that matter, could the West African population have formed the basis for the burgeoning slave trade without such New World crops as corn, manioc, and squash.[25]

HOW *DID* THE INDIANS LOSE THEIR LAND?

When John Smith arrived in Virginia in 1607, he declared that "every man may be master and owner of his owne labour and land."[26] For the latter claim about landownership to evolve into a fact of life, the longstanding connection between the Indians and the earth had to be severed, a process that involved not just violent dispossession but a new system of property relations.

How the Indians understood property in land is not fully known. But we can be certain that Indians never sold land before European colonization. They were less inclined toward an exclusive view of property in land, the *modus operandi* of the colonists. True, among some Indian groups control of choice riverine plots rested in the hands of hereditary rulers. Nevertheless, the indigenous peoples seem to have treated the land as common property.[27] And prior to colonization, no evidence exists that Indians viewed land as a tool for accumulating wealth, as colonial land speculators would. Instead, the Indians relied on mobility to exploit the natural environment's seasonal diversity. Thus, they did not settle permanently and improve property in the way that the English expected. And since mixing labor and land was central to English understandings of private property, the settlers had on hand a convenient rationale for dispossessing the Indians. What the Indians did not improve and own the colonists were free, they reasoned, to take and use for themselves.

"ADVERSE POSSESSION"

According to one seventeenth-century British observer, Indians had "no particular property in any part or parcell of the country, but only a general residencie there, as wild beasts have in the forest."[28] Instead of focusing on exclusive rights to ownership, the Indian concept of property was far more fluid. Indians claimed not the land itself, but what existed on it—the wild berries, acorns, fish, or game animals. The names the Indians gave to different parts of the landscape are suggestive. It was common for Indian place names to describe the kinds of plants or animals that could be found in a particular locale. Abessah in Maine, for example, translated as "clam bake place."[29] Other place names described where eggs could be gathered, where fish could be caught, and so on.

European settlers also named places after elements of the natural world, but in at least one respect they crossed a line that the Indians would not: they named places after individuals, often powerful ones back in Western Europe. That predilection suggests an affinity for individualism that influenced how they related to the land as they clashed with Indians over the question of ownership. Indians often conveyed land to the colonists. But what the Indians thought they were giving and what the colonists thought they were getting were two different matters. Indians commonly believed that they were simply supplying whites with the same rights to land that they themselves had: to use it for planting corn, hunting, or some other subsistence activity. The colonists, of course, thought they were being given the exclusive right to own the property. In Maine, Indians openly sold the same parcel of land to a number of different Englishmen, a move that suggests they viewed the land as a form of common property in which people could share. Indigenous peoples also often remained on the land after they sold it, suggesting that exclusivity was not what they had in mind when they engaged in such transactions.[30]

Although they had a less exclusive understanding of property, the Indians were not at all cavalier about land rights. In fact, they knew the limits and boundaries of their claims. Roger Williams noted that the Native Americans were "very exact and punctuall in the bounds of their Lands, belonging to this or that Prince or People."[31] Although it is tempting to assume that only the colonists possessed the requisite cartographic knowledge to dominate the land, the Indians used their knowledge of the continent to map it and to contest the Europeans' efforts to dispossess them. Some deeds even included graphic renderings of the landscape drawn by Indians themselves that reserved for them rights to continue their subsistence practices. In 1703, for example, the Weantinock, who lived and fished for shad and eels along the banks of the present-day Housatonic River in Connecticut, conveyed land to white settlers. But in a map accompanying the deed, the Indians explicitly reserved the right to continue fishing on the land in question. That six Indians signed the document is evidence that the community as a whole had come together to make the decision to convey the property, rather than a single individual, as was common under English property law.[32]

In Natick, Massachusetts, the Indians continued this community-oriented system of allocating land into the early eighteenth century. In the 1720s, however, this system gave way to one that relied on individual landownership and that placed control over the resource in the hands of a few Indian proprietors, who gained the exclusive right to make decisions about dividing land. In the following decade, some Indians fell into debt and turned to the English market in land to settle their accounts. Instead of the Indian community as a whole

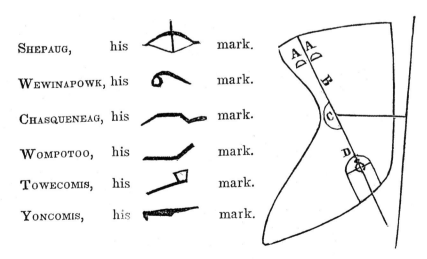

WEANTINOCK DEED

Although the original deed, drawn up on February 8, 1703, is lost, this rendering found in Edward R. Lambert's History of the Colony of New Haven (1838) shows the graphic Indians drew to reserve their right to fish at the falls. (Kelvin Smith Library, Case Western Reserve University)

deciding how to organize control of the land base, land was coming to be treated as an individually owned commodity. And individual ownership of the land made it a lot easier to transfer property, often to non-Indians. Some Indians in the town even began to accumulate more land than they could reasonably use. Though the Indians tried to safeguard common property rights to fish around ponds, even into the 1740s, the creation of a real estate market ended up separating Indians from the land, leaving them with little choice but to become wage laborers, indentured servants, or, worse, so-called wandering Indians, people who had lost their ties to the earth. "In effect," writes historian Jean O'Brien, "the English, who as colonists were rootless people by definition, displaced their own dislocation onto Indians."[33]

The Indians not only lost their connection to the land. They also lost their common property, which had served as a basis for democratic decision-making and control over resource use. Still, one should not exaggerate the differences between the Indian communities and the colonists on the subject of landownership. If the colonists brought with them a property system that allowed for exclusive ownership and land speculation—and they did—they also understood the world of common property. Indeed, there is even evidence that common-property systems survived among the colonists, in Massachusetts at least, until the middle of the eighteenth century.[34] This is an important insight, because these common-property arrangements involved environmental controls, such as limits on the number of animals that could be grazed or rules about when meadow grass could be harvested so as to sustain the resource base.

The Indians lost their land. But the colonists, even as late as the mid-1700s, did not completely favor rampant land accumulation. Many still believed their relationship with the earth was founded on a larger social purpose based on human need and frowned on the view of land as simply a tool for making profits.

THE FUR TRADE

The market in furs was perhaps more far-reaching in terms of immediate ecological consequences than the colonial market in land. North America's incorporation into European commodity markets profoundly impacted the continent. Animals such as deer and beaver that Indians had hunted to survive were swept into the burgeoning fur trade and in places annihilated.

Before the emergence of a full-fledged market in game in the seventeenth century, beavers existed in huge numbers. Beavers survived chiefly on plant species and constructed dams and canals as a way of creating a suitable habitat near food sources. Their projects—and they have been known to erect dams 18 feet high and 4,000 feet long—radically altered ecosystems, creating ponds and changing streamflows. The Europeans chiefly valued beavers because their underhairs made excellent felt hats. In the late sixteenth century, such hats were all the rage in England and France, a trend that led to the eventual obliteration of

Europe's beavers and the shift in focus toward America. Beginning in the late seventeenth century, overhunting in response to the rise of a market in furs caused the beaver population of southern New England to crash.

Some claim that Indians killed beavers, deer, and other game animals because the Europeans had tricked them into giving up the conservation impulse implicit in their elaborate game taboos. In this view, the Indians saw game animals as family members and only killed what they needed to survive. Then the Europeans entered the picture and perverted this relationship by seducing Indians with various trade goods. One historian has even put forth the controversial view that the Indians blamed beaver and moose for the epidemics that raged through their societies, a development that undermined their spiritual relationship with such creatures. This belief then spurred them to embark on an extermination campaign.[35]

When epidemic disease led to the collapse of the Native American population, the stage was set for a change in the way these people related to game animals. Whether or not Indians blamed such animals for their illnesses, when Europeans arrived bearing trade goods, many Indians willingly accepted them in return for beaver pelts, at least in part to enhance their battered political prospects in a period of extreme stress and demographic upheaval. Wampumpeag, or wampum, beads made from the shells of whelks and quahogs, soon took on enormous symbolic significance among the Indians of southern New England, playing a central role in the fur trade. Eventually, Indians realized that beaver pelts could command a price on the market. By killing the animals and exchanging them for wampum, they could bolster their personal power and political prospects.[36]

The decline of the beaver population had ecological effects that radiated out across the New England landscape. Ecologists consider the beaver a "keystone species," an animal on which many other life forms rely to survive. Beavers create ponds and in the process furnish habitats for turtles, frogs, fish, and waterfowl. Woodpeckers and chickadees nest and forage in the trees downed by these creatures. Thus, the decline of the beaver population presaged important changes for species throughout the ecosystem. From the standpoint of humankind, however, the decline had at least one positive effect. With the animals no longer around to tend to them, beaver dams throughout New England collapsed, exposing soils rich in organic matter and creating an ideal environment for grass, which the colonists used as forage for livestock.

In the South, deer more than beaver were key to the emerging fur trade. The warmer climate prevented southern beavers from developing the thick furs so common farther north. That fact made the animals far less viable commodities. Europeans used deerskins, however, to make leather, fashioning gloves, saddles, bookbindings, and other items out of them. Until the early eighteenth century, leatherworkers had relied on European cattle for their raw material. But when disease broke out among the French cattle herds, they turned to America's deer to make up for the shortfall.

Southern Indians, like tribes in the North, killed deer in exchange for a range of goods, including guns, metal kettles, knives, hoes, linen, and silk. As early as 1699, overhunting spurred the Virginia legislature, in an early preservation effort, to ban the killing of white-tailed deer between February and July. Other efforts to regulate hunting followed. Beginning in the eighteenth century, the burgeoning Atlantic economy combined with the Indians' appetite for alcohol to put even heavier pressure on the southern deer population. The Creek controlled an area bursting with deer in large part because their slave-raiding missions had emptied the habitat of people. That fact combined with the establishment of the town of Augusta, Georgia, in the 1730s, to set the stage for an Atlantic trade network that reached from the American South all the way to the factory centers of Britain, a network that may have resulted in the deaths of up to a million deer per year by the middle of the century. In 1801, Mad Dog, a Creek chieftain, remarked, "Our deer and game is almost gone." In all probability, however, the species never went extinct in the southern colonies. That was because Europeans, concerned about the safety of their livestock, also killed wolves and other animals that preyed on deer.[37]

SWEET TOOTH

The significance of the discovery of the so-called New World rested not just on access to vast supplies of new resources such as land, timber, fish, and fur-bearing animals. It also was based on the emergence of a new world of commodity production—tobacco, rice, and sugar—that flourished on soils extending from the northeastern coast of South America to Chesapeake Bay and contributed to the advance of capitalism, a system that ultimately would have profound consequences for the planet as a whole.

No commodity was more central to this process than sugar. The Spanish introduced sugarcane, a grass likely native to New Guinea, to Santo Domingo in the early sixteenth century but failed to develop production to any significant extent. Instead, Spain's northern European rivals were the ones who managed to exploit the environment to its fullest in the name of commodity production. A watershed happened in 1627 when the English settled in Barbados. It took some time, but by midcentury the English sugar industry had expanded across the Caribbean to Jamaica, a considerably larger island than Barbados. The sugar was sent back to England in hogsheads, some 100,000 of them in 1730 alone.[38]

An agro-industrial ecosystem based on slave labor, industrial methods, monoculture, and a geographic split between production and consumption was imposed on the landscape. The soil, climate, and need for an inexpensive source of fuel for boiling down the cane juice into crystals made a forested island such as Barbados a perfect place to set up shop. Making the forest of Barbados into a string of sugar plantations was brutally hard work, however, as was the production of the sugar itself—both tasks being carried out by slaves brought from Africa. The transformation of the island was as thorough as it was ruthless. From

60 percent forest in 1647, Barbados's tree cover plunged so low that in 1666 timber and firewood had to be imported. By 1671, planters found it necessary to obtain coal from England to boil the cane juice, with one observer noting that "at the Barbadoes all the trees are destroyed." If the indigenous people, the Island Caribs, were anything like other native groups in North America, they likely could never have imagined an environment so completely devoid of woods.[39]

The transformation of the Barbados forest into sugarcane yielded great mosquito habitat, as it turned out, and caused yellow fever to thrive.[40] But the implications of the Caribbean plantations extended well beyond their impact on people's physical health. The systematic makeover of a forest into a monoculture to advance the cause of industrial enterprise was an unprecedented development. It reflected an instrumental approach to the natural world that served as a model not just for the rice plantations that would evolve in the lowlands of South Carolina and Georgia but for even more grandiose projects that aimed to incorporate nature into the world of modern wealth creation, in the process cutting people off from more direct and personal interactions with the earth.

CONCLUSION

By bringing the temperate climate of North America and its land and biota into the orbit of their economy, the European colonists secured for themselves an

SLAVES CUTTING SUGARCANE

This watercolor of a Jamaican sugar plantation was painted in the early nineteenth century by artist William Berryman. (Library of Congress)

extraordinary share of the earth's natural wealth. Europe, as historian E. L. Jones once put it, experienced a stunning "ecological windfall."[41]

Europe's tremendous good fortune, however, came at the expense of nature and native peoples. Vast changes ensued as the explorers brought the two continents together. Transformations ramified across the landscape: a horrifying decline in the Indian population resulting from exposure to Old World diseases; the devastation of fur-bearing animals and forests as a result of their incorporation into European markets; and changes in the very meaning of nature itself as the colonists reduced the complexity of the earth into an abstract concept—land—that could be bought and sold in a way never experienced before on the North American continent.

Beyond that, the colonists took the control of nature to a new level. Commodity production on plantations employing slave labor demolished entire landscapes in the service of agro-industrial enterprise, incorporating North American biomes directly into the Atlantic capitalist economy. Nevertheless, even as late as the mid-1700s, a large segment of humanity in the American colonies still did not define human needs in economic or material terms and was inclined to conduct its relations with the natural world directly at the local level for the sake of family and community.

3

UNFETTERED ACCUMULATION

As late as 1750, most of what would ultimately come to be the dominant economic and military power on the earth was still Indian country.

The French, it is true, claimed a hold on land in an arc from the Gulf of St. Lawrence all the way to the Gulf of Mexico. But because the French people never experienced enclosure, as the English did, and instead remained attached to land in Western Europe, they did not migrate in large numbers to North America. As a result, very few French people lived in the Mississippi River Valley or elsewhere in their empire, which was hardly an empire at all given that they occupied this land at the sufferance of the Indians. Meanwhile, the Spanish clung to impoverished New Mexico, where just a few thousand Hispanics lived, mainly in El Paso and Santa Fe, and which served to buffer the Crown's far more valuable Mexican colony to the south. The Spaniards' greatest ecological impact resulted from their introduction of horses, which spread from the Indians of the southern to the northern plains by 1750. Horses dramatically improved the prospects for buffalo hunting and thereby liberated the Indians from the older constraints on material life, enabling them to assert control over the vast grasslands in the center of the continent. Even east of the Mississippi River, though the population of Euro-Americans and African slaves had jumped significantly over the preceding 50 years to 1.25 million by midcentury, indigenous peoples still ruled over the vast expanse between the Appalachian Mountains and the Mississippi River. [1]

In 1750, however, Indian country, at least the eastern portion of it, was on the cusp of monumental change. In the course of the next 40 years, it would succumb to the expansionary ambitions of a rising new state—the United States. Indian population declined further, and indigenous control of the land weakened as military defeats and treaties signed in the 1790s meant that the Indians could no longer rely on Britain, France, and Spain for help they once received in fending off the Euro-American settlers. Separated from the earth, those Indians who remained had to turn to other means of surviving, such as wage labor and indentured servitude.

Nor were the Indians the only ones who found themselves severed from the land that nourished them. Older customary common-property arrangements—to fish, for example—which gave people local control over the wealth of nature, came under assault, as did the idea that land should serve a useful, social purpose and

THOMAS PAINE

An English artisan who was born in 1737, Thomas Paine came of age in a land in the throes of capitalist transformation. His later writings argued for a world of "agrarian justice" in which the fruits of the earth would be shared equally. (Library of Congress)

thereby address the needs of all human beings. This idea came to look increasingly out of place in the lead-up to independence as even revolutionary leaders—Richard Henry Lee, Benjamin Franklin, and Thomas Jefferson, for example—invested in so-called land companies established to profit from the earth. By the end of the century, as more people found themselves divorced from the land, the radical founding father Thomas Paine felt the need to exclaim that uncultivated earth was "the common property of the human race," that society, in other words, had an obligation to support those who found themselves deprived of land.[2]

WORKERS IN THE FOREST

By the middle of the eighteenth century, some Indians in British North America were working as wage laborers, that is, as scouts, hunters, fishermen, and domestic servants. Selling themselves on the labor market was not something that the Indians had previously undertaken. What happened?

Consider the eastern Iroquois, who inhabited what is now upstate New York. Prior to contact with the Europeans, two Iroquois nations named the Mohawk and Oneida interacted directly with the local environment, growing corn, beans, and squash, and hunting game. Communal ownership of resources forestalled the emergence of wealth inequality. In the 1600s, however, as European colonists arrived, a transatlantic trade in furs—shipped to England in return for manufactured goods such as firearms, cloth, and alcohol—steadily grew. After more than a century of this commerce, foreign goods almost completely eclipsed Indian-made items, but even more important, by participating in the fur trade the Indians had entered a new economic world dictated by the market. By the mid-1700s, they were subject to the price mechanism, a form of economic exchange over which they had no real control. When the prices of European wares rose and the Indians could not purchase goods with what they secured in furs, they were out of luck, a point underscored by one Iroquois who lamented in 1761 that he and his people were now "obliged to pay such exorbitant prices, that our hunting is not sufficient to purchase us as much cloathing as is necessary to cover us, & our families."[3]

Ecological decline compounded the Indians' problems, as the supply of beaver in the local environment edged toward exhaustion in the early 1700s. By the middle of the century, the center of the fur trade had shifted west, first to the Ohio River Valley and later to the Great Lakes region.[4]

Worse still, the supply-and-demand calculus of European markets had fallen out of equilibrium as too many furs chased too little demand. The result was that the price of furs plunged. By the 1740s, furs accounted for a significantly smaller percentage of New York's total exports to England than they had 20 years earlier. Instead, the colony was shipping increasing amounts of grain to the slave plantations of the West Indies, which were booming at the time. The deerskin trade in the South suffered a similar fate by midcentury as warehouses bulged with unsold furs.[5]

Agriculture, in other words, was supplanting the fur trade. But for agriculture to thrive—whether on family farms or on plantations worked by slaves—land was, of course, required. And that meant wresting the earth from the Indians. The Creeks living in what had become the new English colony of Georgia in 1733 called the white settlers Ecunnaunuxulgee, which translated as: "People greedily grasping after the lands of the Red people."[6]

In New York, the declining fur trade and consequent rise in capitalist agriculture to supply grain to distant markets compelled Dutch, German, and English settlers to venture into Iroquois country. To keep up with this fast-changing economic world, some Mohawk and Oneida started to view land as a tool for creating wealth, leasing it in return for payments in corn and cash. Others watched as the pillars of their subsistence economy were knocked out from under them. Settlers turned cattle loose to graze on Indian cornfields. Treaties left native populations surrounded by Euro-Americans. Colonists horned in on their hunting grounds. "We know not where to go for subsistence tomorrow. . . . Good hunting is no more known amongst us, since the encroachments of the white people," one warrior reported. In such a context, the appeal of wage work is readily apparent.[7]

CROSSING A LINE

If some Indians turned to wage labor and others entered the world of exchange through the market in land, the capitalist impulse toward the endless accumulation of wealth did not exactly take the native world by storm. In 1736, Iroquois leaders en route to a meeting in Philadelphia fretted that some Indians in their party, whose cultural assumption was that excess personal property ought to be shared with all in need, might simply walk away with any possessions that merchants left unattended. Even as late as 1769, when Richard Smith, a lawyer who would later serve in the Continental Congress, visited an Oneida community on the Susquehanna River, he found a communal tradition of sharing resources. In overseeing a shad fishery, he discovered, the Indians granted "all persons present including strangers, such is their laudable Hospitality [to] have an equal Division of Fish."[8]

Until the early 1760s, the Indians and Euro-Americans managed, whatever their differences, to coexist and share the land, if not always equally, under a transatlantic imperial framework established by Britain, France, and Spain. This was still a world of possibility and of accommodation, and not as yet one marked by relentless European incursion across the frontier to crush indigenous peoples in the land east of the Mississippi River. "We must hang upon our ancient rules," a Seneca leader explained, "and the white people upon theirs. We can then as well agree together as if we followed one rule." Agreeing on what the rules should be was a far cry from the relations that solidified in the latter part of the century, when a treaty system and a different understanding of Indian property all but guaranteed Euro-American domination over the Indians.[9]

The eclipse of whatever chance at coexistence remained began in the 1750s when tensions came to a head over what the Anglo-Irishman Sir William Johnson called "the Pestilential Thirst of Land, so Epidemic thro' all the provinces." Up to this point, individual Euro-Americans had purchased land directly from the Indians themselves. But this system broke down in the face of claims by some Indians to represent the will of the nation as a whole when, in fact, they did not. All kinds of misunderstandings and miscommunications began popping up, a situation made worse by the Seven Years' War between Britain and France, which began in 1754. Indeed, the British authorities thought that their encroachment on the Indians' hunting grounds led the Indians to side with the French in the struggle.[10]

The British triumph in the Seven Years' War was a major turning point for Indians and their relations with the land. With the French driven from the continent, save for some islands, and the Spanish confined to New Orleans and Louisiana west of the Mississippi, the British consolidated their hold on eastern North America, to the Indians' vexation. The Creek, for example, could not understand why land that they thought they had only loaned to the Spanish and French in the South had not been returned to them when the British arrived to take over from their rivals. "People can give away Land that does not belong to them?" the Creek asked. Others evinced more defiance. Ojibwe leader Minivavana lectured an English trader at a British garrison at Michilimackinac, at the straits between Lake Huron and Lake Michigan, in 1761: "Englishman, although you have conquered the French, you have not yet conquered us. We are not your slaves. These lakes, these woods and mountains, were left to us by our ancestors. They are our inheritance; and we will part with them to none."[11]

The war was nevertheless a watershed. No longer could the Indians benefit from the imperial rivalries that had enabled about 50 years of roughly equal coexistence with the Euro-Americans. Instead of the shades of gray that had characterized European–Indian accommodation, a bold frontier line dividing red from white came to define relations between these peoples, a line that gravitated west with the colonial ambitions of the Euro-Americans.[12]

Following the conclusion of the war, the British issued the Proclamation of 1763, establishing a line in the mountains, as it were. The line roughly followed the Eastern Continental Divide. West of that line, the proclamation declared, land grants could not be made and British colonists could no longer settle. East of the line, private purchases of Indian land were banned. Only colonial governors now had the power to negotiate such purchases. The idea was to guarantee Indian possession of land to the west of the line while hemming in the colonists and making them dependent on trade with Britain.[13]

In addition, the proclamation impinged on the right of Indians to alienate—transfer—land to others. Under Anglo-American law, the colonists in North America could sell their land to whomever they wanted. They retained, in other words, full ownership rights to the soil under what was called "fee simple absolute." There was nothing absolute, however, about what the Indians now faced. They could no longer sell land to private individuals, only to colonial governors acting on behalf of the Crown. Indian landownership in this new legal world has been described as "a kind of second-class property right."[14]

Nor was the proclamation line a true line in any meaningful sense. Land hunger drove colonists across the boundary. Illegal settlements and a black market in land sprang up. Even George Washington indulged himself, buying land from Indians who, under the proclamation, no longer had a right to sell it to individuals. Land companies, often peopled with government officials, lobbied hard for colonial governments to buy land and then grant them title, thereby circumventing the requirements of the proclamation. By the 1770s, it was clear that some very powerful, accumulation-minded American colonists had a problem facing up to limits when it came to the land.[15]

THE LOGIC OF EXPROPRIATION

Land occupied a very special place in eighteenth-century Anglo-American political culture. Freedom, it was commonly held, could only result from economic independence. And nothing assured that independence better than ownership of property in land. Not for nothing was property a requirement of voting in both Britain and the American colonies.[16]

But by the 1760s, the landed elite had taken this concern for the value of property in land and turned it into a fetish, a compulsion for endless accumulation that struck some American colonists as not simply wrong, but a sign that morality and economics were going separate ways. In North Carolina, backcountry farmers objected to merchants and land speculators who, fixated on unlimited economic gain, allowed the farmers to squat on and improve land and then sold the very same land back to the people who had done all the work to transform it. The backcountry farmers protested in vain that mixing their labor with the land ought to have resulted in title to the property, much as John Locke, the philosopher of liberalism, had argued. Likewise, in New York, individual landlords accumulated title to hundreds of thousands of acres of land; farmers who had improved the property while cultivating it, often for many years, could only keep it by paying rent to the wealthy owners. The ordinary farmers might have no problem with the idea of private ownership of land, but could not help resenting, and sometimes rebelling against, those hell-bent on monopolizing rights to the earth.[17]

The elites seeking to profit from the stockpiling of land had no patience for the British authorities who wanted to stop them from expropriating the Indians so as to reduce conflict and save on the costs involved in defending the colonies. That's why the grievance surfaces in the Declaration of Independence.[18]

As if to underscore the point, when the colonists emerged victorious in the Revolutionary War, they forewent all the legal niceties involved in purchasing title to Indian land. The government established under the Articles of Confederation held that those Indians who had fought on the British side were to be considered defeated enemies whose lands could now be confiscated without any compensation at all.[19]

With the creation of the United States, the government again began purchasing land from the Indians under the treaty system formerly in use. But by the 1790s, the treaty system had been transformed into a means of colonial domination and a way of separating Indians from the land. Legal safeguards, in other words, did not change the power dynamic, which was tilted heavily in the Euro-Americans' favor, especially in its limits on how the Indians could dispose of their land. "It seems to us that we are not really free men, nor have we had the real disposal of our property," explained Good Peter, an Oneida leader, in 1792. "If we understand what is meant by a person's being free and independent, as to his own property, he may either lend, or sell his property, or any portion of it, as he pleases." The treaty system had by this point evolved into little more than a "license for empire."[20]

The dispossession of the Indians east of the Mississippi was, of course, a violent process. But beyond the brutal subjugation involved in getting the Indians to part with their land, there existed a logic that the leaders of the new republic could use to rationalize their conquests. Henry Knox, George Washington's secretary of war, understood the expropriation of the Indians as part of a civilizing process whereby Indian men would retire from hunting and embrace farming, animal husbandry, and, above all, private property. If they did that, the Indians would not need communal access to hunting grounds extending over vast areas, and the citizens of the new republic would have the elbow room they desired.[21]

REVOLUTION IN LAND

One of the most revolutionary aspects of the American Revolution and the period that followed was the new approach to the land they introduced. The English colonists brought with them the idea that land, under the capitalist system, was a commodity that could be bought and sold, which was something that the Indians had never dreamed of in the years prior to contact. In this way of doing business with the earth, nature was reduced to the abstraction of land—in effect, a commodity that could be exchanged on a market. Nevertheless, many ordinary Americans in the mid-eighteenth century continued to relate directly with the earth and saw in that land the prospect of a comfortable, independent life, not a means of accumulating wealth. By the late 1700s, as the colonists continued to expropriate Indian lands east of the Mississippi, a struggle had broken out between ordinary Americans who viewed the land as a tool to address human need and benefit entire communities and the colonial elite who saw in the land a way of making a profit.[22]

How, then, did the colonists interact with the earth in order to achieve a semblance of material well-being within their local communities? By the eighteenth century, colonial agroecosystems (ecosystems organized around agriculture) in, say, New England, rested on reducing the complexity of the land in order to intensify production. As it turned out, New England's soil had a moisture content that made it especially suited for growing grass to support livestock. Grass played the pivotal role in the region's farm ecology. Grass-fed cattle produced manure that in turn was spread over the fields as fertilizer for growing corn and other crops. Grass and cattle helped to maintain soil fertility—the key to reproducing a sustainable form of farm life—by recycling nutrients back into the fields. It is no wonder then that the colonists especially valued the region's meadows—grassy, uncultivated lowlands found along rivers or salt marshes that absorbed nutrients from higher-situated grazing land and barnyards.

In the eighteenth century, this system of mixed husbandry—centered on livestock fertilizing cropland with manure—produced a "comfortable subsistence." Rather than rushing to cut down the forests for fresh land to crop, farmers lived within the constraints set by the availability of grass from the meadowlands.

The grass made the hay feed that produced the dung that carried the crop nutrients—an agroecological chain that set a cap on the extent of land that could be plowed. This was likely one of the most ecologically sustainable farming ventures in American history, a way of making a living from the land founded not on the creation of endless profits, but on serving human needs within the limits set by the all-important meadowlands.[23]

While agroecosystems along these lines took root in New England and elsewhere in colonial North America (excepting the plantations found in parts of the South, which will be discussed in more detail later), members of the colonial elite began a rather different dialogue with the land. This was an approach that was organized to extract money from the ground by monopolizing it. By the middle of the eighteenth century, men with vast holdings—millions of acres in some instances—such as Lord Baltimore, the Penn family, Lord Fairfax in Virginia, and Lord Carteret in Carolina, had begun effectively taxing those settlers who farmed on property that they had accumulated. They were joined by a new crop of speculators who gained exclusive legal possession of large amounts of land. The speculators also attempted to turn land into money by selling title to lands settled by people whose efforts to intensify food production in the name of human need could yield profits for the entrepreneurs.[24]

A struggle subsequently ensued between those ordinary colonists seeking economic autonomy by farming the land and those dead set on accumulating wealth from the soil. The patriot Samuel Adams spoke up on behalf of the common people, arguing in 1748 that a philosophy of public-spiritedness was necessary to tackle a world in which men undertook "to put a whole Country in Two or Three people's Pockets." The American Revolution in the minds of many had been fought in part to safeguard the natural right of people to improve land for the sake of making ends meet, though it was rarely acknowledged that the Indians, from whom the land had been expropriated, shared a similar goal in their approach to the earth.[25]

In the two generations after 1760, those seeking a small area to farm and call their own locked horns with the elite seeking to profit from the land. This phenomenon took place in the backcountry throughout the new nation. James Shurtleff, for example, began his adult life very poor but managed in 1783 to make it to Litchfield, Maine, where he settled and improved a plot of open ground. However, he could never afford to pay the proprietor enough to secure title to the property. Some years later, near the end of the century, around the time Thomas Paine was advocating for agrarian justice, Shurtleff made it clear that he, too, believed that all people should have an equal right to the earth—to share, in other words, in the wealth of nature. On his own behalf and that of other ordinary farmers who had improved what they took to be their rightful share of land, only to be stymied and harassed by the landed elite, he wrote: "For one man to thus hold thousands of acres, and others pursued and hunted about, and threatened with the utmost severities, who are endeavoring to draw their support by taking possession of, and occupying a single lot, . . . is a despotism so apparent, that it is shocking to humanity."[26]

The lot of the ordinary farmers was worsened by the overcrowding that was coming to characterize some of the older settlements in British North America. Inheritance customs complicated the situation. Typically the eldest son received a double share of the estate left by the deceased; the remaining shares were divided evenly between other sons and daughters. During the first few generations after the original inheritance, the division of land in this way allowed each succeeding generation a sizable enough piece of property to operate a successful farm. But as the eighteenth century wore on, the repeated division led to progressively smaller estates. Inheritance practices began to change. By the 1720s in Massachusetts, for example, some farms were being passed down intact to the oldest son, with the other siblings left either to migrate or to find some other means of support. This practice became increasingly common in the colonies.

It also became harder for the younger generations to gain access to the right configuration of landed resources, that is, cropland, pasture, and especially meadowland.[27] When population pressure and inheritance customs made meadowland inaccessible to increasing numbers of young farmers, the diversified basis of the agroecological system suffered. Overcrowding and a shift toward a less viable agroecology made it imperative that ordinary people be able to migrate out to the frontier to take up a new plot of ground, and all the more unjust when those who were materialistic tried to block them in their pursuit of economic independence.

Even if they had the right resources and could scrounge up enough money to pay for fresh land, farmers confronted other threats to their livelihood. In making a living from the land by arresting forest growth and replacing it with an abridged form of plant life, the New England colonists found themselves battling various pests and diseases. Passenger pigeons, traveling in flocks that grew to millions of birds, descended en masse onto grain fields.[28] So many grasshoppers converged on the grain crops of the first Massachusetts settlements that the colonists took up brooms to sweep them into the ocean. When the colonists brought barberries from Europe to North America to make jam, they also unwittingly imported a fungal parasite known as the black stem rust (or "blast") that devastated the rye and wheat crops. The blast proved so insidious that in some areas of New England it came close to completely annihilating the wheat crop.

Given the perils involved in pursuing agriculture and simplifying nature, combined with the threats from overcrowding and inheritance customs that had cropped up by the eighteenth century, it is not surprising that ordinary Americans turned to hunting and fishing. The estuaries where freshwater and saltwater came together along the coast of North America were enormously productive fisheries. Common-property arrangements evolved over time in these spots. At the heart of this property regime was local control of the resource to serve the interests of the community. Laws and other regulations attempted to prevent overharvesting and other practices that might diminish the public good.

Shortly after the United States declared its independence in 1776, Pennsylvania passed a remarkable constitution to advance the "common benefit, protection and security of the people." To provide for that security, the government endorsed people's rights to hunt and fish "on the lands they hold, and on all other lands therein not inclosed; and in like manner to fish in all boatable waters, and others not private property." But the democratic sentiments seeking to ensure economic security through common rights to the wealth of nature began to disappear in the 15 years that followed as the gentry redefined liberty to mean, as one historian puts it, the right to "amass as much property as one desired." Predictably, a new state constitution in 1790 did not safeguard the rights of people to hunt and fish the commons.[29]

Democratic access to the earth experienced a similar assault in Virginia. Ordinary people argued as late as 1789 that the waterfalls along the James River "ought to be considered as a common." But some wealthy property owners with land along rivers closed off access to the water. Others tried to assert private rights to what had been fishing places open to all. The common people who lived in Henrico and Chesterfield Counties cried out in 1789 as "men called Speculators . . . ransack earth, air, and water for their private emolument" and deprive "a large part of the Community of the Natural rights & privileges." Customary expectations to be able to fish in rivers began to fade before the rising tide of materialism that washed over life in the new republic.[30]

CONCLUSION

After the American Revolution, the capitalist system entered a new phase as more people found themselves bereft of any direct connection with the earth. Lacking access to land and increasingly deprived of common-property rights to North America's wealth of nature, many ordinary Americans were left with little choice but to sell their labor to survive or risk ending up like Mayo Greenleaf Patch and his wife, Abigail McIntire Patch. The Patchs' life story reflects the changing times, during which people lost their connection to the land and had to either make money selling their labor power in the market or starve.

Mayo Greenleaf Patch was born in 1766, the youngest of 10 children, to a father who himself had inherited an 18-acre farm with a small additional amount of meadow and woodland. When his father passed, Patch inherited nothing. Like many others at the time, he owned no land in a culture that attached enormous value to property. Young Mayo Greenleaf went on to live a very checkered life. With no access to land of his own, he descended into debt, alcoholism, divorce, and imprisonment. He survived through various schemes and by dint of family connections and the fact that his wife, Abigail, was able to secure employment in 1807 in the famous mill town of Pawtucket, Rhode Island, where she and her children worked in the production of cotton textiles. The textile work was made possible by the waterfall located in the middle of the town. A new set of social and environmental relations was taking shape.[31]

PART TWO

RATIONALIZATION AND ITS DISCONTENTS

4

A WORLD OF COMMODITIES

It is difficult to imagine that history in the United States, much less the rest of the world, would have unfolded in quite the same way it did were it not for the end of the Little Ice Age. The cold summers and harsh winters that had characterized the Northern Hemisphere since at least the sixteenth century gradually eased in the decades from the late eighteenth to the mid-nineteenth century. Humans became less inexorably subject to climate, pests, and disease. To be sure, the earth erupted periodically in unpredictable ways, with consequences that hit farmers especially hard. For example, hunger became a serious issue in 1789 throughout New England, upstate New York, Pennsylvania, and Canada. A visitor to the Green Mountains remarked: "The year 1789 will be remembered by Vermont as a day of calamity and famine. . . . It is supposed by the most judicious & knowing that more than 1/4 part of the people will have neither bread nor meat for 8 weeks—and that some will starve."[1] Some blamed the gall midge, an insect that thrives in cool, damp weather, its larvae feeding on and destroying wheat. Inclement weather conditions conducive to the spread of the midge surfaced because of volcanic eruptions in Japan and Iceland. Tons of volcanic dust reduced the amount of sunlight reaching the earth, thereby lowering global temperatures.[2]

Likewise, the eruption on April 13, 1815, of Mount Tombora in Indonesia lifted copious rock and ash into the sky. The eruption resulted in severe cold across much of the Western world. Snow and ice were reported in parts of New England for all 12 months of the year. Assessments of the 1816 harvest from every part of the region confirm that the corn crop was nearly a total loss. The effects of the cold were felt as far south as South Carolina, which reported crop deficiencies. These regional problems were part of a much larger calamity that historian John Post has dubbed the "last great subsistence crisis of the western world."[3]

Still, by the early nineteenth century a new form of capitalism was taking shape that would precipitate a far more aggressive approach to the natural world, liberating people from some natural constraints and simultaneously converting features of the natural world into commodities that could be sold for a profit. Historian John Brooke has described the new dynamic as bringing about "human-induced environmental degradation."[4]

This more disruptive form of capitalism caught the attention of a nature writer and anarchist named Henry David Thoreau (1817–1862). Thoreau was one of the nineteenth century's leading critics of progress and its impact on the natural world. After retreating to a cabin on Walden Pond in the woods outside of Boston, Thoreau wrote his most famous book, *Walden, Or Life in the Woods*. Thoreau never believed that landownership conferred any true claim to nature. In one of his journal entries, he wrote of an encounter with a townsman that provoked his distaste for the idea of putting a price tag on nature: "Remarking to old Mr. B——— the other day on the abundance of apples, 'Yes,' says he, 'and fair as dollars too.' That's the kind of beauty they see in apples."[5] Thoreau, for his part, saw in apples not dollar signs, but the wondrous glories of life on earth. The bard of Walden, however, was out of step with the ruling materialism of his time.

It is widely recognized that industrial capitalism spawned a revolution in social relations as people with no access to land or the means of production were compelled to enter the world of wage work. Capitalists profited as workers created more value than they cost their employers in wages. Less well known is that industrial capitalism brought with it a new, more instrumental approach to nature. Corporations emerged to treat the natural world in ways that "externalized" the costs of using land, water, and air, leaving those costs for others to bear. The new capitalists thereby derived profits from the difference between what they paid for natural resources and what the degradation of those resources really cost society.[6]

One of the most powerful tools for rationalizing industrial capitalism's approach to "resources" was the concept of the commodity. By conceiving of such things as water and trees as commodities, rather than as the face of nature, and putting

WALDEN POND

In 1845, Henry Thoreau moved into a cabin on this spot in Concord, Massachusetts, a place where local farmers cut wood for fuel. (Library of Congress)

a price on them, it became possible to efficiently manage and reallocate so-called resources. Reduced to economic units, elements of nature were moved about the country like pieces on a chessboard, redressing resource deficiencies wherever they arose and contributing to the national obsession with economic growth.

FACTORY WATERS

In 1790, the United States was a reasonably prosperous nation of 4 million people—mainly farmers—packed into a narrow strip of land stretching from Maine to Georgia. Seventy years later, the country had become one of the world's leading economic powers, with a population of 31 million. It led all nations in the amount of wheat it exported and ranked third in manufacturing behind only Britain and France. Average per capita wealth boomed in the first half of the nineteenth century; goods once available only to the wealthiest Americans became ordinary, everyday items. Economic growth, in turn, fueled the expansion of cities. Between 1790 and 1860, the urban population increased more than 30-fold from 202,000 to 6,217,000. An industrial revolution swept across the North, transforming the nation into an economic powerhouse.

Factories, machines, railroads—these are the images that typically come to mind when we think about the industrial revolution. But industrial capitalism was not primarily a techno-economic system; it was a socioecological regime based on wage labor and the streamlining of nature. One of the earliest efforts at rationalization involved a shift in the use of rivers.

Long before water became a commodity used to power New England's factories, before the dams and canals produced energy, farmers relied on rivers and streams to provide food for the family economy. In the spring, when winter stores ran low, the colonists went fishing for shad, alewives, and salmon, species of fish that return from the ocean to freshwater streams to reproduce. Salmon were so plentiful during the colonial period that as late as 1700 they sold for only one cent a pound. Shad were even more copious, so much so that some felt embarrassed to be caught eating them. As one observer recalled, "It was discreditable for those who had a competency to eat shad." One New Hampshire farmer visited a fishing place on the Merrimack River for six straight days in June 1772 and returned with a remarkable 551 shad for his efforts. In response to the spring profusion of fish, farmers descended on the region's rivers, turning the most productive fishing spots into veritable carnivals, replete with drinking and card playing. By securing an important supply of dietary protein at precisely the point in the seasonal cycle when they needed it most, farmers may have also been able to relieve feelings of loneliness brought on by a long, hard winter.[7]

In the middle of the eighteenth century, as demographic strains surfaced in New England, fish took on even more importance in the family economy. By this time, inhabitants had lost their embarrassment over eating shad, and the fish sold for a penny apiece in the Connecticut River Valley. It is quite likely that the intensification of fishing led to a decline in the stock of migrating fish even before industrial capitalism and the damming of rivers delivered their own blows to the migrations.

With farmers more dependent than ever on fish, economic change and the rise of a new group of river users set the stage for a bitter and protracted conflict over the handling of New England's waters. By the late eighteenth century, the owners of blast furnaces and textile mills had elbowed their way onto the riverbanks, erecting dams to supply factories with power for production. Their move, combined with the harmful effects of farming on spawning grounds (as soil from plowed fields ran off into rivers), led to the eventual decimation of the spring fish runs.

Located on the banks of streams at those points where the water descended most steeply, mills for grinding grain and sawing logs had existed since the early colonial period. Noisy and cumbersome wooden wheels captured the energy of the water as it rushed downstream and put it to work. The sounds of progress, however, could only be heard on a seasonal basis. The grinding of grain took place mainly in the fall, so it was hardly a problem for mill owners to open the dam gates in the spring when the fish runs began. But the new breed of factories required a continuous supply of water. Blast furnaces relied on a large leather bellows, powered by a waterwheel, to stoke the fire needed to remove the impurities from iron ore. Such furnaces for producing pig iron ran all day. With winters too cold for working out-of-doors, summers too hot, and fall a time of low river water levels, spring proved the ideal season to put a furnace in blast. Fishing suffered as a result.

Textile factories were another story altogether. They raised high dams to create enough energy to power large numbers of machines and presented an even greater barrier for fish. The Englishman Samuel Slater, builder of what is reputed to be the first textile factory in America, constructed a dam in the early 1790s in Pawtucket, Rhode Island, that blocked the passage of fish upstream. In 1792, backcountry farmers petitioned the Rhode Island General Assembly to force Slater to remove the dam. But one of Slater's partners used his political muscle with the legislature to head off the opposition.[8]

In its scale, even the Slater mill was nothing compared with the factories that followed along New England's more powerful Merrimack and Connecticut rivers. These enterprises had vast energy needs and, in the quest for greater production and profit, eventually transformed water itself into a commodity. The construction of mills at Lowell, Massachusetts, on the Merrimack River helped lead to this new conception of water. In 1821, a group of New England capitalists known as the Boston Associates purchased land and water rights at Pawtucket Falls. Over the course of the next 15 years, they built an elaborate waterpower labyrinth consisting of seven power canals and a supporting network of locks and dams to produce the energy to make cotton cloth. The Boston Associates' highly capitalized corporations marked a new generation of business enterprises that outstripped all earlier attempts to control water. But as impressive as the physical infrastructure was, the corporations showed even more creativity and drive when it came to selling the water itself.

In early America, the English common law (a body of legal principles based on court decisions and customs, as opposed to law created by legislative enactments) guided the colonists in their relationship with water. Landowners along a river did not have outright ownership of the waterways, but they did have rights to use the water for fishing or other purposes as long as they did not impede the natural flow to the detriment of others along the stream. When mill owners sold their property, they rarely, if ever, provided precise figures on the amount of water that flowed through it. They simply sold the land with the understanding that the new owner would have whatever rights that the law allowed.[9]

The corporation responsible for distributing water at Lowell, however, disposed of the resource in a completely different manner. One of its chief innovations was the "mill-power" concept. A mill-power equaled the amount of water necessary to drive 3,584 spindles for spinning cotton yarn—the capacity of one of the Boston Associates' earliest factories—plus all the other machinery necessary for transforming the yarn into cloth. The concept enabled the company to easily package water and put it up for sale. By the 1830s, companies at Lowell were even purchasing water without buying any land, breaking with past tradition. Water had morphed into a commodity.

This trend went hand in hand with increasing ecological change, especially in the 1840s, as plans accelerated to build a new textile city downstream from Lowell in Lawrence, Massachusetts. With only a 5-foot drop in elevation at the river site—compared with a 30-foot fall at Lowell—a dam 32 feet high had to be built to supply enough energy to the Lawrence factories. The completion of this monumental structure sealed off the Merrimack River, providing a crippling blow to the already severely compromised spring fish runs. What had once been a free-flowing body of water open to salmon, shad, and alewives had been transformed into one long power canal.

With Lawrence rising along the lower Merrimack and the mills at Lowell running more machinery than ever before, waterpower became an increasingly precious commodity. The unpredictability of rainfall and the increased demand for waterpower eventually spurred the corporations along the lower Merrimack to seek control over the river itself, all the way from its headwaters in New Hampshire down to the sea. By 1859, the factories at Lowell and Lawrence had, by virtue of an elaborate series of land purchases, secured the rights to New Hampshire's largest lakes, an empire amounting to 103 square miles of water.

Using a set of dams placed at the outlets of the lakes, agents employed by the Massachusetts factories stored water in the winter and spring for use between July and October, when a lack of rain often made water scarce. In the past, the mills had been at the mercy of the seasons, with dry conditions dragging down production. The New Hampshire acquisitions, however, liberated the factories from nature's calendar and allowed them to hum all year round.

This grand scheme for efficiently controlling the entire river amounted to a massive redistribution of water wealth from New Hampshire to Massachusetts. Some considered what the Boston Associates had done to be tantamount to theft, and they rose up in defiance. In 1859, a group protested by trying to destroy a dam in Lake Village, New Hampshire, a key structure in the Boston Associates' water system. The attackers included farmers angry over the flooding of their meadows to convenience out-of-state factories; upstream mill owners who resented being forced to follow the waterpower schedule of the lower Merrimack corporations; loggers who wanted the gates lowered to send timber downstream; and many who were poor and dispossessed, incensed that the economic transformation pulsing through the region had left them behind.

Others eschewed violence and turned to the law to redress their grievances. What they found was that the law too was changing, evolving in a direction that encouraged the diversion of water resources for the benefit of the new industrial capitalism. In deciding disputes over access to water, the courts had long held to a so-called natural flow rule: water had to flow as it had customarily flowed. In the nineteenth century, however, as large manufacturing establishments filled in the riverbanks of the North, the courts shifted toward the doctrine of reasonable use. Under this new rule, courts weighed the different interests at stake in the use of water, sacrificing the wishes of some for the larger good of a community. "The rule is flexible, and suited to the growing and changing wants of communities," wrote one New Hampshire judge.[10] Because no one could say exactly what was in the best interests of any community, the rule tended to favor those who used the river most profitably. The doctrine rested on an understanding of water as a commodity in the service of economic growth. Such a view meshed nicely with the needs of the Boston Associates, who in the end had their way with the river.

The industrial revolution meant more than simply the rise of factories, railroads, and new forms of work and social life. It brought about class conflict under the factory roof—strikes and walkouts over wages and hours—but it also involved a struggle over nature, over who would control it and for what ends. The mills along the lower Merrimack incorporated the natural wealth available in the countryside into their designs for production and in so doing produced more than just cloth. They generated a chain of ecological and social consequences that spilled out beyond the factories, affecting places and people more than 100 miles away in a completely different state. Nothing better demonstrates the ways in which industrial capitalism led to a major rationalization and reallocation of natural resources, enriching some at the expense of others.

GRID AND GRAIN

Efforts to commodify water coincided with a far more sweeping attempt to package and impose order on the fertile lands of the Midwest and beyond. Beginning in the 1780s and continuing into the next century, the rich soil of the prairie was neatly divided and sold to farmers. The farmers planted grain and then marketed it throughout America and Europe, extracting the West's soil to create wealth.

More than anyone else, Thomas Jefferson initiated the makeover of the West into a checkerboard. Jefferson believed that small freeholding farmers—yeomen, men who could care for their families on their own without the need of hired hands—formed the basis of a democratic society. "Cultivators of the earth are the most valuable citizens," he wrote in 1785. "They are the most vigorous, the most independent, the most virtuous & they are tied to their country & wedded to liberty & interests by the most lasting bonds."[11] Just the right amount of land was needed to ensure the yeoman's independence and virtue. Too much land would create a nation of tyrants; too little, a country of paupers. Striking the perfect balance between western soil and the people who would farm it preoccupied this founding father.

To execute his plan for democracy, Jefferson proposed something called the U.S. Rectangular Land Survey—familiarly known as "the grid." Under this plan, surveyors were first sent to eastern Ohio with instructions to divide the land into boxes that would measure six miles square. Then they were instructed to divide these larger boxes into smaller ones, one mile square, which were divided yet again into quarter sections measuring 160 acres each, considered to be the approximate size of a single farm. In 1785, Congress passed the grid into law, and from that point on this same checkerboard pattern was etched across the West— one of world history's most far-reaching attempts at rationalizing a landscape.

The grid aided in the rapid settlement of the country, turning millions of Americans into independent landowners, while at the same time turning the land itself—its varied topography, soil, and water conditions—into a commodity, a uniform set of boxes easily bought and sold. But the grid was only the first step in the prairie's journey to distant markets.

Once farmers purchased land, they needed to plow up the existing vegetation. The prairie grasses that thrived on the organically rich, deep soil laid down by the glaciers thousands of years earlier presented a challenge to cut. Wooden plows with edges made of iron proved virtually useless. Only with the development and spread of the steel plow—invented in 1837 by John Deere, an Illinois blacksmith—did the dense sod succumb. In place of the native vegetation, farmers planted corn and wheat, domesticated species of grass that grow best in a monocultural environment, that is, in fields by themselves. These crops tend to grow quickly, socking away carbohydrates in their seeds. With bread constituting a major component of the American diet, wheat would eventually emerge as the West's major cash crop; acres and acres of some of the world's best agricultural land in Ohio, Indiana, Illinois, Iowa, and Kansas were plowed up and given over to the plant.

In the early years of settlement, farmers grew a variety of crops, including wheat, corn, oats, rye, and barley. Increasingly, however, they specialized, as commercial agriculture, aided by improved railroad transportation, proceeded apace. Much of the grain ended up in the Northeast, where by the 1840s population

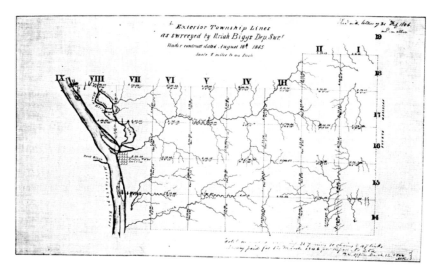

THE GRID

Surveyors finished imposing the geometric logic of the grid on the area east of present-day La Crosse, Wisconsin, in 1845. (Hildegard Binder Johnson, Order upon the Land [New York: Oxford University Press, 1976])

growth had outstripped the local farm economy's ability to provide. In effect, the West's surplus of soil wealth underwrote industrial development farther east.

The railroads not only delivered the products of the rich soils of the prairie into the bellies of easterners. They also changed the meaning of the crops themselves. During the era of water-borne transportation, farmers put their grain into sacks so they could be easily loaded into the irregularly shaped holds of steamboats. The advent of the railroads and steam-powered grain elevators (first developed in 1842) spurred farmers to eliminate the sack altogether. Now grain could move like a stream of water, making its journey to market with the aid of a mechanical device that loaded all the wheat from a particular area into one large grain car. Sacks had preserved the identity of each load of grain. With the new technology, however, grain from different farms was mixed together and sorted by grade. The Chicago Board of Trade (established in 1848) divided wheat into three categories—spring, white winter, and red winter—applying quality standards to each type. Wheat became an abstract commodity, with ownership over the grain diverging from the physical product itself. By the 1860s, a futures market in grain had even emerged in Chicago. Traders could still buy and sell grain in the city as they had long done. But it was now also possible to enter into a contract to purchase or sell grain at a particular price. What was being marketed here was not the physical grain itself so much as an abstraction, the right to trade something that did not yet exist.[12]

The grid helped draw what had been Indian land into the capitalist system. Then the railroads and the advent of grain-grading systems turned the products of the soil itself into something that could be packaged and sold. It would be hard to overestimate the importance of commodities in nineteenth-century America. They played a key part in mediating the relationship between people and the natural world.

THE BUSINESS OF TREES

Although the farmers who settled the prairie found rich soils, one natural re-source was missing from the landscape, and it was a critical one: wood. Wood played a role in the nineteenth century akin to that of plastic and steel in our own time. Just about everything that was built, from homes to roads and bridges, involved wood. Its greatest use was in homes for heat, but it also pow-ered railroads and steamboats and helped make charcoal for the iron industry. In 1839, Americans consumed 1.6 billion board feet of lumber. Thirty years later that figure had risen steeply to 12.8 billion board feet. After 1860, much of that wood came not from New England and New York but from the vast forest reserves of the Great Lakes states of Michigan, Wisconsin, and Minnesota. Yet another major reallocation of the nation's natural resources was under way.[13]

The explosive growth in the population of the central United States, an almost fivefold increase between 1850 and 1890, spawned much of the demand for wood. As one early observer put it, the Illinois prairie, "which strikes the eye so delightfully, and where millions of acres invite the plough, wants timber for building, fencing, and fuel." Urban and industrial change in the Northeast also brought about an equally significant demand for wood. New York City alone, which rose to become what one British newspaper called "the London of the New World" after the opening of the Erie Canal in 1825, required huge amounts of lumber. At first the city drew on the Adirondack Mountains to supply its building and energy needs. But rapid economic growth stimulated the need for more distant sources. Canals such as the Erie and others that linked eastern rivers with the Great Lakes opened up the pine forests of the central states to consumers in New York City.[14]

Pine is a durable and strong wood that is soft enough to be easily worked with even the simplest of hand tools, making it especially attractive for building purposes. It also floats nicely on water, making it easy to transport. The central and northern reaches of Michigan, Wisconsin, and Minnesota all contained ex-tensive pine forests, as well as many large rivers for floating logs into the Great Lakes. What the Erie Canal did for markets in the East, the Illinois-Michigan Canal (which connected the Chicago and Illinois rivers in 1847) did for markets in the West. The canal put an end to the log cabins that dotted the plains. Balloon-frame houses replaced them, structures whose lightweight, milled lumber drew down the forest reserves of the Great Lakes states.[15]

The Illinois-Michigan Canal further solidified Chicago's position as the country's dominant wholesale lumber center. In 1847, some 32 million board feet of lumber passed through the city; after the canal opened, the figure rose to 125 million in 1851 and more than 1 billion in 1869. Chicago was well positioned to mediate exchange between the forested regions north of the city and the largely treeless prairie to the south and west. The city acted like a huge magnet for timber originating along rivers such as the Peshtigo and Menominee in eastern Wisconsin and the Muskegon, Grand, and Manistee in western Michigan. These rivers carried lumber directly into Lake Michigan. From there the wood made its way to Chicago, where wholesalers sorted it and sent it west as far as Colorado and south as far as Texas.[16]

By 1860, the settlement of the West along with timber shortages in the East had converged with ever-widening impact on the pine forests of the Great Lakes states. Over the next 30 years, lumbering evolved into a full-fledged industrial enterprise in Michigan, Wisconsin, and Minnesota. Instead of simply cutting down individual trees and sending them to market, which the colonists had done as far back as the seventeenth century, newly formed lumbering corporations bought up prodigious tracts of pineland and set wage laborers to work systematically cutting down the trees. The industrialists adopted a far more thorough and calculating approach to removing trees than the colonists had. In this sense, what happened between 1860 and 1890 represented a significant break with the past. No longer were farmers who needed extra income the main source for shingles, firewood, and other wood products. By the 1870s, farmers and city dwellers alike were purchasing forest products at a distance from large, concentrated manufacturing concerns located in the Great Lakes states rather than chopping wood themselves or buying it locally.[17]

The creation of wealth by extracting profits from wage laborers, who exploited the raw material served up by the forests, received a hand from technological change. The early, thick saw blades tended to waste significant wood, with perhaps as much as a third of the log left behind on the floor as sawdust or scrap. In the 1870s, however, the British-invented band saw, with its thinner blade, became standard issue in the Great Lakes states' lumber factories. Meanwhile, the rise of steam-powered mills simplified production by allowing more efficient, centralized, and continuous cutting of lumber. Steam helped to automate a variety of tasks, from cutting to the carrying away of waste. Friction feeds, for instance, automatically sent the logs directly past the saws. Mills also employed steam to heat log ponds, preventing them from freezing and making possible year-round lumber production.[18]

For industrial capitalist lumbering to succeed, a way had to be found to neutralize the effects of the seasons on production. Traditionally, cutting took place in the winter, when snow and ice made it easier to drag logs to the banks of streams. Once the streams and lakes thawed, workers rafted the logs to mills, where they were cut into lumber in the summer. If nature did not cooperate—if the winter proved dry and warm, or if the spring thaw was delayed—production would suffer. To counter the effects of climate on lumber production, loggers experimented with a variety of techniques for transporting trees out of the woods. In the 1870s, loggers in the Great Lakes states began sprinkling water on sleigh roads, giving them an ice coating to facilitate travel. The ice reduced the friction and allowed workers to move larger and heavier loads, with some sleighs capable of carrying over 100 tons of timber.[19]

But all the sprinkling in the world would not save a logger from the threat of a warm winter. Without snow the sleigh roads turned to mud. In the 1870s, several snowless winters left lumber companies to ponder ways of liberating themselves from the seasons. Railroads offered one possibility. At first, the remoteness of the pine forests discouraged common carriers from laying track. But rising lumber prices in the late 1870s combined with periodic warm, dry winters compelled logging companies to take advantage of railroads that had penetrated the forest. By 1887, 89 logging railroads crisscrossed Michigan, transforming logging from a winter activity into a year-round one.[20]

Once the logs arrived at a river, the trip downstream to a mill could be long and tortuous. Logjams—at times stretching for 10 miles—happened frequently as pressure on the northern Midwest pinelands increased in the 1860s. To help keep the logs moving efficiently, workers built barriers out of chains of floating logs called booms to control the direction of the timber. By the 1870s, booming companies existed in all the major logging areas of the northern Midwest.

Frederick Weyerhaeuser of Rock Island, Illinois, epitomized the new industrial capitalist approach to lumber. Weyerhaeuser had a stake in 18 lumber manufacturers and oversaw the cutting of timber throughout a large part of the Chippewa, St. Croix, and Upper Mississippi watersheds. By buying up other milling companies and controlling all the processes of production from the felling of the tree to the making of mass-produced lumber, Weyerhaeuser and his associates achieved a large degree of both horizontal and vertical economic integration. "In his way," geographer Michael Williams has written, "Weyerhaeuser was the counterpart of Rockefeller in oil or Carnegie in steel."[21]

Lumber capitalists like Weyerhaeuser owed their success in large measure to help from the federal government, which subsidized large-scale lumber production mainly through the sale, at bargain prices, of federal timberland. By allowing lumber companies to amass huge quantities of inexpensive land, the government underwrote the industry's growth. Even land granted to railroad and canal companies eventually came under the control of large lumber interests. Perhaps most surprising of all, this enormous giveaway of what one commissioner of the General Land Office in 1876 called our "national heritage" took place without any deliberate decision on the part of Congress.[22]

Of course the lumber companies really had no interest in the land per se. What they wanted was the right to cut the timber. Once the trees disappeared, the companies willingly relinquished their land claims, often defaulting on their taxes or selling the land cheaply. Lumber barons simply sought the ability to cut wood. They received, in effect, unconditional licenses to fell timber.[23] The forest and the soil parted ways as the objectification of trees brought them even more squarely in line with the abstract world of prices and markets.

LOGJAM

Logjams often developed in the spring as workers floated logs downstream to mills. Men risked their lives trying to dislodge what sometimes amounted to tens of thousands of logs stacked as tall as 10 feet high. The jam pictured here occurred on Wisconsin's Chippewa River in 1869. (Library of Congress)

This calculating and systematic approach to the removal of trees went on with little to no regard for future yields. The end result was the eventual destruction of the forests. By 1900, the pinelands of the northern Midwest had been logged out. With the consuming public more reliant on pine than ever before, it would not be long before the timber capitalists of the Great Lakes states set off in search of new woods to cut. By the 1890s, they had targeted the American South, and a decade later the far West, where the name Weyerhaeuser would soon become synonymous with timber.

As the lumber barons left the upper Midwest, they gave over their abandoned stumplands to settlement companies, which tried to entice people into farming the cutover land. But the land, so full of stones and stumps, proved difficult if not impossible to plow. And in any case, the climate was too cold for agriculture. But none of this gave speculators such as the infamous James Leslie "Stump Land" Gates reason for pause as they misled prospective settlers into thinking that financial success lay just around the corner.[24]

The wholesale logging of the northern woods created the perfect setting for fires. The loggers, in their haste to remove those trees with commercial value, produced an incredible amount of slash, the branches and other debris left behind in the cutting. In 1871, a Port Huron, Michigan, man reportedly walked for an entire mile stepping from one branch to the next without ever setting foot on the ground. When farmers moved into the region they set fire to the slash

PESHTIGO FIRE, 1871

The late nineteenth century witnessed some of the worst wildland fires in American history, as steam locomotives, throwing sparks, wound through logged-out landscapes littered with downed branches. (Wisconsin Historical Society)

to remove it—only the fires burned out of control. In the 50 years after 1870, massive conflagrations swept across the landscape. In 1871, referred to as the "Black Year," fires scorched Illinois, Wisconsin, Michigan, and Indiana. Indeed, the word firestorm was actually coined in response to these disasters, only to be rediscovered during World War II. Fifteen hundred people may have died in a fire around Peshtigo, Wisconsin. Many were asphyxiated in their cellars, where they fled to escape the smoke and heat. Other major fires singed Michigan in 1881 and Minnesota, Wisconsin, and Michigan in 1894.[25]

One survivor of the 1871 Peshtigo fire recalled that many people saw the event as proof that Judgment Day had come, falling to the ground and prostrating themselves before God. "Indeed this apprehension, that the last day was at hand, pervaded even the strongest and most mature minds," one writer recorded.[26] But far from being acts of God, the fires were, in fact, a testament to the unintended ecological consequences that derived from the systematic attempt by timber capitalists to create wealth by combining wage labor and the riches of the northern forests.

PIGEON FEVER

The transformation of the northern woods into stumpland was rivaled by another equally impressive vanishing act: the sudden extermination of the most prolific bird on the face of the earth. In early America, flocks of passenger pigeons—a

16-inch-long, slate-colored bird with violet, gold, and green about the neck and a wedge-shaped tail—literally darkened the sky. A swarm of pigeons passing near Cooperstown, New York, "extended from mountain to mountain in one solid blue mass," wrote James Fenimore Cooper in his 1823 novel The Pioneers, "and the eye looked in vain over the southern hills to find its termination." A decade later, ornithologist Alexander Wilson, working at a site near the Ohio River, wrote of being "suddenly struck with astonishment at a loud rushing roar, succeeded by instant darkness." He likened the pigeons passing overhead to a tornado and calculated the entire flock to be about 2 billion birds.[27]

Periodically, the birds made a nuisance of themselves, feasting on the colonists' grain fields. But sometimes the pigeons arrived during a period of scarcity and the colonists managed to kill enough of them to stave off famine, as happened in 1769 during a Vermont crop failure. By the mid-nineteenth century, however, the birds were being pushed to extinction. A number of factors contributed to their decline. The growth of cities played a role. Farmers, who had long been in the habit of killing the birds for food, took to packing them up in barrels and shipping them off to urban areas. Meanwhile, deforestation destroyed habitat and nesting areas. Even the pigeons themselves played a part in their own demise. The birds produced only one egg, limiting their reproductive potential. They also tended to roost in such great numbers that they caused tree branches to snap off, killing their young. The last significant nesting in New England happened in 1851, near the town of Lunenburg, Massachusetts. The following year, Henry David Thoreau wrote: "Saw pigeons in the woods, with their inquisitive necks and long tails, but few representatives of the great flocks that once broke down our forests."[28]

By the second half of the nineteenth century, the northern Midwest had become the pigeon's last refuge. In 1871, south-central Wisconsin witnessed an immense nesting; perhaps as many as 136 million pigeons fanned out over a 750-square-mile area. Seven years later, another humongous nesting took place, this time near Petoskey, Michigan. Then, quite suddenly, over the course of just a single generation, the great flocks vanished. In 1890, one observer wrote: "I have often stood in the farm-yard, gazing in rapt admiration, as the setting sun was darkened by the traveling flocks. We miss them more than any other birds."[29]

Why the end came so rapidly remains something of a puzzle. Certainly the rise of market hunting, aided by the spread of the railroad and the telegraph, played an important part. While colonial farmers had relied on the pigeon to supplement their own diets, shipping the occasional barrel to the city, the market hunters reduced the pigeons to a pure commodity, with little meaning beyond the price they would bring. Alerted by the telegraph to the start of a major passenger pigeon nesting, market hunters piled into trains, which by the 1850s had expanded throughout the northern Midwest. The trains also allowed the hunters to ship the pigeons back to consumers in cities, including Chicago, St. Louis, Philadelphia, Boston, and New York.[30]

HUNTING PARTY

Sportsmen took special trains, like the one pictured here in Minnesota in 1880, to wetlands and other environments, where they hunted birds. (Minnesota Historical Society)

But technological change and commodification alone probably would not have led to the pigeon's demise had not ecology also intervened. The pigeons fed on the nuts produced by beech, oak, and hickory trees and congregated in gigantic colonies; they were living proof of the dictum that there is safety in numbers, at least against such predators as hawks and raccoons. Such immense numbers of birds ensured that at least some eggs and young birds would always survive. But when market hunters severely thinned out the flocks, the last remaining pigeons may have been unable to stave off their predators.[31]

Measuring the ecological effects of the pigeon's decline is difficult. Pigeon dung may seem like an inconsequential thing. But the gargantuan quantities produced by the vast flocks of birds had the power to influence the ecology of entire regions, providing an important source of nutrients in roosting areas. The pigeon's demise cut off this fertilizer source, with potentially far-reaching effects on plant and forest life.

The bird's extinction may have had an even more profound effect on the relationship Americans had with the land's natural rhythms.[32] We can only imagine how it felt to have spring arrive and look up into the sky at thousands, even millions, of birds. When the birds vanished, joining the spring migrations of salmon and shad in the annals of destruction, there was one less natural event to mark the onset of this season. Farmers and urbanites alike grew further detached from the cycles of nature.

Industrial capitalism involved a kind of war waged against seasonal variation. Whether this meant getting water to flow when industrialists, not nature, demanded or building tram roads so that loggers could cut and transport trees all year round, the result was the same. Seasonal change gave way to the mechanical ticking of the clock in a new era, in which time had become money and workers and nature both required discipline in the name of the endless quest for more production and profit.

CONCLUSION

The passenger pigeon's decline was simply one example of the power of industrial capitalism to package the components of an ecosystem and deliver them to wherever demand was greatest. In the process, resources such as cotton cloth, pigeon meat, and lumber lost their binding ties with their place of origin and the human and natural processes responsible for their existence. When the cotton cloth produced at Lowell found its way into a shirt, who, aside from perhaps a mill agent or a disgusted fisherman, would ever think to inquire about the true costs of what went into it: the slave-grown cotton, the overworked machine tenders, the water that was literally drained away from farmers in one state and made to flow according to a capitalist production schedule? Who would possibly see in a roofing shingle the complex set of processes—the federal government's land subsidies, the fires that plagued the land—bound up in this small but essential piece of wood?

Conceiving of things as commodities allowed people to reduce all that was complex and unique, whether pigeon meat, lumber, apples, or oranges, to a single common denominator: price. In a world moving toward such a system, in which something as elusive as water could be owned and sold, grain that did not yet exist could be purchased, and so many aspects of the natural world fell equal before the almighty dollar, it was easy to overlook what separated one thing from another. Commodities have a special ability to hide from view not just the work, the sweat and blood, that went into making them, but also the natural riches, the soil, water, and trees, without which they would not exist. Money, to quote German sociologist Georg Simmel, had become the "frightful leveler," reducing the uniqueness and incomparability of objects to a state of "unconditional interchangeability."[33]

KING CLIMATE IN DIXIE

April 15, 1849, was one of the strangest spring days on record in Dixie. From Georgia west to Texas, a snowstorm and subsequent frost killed cotton, corn, and other crops, as winter refused to relinquish its grip on the land. "The damage done by the late frost you can hardly form an idea unless you were here to see," lamented one South Carolina planter. By all measures, the cold spell was an exceptional event, although it seemed to confirm what James Glen, colonial governor of South Carolina, had said about a century before: "Our Climate is various and uncertain, to such an extraordinary Degree, that I fear not to affirm, there are no people on Earth, who, I think, can suffer greater extremes of Heat and Cold."[1]

It has long been realized that climate has played an important role in southern history.[2] The cultivation of such staple crops as tobacco, rice, and cotton would have been impossible if not for the region's long growing season, its ample rainfall, and its warm weather pattern. Beyond this obvious and important insight, however, climate has largely been taken for granted, with most students of the South viewing it as a largely stable and unchanging aspect of life in this region. And yet it bears noting that slavery and the plantation economy grew fastest during the tail end of the Little Ice Age, a period of erratic weather conditions. Growing any kind of crop is a chancy enterprise, made even more unpredictable by a volatile weather regime, a point not lost on the antebellum South's planter class, which suffered through the 1849 freeze and other cold weather outbreaks, including a devastating episode in February 1835 that killed Florida's entire citrus crop.

Southern plantations based on racial slavery were integral to the United States' emergence as the world's paramount capitalist economy. They played an important part in the trend toward intensification and discipline that increasingly characterized human social relations and interactions with the earth in the name of profits. We cannot fully understand the slave-based plantation economy without recognizing the important role that natural forces played in it.

A MATCH MADE IN VIRGINIA

Located at the northern end of a plantation region stretching as far south as Brazil, the southeastern United States was part of a set of tropical and subtropical environments well suited to growing commodities for European consumption. In Virginia the commodity of choice was tobacco.

From the start, a business mentality informed life in the colony. While the New England colonists held lofty religious ambitions in mind as they ventured across the Atlantic, Virginia's colonists had more mundane goals. They aimed for a comfortable rural existence that would improve on their more meager prospects back home. New Englanders wrote sermons; Virginians published promotional tracts. They tried to sell their newfound home to English people seeking to rise to the status of gentlemen. To secure a decent standard of living, the southern colonists had to import a variety of foods and finished goods from across the Atlantic. And to generate the money needed to purchase them, they produced tobacco, a crop of New World origin demanded by smokers in Europe.[3]

In growing tobacco, southerners, like all good farmers, tried to load the dice in their favor. In the first stage of cultivation, they planted many different beds with the crop, often separated by great distances to fend off pests and disease. But some important aspects of tobacco cultivation were beyond the planter's control. In order for the seedlings to be successfully transplanted, for example, a good, soaking rain was needed so farmers could move the tiny plants without damaging their root structures. In the decision as to when to cut tobacco, planters again gambled with nature. To fail to cut before a frost would lead to the crop's destruction, yet cutting too early to beat the cold could mean harvesting an unripe crop that might fail to cure properly. Successful tobacco planting thus demanded a great deal of luck, a point not lost on eighteenth-century Virginia planter Landon Carter, who in 1771 lost his tobacco to drought, despite his best efforts to ward off disaster. "Had I not been honestly sensible that no care had been wanting nor diligence neglected," he wrote in his diary, "I should be uneasy more than I am; but as I have nothing of this sort to accuse myself with, I must and do submit."[4]

As crops go, tobacco is extremely demanding of the soil. Even the slightest deficiency in a single element—be it nitrogen, potassium, or phosphorus—tends to result in small yields. The problem in the colonial era was that although the South offered ample rain and a long growing season, its soils left much to be desired. The region had escaped the most recent glaciation and thus failed to benefit from the minerals pulverized by the large masses of moving ice. In addition, the area's abundant precipitation tended to cause minerals to leach from the soil. Worse yet, the soil, especially in the Piedmont section comprising the rolling hills between the Appalachian Mountains and the Atlantic coastal plain, was weathered and extremely susceptible to erosion. The poor soil proved no match for the tobacco plant's tremendous mineral appetite. As one observer put it in 1775, "There is no plant in the world that requires richer land, or more manure than tobacco." Faced with such a demanding crop, the colonial tobacco planter was "more solicitous for new land than any other people in America," moving on to fresh soil once the old land became exhausted.[5]

Tobacco demands much of the soil, but it also asks a lot of those who cultivate it. Few crops are quite as labor-intensive. That was a serious problem in land-rich America, where the price of free labor was high. To deal with this dilemma, planters tried to legally bind laborers to their masters to prevent them from seeking out their own land. White indentured servants, bound by contract, worked to clear the land, using hoes to make small hills for planting tobacco or corn. After the soil eventually wore out, the servants went about the laborious task of clearing more land. This system worked reasonably well until the latter part of the seventeenth century, when the price of servants rose while tobacco prices fell. As labor for felling trees became scarce, the supply of fresh land dwindled. Planters continued to cultivate the same plots of soil. By the last third of the century, the older colonial settlements had entered an ecological decline.

SHIFTING AGRICULTURE
Southerners often began the regime of shifting agriculture by burning the woods to help release nutrients into the soil. (Clifton Waller Barrett Library of American Literature, Special Collections, University of Virginia Library)

Trapped by the reality of failing soils, planters eventually exercised their imaginations. Beginning in the 1680s, Chesapeake tobacco planters turned to their Indian predecessors for inspiration, adopting a system of land rotation that has come to be called "shifting agriculture." Under this new regime, servants cleared a handful of acres in a haphazard manner. They then planted corn or beans (in between the leftover stumps) during the first year of cultivation, followed by two to three successive years of tobacco. After that, corn was combined with beans or peas in years four through seven, followed often by a year devoted to wheat. They then abandoned the field for a generation to restore its soil fertility.[6]

The success of this system—which was in widespread use throughout the Chesapeake region by the 1740s—depended on the clearing of new tobacco lands every three to four years. A servant might be available to do the initial work, but once his contract expired, planters scrambled to find labor to clear more land. It is perhaps not coincidental that this more ecologically sustainable form of farming arose at roughly the same time that southern planters were replacing indentured servants with black slaves from Africa. The West Africans were deeply knowledgeable about hoe agriculture and quickly learned the intricacies of tobacco and corn, which had become staples in the Chesapeake by the end of the 1600s. Slavery and shifting cultivation made a perfect match from the planter's standpoint. The land rotation system required the clearing of new tobacco land every three to four years in perpetuity; slavery offered planters a guaranteed labor supply.[7]

The ecological virtues of this new way of relating to the land extended beyond its regenerative effect on soil fertility. It also helped to ward off erosion. Slowly the landscape evolved into a patchwork, with some land in cultivation, some in various stages of abandonment, and some filling in with grass and eventually pines and other trees. With no large expanses of open field, the soil could not fall victim to wind erosion. The fields also contained leftover stumps that acted to check erosion. And with field hands using hoes (not plows) to form hills for planting, the uneven surface trapped water before it disappeared with even more soil. Although this system of land use remained ecologically sound, it depended on continued access to fresh land, something not available on small plantations. Resistance to the system also had some less obvious roots. Allowing land to lie idle offended the moral and aesthetic sensibilities of some southerners, who saw it as their civic duty to transform such barren land in the name of civilization.[8]

Although the land rotation system proved a success in the short run, it eventually broke down under the pressure of population growth and the emergence in the 1700s of large landed estates such as that of William Byrd II, who by 1739 had accumulated 179,000 acres in Virginia—an area nearly the size of all of New York City today.[9] By the last quarter of the eighteenth century, planters in the Chesapeake region had run out of land and were forced to shorten the fallow period. This move hindered the land's ability to replenish itself. Shifting agriculture would soon give way to a more intensive form of farming that proved considerably less stable from an ecological perspective.

The imbalance between population and land generated a number of responses. Some men migrated. Some deferred marrying until they had amassed enough land to raise a family. Others believed that agricultural reform was the answer. People such as John Taylor of Caroline and Edmund Ruffin urged the adoption of a more modern and enlightened set of farming practices. Put aside hoes and axes, they advised, and replace them with plows. Remove stumps and other debris from fields and give them a clean and ordered appearance. Fertilize those fields with manure and add lime (to counteract the acidity of southern soil) and thus use the land continuously rather than abandoning it to lie fallow. But agricultural reform made few inroads in the South. Any reform measure that diverted land, labor, or capital from the production of staple crops raised eyebrows among the planter class. "Our want is the cheapest system of enriching and preserving large plantations," explained one southern planter, "for it is outrageous humbuggery to talk of hauling manure over them."[10]

With the soil no longer allowed to rest for 20 years between plantings, the amount of land in cultivation increased markedly. Land planted with crops in southern Maryland rose from roughly 2 percent of the region's total area in 1720 to almost 40 percent by the early 1800s. When lands became exhausted, some planters sold their Tidewater plantations and ventured into the Piedmont. There they cleared fresh land and then broke out plows to ready the ground for planting tobacco and corn. But farming the Piedmont, with its steep slopes and soils susceptible to erosion, had significant ecological consequences. Sediment soon sluiced into rivers and streams. During a 1779 flood, one observer called the clay-choked James River a "torrent of blood." Beginning in 1780, the port at Baltimore had to be dredged on a regular basis to combat all the silt. The sediment must have destroyed spawning grounds frequented by migrating fish and, with its high concentrations of phosphorus and nitrogen, probably affected other bottom-dwelling organisms as well. Eventually, the fertility was literally mined out of the soil, as planters, in the words of one scholar, "bought land as they might buy a wagon—with the expectation of wearing it out."[11] Commercial farming and ecology had, for the moment, parted ways.

HARNESSING THE TIDES

While the Upper South turned increasingly to plows and continuous cultivation in the years after the American Revolution, planters along the coasts of South Carolina and Georgia experimented with other means of making the landscape bear fruit. Beginning in the 1720s, South Carolinians focused on rice, growing the lucrative crop on dry soil and relying on rainfall for moisture. They soon discovered that yields increased dramatically if the rice crop were grown on marshlands near the coast, where it could be irrigated with reservoirs and ponds. Slaves imported into the colonies from West Africa, where rice had long been grown, played the pivotal role in helping southern planters organize their economy around the grain.

However, rice farming was seldom an easy enterprise. Floods and droughts in the Low Country upset planters' designs for water control. Weeds fed off the rich supply of nutrients and water and posed an even more significant threat. By late spring, slaves were forced to toil away in knee-deep mud in an effort to keep the weeds at bay. Slaves commonly ran away to escape the backbreaking work. At times, plantation managers even resorted to bribery to secure the necessary labor, lest fields be overrun with unwanted vegetation. South Carolina planter Josiah Smith, Jr., found himself forced to offer his slaves the enticements of beef and rum to keep them from fleeing when "the Grass was very bad."[12]

Then, in the 1740s, planters tapped the know-how of their West African slaves and discovered a means of recruiting nature to their cause. Huge numbers of blacks skilled in the cultivation of rice in wetland environments came to South Carolina in the 20 years following 1750. Together, slaves and planters reengineered the landscape to make use of the ebb and flow of ocean tides for flooding and draining rice fields. The tidal flow helped in at least two ways. First, it killed weeds. Second, it drastically reduced the need to hoe. Tidal irrigation amounted to one huge energy subsidy for rice planters. The energy came courtesy of the gravitational attraction of the sun and moon, and it lowered the workload. In 1802, one observer wrote, "River swamp plantations, from the command of water, which at high tides can be introduced over the fields, have an undoubted preference to inland plantations; as the crop is more certain, and the work of the negroes less toilsome."[13]

SOWING RICE

Although we tend to associate rice with "Uncle Ben," in reality it was African women who played the main role in showing Americans how to plant and raise the crop. (Patience Pennington, A Woman Rice Planter *[Cambridge, MA: Harvard University Press, 1961])*

Although the technique had been discovered in the mid-eighteenth century, it was not until after the American Revolution that tidal irrigation spread widely over the Low Country. The lands surrounding rivers such as the Ogeechee and the Altamaha in Georgia, with large watersheds and deep enough channels to create the right combination of freshwater and saltwater flow, provided ideal locations. Wealthy planters adopted the technique mainly because they had the time and money to build the proper water control systems. Planters had to attend carefully to the direction and flow of the water, since the intrusion of saltwater onto the rice fields would spell disaster for the crop. In the 1790s, a group of South Carolina planters made the mistake of building a canal to connect two rivers and inadvertently caused saltwater to encroach on the rice fields; the value of some of this land plummeted to a mere fraction of its original price. To avoid such calamities, planters relied on slaves to erect elaborate systems of embankments and canals, a costly and labor-intensive process but one that greatly profited those who could afford the expense. While inland rice plantations produced roughly 600 to 1,000 pounds of rice per acre, tidal facilities yielded 1,200 to 1,500 pounds.[14]

The blossoming of tidal rice cultivation in the years after the American Revolution was part of the larger national trend toward a capitalist market economy wedded to the rationalization of agriculture. Just as the U.S. government employed the grid in the Midwest to divide the land into tidy little boxes so it could be sold and converted into farmland, surveyors with the same rectangular logic in mind descended on the Low Country, parceling it out into quarter-acre squares. Slaves leveled the ground and built embankments around these squares as well as trunk lines to carry the water from the rivers to the fields. A staggering amount of work went into reshaping the land for tidal rice cultivation. By 1800, the rice banks on a plantation located on a branch of South Carolina's Cooper River extended for 55 miles and consisted of more than 6.4 million cubic feet of dirt. In other words, slaves with nothing but shovels and hoes hauled approximately the amount of earth it would take to fill the planet's largest pyramid, Egypt's Cheops, three times. The end result was a reengineered landscape designed to maximize rice production—a "huge hydraulic machine," in the words of one planter.[15]

The impact of the hydraulic grid extended beyond the land into the realm of labor. Slaves on rice plantations worked under a code of conduct known as the task system. Unlike slaves on tobacco and sugar plantations, where gangs performed a specific job under the watchful eyes of an overseer, blacks who produced rice received a certain amount of work, a "task," for each day. After completing the assigned job, they could do as they liked with their time. Why the task system emerged in the Low Country is not entirely clear, but the unique demands involved in growing rice may account for its rise. Tobacco required meticulous care, while rice, a hardier plant, demanded somewhat less attention. More important, much of the work involved in rice cultivation centered on the digging of ditches and embankments—discrete, easily measured tasks. And with

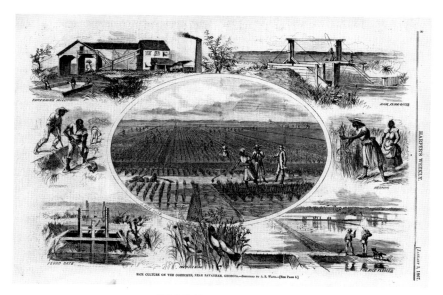

RICE PLANTATION

Slaves cultivating rice on a plantation situated on Georgia's Ogeechee River. (Special Collections and Archives, Georgia State University Library)

the aid of the grid, which imposed geometric order on the landscape, plantation managers could assign slaves the jobs of weeding and hoeing in self-contained areas. A slave could generally perform any operation to completion on a quarter-acre piece of land. As one master put it in the late eighteenth century, "A Task was a quarter of an Acre to weed p. day."[16]

The task system clearly predated the emergence of tidal irrigation. But the development of this new energy source spurred planters to impose even more order on the landscape, as they enlisted geometry to help them get the maximum work from slaves. Tidal energy relieved field hands from hoeing during the summer, but then planters turned around and raised the amount of land a slave tended to half an acre. As the summer workload declined, winter chores increased, with slaves pressed into service maintaining ditches and canals. The surplus energy supplied by the tides did little to improve the quality of slaves' lives, but instead went to fatten the profits of the already wealthy planter class. If anything, working conditions in the fields declined. "No work can be imagined more pernicious to health," wrote South Carolina historian Alexander Hewit, "than for men to stand in water mid-leg high, and often above it, planting and weeding rice" while "the scorching heat of the sun renders the air they breathe ten or twenty degrees hotter than the human blood."[17]

If tidal irrigation offered less in the way of freedom for slaves, it also imposed strictures on the planters themselves, tying them more closely to a schedule not of their own making. Georgia planters, for example, had slaves plant the rice seeds in March, just before the first full spring tide. Later plantings were timed to coincide with the new and full moons, when tides provided enough water to make the seed wet.[18]

Even before the rise of tidal irrigation, rice planters felt compelled to organize the production schedule around the rhythms of nature. Like one-crop agriculture anywhere, rice remained susceptible to attack by predators. No animal presented more problems than the bobolink. These birds swarmed over the rice fields as they migrated north in the spring, returning south for yet another visit in August and September. Planters who were late getting the rice in the ground used water to help the crop ripen more quickly before the birds descended again in the summer. But this technique cost them by reducing yields.[19]

Reengineering the landscape to produce rice also spawned at least one unintended ecological consequence. Tidewater areas bred mosquitoes. Rice plantations, with their carefully designed systems for flooding and draining the land, made the habitat even better for mosquitoes, especially for the malaria-carrying *Anopheles* species. The connection between the cultivation of rice and the increase in malarial conditions did not escape notice among contemporary observers. "These exciting causes of disease lie dormant in the native state of new countries, while they are undisturbed by cultivation," wrote one, "but when the ground is cleared and its surface broken they are put into immediate activity." Although a substantial percentage of Africans were immune to one common strain of malaria, the Euro-American population was not, a fact that compelled many masters to flee the plantations during the warm months.[20]

Despite some disadvantages, tidal cultivation proved enormously successful in boosting rice yields. In part, the surplus energy provided by the tides increased output by allowing slaves to tend to as much as five times the amount of rice they had customarily cultivated on inland plantations. But the success of tidal agriculture stemmed from more than simply an increase in energy. Low Country rice planters also benefited from changes afoot in the Up Country, shifts explaining why soil exhaustion was rarely an issue for those in the tidal zone. The settlement and clearing of forest from the steeply sloped Up Country sent fertile topsoil into rivers and eventually on to the rice plantations. As one South Carolina geologist put it in 1860, "The Up-country since its cultivation was first commenced, has been going steadily downstream."[21] Low Country planters, aware of the sediment-rich water being sent to their doorsteps, would use a full tide to flood the land, causing the river water from upstream to deposit its load of fresh soil on the fields.

But the same forces at work redistributing the Up Country's soil wealth—the clear-cutting and settlement of the forest—also increased the threat of floods. Indeed, Georgia rice planters lamented the increasingly severe deluges that damaged their bank and canal systems—and of course, their crops—in the years after 1830, especially the devastating inundations of 1833, 1840, 1841, and 1852. On balance, however, the settlement of the Up Country generated a nice bonus for the downstream planters, providing a new source of rich soil to accompany the infusion of energy they received courtesy of the earth's relative position in the solar system.

THE OTHER SOUTH

The steady disappearance of the Up Country's soil into the account books of the Low Country is perhaps an apt metaphor for the divergent economic courses these two regions took in the antebellum period. Although large-scale plantation agriculture was a major component of the Low Country economy, such plantations made up barely one-fifth of all the farmsteads in the South by 1850. While rice and tobacco planters engaged in single-crop agriculture for market, small farmers in the Georgia and Carolina highlands practiced a more diversified form of agriculture centered on family survival. Yeoman farmers, who had few if any slaves, worked hilly and sandy soils and often had little choice but to put the security of their families ahead of the desire to export products for market. The yeomen and planters thus had two entirely different goals for and approaches to relating to the land, a situation that at times brought them into conflict. Although there were many fewer planters than yeomen, the former had far more power and political muscle. As a result, more than just soil disappeared from the Up Country landscape.

Consider what happened to the fish that once swarmed upstream in southern rivers. Although the use of water to power mills occurred in the South on nowhere near the scale that it did in the North, in the period leading up to the Civil War, the South flirted with industrial transformation. Traditional sawmills and gristmills, in existence since the colonial period, became better capitalized and began producing for more distant markets. Rice planters used some of their newfound wealth to build rice mills. Even textile mills, that staple of northern factory production, showed signs of expanding throughout the South beginning in the 1810s. Much as had happened in New England, conflict broke out as mill owners, many of them serving the needs of the slave-based plantation economy, dammed rivers for power, blocking the passage of fish and cutting off upstream farmers from an important food source.

Shad and herring, the main species harvested by farmers, normally spend most of their lives at sea, returning in the spring to freshwater rivers to deposit and fertilize eggs. When they returned, they became easy prey for farmers throughout the southern Piedmont. Reaching at points hundreds of miles upstream from the ocean, the fish, once salted down, composed a major component of the southern diet, especially for the poor. During the eighteenth century, the fish were readily available, easy to catch, and, according to one source, "cheaper than bacon."[22]

Farmers in the Up Country turned to the annual spring shad and herring runs to round out a diet based mainly on corn, deer, rabbit, and squirrels. But in the period after the American Revolution, the intrusion of a market economy organized in the interests of capitalists undermined the pioneers' subsistence regime as the damming of rivers to produce flour and lumber for export or for sale to plantations cut off fish from spawning grounds and led to their decline.[23]

As production for the capitalist market economy made further inroads, those who depended on communal access to the fish to satisfy human need cried out. In 1787, a group of South Carolina yeoman farmers joined together to oppose a milldam across the Edisto River that left them "totally cut off from availing themselves of the common Rights of Mankind." The mill, which cut lumber for sale to Sea Island plantations, blocked the passage of fish, depriving people upstream "of *a necessary of Life*, which their fellow citizens living upon other water courses 200 miles above the said Mills enjoy in the Greatest plenty."[24] Such rhetoric resonated among citizens across the nation in the supercharged atmosphere of the revolutionary era. Up Country yeomen readily employed it to protest the rising system of slave-based plantation agriculture coming to the fore.

The rebellious southern farmers argued that the rush to preserve the economic interests of mill owners trampled their common rights. Fish, the farmers declared, derived from either God or nature and by right existed to serve the public good. In fact, the fish did not owe their existence to the abstractions of nature or God. Ecological factors determined whether the fish would lay eggs, as well as whether a river system remained healthy enough to support such reproductive efforts. Changes occurring in the ecosystem at large affected the ability of shad and herring to reproduce. Ironically, the yeoman farmers themselves may have contributed to their own troubles, undermining the fish that formed the basis of their subsistence by chopping down the forest and settling more of the Piedmont. Extensive deforestation took place in the South between the American Revolution and the Civil War, especially in the decade of the 1850s. Erosion increased, as did the sediment load of rivers, benefiting tidal rice plantations but also burying spawning grounds.

The final blow to the fish runs came during the mid-nineteenth century when commercial fishermen erected seines across rivers, systematically exploiting the catch to the point at which it could no longer reproduce. As far as migrating fish went, both the North and the South ended up with rivers that were, for all intents and purposes, dead, made over into biologically impoverished power and navigation canals. Those who had formerly depended on water for food were forced to turn to new ways of earning a living from the land. In New England, the possibility of factory employment provided farmers with one way out of this dilemma. But few such opportunities existed for their southern counterparts. There, the evolution of capitalism involved the further expansion of slavery, not more wage work in factories.[25]

SOIL MINING

In the late eighteenth century, when Britain embarked on its industrial revolution, Low Country planters began searching for a variety of cotton to meet the needs of British textile mills. Georgia planters eventually discovered a kind of long-staple cotton (perhaps brought to the United States from the Bahamas) that flourished along the coast in an area known as the Sea Islands. Extending from South Carolina all the way to northern Florida, the islands proved an ideal environment for cultivating cotton. The long-staple variety required a protracted growing season, in excess of 250 days without frost, and grew best when nurtured by moist ocean breezes. In both these respects the Sea Island environment cooperated. Between 1785 and 1795, island planters saw their profits from long-staple cotton rise dramatically.

Cotton fabrics appealed to consumers in search of clothes that were washable, comfortable, and moth-proof. In an effort to cash in on the burgeoning cotton market, planters farther inland tried to plant the crop but found that only the short-staple variety grew away from the coast. Short-staple cotton had one serious drawback: the cotton seeds had an annoying habit of clinging to the lint, requiring as much as an entire day to clean a pound by hand. In 1793, however, Eli Whitney invented the famed cotton gin for separating the cotton fibers from the seeds. From this point forward, the South's fortunes remained tied to the textile-driven industrial transformation that eventually spread from Britain to America.

While northerners moved toward abolition in the 1790s, southerners headed in precisely the reverse direction: a marked expansion of slavery, fueled by the booming cotton economy. Short-staple cotton could be successfully grown in nearly all of the South located below the 77-degree summer isotherm (a line drawn on weather maps to connect places with the same temperature). That fact allowed the slave system to spread beyond its coastal confines throughout the Piedmont and eventually as far west as eastern Texas. Cotton could be grown at some distance from the rivers required to transport the crop to market because it was a nonperishable item and relative to, say, grain, far more valuable per unit of weight. It was also perfectly suited to single-crop plantation agriculture supported by slave laborers, who carried out the necessary planting, hoeing, and picking under the supervision of an overseer.

Apart from having the requisite number of frost-free days (roughly 200), the South also possessed enough rainfall (approximately 20 inches per year) and the right precipitation pattern for growing cotton. Too much spring rain and the crop's root system might not anchor properly in the soil; too much rain at harvest time and the boll might fall off before being picked. With their gentle spring rains, which increased through the middle of the summer and then tailed off, the southern states made perfect cotton country. Climate helped to forge the cotton South, as the region rose to become the world's leading supplier of the fiber, bolstering the industrial transformation of the North and Europe in the process. By the 1850s, cotton not only fed northern mills but accounted for two-thirds of U.S. exports.[26]

Cotton planters, like their counterparts who grew rice, tried as much as possible to streamline the production process. One of their greatest advances involved a shift in the species of cotton grown. By the early nineteenth century, planters

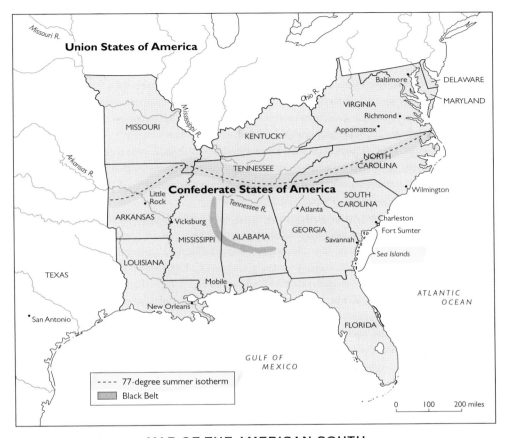

MAP OF THE AMERICAN SOUTH

The region south of the 77-degree summer isotherm is the part of the eastern United States best suited climatically for growing cotton. Within that region, the Black Belt—an area noted for its dark and especially rich soil—led the nation in cotton growing during the antebellum period.

had moved from black- and green-seed varieties to Mexican cotton. Unlike these earlier types, Mexican cotton had large bolls, allowing slaves to pick as much as five times more per day than they could with the inferior black-seed kind. From a profit standpoint, this development nearly rivaled the invention of the cotton gin.[27]

Planters also standardized many of the routines and tasks associated with cotton production. In the early years of the crop's cultivation, slaves used their feet or a wooden tamper to stuff cotton into bags of different sizes. In 1779, a lever press was invented in the South that produced neat square bales. By the mid-nineteenth century, large plantations with the latest equipment were packing anywhere from 40 to 50 bales per day.[28]

The rise of the Cotton Belt—the name for the vast stretch of South Carolina, Georgia, Alabama, Mississippi, and Louisiana devoted to the crop—rested on more than simply climate and efficient production. As of 1800, cotton had spread very little from its initial coastal confines, blocked in large part by the presence of 125,000 Indians located east of the Mississippi. Many of the South's leading planters thus pushed for their removal. European and American traders had since the late eighteenth century helped to weaken these southern tribes, introducing disease, liquor, and a capitalist market for deerskin, all of which undermined their subsistence economies. In the quarter-century following 1814, Andrew Jackson delivered the finishing blow. Jackson, first as a military officer and later as president, masterminded a systematic removal campaign. The treaties he dictated between 1814 and 1824 alone aided the United States in acquiring three-fourths of Alabama, one-third of Tennessee, and one-fifth of Mississippi and Georgia.

Jackson succeeded in transforming the communally held lands of the southern tribes into private property available for sale. "No one will exert himself to procure the comforts of life," Secretary of War William Crawford explained in 1816, "unless his right to enjoy them is exclusive." By 1844, only a few thousand Indians remained east of the Mississippi, and even they had in large measure been forced to accept life under a society based on private property. In the process, they abandoned the communal obligations toward the environment that once undergirded their culture. By the 1840s, the few remaining native people found themselves surrounded by profit-maximizing cotton growers. Unlike the Native Americans, the southerners were content to farm hillsides, a trend that over time led to an increase in soil erosion.[29]

Southern planters intent on growing cotton streamed into Alabama, Mississippi, and Tennessee in the 1820s and 1830s. Clearly, the superior soils available in parts of what was once the nation's Old Southwest attracted the attention of settlers. Some people may have abandoned perfectly adequate farmland in search of the greater returns to be found in the Black Belt, a land of dark, fertile soil extending from central Alabama northwest into Mississippi. But far more evidence suggests that between 1780 and 1840, many cotton planters fled into such regions because of the growing problem of soil depletion, a development that eventually led to the forced relocation of more than a million slaves from the Upper South.[30]

Buoyed by sharply rising cotton prices, especially in the 1810s, planters in the eastern parts of Georgia and South Carolina became mired in a profit-driven cycle of clearing and land abandonment that left the landscape in a state of disarray. "Tens of thousands of acres of once productive lands are now reduced to the maximum of sterility," wrote one resident of South Carolina's Piedmont in the 1850s. "Water-worn, gullied old fields everywhere meet the eye." In the Georgia Piedmont, some of the gullies on old cotton lands extended 150 feet in depth.[31]

Some abolitionists attributed the South's problem with soil depletion to slavery, arguing that bondsmen had little motivation to sustain the fertility of the land. In the period leading up to 1860, the regions of the Piedmont with the highest slave population density correlated nicely with the worst areas of soil erosion. But the problem, according to geographer Stanley Trimble, stemmed not from slavery as much as from single-crop agriculture and the lack of a "land-ethic" among profit-driven southern planters.[32]

It seems unlikely that slavery alone was to blame for the depletion of southern soils, if for no other reason than that family farms in the North also severely depleted the soil. But slavery did create a context for soil exhaustion to take place. With slaves themselves (a form of personal property) constituting over half of the agricultural wealth of the cotton South, land took on secondary importance for planters. Slavery and soil erosion were correlated: planters had few incentives to maintain the fertility of the land when they could just as easily head off toward fresh soil with their most valuable personal property (the slaves) in tow.[33]

Thus planters failed miserably when it came to maintaining the land's fertility. Very little nutrient-rich manure made it back to the soil for two reasons. First, stockpiling and spreading manure over large southern fields required a significant amount of labor. One source summarized the dilemma confronting planters by noting that northern farmers "can well afford to fertilize their little spots of ten or a dozen acres; but a Southern plantation of 500 or 600 acres in cultivation would require all the manure in the parish."[34]

Second, there was not much manure to spread around in any case. As South Carolina state geologist Oscar Lieber put it in 1856, "no manure worth mentioning is saved under the present system." The shortage resulted from a combination of climate, soil, and epidemiological conditions. Unlike the North, the South was not a good environment for growing grass. And without grass, there was little feed for cattle, a major source of manure. Acidic soil, combined with the persistent threat of rain at precisely the point in time when fodder crops such as timothy and red clover needed to be cut, made raising grass difficult. Even worse, a parasitic animal infection (babesiosis) spread by ticks further dampened southern cattle-raising prospects. With labor dear and the supply of livestock limited, manure played a minimal role in antebellum southern agriculture.[35]

For a brief period, southern planters had high hopes for Peruvian guano, a fertilizer made up of bird droppings found in various coastal reaches of South America. Guano contains substantial amounts of nitrogen, a key nutrient for plant growth. Reform-minded farmers in the United States had formerly been harvesting nitrogen locally by feeding livestock leguminous fodder crops rich in the nutrient and dutifully spreading the resulting manure over the fields. Now, however, the prospect of Peruvian guano offered farmers a chance to escape the hard work involved in sustainable farming by introducing plant food from outside the local ecosystem—indeed, from another country altogether.[36] It was an approach with a great deal of appeal, so much so that in the 1850s, declining agricultural prospects and high guano prices caused southern farmers to clamor for federal intervention.

In 1850 President Millard Fillmore made bird feces a subject of his State of the Union address. Six years later, Congress passed legislation allowing anyone who discovered the much-sought-after excrement on an unclaimed island or rock, anywhere in the world, to receive government protection of the claim. The legislation set off a veritable bird-droppings rush, with Americans laying claim to 59 rocks and islands in the Caribbean and Pacific in the seven years following the act's passage. But in the end, guano failed to rescue the South from soil degradation. Guano imports peaked in 1854 and then experienced a rapid decline as a result of the expense of the material combined with the massive quantities needed to revitalize exhausted cotton fields. Still, the guano rush is significant. The days of growing fodder crops rich in nitrogen and managing cattle and manure to husband the nutrient would soon fade fast before the rise of industrial agriculture and its newfangled chemistry. Farming began to lose its attachment to place the moment some obscure planter ripped open that first bag of guano, provided courtesy of the birds of Peru.[37]

Slavery, monoculture, climate—all these factors help explain why soil exhaustion threatened southern agriculture in the period before 1840. But to some extent, the focus on cotton is misplaced. Cotton was not particularly demanding of soil nutrients, certainly not when compared with corn. In the 1840s, as the North moved toward a more diversified diet (aided by an integrated transportation system), corn remained a mainstay of southern cuisine. Corn is a very versatile crop that can flourish in a variety of different settings. It meshed well with cotton, requiring little care during the season when the cash crop needed harvesting and making up as much as 40 to 50 percent of a plantation's farm value. But it made great demands on the soil, requiring as many as 13 nutrients to thrive. Planting so much of it thus only added to the South's soil woes.

CONCLUSION

What is the relationship between slavery and the environment? Slavery has not flourished in very cold climates, and in the antebellum South at least, it owed its rise to a clime that favored the growth of short-staple cotton. The development of the Cotton Belt rested on a set of climatic conditions; without them, it is hard to imagine slavery taking on the role that it did in southern political culture.

If nature shaped the evolution of slavery, the reverse proposition—that the slave system had significant environmental implications—seems even more persuasive. Land played a secondary role in a society in which so much wealth remained tied up in owning and trading slaves. It follows that little incentive existed for planters to maintain soil fertility, especially with fertile land always available farther west. Thus the stage was set for the brutal cycle of clearing, ecological degradation, and eventual abandonment that characterized southern agriculture in the 60 years after 1780.

Slavery created favorable conditions for this abusive pattern of land use to emerge. But it was the short-term capitalist orientation of planters, especially the fixation on profits that could be made by growing cotton, that drove a reckless tear through the land, leaving a trail of gullies behind. In this respect, the South and the North were not all that dissimilar. In both regions, agriculture answered to a higher force, be it the price of wood, furs, tobacco, or cotton. Southern land and soil came to be looked upon less as a meal ticket and more as a resource organized around the profit motive, with the planter elite content to mortgage Dixie's ecological future.

In the end, however, the South's ultimate ecological legacy rested on its path-breaking role in the emergence of specialized, one-crop agriculture. The commercial farming of staples split production off from consumption, making it difficult, if not impossible, for the end users of these commodities to grasp the enormous social and environmental costs involved in devoting vast areas to growing a single set of plants. Here the southern states did diverge from the northern ones. By focusing so intently on producing tobacco, rice, and ultimately cotton, the region forged a new, more indirect relationship with the earth, the consequences of which are still felt today.

6

THE GREAT FOOD FIGHT

Spring 1865 brought misery and death to the beleaguered Confederacy. All that remained of the formerly invincible Army of Northern Virginia was 55,000 desperate and starving troops. The indignities of war mounted. In April, the men trudged toward Amelia Courthouse, Virginia, driven on by the prospect of a rendezvous with rations arriving by train. But a snafu caused ammunition to be delivered instead of food. As the men dragged themselves forward, they were reduced to eating horse feed—the corn on the cob commonly fed to the animals. "Two ears were issued to each man," one soldier wrote. "It was parched in the coals, mixed with salt, stored in the pockets, and eaten on the road. Chewing the corn was hard work. It made the jaws ache and the gums and teeth so sore as to cause unendurable pain." One of the first things Gen. Ulysses S. Grant did after the South surrendered was to send three days of rations to the rebels.[1]

The Civil War interrupted many of the normal routines of daily existence. But one basic fact of life remained the same: people still had to feed themselves and the animals on which they had come to depend. The eternal quest to survive biologically, to derive the requisite number of calories from food, was as relevant for soldiers on the battlefield as it was for plantation slaves and factory workers. Biological existence in turn depended on the land, soil, weather, and countless other natural factors that went into getting the earth to yield fruit.

Politically speaking, two different conceptions of life under capitalism—a socioecological order in which people had to make money or risk starvation, foreclosure, or bankruptcy—collided in the years leading up to the Civil War. For northerners, only landownership and the freedom of men to benefit from the product of their labor would ensure economic independence. Southern slaveholders preferred that paternalistic masters control others and what they produced. These two competing worldviews found expression in two different philosophies toward the land. These differences, it turned out, helped to shape the outcome of the war, as Union forces exploited access to industrial production in lands far from the frontlines, while the South struggled as its soldiers found that the need for food, water, and clothing outstripped the region's household production, based as it was on direct interaction with the earth near the battle lines.[2]

MUD WRESTLING

"After four years of arduous service marked by unsurpassed courage and forti-
tude, the Army of Northern Virginia has been compelled to yield to overwhelming numbers and resources."[3] Those were the words of Gen. Robert E. Lee,
summing up the reasons behind the South's defeat. With 22 million people to
the Confederacy's 9 million (over one-third of whom were slaves), 70 percent
of the nation's railroad mileage, and 110,000 factories (to the South's 18,000)
producing nearly all of the firearms available in the country, the North, with
moral reason on its side to boot, may seem to have been predestined to win the
war. But in 1861, as the first shots rang out, the outcome seemed far less certain.

At the start, the South had a number of advantages over the North. It was no
secret that the Confederate troops retained a significant edge during the early
years of the war in terms of horsemanship, a benefit bestowed on them at least
in part by climate, specifically the mild winters that allowed them to spend
nearly the entire year outside practicing while their adversaries kept warm by
the fire. One British observer went so far as to reckon that the Yankee soldiers
could "scarcely sit their horses even when trotting."[4]

The South also had the home-field advantage. Confederate troops fought a
defensive war on their own territory, a land where many soldiers had been born
and raised. Fighting on their home turf also allowed the southern forces to conduct maneuvers in places within easy reach of ration and ammunition stockpiles. Union soldiers, in contrast, had to carry what they needed with them.
Imagine for a moment the logistical problems faced by the northern forces.
Every 100,000 troops required each day no less than 600 tons of supplies, 2,500
supply wagons, and 35,000 draft animals, horses and mules that themselves
required feed and forage. That the Union Army was able to master these logistics
and supply its forces with industrial products from distant locales in part explains the North's success. But this only became clear in hindsight.[5]

As the North soon learned, the rebels had a secret weapon in store: the environmental conditions that made travel arduous, especially in the winter. Unlike
in the North, the ground south of the Mason-Dixon line froze to only a shallow
depth. Poorly drained and consisting of soil composed largely of red clay (at
least in Virginia, where much of the fighting went on), southern roads turned
into quagmires when it rained, leaving Union supply trains to slog through
muck that at times buried mules so deep they could not move.

No one knew better the problems of southern roads than Union Gen. Ambrose
E. Burnside, whose failures are legendary among Civil War buffs. In January
1863, still smarting from the slaughter of his troops at Fredericksburg late in
the year before, Burnside drew up a plan to outflank Lee's army by crossing
Virginia's Rappahannock River. Dry weather, unusual for that time of year, gave
Burnside reason to feel hopeful. On January 20, Burnside and his men moved
out. By dusk, however, it was raining. For the next 30 hours rain pummeled the

UNION WAGON TRAIN

The massive supply trains required by northern forces often fell prey to the South's bad roads and inclement weather conditions. (Library of Congress)

region, turning the roads to mush. "The mud is not simply on the surface, but penetrates the ground to a great depth," wrote the Union officer Régis de Trobriand. "It appears as though the water, after passing through a first bed of clay, soaked into some kind of earth without any consistency. As soon as the hardened crust on the surface is softened, everything is buried in a sticky paste mixed with liquid mud, in which, with my own eyes, I have seen teams of mules buried." Trobriand concluded: "The powers of heaven and earth were against us."[6]

Muck became public enemy number one for the Union forces. "Virginia mud," another northern officer pointed out, "is a clay of reddish color and sticky consistency which does not appear to soak water, or mingle with it, but simply to hold it, becoming softer and softer." As they watched the northern forces struggle through the slop, Confederate soldiers flashed homemade signs that read "Burnside Stuck in the Mud" and "This Way to Richmond."[7]

Calling attention to the poor weather and soil conditions in the upper reaches of the South, the New York *Evening Post* opined that "operations in a country and climate like Virginia are more destructive and wasteful than advantageous to an invading force."[8] The disaster along the Rappahannock would be dubbed the Mud March. The North had learned a lesson: never again would the Union launch a major military campaign in Virginia during the wintertime.

FOOD FOR THOUGHT

When the end came for the Confederacy, Gen. Lee and his troops headed for Appomattox, with all but the officers forced to eat horse feed. Sometimes, even, the men had to make do with horse leftovers. C. Irvine Walker, a southern officer, claimed that he "frequently saw the hungry Confederate gather up the dirt and corn where a horse had been fed, so that when he reached his bivouac he could wash out the dirt and gather the few grains of corn to satisfy in part at least the cravings of hunger." Other desperate soldiers tried to develop a taste for rodents. "We were keen to eat a piece of rat," one soldier wrote. "Our teeth were on edge; yea; even our mouth watered to eat a piece of rat."[9]

Lee himself had wondered as far back as 1862 whether starvation might prove a greater threat than enemy forces. Camped out in Northern Virginia, Lee and his troops found the winter of 1862–1863 especially grueling. In 1862, a drought in the South severely depressed the corn supply, compounding the effect of the already meager meat provisions. Throughout the war, Lee was repeatedly forced to shift his military strategy to make sure that supply lines remained open; at one point he warned the Confederacy's secretary of war of the army's impending doom if it could not be furnished with regular and adequate rations. With bacon and other meat in very short supply, the southern forces ate mainly cornmeal. Demoralized by the lack of variety in their diet, some Confederate soldiers talked of the "Fed and the Cornfed." In 1863, Lee said, "The question of food for this army gives me more trouble than anything else combined." Indeed, concerns about the sparsity of food for his troops explains in part Lee's questionable decision to challenge the Union Army at Gettysburg.[10]

The horses pressed into military service suffered as much or worse than the men they served. No one regretted this more than Gen. Lee, a man so fond of the animals that he once lectured his officers on how to adjust a saddle to care properly for a horse's back. Some horses, desperate for food, chewed the bark from trees and ate small scraps of paper strewn about base camps. Lee did everything he could to find food for the creatures. He directed that forage in large sections of land near campaigns be reserved for the army. He forbade farmers from retaining more than six months' worth of corn for use as feed. He even sent cavalry to distant points to save the forage in a given area for the animals pulling the supply train.[11]

In July 1863, as the tide turned militarily against the South, the quartermaster general reported a need for somewhere between 8,000 and 10,000 horses to take the place of those killed or ruined by starvation. When Jefferson Davis, the president of the Confederacy, ordered troops to Georgia in the wake of the defeat at Gettysburg, Gen. James Longstreet, who was placed in command of the mission, had to relinquish some of his artillery units because he lacked the draft animals necessary to haul the equipment. As the war wound down, so little fodder remained near the Confederate army camp on the Rappahannock that Lee had to send men and horses on forage sweeps as far south as the North Carolina border. "There can be little doubt," wrote Douglas Freeman, Lee's foremost biographer, that the great general "saw in the prospective failure of the horse supply one of the most serious obstacles to the establishment of Southern independence."[12]

Barely able to feed themselves, much less their mounts, both armies, North and South, dealt with the limited rations by foraging. Although under orders to compensate those from whom they took food or animals, in practice soldiers pillaged the countryside. "The government tries to feed us Texains on Poor Beef," wrote one soldier, "but there is too Dam many hogs here for that, these Arkansas hoosiers ask from 25 to 30 cents a pound for there pork, but the Boys generally get it a little cheaper than that I reckon you understand how they get it."[13]

As early as 1863, Lee worried that the meager rations—18 ounces of flour and 4 ounces of bacon per day—might be weakening troop morale. One Confederate officer observed that the Union could easily track the movement of the southern forces by simply following "the deposit of dysenteric stool." In the autumn of 1863, when President Jefferson Davis visited the Confederate Army of Tennessee, troops shouted, "Send us something to eat, Massa Jeff. Give us something to eat, Massa Jeff. I'm hungry! I'm hungry!"[14]

With respect to provisioning its troops, the Union unquestionably had an advantage. Although hardly immune from hunger, northern soldiers received more food per person than any other army in the history of warfare. Bumper yields even allowed the North to earn valuable trade surpluses by doubling the amount of wheat, corn, beef, and pork it exported to Europe. How did the North achieve such a high level of agricultural production with a third of its farm workforce off at the front? Mechanization in large part compensated for the shortage of labor. "The severe manual toil of mowing, raking, pitching, and cradling is now performed by machinery," *Scientific American* reported in 1863. Women, their husbands off at war, embraced the new technology. "Yesterday I saw the wife of one of our parishioners driving the team in a reaper; her husband is at Vicksburg," an Illinois minister wrote. Furthermore, Union forces had not only more food but also a better variety of foodstuffs at their disposal. Items such as canned fruit and condensed milk had existed prior to the outbreak of hostilities, but wartime demands racheted up production. In 1859, Gail Borden opened his first factory for producing condensed milk; by 1863, army contracts had boosted Borden's production level to 17,000 quarts per day.[15]

By mastering logistics, the Union Army escaped the constraints of local ecology and supplied troops with industrial products manufactured far from the battlefields, right down to the standard issue blue trousers that held up better than the homemade pants the rebels wore. This is why the Civil War is considered the first modern war.[16]

Civilian populations in the South sometimes suffered as much as Confederate soldiers did. Food shortages and even periodic riots broke out in the Confederacy. Salt in particular was in very short supply, especially after the Union naval blockade kept ships, which used it as ballast, from entering southern ports. In December 1862, some 20 women in Greenville, Alabama, cornered a railroad agent yelling, "Salt or blood" and ultimately forced him to hand over a bag of the preservative, an absolute necessity in these days before refrigeration. The

NOTICE.

To the Farmers of Campbell, Franklin, Henry, Patrick, Grayson, Carroll, Floyd, the Western part of Pittsylvania and Halifax, and the Southern part of Bedford Counties :

The surplus Forage in the above district has been set apart for the purpose of feeding the Public Animals not in service.

All the Corn, Rye, Oats, Hay, Fodder and Straw, not required for the use of the people in the above Counties and parts of Counties, will be wanted by the Government for the purpose above stated.

Stables are being erected at suitable stations in the District, at which Farmers will be expected to deliver their surplus Forage, and for which they will be paid the prices fixed by the State Commissioners. The following are the Schedule Prices at present :

Corn unshelled, $3,95 per bushel ; Corn shelled, $4,00 per bushel ; Rye, $3,20 per bushel ; Oats, $2,00 per bushel ; Sheaf Oats, $3,70 per 100 lbs. ; Hay, per 100 lbs. $3,00; Wheat Straw, $1,30 per 100 lbs ; for baling Long Forage, 50 cts. per 100 lbs. ; for hauling Long Forage, 8 cents per mile per 100 lbs. ; for hauling Corn, 4 cents per bushel per mile.

It is with great difficulty that the necessary transportation for armies in the field can be furnished. The Government, therefore, cannot supply the teams to haul the Forage from the farms to the stations at which it is needed. It will be necessary for the farmers to do the transportation, for which, they will be paid liberal prices.

JAS. G. PAXTON,

Maj. and Q. M.

Fair Grounds, near Lynchburg, Nov. 13th, 1863.

JOHNSON & SCHAFFTER PRINTERS LYNCHBURG. VA.

FORAGE CALL

Constantly short of feed for their horses, the Confederacy called on farmers to supply its army with whatever surplus forage they had available. (Lamont Buchanan, A Pictorial History of the Confederacy [New York: Crown, 1951])

following year, in Salisbury, North Carolina, 40 to 50 hungry women wielding hatchets sacked several stores and escaped with over 23 barrels of flour plus salt, molasses, and money.[17]

The most famous food riot occurred on April 2, 1863, in Richmond, Virginia, where Lee's forces had stretched the local food supply to its limit. In the latter part of March, a snowstorm dumped a foot of snow on the Confederate capital, rendering roads used by farmers impassable and adding to the food shortage. When the snow melted later in the month, it damaged pumps at the city waterworks and inconvenienced residents, mainly from working-class areas, who now had to trudge all the way to an old well in Capitol Square to get water instead of receiving it from a hydrant. The food and water shortages, combined with an explosion on March 13 at an ordnance laboratory that killed 69 people (most of them women), all helped to bring on the bread riot. From all over the city hundreds of women and boys converged on the square screaming, "Bread or blood." The mob, armed with "those huge old home-made knives with which our soldiers were wont to load themselves down in the first part of the war," as an observer noted, then proceeded to loot bacon, flour, and other items in short supply.[18]

More than simply hunger drove southerners to engage in mob violence. Principles too figured in the decision. In St. Lucah, Georgia, women protestors—their husbands away at war—called attention to the unlimited material gains of those storekeepers who stayed "back at home speculating." "Unrelieved suffering," read an editorial published in a soldiers' newspaper on the first anniversary of the Richmond revolt, "asserts an absolute right to what is necessary for its removal."[19] In other words, the protestors rose up to defend an older, and to their minds more just and moral, economic arrangement that entitled everyone to such basic necessities of life as food.

A number of factors lay behind the South's wartime shortage of comestibles. The North's naval blockade, proposed by Lincoln in April 1861, proved extremely effective in cutting off outside trade with the southern states. Equally important, the decisions of the border states of Kentucky, Missouri, and Maryland not to secede from the Union dealt a devastating blow to the southern cause. Loyalty to the republic translated into lost meat and flour in the South, with the three states together representing one-third of both the grain and livestock supply present in the slave South on the eve of war.[20]

Food scarcity in the South also had some less obvious sources. Poor weather was one of them. In 1862, drought reduced corn yields throughout large parts of the southern states. "Hundreds of families will not make enough corn to do them and many will make none of consequence," a newspaper based in Greensboro, Alabama, reported. To make matters worse, the heavy rains that preceded the drought created conditions congenial for the development and spread of a rust fungus. The plant parasite devastated the wheat crop, in some places reducing it by a factor of six.[21]

In Mississippi, flooding combined with the 1862 drought to add to the South's woes. High water—higher in places than at any time since 1815—breached levees along the Mississippi, Yazoo, and Ouachita rivers, laying waste to some of the region's most productive land. "There is more to fear from a dearth of food than from all the Federal armies in existence," declared a Jackson, Mississippi, newspaper. Union forces finished what nature started. In the spring of 1863, Grant instructed his troops "to weaken the enemy, by destroying their means of subsistence." And as southerners joined the call to battle, they left behind vast stretches of farmland soon to be taken over by weeds, adding to the scarcity of food. When Confederate soldiers capitulated at Vicksburg in the summer of 1863, Union soldiers refused to taunt their captives, knowing full well, in the words of one observer, that they "surrendered to famine, not to them."[22]

Then came the extremely harsh winter of 1863–1864, described by one meteorological expert as "the outstanding weather event of the Civil War." In Texas, the Arctic outbreak killed half to perhaps as much as nine-tenths of the cattle found on some farms. Confederate troops went two whole days without any food at all that winter. A soldier forwarded his meat ration to Gen. Lee with a note lamenting that, despite his aristocratic heritage, he had been driven to steal in order to survive.[23]

Apart from bad weather conditions, southerners themselves played a hand in bringing on the chronic shortage of food. No trend contributed more to the dilemma than the move toward cotton monoculture. Cotton specialization would take a giant step forward after the war. But even before the war, when cotton prices rose dramatically in the 1850s, planters invested heavily in the crop—so heavily that per capita production of such essential foods as corn and sweet potatoes fell over the decade. When the Civil War began, many southern agricultural leaders called upon people to support the Confederacy by abandoning cotton and growing more corn. "Plant Corn and Be Free, or plant cotton and be whipped," one Georgia newspaper declared. Confederate soldiers, the paper went on to explain, "will be powerless against grim hunger and gaunt famine, such as will overwhelm us if we insanely raise Cotton instead of corn." It was hard, however, for the planter elite to give up their money crop and risk the region's near-monopoly over world cotton production, especially because many believed that foreign dependence on southern cotton would help bring Britain into the war on the South's side. Some planters went so far as to grow corn near roads and cotton out of sight.[24]

The reluctance of southern planters to grow food stemmed from more than simply economic self-interest. A major concern involved what to do with their slaves, who would have more time on their hands if they were not out tending cotton. Planting corn exacted much time during the planting and cultivation stages, but the length of its harvest phase came nowhere near matching the long cotton-picking season, which typically lasted four and often five full months. As one Georgia newspaper put it, "No grain crop in this climate needs cultivation more than four months of the year, the remainder of the working season is unemployed. Can the farmer afford to keep his negroes, horses and other capital idle and 'eating their heads off' for the balance of the season?" To deal with this issue, the states of Arkansas and Georgia felt compelled to pass laws restricting the amount of land planted with the money crop.[25]

Meat also remained a scarce commodity throughout the war, not just on the battlefield, but on the plantation as well. The South had always had more limited livestock prospects than the North, and the corn shortage could not have helped that situation any. Planters took to reducing the amount of pork they provided slaves, instead encouraging them to maintain vegetable gardens. One planter ventured that the gardens would allow blacks to "pass through the year on a small supply of bacon with much less inconvenience and suffering than the peasantry of the balance of the civilized world."[26]

The ineffectiveness of this substitution soon became apparent. As the war progressed, slaves and planters struggled over game in the southern woods. Slaves had long been known to hunt deer, rabbit, and raccoon in order to supplement plantation provisions. But the reduction in rations may have spurred them to hunt farther afield, at times bringing them into conflict with planters, who charged them with killing hogs that the planters had set free in the woods to forage. Although bereft of the glory and theatricality of battle, the struggle to survive biologically in wartime was every bit as important.

CONCLUSION

The Civil War made the American people into a nation. It also marked a shift from direct interactions with local ecology—the South's primary approach—toward more indirect relations with the earth based on industrial production and complex logistics—the forte of the North—overseen by a budding American nation-state.[27]

The war put the United States firmly on a path away from a system of household production, in which ordinary people interacted directly with the land to meet human needs, and toward a full-fledged capitalist economy founded on unlimited accumulation of wealth. On the strength of these changes and the enormous expansion in material goods they produced, the United States eventually ascended not just to a position of world military dominance, but to a vantage at which it would have an outsized impact on the ecology of the earth as a whole.

7

EXTRACTING THE NEW SOUTH

With the war at an end, one rebel captain returned home to his father's plantation. He was in for a rude awakening. "Our negroes are living in great comfort," he wrote. "They were delighted to see me with overflowing affection. They
waited on me as before, gave me breakfast, splendid dinners, etc. But they firmly
and respectfully informed me: 'We own this land now. Put it out of your head
that it will ever be yours again.'"[1] As events unfolded, the captain had less to fear
than he thought. The struggle over slavery had ended, but the former slaves lost
the subsequent battle to control their political and economic destinies.

It is one of history's great ironies that a region that once enslaved an entire
group of people later found itself reduced to semicolonial status, its resources
ravaged by outsiders. The South emerged from the war economically crippled —
its fields and livestock plundered, its forests cut down for firewood and barrack
timber. The cotton monoculture, which had gained a strong foothold during the
antebellum period, now advanced across the landscape at a pace that would have
challenged even the most swashbuckling Confederate cavalryman. In its wake,
it left the land scarred, its people heavily dependent on outside sources of food
as well as capital. As the region descended into poverty, people from outside the
region—northern capitalists, midwestern lumbermen, and British financiers—
siphoned off its natural wealth, especially its forests and minerals. The ecological
origins of the New South centered squarely on the extraction of resources for
the benefit of the capitalist economy. Blacks were set free in a region enslaved.

FAST FOOD FARMING

King Cotton emerged from the war more imperious and despotic than ever
before. As the single most important cash crop in the postbellum South, the
staple soared in importance, turning the stretch from South Carolina to east
Texas into a sea of white. Like addicts unable to control themselves, southern
farmers grew so much cotton that they continually undercut their ability to feed
themselves. By 1880, per capita corn and hog production in the Deep South
had plummeted to nearly half of 1860 levels, forcing farmers to import food
from the Midwest. Wisconsin flour, Chicago bacon, Indiana hay—all flowed in
to shore up the region's food deficit when in fact, as one observer noted, these
items could have been grown in Dixie "at nothing a ton."[2]

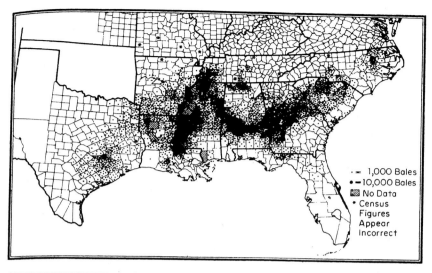

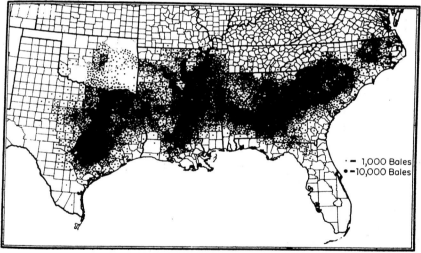

COTTON PRODUCTION, 1859 AND 1899

Although cotton was a major crop in the pre–Civil War South, it was even more widely grown in the postbellum period. (U.S. Department of Agriculture, Atlas of American Agriculture *[Washington, DC: Government Printing Office, 1918])*

On one level, the attraction of cotton is easy to understand. The economic profit attached to cotton was simply far greater than that associated with any other grain crop. With its acidic soil conditions and heavy rainfall, the South, unlike the temperate northern states, was ill suited to raising grains and grasses. Add to this the animal parasites that dragged down livestock prospects, and the magnetic appeal of cotton is easily understood. Still, two other factors—the rise of sharecropping and the growing commercialization of farming—furthered cotton's eventual chokehold on the region.

Sharecropping developed as blacks found few prospects for owning land after the war. In 1868, the same white planter class that had controlled the best land in the antebellum period still retained its title to the region's most valuable resource—only now the slaves had been set free, and planters could no longer count on their labor. This proved especially problematic for those planters who raised cotton, because the crop must be picked in a timely way or risk serious damage by rainfall. Freed from their chains, blacks sometimes left planters in the lurch, moving on at the peak of the picking season. Sharecropping helped to resolve this problem by tying laborers to the land for a specified period of time. Planters divided plantations into 30- to 50-acre farms and rented them out to freedmen, providing tenants with land, seed, and tools and, in return, taking a half-share of the crop at harvest. The arrangement appealed to planters and also to freedmen, who, unable to buy land on their own, found that sharecropping at least got them out from under the thumb of white supervision. Landlords, however, reserved the right to dictate the crop mix to tenants; with their own personal fortunes tied to what the sharecropper raised, they chose cotton because it was more profitable per acre than any other crop.[3]

Sharecropping and the cotton monoculture went hand in hand with the increasing commercialization of farming, spurred by the spread of railroads and merchants. In the 1870s, railroads began laying track in the Georgia Up Country, tying this region more closely to markets in the North. With the railroads in place, merchants moved in to buy locally grown cotton and sell goods on credit. Under crop lien laws passed in the 1870s, merchants loaned farmers money with a future crop as collateral. For obvious reasons, they insisted that farmers plant cotton. "If I say 'plant cotton' they plant cotton," one merchant said. With the system stacked in cotton's favor, sharecroppers tripped over each other as they rushed to plant more of the crop. But the more they planted, the less food they produced on their own—and the more they had to turn to stores for food as well as supplies, drawing them into a vicious cycle of indebtedness.[4]

Nothing was more critical to cotton production under the sharecropping system than fertilizer. Landlords and renters alike had little incentive to invest in the long-term health of their land and thus little interest in crop rotation or manuring. Current yields were what mattered most to them, with the land simply a vehicle for raising cotton for cash. Such present-mindedness encouraged farmers to mine the soil relentlessly, using fertilizer to pump up yields in the short run.[5]

Beginning in 1867, with the establishment of large phosphate mines in South Carolina, commercial fertilizer use boomed. Much of the soil in Georgia and South Carolina suffered from a natural deficiency in phosphorus, a problem the fertilizer addressed with a great deal of initial success. Cotton yields climbed as this powerful chemical input bolstered fertility. Fertilizer also accelerated crop growth, causing cotton to mature more quickly and uniformly. The speedup shortened the cotton harvest to as little as five weeks and lowered the threat posed by rain and frost. Given the virtues of fertilizer and its pivotal role in the cotton monoculture under the sharecropping system, it is no surprise that the South consumed more of it per acre than any other part of the nation.[6]

Sharecroppers funneled a mix of inorganic chemicals into ecosystems across the South, ratcheting up yields from the region's soils. No longer self-contained entities sustained by their own nutrient cycle, southern farms increasingly became receptacles for various outside inputs in the quest for more cotton. For a time, phosphorus-based fertilizer worked, but what the cotton plants needed most was nitrogen, a chemical not yet incorporated into plant food mixtures. Worse still, as sharecroppers fell further into debt, they bought greater amounts of commercial fertilizer from merchants on credit to boost output and generate the cash to pay off their loans—a self-defeating process that pushed the soil to its ultimate limit. "Who said fertilizer? Well, that's just it. Every farmer says it, every tenant says it, every merchant says it, and even the bankers must speak of it at times," one observer noted. "The trouble is that in times past the easy purchase and use of fertilizer has seemed to many of our Southern farmers a short cut to prosperity, a royal road to good crops of cotton year after year. The result has been that their lands have been cultivated clean year after year, their fertility has been exhausted." While some areas turned to more ecologically stable crop rotation practices, much of Georgia and South Carolina, as well as portions of Alabama

SOIL EROSION

Increasing fertilizer use promoted the constant planting of cotton, which eventually took its toll on the land. The gullies shown here were on a farm in North Carolina. (Library of Congress)

and Mississippi, fell prey to the fertilizer craze. The trend made the late nineteenth century the worst period of soil depletion in the South's entire history.[7]

Single-crop farming is always a perilous enterprise facing multiple threats. In 1892, the boll weevil, a small insect whose larva feed on the cotton boll, made its way out of Mexico into Texas. Eastward it crawled, reaching Louisiana in 1904, crossing the Mississippi five years later, and arriving in South Carolina by 1917. The pest left destruction in its wake, dramatically reducing cotton yields just about everywhere it went. In Greene County, Georgia, farmers picked 11,854 bales of cotton in 1916, the year the boll weevil first arrived. Six years later, the county produced just 333 bales.[8]

The boll weevil was especially devastating for black tenant farmers. Under the thumb of creditors who demanded cotton, black tenants had little say over the mix of crops they planted. The weevil figured in the great exodus of blacks to the North that began in 1910—one of the largest migrations in the history of the world. Between 1910 and 1920, it is estimated that as many as 500,000 African Americans left the South for northern cities. The weevil was not the only cause of the migration—other factors included the higher wages that came with the tight World War I–era labor market and rampant racial discrimination in the South—but the frustrations of southern farming were front and center. In the early 1910s, one woman from Mississippi spoke of a "general belief [among blacks] that God had cursed the land." But more than just the weevil caused blacks to wonder whether God was speaking up. Devastating flooding along the lower Mississippi River in 1912, made worse by the policy of building levees, broke records at nearly all of the river gauges between Cairo, Illinois, and the Gulf of Mexico.[9]

The boll weevil's consequences for southern agriculture were, in the long run, mixed. On the one hand, it drove farmers to use even more fertilizer to help the cotton crop mature before the weevil attacked it, solidifying the shift away from organic farming. And it caused cotton yields to decline precipitously. The number of acres devoted to cotton in the Deep South (Louisiana, Mississippi, Alabama, Georgia, and South Carolina) declined an average of 27 percent over the four years surrounding the infestation. On the other hand, the weevil broke cotton's grip on the region, heralding the move to a more diversified form of agriculture centered on corn, peanuts, and hogs—creating, in other words, a way out of one-crop farming. Citizens in Enterprise, Alabama, actually erected a statue in honor of the beetle, one of the more curious national monuments to dot the American landscape and a testament to the insect's role in forcing southerners to abandon their single-minded and ill-fated relationship with the land.[10]

Blacks too sometimes welcomed the weevil. Blues singers immortalized the insect, most famously in this song by Huddie Ledbetter (Lead Belly), who was born in 1888 in Shiloh, Louisiana:

First time I seen the boll weevil, he was sitting on a square.
Next time I seen a boll weevil, he had his whole family there.

He's a looking for a home.
He's a looking for a home.

The old lady said to the old man, "I've been trying my level best
Keep these boll weevils out of my brand new cotton dress.
It's full of holes.
And it's full of holes."

The old man said to the old lady, "What do you think of that?
I got one of the boll weevils out of my brand new Stetson hat,
And it's full of holes.
And it's full of holes."

Now the farmer said to the merchant, "I never made but one bale.
Before I let you have that last one, I will suffer and die in jail.
And I will have a home.
And I will have a home."[11]

OPEN AND SHUT RANGE

If cotton's stranglehold impoverished the ecology of the postwar South, it also helped to drive many people deeper into poverty. In 1880, federal census takers described black farmers as "sometimes without bread for their families" and declared that "many are in a worse [economic] condition than they were during slavery." As the quality of their diet declined, poor southerners, both black and white, turned to the region's common lands—unenclosed woods and pastures. There they could fish, hunt game, and turn out whatever few hogs and cattle they owned to find forage. Now, however, with increased sport and market hunting placing more intense pressure on the South's common resources, many landlords, merchants, and planters, using the law as their weapon, sought to seal off the range.[12]

In the antebellum period, slaves, especially those on tidewater plantations, had headed for rivers and forests to procure food and supplement their rations. "My old daddy," Louisa Adams of North Carolina recalled, "partly raised his chilluns on game. He caught rabbits, coons an' possums. He would work all day and hunt at night." Slaves also hunted and fished for sport, these being among the few recreational activities afforded them. In the woods of the South Carolina Low Country, slaves hunted deer, rabbits, squirrels, opossums, bears, ducks, turkeys, pigeons, and other animals. "Possum and squirrel all we could get," recalled one slave. "Wild turkey, possum. Don't bother with no coon much." In 1831, a visitor from the North observed, "The blacks are never better pleased than when they are hunting in the woods; and it is seldom that they have not in the larder the flesh of a raccoon or opossum." In the Georgia Low Country almost half of the slaves' meat, it is estimated, came from game and fish.[13]

Slaves had also counted on the woods as a source of fodder for livestock. Curious as it may sound, although themselves owned by others, slaves possessed property, including animals like cattle and hogs. One slave, described by a planter as "more like a free man than any slave," claimed in the mid-nineteenth century to have had 26 pigs, 16 sheep, and 8 cows.[14]

It was to the pine forests and patches of cane commonly found along streams that slaves and poor farmers alike went to run their hogs and cattle. "We raise our hogs by allowing them to range in our woods, where they get fat in the autumn on acorns," explained one resident of the South Carolina Piedmont. Cattle were raised "with so little care, that it would be a shame to charge anything for their keep up to three years old." The open range thrived in the South in large part because the mild winters allowed herders to leave stock on the range all year round (in contrast, farmers in the North had to bring in the animals to prevent them from freezing to death, and thus barn size limited the number of animals on common lands).[15]

"The citizens of this county have and always have had the legal, moral, and Bible right to let their stock . . . run at large," declared one Georgia Piedmont farmer in the 1880s. Private property in land existed in the South from the colonial period forward. But the customary right to use unimproved land for hunting and grazing coexisted with private landownership. The law itself respected the customary practice of grazing livestock in unfenced areas, regardless of who the "owner" of the land might be. So-called fence laws dating from the colonial period put the burden on farmers to enclose their crops with adequate fences or risk liability for damage from roving livestock. Early laws prescribing a death sentence for livestock theft were later reduced in severity when lawmakers realized that the customary practice of running cattle and other animals on the commons made it very hard to determine who owned a particular animal. The customary right to use the commons for a variety of subsistence activities persisted in the South until shortly after the Civil War. As the Virginia legislature put it: "Many poor persons have derived advantage from grazing their stock on the commons and unenclosed lands, and to whom the obligation to confine them, or a liability to damages if not confined, would operate as a great hardship."[16]

With emancipation, however, things began to change. Planters wondered how they would ever make a living growing cotton if their labor force spent valuable time hunting and fishing. In 1866, one Virginia newspaper bemoaned the fact that planters "suffer great annoyance and serious pecuniary loss from the trespasses of predacious negroes and low pot hunters, who with dogs and guns, live in the fields . . . as if the whole country belonged to them." Slowly, planters called for making private property more private and less open to customary hunting and fishing by commoners. "The right to hunt wild animals is held by the great body of the people, whether landholders or otherwise, as one of their franchises," lamented wealthy South Carolina planter and sportsman William Elliott. One observer who toured the South in the 1870s found that blacks "are fond of the same pleasures which their late masters gave them so freely—hunting, fishing, and lounging; pastimes which the superb forests, the noble streams, the charming climate minister to very strongly."[17]

Planters eventually pushed for the passage of game laws. Beginning in the 1870s, counties in the Black Belt passed statutes that regulated hunting. In 1875, three Georgia counties made it illegal to "kill or destroy" partridges or deer any time between April and October. The new law also prohibited people from using poison to catch fish. Although planters enjoyed a good hunt at least as much as their ex-slaves did, many supported such laws because they sensed, correctly, that wildlife was being depleted in the postbellum South. And, for example, a fawn that lost its mother in the early fall might be too young to survive the winter. But more likely, planters supported the game laws in order to further control the freedmen and get them back to work in the fields. Alabama's passage of a game law in 1876 that only applied to 14 Black Belt counties supports such a view. To some extent the laws may have improved the prospect for game. Like other such laws, it prohibited hunting in exactly the season of the year when planters needed agricultural laborers the most.[18]

In truth, wildlife in the postbellum South experienced a devastating decline. The depletion, however, was not solely the work of freedmen and other poor farmers. The rise of market and sport hunting also came into play. Wildlife had an incredibly powerful hold on the imagination of late-nineteenth-century Americans. A source of both food and fashion, wild game occupied a place in the hearts of urban consumers and rural poor alike. While trains transported ducks, geese, and pigeons from the Midwest to the tables of New Yorkers, game birds hung from the rafters in Atlanta, Norfolk, and New Orleans. Women wore feather hats and sometimes even sported entire birds. In the 1880s, the millinery trade spurred on market hunters who brought about the collapse of the heron population south of Tarpon Springs, Florida. By 1896, hunters had destroyed 99 percent of the terns nesting on Cape Hatteras.[19]

It was the railroads, under northern capitalist control by the 1890s, that brought the meat and feathers to market. The railroads also encouraged sport hunters "to visit the South and hunt game where it is more plentiful than in any other section of the United States." Access to new weapons such as the breech-loading shotgun and to better ammunition also improved the success of hunters.[20]

By the late nineteenth century the southern commons was in turmoil. Market and sport hunters descended on it in search of game, while cattle and pigs overran it in the quest for forage. Few animals inspired more resentment than the hog, described by one Mississippian, in a fit of anger, as an "old, pirating, fence-breaking, corn-destroying, long-snouted, big boned and leather-bellied" beast. Apart from planters, railroads also suffered from the effects of roaming livestock. Under the law, a railroad was liable if animals became injured on its tracks. The legal nicety reportedly drove some stockowners—eager to collect damages—to apply salt to the rails so as to lure the hapless creatures into the path of oncoming trains.[21]

Egged on by the railroads, landlords, merchants, and planters took action against the old fence laws in the 1870s. No longer should the farmer be called on to fence his crops, they cried out, while livestock roamed willy-nilly across the landscape.

"Why in the name of common sense," one planter asked, "am I compelled to maintain 12 or 13 miles of hideous fence around my plantation at an annual cost of upwards of a thousand dollars, in order to prevent the cattle and hogs which my neighbors turn loose . . . from destroying my crops and robbing my property?" Of course those who favored the open range saw things differently. "Poor man, without a farm of your own; what must become of that cow that gives milk for your prattling babes?" one pro-range advocate from Georgia wondered. "What is to become of the poor widow who is homeless? Freedmen, what is to become of you?"[22]

Although those opposed to the old fence laws objected to them on the grounds of principle, other more practical matters also influenced their view. The peculiar design of southern fences required a great deal of wood, an increasingly scarce resource in the postbellum years. The most common fence was the so-called Virginia or zigzag fence. It required much less labor than the post-and-hole fence to construct, it could be easily removed to another location if the soil wore out, and it was strong enough to resist marauding bands of swine. The Virginia fence, however, used a great deal of wood in a timber-poor environment, and because of their zigzag design, also took up much more land—which could have been used to plant crops—than the straight post-and-hole variety. Although barbed wire, invented in 1873, could have been substituted for wood, as happened in the West, it and made few inroads in the South, probably because pigs (unlike cattle) could get through it.[23]

ZIGZAG FENCE

Common throughout the South, this type of fence snaked through the land, taking up more room than the straighter post-and-hole variety. (Library of Congress)

compare to
"enclosure
movement
in
England"

It would take decades, in some places until the 1970s, before the range was fully closed, but the momentum was clearly established in the post–Civil War decades. By the 1890s, a new set of fence laws, often called stock laws, had emerged in counties across the South. The laws required farmers and stockmen to pen in their livestock, making them legally responsible if the animals somehow escaped and caused property damage. The stock laws penalized the poor, who had formerly relied on the unenclosed stretches of land. People with power and money used the law to preserve the sanctity of their property and make it more private. Those who had once counted on such land had to turn to other means to survive.

The stock laws had ecological and biological consequences as well as social ones. Animals formerly allowed to run loose in the woods now became true domesticates. Penned up in barnyards and no longer free to wander the land, the animals were either fattened on feed or forced to graze on self-contained pastures, where overuse, especially on hillsides, contributed to the South's already intense erosion problem. The closing of the range also brought another, more complicated effort. It helped to limit the spread of the cattle tick, carrier of the parasitic infection babesiosis (eventually named "Texas fever" by midwesterners who feared the Lone Star state's infected livestock). In the early twentieth century, with animals no longer able to roam the landscape and infect one another at will, the federal government introduced a program for eradicating the tick, a move that greatly benefited large commercial stock raisers. Tragically, the high capital costs involved in purchasing the technology to eliminate the cattle tick, plus the huge expense of fencing-in livestock, combined to further disadvantage southern yeomen who raised just a few cattle for household use. The stock laws, a social development, brought about a biological shift (a less congenial environment for the tick) that led to still more social changes, harsh ones for struggling small farmers.[24]

The fencing controversy, which ultimately worked its way as far west as Texas, figured indirectly in the rise of the late-nineteenth-century agrarian protest movement known as Populism. The Populists formed a third political party, the People's Party, opposed to the business-dominated organizations run by the Democrats and Republicans. Their critique of American society stemmed in part from changes in the land, for it was there that the yeoman farmer's earlier subsistence lifestyle, resting on the cultivation of corn and some cotton, and the pasturing of hogs in woods and bottomlands, gave way to the single-minded pursuit of cotton by the 1880s. Now the logic of distant markets in New York, St. Louis, and Liverpool, not the dietary needs of families, combined with the enclosure of the commons to force such farmers deeper into poverty. Driven from a safer and more ecologically sound form of farming to embrace monoculture, small farmers lost control of their livelihoods with the end of the open range.[25]

THE INVASIONS

Next to the closing of the range, the rise of industrial lumbering made the greatest contribution to the dispossession of the poor. Lumber production in the South skyrocketed in the 40 years after 1880, with the South overtaking the depleted Great Lakes states as the nation's major lumber-producing region. As industrial logging, aided by the increasing penetration of the railroad, boomed, the original forest cover in the southern states declined by an astonishing 40 percent, falling from roughly 300 million acres to just 178 million by 1919. One lumberman recalled, "You hardly ever left a tree of any size standing and all the little [ones] was torn down." Destruction of the woodlands habitat depressed game and plant populations, further undermining hunting and gathering as an element in survival. Of course it was becoming even harder to enter the woods in the first place, as logging and coal companies monopolized the land. By 1930, industrial enterprises, many serving the interests of distant corporations, controlled nearly two-thirds of all the privately owned land in the southern Appalachians.[26]

The federal government's land policies played a major role in aiding the logging companies' quest for control of the South's timber, much as they had done in the Midwest. In 1866, Congress passed homestead legislation designed to aid freedmen (as opposed to speculators) that limited the amount of land a person could claim (after settling on it and paying a nominal fee) to 80 acres. But in 1876, southern legislators, emboldened by the end of Reconstruction, won repeal of the law. Nearly 6 million acres of land passed out of the federal domain between 1877 and 1888 as the American state bankrolled private accumulation. Moroever, the federal land sales were as nothing compared to the tens of millions of acres of state land sold off, sometimes for as little as 25 cents an acre. By 1885, an astounding 32 million acres of state land passed into private hands in Texas alone.[27] With the southern lands open to unrestricted sales, the great giveaway began.

Combined with the assault on common-use rights, the steep decline in public domain land further undermined the efforts of yeoman farmers to survive off the land. Ownership of vast stretches of the southern landscape now rested with a relatively small number of individuals and companies, who valued it in part for its speculative value as farmland but mainly for its timber or mineral potential. Railroads ran trains for the express purpose of aiding so-called land lookers. Boarding in Chicago, those with money to spend headed south to Mississippi and Louisiana in search of prime timberland. Lumber barons from the Great Lakes states, northern capitalists, and British land moguls all rushed south in the 1880s to cash in on the red-hot land boom.[28]

The natural wealth of the countryside, after all, was worth little if it could not be transported to markets elsewhere in the nation. To meet this need, new railroads crisscrossed the region, forming a network so vast and all-consuming that it almost defies comprehension. The combined amount of track in 13 southern states rose from slightly over 9,000 miles in 1865 to nearly 39,000 miles by 1910. The railroads, one West Virginia historian observed in 1913, "carried into the silence of primeval woods the hum of modern industry." Some lines left no doubt about their mission, with one railway dubbing itself "the great lumber route."[29]

The railroads spurred the loggers on as they harvested timber and then turned around and burned what was left. Stripped of pines (the most commercially valuable stands) and hardwoods, the southern forests piled up with slash; all it took was for a stray spark from a locomotive to ignite it. Somewhere between 800,000 and 1.2 million acres of North Carolina woodland erupted in flames in 1891. In 1908, one-tenth of West Virginia felt the effects of forest fires.[30]

Southerners, however, remained largely unmoved by the smoke and flames. In 1898, when fire raged over 3 million acres of North Carolina, the episode rated barely a mention in Raleigh newspapers. The nonchalance likely derived from the historic role that fire played in the lives of those who raised stock on common lands. Burning the woods was an annual ritual in many parts of the South. In keeping down the "rough" (grasses and saplings), burning allowed stockmen to drive cattle from one place to another and, most important, encouraged the growth of grasses and other vegetation on which cattle fed. As the lumber industry tried to check the spread of fires, it allowed the rough to flourish and contributed, inadvertently, to the spiraling downward of those raising stock.[31]

Industrial logging also contributed more directly to the demise of subsistence practices by altering the habitat. Deer, bear, and turkey disappeared as the woodlands vanished. Ginseng, mayapple, and other plants, which mountaineers had historically collected and exchanged at stores for cash, met a similar fate.[32]

The forest and its wealth of plants and animals figured centrally in the lives of southern Appalachian mountaineers, which is why they left so much of their land—in some areas as much as 90 percent—unimproved. When northerner George Vanderbilt, scion of the famed railroad family, bought 100,000 acres of land in North Carolina in order to pursue hunting and forestry, Gifford Pinchot, conservationist and forester for the estate, said this about those displaced by the purchase: "They regarded this country as their country, their common. And it was not surprising, for they needed everything usable in it—pasture, fish, game—to supplement the very meager living they were able to scratch from the soil."[33]

The entry of northern industrial loggers into the southern forests was not the only incursion that the common people had to endure. An alien invader compounded their problems: the chestnut blight. By 1912, the fungus, brought accidentally to the United States in 1904 in a shipment of Asian chestnut trees, had destroyed all of New York City's stock. Then the fungus, which starved the chestnut tree by colonizing the food-storing cortex cells underneath the bark, worked its way south, carried there on the boots and axes of loggers. By 1913, the blight had entered North Carolina. Some experts describe the chestnut tree's near-total annihilation in North America as one of the most profound changes in plant life ever recorded in human history.[34]

SHELTON FAMILY

Southerners who depended on chestnut trees like this one for their livelihood were severely affected by the blight. (Great Smoky Mountains National Park)

One of the most important and abundant trees in the eastern forests, the chestnut, once found on 200 million acres of land, played a far more critical role in the lives of southerners than it did for New Yorkers promenading around Central Park. The poor seeking to survive off of the southern woodlands found the blight devastating. Prior to the incursion of the fungus, edible chestnuts commonly mounted to a height of four inches on the forest floor, providing a crucial source of food for wild game and grazing livestock. "The worst thing that ever happened in this country was when the chestnut trees died," lamented one

Tennessee resident. "Turkeys disappeared, and the squirrels were not one-tenth as many as there were before." Another mountaineer from Virginia recalled that before the blight it "didn't cost a cent to raise chestnuts or hogs. . . . It was a very inexpensive way to farm. The people had money and had meat on the table too." Children also gathered the nuts, supplementing the diet of mountain families. "The chestnut tree was the most important tree we had," recalled one Kentucky woman. "We needed those chestnuts."[35]

If the blight provided yet another threat to the yeoman farmer's subsistence, it did not stand in the way of the lumber barons. Timber harvesting actually increased in the wake of the epidemic, which eventually infected enough trees to produce 30 billion board feet of chestnut wood. By this point the South had eclipsed the Great Lakes states as the chief purveyor of the nation's lumber, underscoring the fact that the accumulation of wealth required both human labor and a steady supply of raw materials.[36]

AMERICA'S INTERNAL COLONY

No part of the South felt the effects of resource extraction more than Appalachia—the mountainous region spanning from western Maryland to northeast Alabama whose very name is now synonymous with poverty and desperation. This impoverishment and accompanying ecological damage was not an accident. It was the product of an unfolding capitalist tragedy that began as far back as the eighteenth century, when the transformation of land into a commodity led not just to the expropriation of the Indians but to a frenzied land grab that by 1810 had left three-quarters of the land—nearly 40 million acres in all—in the hands of absentee landholders. The speculators, who included such luminaries as George Washington and Robert Morris, accumulated so many deeds that the less fortunate who entered the region had little choice but to rent small parcels or turn to wage labor in order to eke out a living.[37] If not for the large number of these people, divorced from the land and forced to sell their labor power to those who saw in the mountains vast natural riches that could be extracted for profit, the capitalist system never could have thrived.

Those commodities extracted from the region, shipped primarily to the North and to Western Europe, helped to fuel the growth of industrial capitalism. Before California entered the national picture, for example, southern Appalachia was the country's leading source of gold. Vast reserves of coal also rested beneath the earth, black rock that was hauled out of the ground by wageworkers and slaves and sent to far-off markets in the Midwest and South to be burned. There seemed no end to the resources that could be extracted—from manganese and saltpeter to copper and timber. Even the region's water was bottled up and shipped off to distant locales.[38]

Eclipsed by gold from California and battered by deindustrialization as the region's iron manufacturers lost ground to European mills (which supplied the Northeast by the 1840s), southern Appalachia concentrated on exporting raw materials scrounged from the earth by the growing class of landless workers. By the latter part of the nineteenth century, as Thomas Edison developed the first coal-fired power plant and electrification began in earnest, workers had begun blasting through the mountains, inaugurating another round of changes to the land.[39]

The story of coal was much the same as that of trees: the invasion of outside capital from the North and abroad, the penetration of the railroad, the relentless mining of the resource, sweeping ecological change, and the dispossession of ordinary people. The region assumed the status of an internal colony.

The origins of Appalachia's decline and reincarnation as a huge coalpit for supplying energy to the North and Midwest go back to the period just before the Civil War. As population surged between 1850 and 1880—rising 156 percent on the Appalachian Plateau—the eternal struggle to farm the land in an ecologically viable manner became harder. Farm size plummeted and steep hillsides swelled with people, forcing farmers to improve more land.[40] Living standards soon began to fall, making farmers seek wage work.

Northern and foreign capitalists were eager to harvest the natural riches of the mountains, the product of geological forces that had compressed what had once been swampland with ferns the size of trees into one of the world's great sources of energy: bituminous coal. Unlike anthracite coal (a less accessible resource because of the steep pitch of the folds in which it rests), Appalachia's bituminous fields, extending over 72,000 square miles from western Pennsylvania to northeastern Alabama, are positioned horizontally, parallel to the surface, and can be mined with relative ease, though not with safety. These miners were caught in the clutches of a capitalist dilemma that forced them to work for low wages or risk starvation. Were it not for their blood and sweat, bituminous coal—an expensive item to transport to northern markets—would never have been economically competitive.

CONCLUSION

By the turn of the century, Appalachia and many other parts of the South had moved from self-sufficiency in food production to economic dependency. A region whose people could once feed themselves on their own now became dependent on other places and ecosystems and thoroughly entrenched in a market economy overseen by capitalists pursuing the private accumulation of wealth. The reasons for this shift are multiple. The steady spread of the cotton monoculture in much of the South, fueled by the addition of large amounts of phosphorus-based fertilizer, clearly played a role. It drove farmers into debt as they bought more chemicals to speed crop maturation and fight off the boll weevil, inaugurating a cycle in which they struggled to pay for a product that briefly boosted yields but could never deliver the nitrogen that the cotton plant needed most. Busted yeoman farmers might have looked to the woods to survive, had not planters and merchants been cracking down on the system of common rights to hunt and forage—precisely when the federal government, in league with the states, sold off these very same lands to lumber and mineral companies. The chestnut blight delivered an additional, perhaps final, blow to those seeking to survive from what little common land remained.

All these trends conspired to leave southern farmers dependent and dispossessed. The compound tragedy affected the poor, but it was especially ruinous for blacks, who had been promised freedom after years of bondage. In addition to facing crippling racism, reflected in the rise of repugnant segregation laws and lynching in the late-nineteenth-century South, blacks found themselves enslaved to a culture that mediated their relations with the land through the institutions of private property and a market economy controlled by a capitalist elite who aimed not to meet human needs, but to advance their own pecuniary interests.

8

THE UNFORGIVING WEST

In at least one respect, the American West—the vast expanse of land running from the 98th meridian bisecting the Dakotas, Nebraska, Kansas, Oklahoma, and Texas to the Pacific Ocean—was all a big mistake. Following the Civil War a period of unusually wet weather that lasted roughly two decades inspired Americans to head west in droves. Urged on by scientists such as Cyrus Thomas, who pronounced the ample rainfall a permanent feature of the climate and "in some way connected to the settlement of the country," Euro-Americans forged into the region under the delusion that moisture would increase in proportion to population. As late as 1884, one Chicago reporter wrote, "Kansas was considered a droughty state, but that day is past, and her reputation for sure crops is becoming widely known."[1]

One of the few people urging restraint as settlers rushed across the continent was a man by the name of John Wesley Powell. A Civil War veteran who had lost his right arm in the Battle of Shiloh, Powell went on in 1869 to successfully navigate the Colorado River. But his greatest contribution stemmed not from his explorations but from his deep understanding of the hard reality that character-ized the lands west of the 98th meridian. The West might seem wet and inviting at the moment, Powell argued in the 1870s, but aridity—a fundamental inability to support agriculture without an artificial infusion of water—defined its true character. As the rain charts available at the time made clear, this was a land sub-ject to fewer than 20 inches of precipitation annually, a finding that amounted to two-fifths of the nation being bereft of the moisture necessary to grow wheat and corn without a supply of irrigation water. We now know that it is the Rocky Mountains, in league with the coastal ranges farther west, that, by blocking the passage of storm fronts and squeezing water from the clouds, make the West so dry. But Powell, in his day, understood enough to realize that it was folly to expect the rains to continue forever, that soon the cycle of drought would come around again. As he wrote, westerners "shall have to expect a speedy return to extreme aridity, in which case a large portion of the agricultural industries of these now growing up would be destroyed."[2]

In this land of little rain, Powell argued, the geometric logic of Jefferson's grid made little sense. No settler could expect to succeed on 160 acres—the survey's magic number—if that land lacked water for farming and ranching. In-stead, in 1878, Powell proposed organizing the region into two kinds of land-use

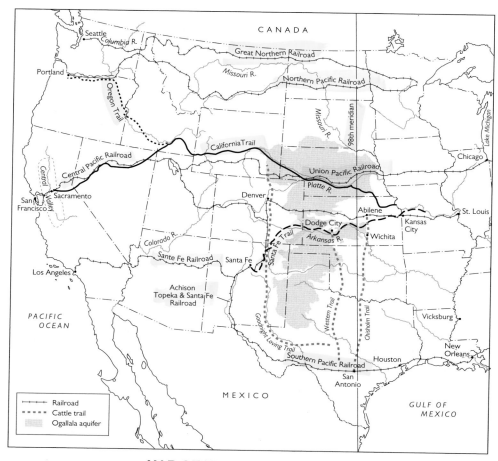

MAP OF THE AMERICAN WEST

arrangements: small, 80-acre farms and large, 2,560-acre livestock ranches, each attached to a respective irrigation and grazing district. Nobody paid any attention. Nor did anyone heed his gloom and doom prediction of drought. But history would soon vindicate his doomsaying, as drought returned in the 1890s. The reasons for this and other such misfortunes arose from the clash between an inherently unforgiving and at times unpredictable land and the strivings of a socio-ecological order organized to defy limits in the name of endless economic growth.

GOLD!

On January 24, 1848, a carpenter named James Marshall, while building a saw-mill on the American River, discovered a small nugget of gold, an event that drove pioneers, brimming with hope, to hitch up wagons and head for California. Thus began the Gold Rush, one of the earliest and most formative chapters in the history of the West. Or so the textbooks say. In fact, officials in Washington, DC, knew about California's gold as early as 1843, when almost 2,000 ounces arrived in the city from mines in Southern California.[3]

The problems with the myth of an otherwise obscure carpenter "discovering" gold extend well beyond its implications for fully comprehending the mineral's importance to the nation's expansionist crusade. The Marshall story renders the people who preceded the Euro-Americans on the land all but invisible. It is as if Marshall and his boss operated in a virtual wilderness, a place awaiting the arrival of clever and industrious people to mine and profit from the landscape. Nothing could be further from the truth. The Indians unquestionably knew about the region's gold. They had to have known about it, busy as they were pruning, transplanting, and burning the landscape, shaping the plant and animal life on which their survival depended. By the time whites arrived from the east, the Indians, decimated by the arrival of European diseases, no longer preyed on animals and worked the landscape to the extent they once had. Native game populations thus rebounded just in time for the Gold Rush, as did the underbrush in many forested areas. The rising number of deer, antelope, and elk furnished the forty-niners with ample food, but the growth of a tangled understory in the woods hindered travel and increased the risk of fire.[4]

Before John Marshall made his so-called historic find, there were already 26 gold mines or sites where gold had been discovered, most of them by Spanish and Mexicans. These Spanish-speaking residents of California sought placer gold, bits of the mineral that harsh weather had torn from its parent rock and sent tumbling into rivers. The Spanish word "placer" means "sandbank," and that is precisely where miners found the gold, a very heavy metal that settled out of the stream along its edges, where the current slowed down. When the forty-niners arrived they also took up placer mining, using pans, picks, shovels, and sluice boxes to search for dust and nuggets. But the real money was made not by the miners but by the merchants who supplied them and by land speculators.[5]

Placer mining lasted just a short time, as the surface gold slowly ran out. Individual enterprise then rapidly gave way to corporate mining, mainly because it took large amounts of capital to get the earth to yield the precious metal. The companies literally moved rivers, diverting the water with dams into wooden chutes so that workers, many of them Chinese, could be sent in to hack at the now dry riverbeds. The threat of flooding in the winter, a common occurrence in northern California, forced laborers to work with enormous speed or risk the possibility that the chutes would be washed downstream during a heavy rain. By 1853, nearly 25 miles of the Yuba River had been diverted from its channel. One company on the Feather River built a chute extending 3,200 feet and then sent 260 workers into the abandoned channel to strike it rich.[6]

River mining produced gold, but in nowhere near the amounts to be found in old, dried-up stream channels. Some 70 million years ago, when the Sierra Nevada range was an anemic version of its present monumental splendor, the climate of northern California tended toward the subtropical. For millions of years, this climate subjected the mountains to intense weathering, producing huge quantities of sand, gravel, and gold. In the Eocene period (55 million to 38 million years ago), the mountains began to rise up, and the accumulated mineral wealth along with the rest of the debris slid downstream toward the ocean. Gold was so heavy that it took much longer to make that journey than did gravel or sand. Thus, when later volcanic eruptions sent torrents of ash onto the landscape, rerouting old streams, much of the gold settled into abandoned river channels, where it hardened and remained—until 1853, that is, when a man named Edward Matteson, a New Englander, discovered that a stream of water delivered by hose could tear apart an ancient hillside, freeing the precious metal in the process. What many miners with picks and shovels took weeks to accomplish was just a day's labor for a few workers who tapped the energy supplied by a large volume of water.

Hydraulic mining, as the technique came to be called, sent miners scrambling for water, a resource unleashed with reckless abandon on the foothills of the Sierra Nevada. The force of the water amazed onlookers. "Trunks of trees lying in the mine can be made to spin like straws or be hurled away many feet distant," said one. "The amount of soil removed in hydraulic mining must be seen to be believed," another added. Miners along the Feather, Yuba, American, and Bear rivers bombarded the hills with water, eventually producing nearly 1.3 billion cubic yards of gravel debris, enough material to bury the city of Washington, DC, to a depth of 19 feet. Hydraulic mining caused more erosion than any other event in the history of the Sierra Nevada, stretching back nearly 600 million years.[7]

Thousands of miles of ditches brought water from the Sierra Nevada to bear on mines located in northern California watersheds. By 1857, some 700 miles of canals crisscrossed the Yuba alone. Billions of gallons of water tore apart the mountains, with the leftover debris coursing into rivers, raising their beds and destroying salmon spawning grounds. In 1869, a tourist from the East noted, "Tornado, flood, earthquake, and volcano combined could hardly make greater havoc, spread wider ruin and wreck, than are to be seen everywhere in the track of the larger gold-washing operations."[8]

The entire hydrological network of northern California received a huge face-lift as a result of hydraulic mining, with devastating results. Massive amounts of debris—the excavated remains of the Tertiary period (66 to 1.6 million years ago)—settled in riverbeds downstream from mines, leaving less room for water and forcing the river to spill across the floodplain, killing people and destroying property. Massive rains in the winter of 1861–1862, which dropped six feet of water between November and January, put much of the Sacramento Valley under water so deep that Leland Stanford, the state's newly elected governor, had to take a rowboat to his inauguration. The downpours scoured the mountains, flushing debris downstream, where it buried some of the richest farmland in the state. By 1868, the Yuba and Feather rivers contained so much mining sediment that at Marysville, California, where the two waterways intersected, their

HYDRAULIC MINING
Mining in French Corral, California, in the foothills of the Sierra Nevada Mountains. (Library of Congress)

beds rose higher than the streets of the town itself. The town built levees to contain the floodwaters. By 1874, after a generation of hydraulic mining, the Yuba River's bed had risen an astonishing 16 feet.[9]

Important legal changes helped propel the rise of hydraulic mining. Hispanic mining law, based on the idea of public rights to mineral resources, ruled initially. Even the 1848 Treaty of Guadalupe Hidalgo, which followed U.S. victory in the Mexican War and ceded control of the Southwest, including California, to the United States, respected the then-prevailing Hispanic property rights regime. Under that regime, landowners did not have automatic title to mineral rights below the land. Those rights resided in the public domain. Between 1859 and 1861, however, a set of leading California cases overturned the right of the state to license mineral prospecting on private land. These cases held that rights to the subsurface minerals belonged to the owner of the surface land and would "pass with the transfer of the soil in which they are contained." The rulings denied the public nature of mineral resources and were of a piece with the changes to water law then occurring in New England. Both sets of changes privileged private control over natural riches from the earth in the name of industrial expansion. And both led to much more heavily capitalized industry and significant changes to the land.[10]

SANTA FE TRAIL

The Santa Fe Trail ran from Independence, Missouri, to Santa Fe, New Mexico. (*Granger Collection, New York*)

The devastating floods of the late nineteenth century flowed from this new privatized legal regime. A deluge in 1875 finished off the remaining farms on the fertile Yuba floodplain, a development that angered many in a state fast becoming known for its rich agricultural land. Farmers and others in Yuba and Sutter counties soon banded together to fight the hydraulic mining companies in court, emerging victorious in 1884 when a federal judge closed down one of the most powerful companies. Severe flooding in the 1880s—largely the result of the monumental changes to land and water brought about by hydraulic mining—also compelled the California Supreme Court to overturn a decidedly pro-business legal understanding of liability. The court instead made it easier for negligence claims by plaintiffs suing industry to succeed.[11]

The ecological significance of the Gold Rush, however, was not confined to northern California alone. People had to get to the gold and thus had to traverse the continent. For the first time, ordinary Americans tramped west in large numbers—80,000 just in 1849. They brought major changes to California. But they also figured centrally in a significant environmental disaster on the Great Plains, a crisis of subsistence for Indians that was rooted in the expansion of human and animal populations beyond what the land could handle.

Gold seekers took two main trails west across the Great Plains, the vast grassland that occupies the nation's midsection: the Oregon–California road and the Santa Fe Trail. The traffic along these routes was enormous. Some 300,000 people with more than 1.5 million four-legged creatures—cattle, horses, and oxen—set off along the Oregon–California road between 1841 and 1859. The Santa Fe had been plied by almost 2,000 wagons by the end of the 1850s.

The stream of emigrants—human beings and animals—took their toll on the Platte and Arkansas watersheds. Pioneers cut down timber on the river bottoms to cook and keep warm. Oxen, cattle, mules, and horses chewed up the region's forage, putting a significant dent in what had once seemed like an almost limit-less supply of grass that thrived in the dry environment. The gold seekers even timed their journey west to coincide with the availability of grass. They tried not to leave before it had sprouted enough to support their herds but feared setting off too late, when all the forage would have been eaten. All the foot and hoof traf-fic also trampled a great deal of vegetation. Then there was the damage caused by wagon wheels. Sometimes bunched together in groups with 12 wagons abreast, the caravans moved across the region like giant steamrollers.[12]

The central plains environment perhaps would have rebounded from the pio-neer invasion but for another mass migration. While gold seekers trudged across the plains, Indians, led by the Cheyenne, headed there to capitalize on the large herds of bison and to assume a role as middlemen in a trading network that stretched from New Mexico into Canada. Despite being battered by European diseases, the Indian population grew significantly, to perhaps as many as 20,000 people by the 1850s.[13]

The Cheyenne counted on their horses—animals acquired from the Spanish—to track and hunt the mobile buffalo herds. Large numbers of horses, perhaps as many as 5 to 13 for each person, required lots of forage. Forage was especially scarce on the plains in the winter, when rainfall tapered off and grama and buffalo grass became less nutritious. That forced the Indians to retreat to river locations where moister conditions and protection from the weather kept grass alive. Indeed, survival on the plains depended on finding adequate forage, fuel, water, and protection from the severe winters. River bottoms such as the Big Timbers, a large stretch of cottonwoods along the Arkansas River in present-day Colorado, served well for a time. But then the pioneers arrived with their horses and oxen in the summer months. When white emigrants approached the Big Timbers in the latter part of the 1850s, they found it scalped, prompting one pioneer woman to write: "Cattle were nearly starved for grass."[14]

A climatic change made matters worse. The central plains experienced unchar-acteristically wet weather between 1825 and 1849. A lush, inviting environment resulted, precisely in time to greet both the Indians and pioneers. But in 1849 drought descended across the Arkansas River Valley. A more extensive dry spell wracked the central plains in 1855, followed by two even worse droughts in the early 1860s. The Indians turned increasingly to river locations for water and forage, putting additional pressure on an environment already stretched to its limits.[15]

By the 1850s, the central plains were in ecological turmoil, with more people and animals dependent on a shrinking supply of natural wealth. The drought only intensified the suffering, driving Indians to beg whites for food as they passed west. Some Indians even stole in order to eat. In 1855, a group of Arapaho made off with more than 2,000 sheep. The following year, Indians reportedly demanded food in return for safe passage along the Santa Fe road.[16]

Then, in 1858, gold was discovered in what became Denver, Colorado. Twice as many people picked up and crossed the continent as had in 1849. Wagon traffic on

BISON

The West's most famous animal species, bison survived on the region's shortgrass, which had just the combination of protein and carbohydrates they needed to thrive. (Library of Congress)

the Santa Fe Trail boomed. By the mid-1860s, Denver alone depended on the shipment of tens of thousands of tons of supplies each year from back east. The bottomlands continued to decline ecologically. The summer of 1859 became known as the "timber clearing sun dance," a name bestowed by the Kiowa, who showed up for their yearly ritual on the Smoky Hill River expecting to see a forested grove and instead found stumps. Previously, Euro-Americans had avoided the area, but now the search for forage and timber to support the overland trek had forced them farther from the main trail west, bringing them into conflict with Indians.[17]

As the number of such conflicts rose, so, in response, did the U.S. military presence. As during the Civil War, the army worried about feeding its horses. It sought out locations at precisely those wintertime haunts so cherished by Indians. Military posts sprouted at the Big Timbers of the Arkansas (Fort Wise) and at other such sheltered sites rich in wood and grass, further undermining the ability of Indians to survive.[18]

To move from gold mining to Indians, to horses and mules, and then to drought, forage, and timber seems like helter-skelter history. But this seemingly disconnected chain of topics reminds us of the interdependency of the various aspects of the natural world. This one change in human behavior—the rush to mine gold—had consequences that ramified throughout the continent, in ecosystems far removed from the site of the gold itself.

LAST OF THE BISON

Virtually everyone knows about the decline of the buffalo, one of the most studied blunders in the nation's environmental past. When the buffalo vanished, so did the hopes and dreams of the Plains Indians, who for more than 150 years had organized life around the animal. Sitting Bull put it this way: "A cold wind blew across the prairie when the last buffalo fell—a death-wind for my people."[19]

As improbable as it may seem, herds of bison could be found in the eastern part of the United States as late as the 1830s. From then on, the buffalo population retreated to the grasslands of the plains—its primary home since the end of the Ice Age, when climatic change spurred the shift from trees to grass in this vast region. Unlike such large animals as mammoths and mastodons, the bison—a prolific reproducer that was quick on its feet and able to subsist on less forage than other megafauna—survived the Pleistocene extinctions. With its competitors now out of the way, the bison multiplied, gobbling up the aptly named buffalo grass, while fertilizing the soil with its dung and thus helping to sustain its habitat.

How many bison existed on the plains has been the subject of much debate. But whatever the actual number, it was high, at least before the late nineteenth century. George Catlin in the 1830s found bison so thick that they "literally blacken the prairies for miles together." As late as 1871, one observer witnessed a herd of buffalo in Kansas that reportedly took five full days to venture past. One Indian asked in the late nineteenth century to recall the glory days of the bison simply signed the words, "The country was one robe."[20]

Estimates of the total bison population have ranged as high as 75 million, but historians and ecologists have recently scaled down that figure considerably, and for good reason. The bison depended on grass to survive: as went the grass, so went the bison. By taking into account the carrying capacity of the grassland, it seems reasonable to assume that the Great Plains supported a population of about 27 million such creatures. Significant threats, however, ranging from drought, perhaps the most important, to predation by wolves (1.5 million of which may have roamed the plains in the early nineteenth century) affected the buffalo's numbers. The more such threats, the more volatile the animal population. Like their human counterparts, the bison also had to face the facts of life in this unforgiving land.[21]

Before the eighteenth century, Indians ventured to the plains to hunt buffalo, but the animal remained just one element of their subsistence regime. They also gathered a variety of plants—roots and berries—and, in some cases, turned to agriculture as well. Like southern yeoman farmers in the years before the Civil War, Native Americans opted for a safety-first strategy, engaging in a diverse set of practices to feed themselves. And like the South's small farmers, the Plains Indians were eventually driven to specialize—in this case, not in cotton but in buffalo. More than anything else, perhaps, specialization sealed their fate and set the stage for the decline of both the bison and the people who depended on them.

Nothing did more to encourage the Indians to throw their fortunes in with the bison and engage in year-round hunting than the arrival of the horse. The Spanish brought horses to America in the early sixteenth century, but it took well over 100 years for the Plains Indians to adopt them. Horses greatly expanded the Indians' ability to hunt buffalo, freeing them from the punishing task of chasing after the animals by foot. Horses were also a huge improvement over the dogs the Indians had formerly depended on for transport. Dogs are carnivores, and during the winter Indians found it difficult to find enough meat to feed them. The horse, however, eats grass, which was plentiful on the plains.

When the Indians discovered the horse they found the key to unlocking the grasslands' huge storehouse of energy. This energy allowed the Indians to fortify their mounts and set off to hunt buffalo, to the exclusion of other subsistence activities save the gathering of berries and roots.[22]

By the eighteenth century, the bison had assumed a place at the center of Plains Indian culture. The Indians roasted and boiled it for food, consuming nearly the entire animal right down to its testicles and marrow. They made bedding, clothing, and rope from it. They used the intestines as containers, the penis for making glue, and the horns for cups. The bison served so many different dietary and cultural needs that one scholar has referred to the animal as a "tribal department store."[23]

What impact did the Indians have on the bison population? According to one estimate, Plains Indians killed only about half a million buffalo every year, a sustainable figure in light of the bison's reproductive habits. Indians may have even looked down on those who wasted bison. "Don't kill more meat than you think you can skin and your horse can pack home," one Kiowa told another in 1861 on the occasion of his first buffalo hunt. Other evidence, however, indicates that the Indians' belief system may have encouraged them to overhunt the species. When buffalo disappeared for the year, the Plains Indians believed, they went to underground prairies, reemerging in the spring "like bees from a hive," as one settler put it. If they failed to appear in adequate numbers one could still hunt with abandon, safe in the knowledge that other buffalo grazed happily in the land down below.[24]

In reality, a group so deeply dependent on bison was capable of diminishing its numbers. Well before commercial shooters descended in droves on the plains, Indian hunting had taken its toll. At one time, contested grounds—places where no single Indian group dominated—sheltered the bison there from attack. Indians, fearing for their lives, tended to shy away from those areas. But in 1840, a number of Native American groups on the western plains agreed to peace. No longer looking over their shoulders, Indians waged war against the bison. As a result, by the 1850s the bison had begun vanishing from around Denver.[25]

A mere 30 years later, the buffalo would be virtually annihilated. Nothing the Indians did rivaled in importance the role of the capitalist market economy in the animal's demise. Plains Indians had long traded with other Native American groups, often bartering buffalo for corn. But by the 1830s, the demand for buffalo skins had begun to rise sharply, as Euro-Americans increasingly used them to keep warm. In the past, Indians had valued the entirety of the animal. To them, it had use-value, a unique ability to serve a variety of different needs ranging from food and clothing to much more, and could be acquired without any monetary cost. The rise of a market in robes to benefit the pecuniary interests of speculating capitalists, however, drove the Indians to kill bison for their skins alone, leaving the rest of the carcass for wolves to devour. The Indians and the buffalo had entered a new economic world in which exchange value—the idea that buffalo could result in speculative profits when sold on a market—was the dominant force. In the 1850s, the evolving political economy of bison hunting combined with drought—which dried up creeks and stunted the growth of grass—to make life even more difficult for the buffalo. "The buffalo is becoming scarce and it is more difficult from year to year for the Indians to kill a sufficient number to supply them with food and clothing," one observer along the Platte River reported in 1855.[26]

The transformation of the buffalo into a commodity to be sold on the market propelled Euro-American market hunters out to the plains. Beginning in the 1870s, they flooded into the region to meet the burgeoning demand for leather in industrial America. The growth of industry called for leather belting for power machinery, with demand outstripping the domestic supply of hides. Tanners, hard pressed for skins, initially imported them from as far away as Latin America. Then, in 1870, tanners in Philadelphia discovered a method for turning bison skin into leather. The production of industrial leather required green, unprepared buffalo hides. In the past, Indian women had fleshed the hides, transforming them into buffalo robes for markets in the East. This was a time-consuming process, and bottlenecks occurred, inadvertently protecting the buffalo against overhunting. The demand for green skins removed the threat of such slowdowns, but there was one hitch: they weighed about five times as much as a robe, possibly as much as 50 pounds each. It would take something far more powerful than the back of a horse to transport them to market in the numbers required to satisfy American industry.[27]

That something turned out to be the railroad. The roads pushed through the plains in the years following 1867; the buffalo declined everywhere the trains went. Scarcely a generation later, the bison would be all but gone. The Santa Fe, Kansas Pacific, and Union Pacific railroads shipped over a million hides in just two years (1872–1874). The bison, recall, had few predators and thus little experience with being attacked. The animal also tended to stampede or stand pat when faced with an aggressor. The gun-toting market hunter could not have asked for more cooperative prey. Hunters commonly bagged 2,000 to 3,000 hides per season. In 1876, one hunter killed nearly 6,000 bison in just two months, firing his .50-caliber rifle so many times that he went deaf.[28]

Aiding the market hunters was the U.S. Army. Military leaders believed that the best way to subjugate the Plains Indians was through the elimination of the buffalo. Lt. Gen. John M. Schofield, who was in charge of the Department of Missouri from 1869 to 1870, put it this way: "I wanted no other occupation in life than to ward off the savage and kill off his food until there should no longer be an Indian frontier in our beautiful country." Gen. William Tecumseh Sherman, of Civil War fame, wrote in 1868 that "as long as Buffalo are up on the Republican [River] the Indians will go there. I think it would be wise to invite all the sportsmen of England and America there this fall for a Grand Buffalo hunt." Sherman's comrade in arms, Gen. Philip Sheridan, pointed out that market hunters had done more "to settle the vexed Indian question than the entire regular army has done in the last thirty years. They are destroying the Indians' commissary.... Send them powder and lead, if you will; but for the sake of lasting peace, let them kill, skin and sell until the buffaloes are exterminated." The Army even went so far as to distribute free ammunition to hide hunters, thereby underwriting the private accumulation of wealth.[29]

With the bison gone from the southern plains by 1878, the hunters moved north. There the fate of the buffalo rested as much on the commodification of the animal as on the combined forces of ranching and drought. The huge number of cattle imported into the region (Wyoming's cattle population increased from 90,000 to more than 500,000 between 1874 and 1880) competed with the bison for grass, closing off areas to which the animal had retreated for food and water. When dry spells struck beginning in the 1870s, the bison had nowhere left to turn. In 1882, hunters took the remaining 5,000 survivors present on the northern plains.[30]

Only their bones remained, and, fittingly, even these were turned into cash. Dispossessed Indians (and others) collected the skeletal remains of the once vast bison herds, piling them 10 feet high along railroad tracks, where bone dealers arranged to ship them east. There they were crushed up, made into phosphate fertilizer, and spread on the soils of the cotton South and the Corn Belt, providing a nutrient subsidy to distant ecosystems.

TR'S TROPHY ROOM

Theodore Roosevelt's trophy room at his home on Long Island, with bison heads shown on each side of the mantle. (Library of Congress)

In those bones lay a lesson on where economic specialization in a capitalist market economy might lead. When the Plains Indians engaged in the single-minded pursuit of bison, they foreclosed other avenues for making a living from the land and put their future at risk in a region prone to climatic extremes.

THE GREAT CATTLE BUST

The death of the bison was the prelude to one of the most stunning transformations of a North American biome ever known: the makeover of the Great Plains grasslands into pastures and farms. Cattle drovers and wheat farmers delivered a one-two punch in the post–Civil War years, stripping the region of its original vegetative cover, loosening the soil, and making it far more prone to wind erosion. No shortage of food compelled cowboys, cattle companies, and wheat farmers to exploit the plains by grazing more cattle or planting more wheat. It was, instead, the quest to incorporate grass into products such as wheat and cattle that could be sold at a profit that set them to work rearranging the landscape. The approach to the land, in other words, changed from a focus on use value—employing grass to support animals eaten or otherwise used in the local context to satisfy human needs—to a concern with exchange value—working the land to produce speculative profits through participation in the market system. By the time they were through, they had set the stage for some of the worst ecological calamities to ever befall the region.

To the rancher, cattle were less a source of food than a means of accumulating wealth. Indeed, the word "cattle" has the same etymological roots as "capital," the so-called stock of life. As one of the world's earliest mobile assets, cattle were money, but only if the animals could be fed. When it comes to cattle, grass is the currency of accumulation. If the grass is free, as it was on the plains during the postbellum years, then all the better. "Cotton was once crowned king," proclaimed one eastern livestock journal in the 1870s, "but grass is now. . . . If grass is King, the Rocky Mountain region is its throne and fortunate indeed are those who possess it."[31]

Ranching began in the early nineteenth century in southern Texas. It was there that the mixing of Anglo-American cattle from the South and Spanish stock from Mexico produced the breed known as the Texas longhorn. Hardy, able to thrive on grass, and famous for its long horns, the longhorn reproduced with abandon during the Civil War. The animals roamed the range unsupervised as the men who once raised them went off to fight; other ranchers simply gave up tending them as hostilities cut off the market for their meat in southern cities like New Orleans. By 1870, as ranching spread northward in Texas, one county had 57,000 cattle; another had 159 head for every inhabitant. Closed off from southern markets, ranchers shifted their product to the North, where cattle commanded higher prices. After the war, railroads began to work their way across the plains, and towns such as Abilene, Kansas, emerged to wed the southern cattle drover with buyers in the North. Setting off along the Chisholm Trail and other routes, drovers brought livestock to rail depots and transferred them to trains headed east to meet the demand for beef in St. Louis and Chicago. By 1871, Abilene was processing nearly 750,000 longhorns every year, dispatching them to slaughterhouses in cities farther east.[32]

Slowly, the Texas ranchers gravitated northward, attracted by the vast stretches of shortgrass they found on the Great Plains. It is estimated that something on the order of 5 million head of cattle were driven north and west onto the plains between 1866 and 1884. From New Mexico to Montana, the Texas cattle system spread, spurred on by a period of wet weather in the 25 years following 1860. Texas cattle culture evolved in the South's subtropical climate; had not the wet conditions prevailed, the move onto the arid plains would almost certainly have been forestalled.[33]

The Texas longhorn—a product of the warm and wet South—was ill adapted to the arid conditions and bitter winters found on the plains. In Kansas, the number of calves surviving to adulthood was only four-fifths of what ranchers expected in Texas. The survival rate declined still more farther north. Unlike buffalo, cattle are not well equipped physically to deal with snowy conditions. Bison have gigantic flat heads that they swing from side to side, clearing the ground to access the grass. Not so the longhorn, which stood around and starved when confronted by snow cover. The winter of 1871–1872 was so severe in Kansas and Nebraska that mortality rates for cattle in some areas exceeded 50 percent.[34]

Despite these warning signs the ranchers pushed on, joined in the 1870s and 1880s by investors from overseas, especially Britain. In nineteenth-century Europe, fatty cuts of beef symbolized power and privilege, but with the pastures of Scotland and Ireland overgrazed, the British turned to the American plains. As early as 1868, cattle were transported live across the Atlantic. The introduction of refrigerated transportation technologies in the following decade helped to solidify the link between the plains grasslands and the British consumer. In 1875, a New York inventor named John Bates employed a large fan and ice to ship 10 cattle carcasses across the Atlantic, with good results. By 1877, one shipping outfit was sending 3 million pounds of American beef to Britain every month. The beef bonanza was on, as English and Scottish entrepreneurs launched cattle ventures that gobbled up huge swathes of land in the American West. By the early 1880s, foreign investment in the grasslands had elicited so much opposition that both the Democratic and Republican parties supported a reduction in alien holdings. "America for Americans," presidential candidate James Blaine trumpeted in 1884, tapping into the anti-British sentiment rife across the West.[35]

Driving the land grab was the ease with which one could arrive on the plains and set up a cattle business. In the early years of ranching, the range was free and open to everyone. If a drover arrived in a valley and discovered cattle, he simply moved on. The range remained, in other words, common property. But as American and foreign investors descended on the grasslands, overcrowding soon became a problem. In response, some ranchers purchased barbed wire (invented

COWBOYS

Until fencing, disastrous weather, and other changes put an end to the open range, cowboys of Anglo, Indian, Hispanic, and African American descent tended large herds on the grasslands of the West. (Library of Congress)

in 1873) to close off parts of the public domain from intruders. American factories produced 40,000 tons of wire by 1880; much of it was strung across the plains. Between 1881 and 1885, ranchers in the Texas Panhandle laid out 200 miles of fence to prevent cattle from drifting during a storm.[36]

Fencing had some untoward ecological consequences. First, it concentrated cattle in specific locations, a development that led to overgrazing. In the 1880s, one ranch manager from Texas lamented the increase in both cattle and fences: "With this the character of the grass completely changed; where formerly there was long luxuriant grass that would fatten an animal without his having to do too much walking; there is now only short grass at the best of seasons." Second, fences made the already severe winters all the harder for the animals. When the range remained open, cattle caught in a snowstorm could drift across the plains, perhaps escaping the worst conditions. If the animal reached a barrier, however, it remained trapped. As one critic of the fencing mania put it in 1883, "Under the old regime, there was a loose adaptability to the margins of the ranges where now there is a clear-cut line which admits of no argument, and an overstocked range must bleed when the blizzards sit in judgment."[37]

And bleed it did. Huge numbers of cattle died in Utah during the winter of 1879–1880. The same happened in Colorado and Nebraska the following winter.

In 1884–1885, cattle die-offs killed as much as 90 percent of the population as extreme cold plunged south all the way to Texas. Ranchers on the southern plains suffered through another harsh winter the following year. In the spring of 1886, the cattle "died of hunger; they have perished of thirst, when the icy breath of winter closed the streams; they have died of starvation by the tens of thousands during the season when cold storms sweep out of the North and course over the plains, burying the grass under snow."[38]

By the mid-1880s, the western range had been abused for over a decade. Noting the deteriorated state in 1885, a U.S. government official remarked, "Cattlemen say that the grasses are not what they used to be; that the valuable perennial species are disappearing, and that their place is being taken by less nutritious annuals."[39] Free grass combined with a speculative fever had led ranchers to stock the range with far more cattle than it could reasonably support.

The final blow came in 1886. After a dry summer the year before, fire broke out on the southern plains, reducing the available forage and weakening the animals as winter approached. And what a winter it was. Gale-force winds and blinding snow reduced visibility in some areas of the southern plains to 16 feet. The cold extended as far south as Austin, Texas, where below-zero temperatures (Fahrenheit) were reported in January 1886. From Montana all the way to Texas, vast numbers of cattle died, their carcasses piling up in precisely the places one would expect: the cattle drifted south as the blizzards rolled in, and they stopped when they came to a fence, pressing in on each other and scrounging the ground for every last blade of grass. According to a firsthand account of the blizzard by O. P. Beyers, following the right-of-way fence erected by the Union Pacific Railroad, one could walk 400 miles from Ellsworth, Kansas, to Denver stepping only on carcasses.[40]

Farther north in the Badlands of North Dakota, an even worse disaster unfolded. On New Year's Day 1887, the temperature plunged in the southwestern part of the state to minus 41 degrees. Gale-force winds and blinding snow arrived on January 28. "For seventy-two hours," one victim wrote, "it seemed as if all the world's ice from Time's beginnings had come on a wind which howled and screamed with the fury of demons."[41]

Spring 1887 arrived with a vengeance. As the land began to thaw, rivers filled with water, a trickle at first that eventually rose to a torrent. Floods overtook the land, precipitating one of the longest funeral processions in history: tens of thousands of animal carcasses all flowing downstream. On the Little Missouri River, one man, shocked by what he saw, wrote as follows: "Countless carcasses of cattle [were] going down with the ice, rolling over and over as they went, so that at times all four of the stiffened legs of a carcass would point skyward, as it turned under the impulsion of the swiftly moving current and the grinding ice-cakes."[42]

It must have been a stomach-turning scene for many ranchers, watching as their investments disappeared downriver in a roar of bankruptcy. In the end, the ranchers, hungry for profits, fell victim not simply to nature, but to their

BLIZZARD, 1886

With the range overstocked, a blast of cold weather delivered a punishing blow to western ranching.
(Harper's Weekly, February 27, 1886; Library of Congress)

defiance of natural limits, which caused them to persistently funnel more stock onto the range. That speculative impulse joined with the trail of fences that now gripped the land to deny the Texas cattle—poorly adapted to the cold and dry weather conditions present on the plains in any case—its mobility, its best defense against the weather.

The die-offs of the late nineteenth century offer a textbook lesson on the perils of overstocking the range. No one, however, should see in the disaster an argument for ridding the plains of cattle. Ecologically speaking, the grasslands need cattle or some other herbivore so that the plants and grasses that live there can experience the level of disturbance they need to survive. From the days of the mastodons through those of the bison, plant life in the grasslands evolved in tandem with the creatures that browsed the earth. Too much grazing is a problem, but so also is too much rest for the land.[43]

Sustainable ranching can be conducted on the plains, as the Hidatsa of North Dakota proved in the waning years of the nineteenth century. This Indian group operated small-scale communal ranches, cutting and storing hay to get their animals through the winter. Not out for big money, they reveled in the freedom and thrill they experienced in rounding up cattle, in living a cowboy life out on the plains. The Hidatsa offer proof that sustainable use of the land does not have to mean forsaking significant economic development, as long as people can content themselves with a competent living designed to preserve their material well-being as opposed to questing for endless accumulation of profits.[44]

O STARVING PIONEERS!

As calamities go, the great cattle bust was just one of a number of disasters that put an end to the dreams of those who imagined the plains as one vast field of opportunity. In truth, the ecological perils of westward expansion have yet to be fully recognized. Perhaps this is because they have been obscured by stories—like those of the demise of the buffalo—that have made it seem as if Euro-American settlers could simply have their way with the animal world. In fact, settlers at times found their futures mortgaged to something as seemingly small and inconsequential as an insect. The devastating locust outbreaks of the late nineteenth century are a case in point.

The Rocky Mountain locust, a grasshopper that can reach incredibly high population densities and travel long distances, is estimated to have caused 200 million dollars in damage to agriculture (well over 100 billion dollars in today's money) between 1874 and 1877. Not for nothing does the word "locust" derive from the Latin term for "burnt place." Drought conditions in the mid-1870s precipitated the locust swarms, as the dry weather sped up the maturation of the insect. Although westerners tried everything they could to get rid of them—from flamethrowers to the Peteler Locust-Crushing Machine—the swarms caused horrific starvation. During the winter of 1874–1875, the U.S. Army supplied 750,000 people with rations in Nebraska alone. The Department of the Interior called the locust "the greatest obstacle to the settlement of [the] country between Mississippi and the Rocky Mountains."[45]

Within little more than a generation, however, the locust had disappeared. It was a breathtaking ecological change. One entomologist has shown that even a conservative estimate of the number of locusts present in the West in the 1870s would give them a biomass (collective amount of living tissue) outstripping the 27 million bison then inhabiting the plains.[46]

In all likelihood, Euro-American settlers bearing plows and cattle perpetrated the slaughter. Farmers and locusts collided in the river valleys of the Rocky Mountain region, where in the 1870s almost 2 million people flocked. Settling near rivers to supply their livestock and crops with water, the farmers destroyed the locusts' habitat. Their plows jeopardized the insects by overturning the soil and exposing the locusts' eggs to cold temperatures. Their irrigation projects drowned the eggs. And their cattle overgrazed the land, contributing to both erosion and flooding and sealing the fate of this once spectacularly prolific creature. By 1902, the Rocky Mountain locust was extinct.[47]

The locust's demise eliminated one major hurdle to the settlement of the West. There were, however, other obstacles. In terms of the suffering and hardship it caused, the drought of the 1890s went down as one of the worst in the history of the region. The groundwork for the calamity was laid between 1878 and 1887, when the same wet weather that gave rise to the beef bonanza also sent farmers from the eastern part of the country out to the plains to plant wheat, causing the population in some areas to explode. The population of the western third of Kansas alone rose from 38,000 people in 1885 to 139,000 people in 1887. Optimism ruled the day as railroads and other western boosters, with prevailing scientific theory on their side, promoted the catchphrase "Rain follows the plow."

In 1887, however, wheat yields tumbled in response to the dry weather, which extended into the following decade. Widespread reports of drought-induced starvation and malnutrition began to trickle in, with some talking of "Anderson fare," a reference to the South's brutal Civil War prison, Andersonville. In Miner County, South Dakota, 2,500 people faced death from starvation, with corn yields averaging just a meager two to three bushels per acre. Unable to survive, many simply walked away from the land. Some areas experienced population losses of half to three-quarters. Suddenly pessimism replaced optimism, with one songwriter telling of "starvin' to death on my government claim." The government, under the provisions of the Homestead Act (1862), sought to open the Great Plains by conferring title to anyone who settled 160 acres and remained there for five years. In the late nineteenth century, however, they were more likely to starve first.[48]

SANDSTORM, 1894

Although most people associate blowing dust with the 1930s, severe drought afflicted the Great Plains in the 1890s, leading to dust storms like this one in Midland, Texas. (National Archives)

CONCLUSION

A wide range of ecological changes followed the incorporation of the West's natural riches into the capitalist market economy. Industrialized extraction transformed the hydrology of the Sierra Nevada mountain range by scattering debris throughout California's watersheds, but other stunning environmental transformations had less obvious roots. Gold seekers headed to the central plains were unaware that their migration would impact the region's river valleys, robbing them of wood and grass and thereby depriving Indians of important natural resources. Nor did the later Euro-American settlers of the Rocky Mountain region have any idea that their plows and livestock would help kill off the locusts. A volatile political economy that unleashed the entrepreneurial spirit proved to have unexpected results in an unforgiving land.

9

CONSERVATION RECONSIDERED

One of the ranchers who watched the Blizzard of 1887 wipe out his herd of cattle was Theodore Roosevelt, a New Yorker who had built a ranch in North Dakota's Badlands, stocked it with animals, and hired two cowboys to oversee the venture. In the spring of 1887, he headed west to check on the status of his investment, arriving in the Little Missouri Valley only to find that death had beaten him there. He saw cattle carcasses—23 in just a single spot—and found his once-glorious herd reduced to just "a skinny sorry-looking crew." The ground itself was in no better shape. "The land was a mere barren waste; not a green thing could be seen; the dead grass eaten off till the country looked as if it had been shaved with a razor."[1]

In the fall of 1887, Roosevelt returned to the Badlands, this time on a hunting trip. Not much had improved since his last visit. The region's prairie grass had lost its battle with ranchers, ever eager to stock the range with more animals than it could reasonably bear. The remaining grass had fallen victim to desperate cattle seeking whatever little forage they could find in the wake of the death-dealing blizzard. An eerie silence spread over the land. Four years earlier, on a visit to this spot, Roosevelt had found few, if any, buffalo. In 1885, he lamented the loss of wild sheep and antelope. In 1886, he worried about the disappearance of migratory birds. Now, on his two visits in 1887, the Badlands offered a melancholy sight, and Roosevelt proposed to do something about it. He returned to New York to invite 12 of his animal-loving friends over for a meal, and in January 1888 they established the Boone & Crockett Club, named in honor of Daniel Boone and Davy Crockett, legendary frontiersmen whom Roosevelt worshipped. The club was one of the first organizations in the country dedicated to saving big-game animals. And it was the work of a young man who would go on to become president.[2]

Roosevelt made conservation a cornerstone of his administration (1901–1908) and helped to solidify the nation's reputation as a world leader in this area. In 1872, when Congress created Yellowstone National Park, the United States had become the first country ever to take such action. Now, Roosevelt elevated conservation into a national political priority, expanding the park and forest systems and designating the first federal wilderness refuge. The effects were long-lasting. When it came to conserving nature, it was to the United States that other nations across the world eventually turned.[3]

Roosevelt himself looked to two men—Gifford Pinchot and John Muir, each of whom represented a different strand in conservation thinking. In 1905, Roosevelt named Pinchot, a professional forester with inherited wealth, to head the newly formed U.S. Forest Service. Pinchot and like-minded colleagues in the conservation movement, many drawn from fields such as forestry, geology, and hydrology, felt that a rational plan for organizing the nation's use of natural resources was urgent. Business leaders, driven by unrestrained competition for timber, water, and grass, they held, should cede their authority to expert government planners with scientific backgrounds. Only such new leadership could ensure the most efficient, profitable use of the country's natural wealth. Pinchot was less interested in preserving nature untouched than in standing guard to make sure it was used in the wisest, most efficient way possible.[4]

Opposing the "efficient use" brand of conservation were the preservationists, the most famous of whom was John Muir, founder of the Sierra Club in 1892. Born in 1838 in Dunbar, Scotland, and brought by his parents to Wisconsin at age 11, Muir, who experienced a devout upbringing, would go on to adopt what was in effect his own religion. This faith was based on the idea that we are "all God's people"—"we" referring not just to human beings but to foxes, bears, plants, and, indeed, all elements of the natural world. In this view, humans had no more right to exist than other species of life did. Often touted as the founder of the environmental movement, Muir strongly disagreed with Pinchot and the practical philosophy that informed the latter's view of conservation. He proposed instead that wilderness areas enriched human life, by providing sacred refuges, antidotes to the stresses of modern society. "Climb the mountains and get their good tidings," he once remarked. Muir felt that government had a moral responsibility to preserve nature, not simply to use it wisely in the name of industry. He urged Roosevelt to lock away America's wilderness areas and throw the key as far from business as humanly possible, though he came to modify that stance as he ventured increasingly into the practical world of politics.[5]

In the early years of the twentieth century, these two philosophies—utilitarianism versus preservationism—collided in the beautiful Hetch Hetchy valley in California's Sierra Nevada. In the aftermath of a devastating earthquake and fire in 1906, the city of San Francisco to the south proposed the construction of a dam to bring water to the growing metropolis, a project that would flood the valley in the process. Pinchot supported the city's proposal on practical grounds. He faced off against the preservation-minded John Muir, whose eloquence was not enough to stop the project. The dam was built and the valley inundated.

This is the standard portrayal of conservation as primarily a battle over philosophies of nature. Less has been written about the impact of conservation measures—such as the establishment of national parks, forests, and wildlife preserves—on the ecosystems themselves. Oftentimes the West's plants, trees, and animals simply thumbed their noses at the supposed experts sent to manage them. Conservationists found themselves unable to fully grasp the complexity of ecological forces and unwittingly took steps that caused nature to strike back

ROOSEVELT AND MUIR

Shown here posing at Yosemite National Park in 1903, these two key figures in the conservation movement disagreed over the best approach to achieving peace with nature, with Theodore Roosevelt embracing a utilitarian stance and John Muir a more spiritually oriented approach. (Library of Congress)

with devastating wildfires and game explosions. Even less recognized has been the reality that conserving nature favors some groups of people over others. As the federal government moved in to try its hand at managing the forests and range in the name of tourism, ranching, and logging, the interests of Indians and poor whites, who had depended on such lands for food, were often shoved to the side. What was being conserved was not so much the natural world, but a socioecological order that produced monumental material gain at the expense of some vulnerable wildlife and people.

TAYLOR-MADE FORESTS

While the conservationists were off dreaming up ways of conserving nature in the name of efficiency, engineer Frederick Winslow Taylor was busy inventing a strategy for bringing efficiency to the workplace. Rarely spoken of in the same breath, the two philosophies ought to be. Taylorism tried to help corporations increase productivity and cut costs by engineering a new kind of worker, one who would use the most efficient set of motions possible to complete a given task. It was a philosophy of management that deskilled workers by forcing them to yield before the supervisor and his stopwatch.[6] Conservation, at least in the form that Pinchot espoused, tried to reinvent not the shop floor but the forests and save costs by eliminating any disorderly tendencies. It sought the most efficient way of producing crops of timber and animals. Taylorism controlled workers, conservation controlled nature, and both relied on the science of management. Frederick Taylor and Gifford Pinchot were cut from the same cloth.

Before Pinchot's view of conservation rose to dominance, an ecologically informed group of foresters had tried to understand the forest on its own terms. Bernard Fernow, one of the earliest scientific foresters, believed that forests did more than simply serve the immediate economic needs of the American people. As interdependent entities, the woods, if managed properly, could help fend off floods and soil erosion. Forestland, he once wrote, played an important part "in the great economy of nature." Early conservationists, concerned with the overall ecology of federal forestland, evinced an anti-industry stance, opposing the timber companies in their disastrous quest for short-term profits. Conservation, in other words, got off to a promising start, seeking a holistic view of the natural world.[7]

Eager to please the timber companies, however, Pinchot, who replaced Fernow as chief of the Department of Agriculture's Division of Forestry in 1898, elevated economics over ecology. "The first principle of conservation is development," he wrote in 1910, "the use of the natural resources now existing on this continent for the benefit of the people who live here now." Pinchot pledged loyalty to his own generation of Americans "and afterward the welfare of the generations to follow." Like Fernow, he opposed the unrestrained destruction of the nation's vast forest reserves. But unlike Fernow, he aimed to replace the timber companies' approach with a scientifically grounded one that emphasized renewal of the resource as a way of serving economic—not ecological—ends.[8]

Pinchot believed forests existed to serve the demands of capitalism, and to do that the lumber industry needed to cede authority to the experts at the Forest Service, who would tell them when it was acceptable to cut down trees. "The job," as Pinchot put it, "was not to stop the axe, but to regulate its use." Trees, in this view, were to be managed in a way that preserved their ability to continue to reproduce raw materials so that the capitalist system would be able to continue to extract profits from workers. Frederick Taylor studied the behavior of workers in order to find the most efficient least expensive path to more production and profit; Pinchot and his colleagues studied trees with the same end in mind.[9]

At the outset, Pinchot galvanized the American public behind his forest initiative by calling attention to an impending resource scarcity. By the turn of the century, the nation's timber frontier was closing, as lumbermen ventured to the Pacific Northwest, having already cleared vast portions of the Great Lakes states and the South. In 1906, annual lumber consumption reached 46 billion board feet, a record that has yet to be broken. With prices rising, Pinchot and Roosevelt both raised the prospect of a wood shortage. "A timber famine in the future is inevitable," Roosevelt declared in 1905. Clearly the nation's original forest cover had decreased, from 850 million acres in the early seventeenth century to roughly 500 million by the dawn of the twentieth century. Famine or not, the context was ripe for intervention, a point Pinchot clearly grasped.[10]

"Forestry is handling trees so that one crop follows another," Pinchot was fond of saying. What he meant was that left to its own devices, nature was far too inefficient to serve the demands of a modern, industrial capitalist economy. Nothing irritated Pinchot and his fellow foresters more than the sight of an old-growth forest filled with mature, dead, and diseased trees. Those old and disorderly forests needed to come down to make room for a new crop of timber. "To the extent to which the overripe timber on the national forests can not be cut and used while merchantable, public property is wasted," intoned Henry Graves, who followed Pinchot as chief of the Forest Service. As workers prone to distraction and sabotage became the target of efficiency experts, so too did the forest figure in the designs of managers bent on ensuring a steady, inexpensive supply of raw material to aid maximization of production and profits.[11]

Anything that got in the way of a speedup in forest production—old growth, disease, insects, fire—had to be extinguished. What Pinchot and his disciples either failed to fully comprehend or chose to ignore was the complexity and, above all, the interdependency of the forest. The various elements that made up the woods—trees, plants, insects, and animals—functioned as a unit. Small changes could have enormous impacts. A change to one element in the mix—removing a dead tree, for example, or ridding the forest of an insect—had consequences that could ramify throughout an ecosystem, at times, ironically, even interfering with the business-oriented goals of the conservationists. A kind of moth, for instance, fed on the needles of Oregon's Douglas fir trees, a sight that drove the Forest Service wild. But behind the scenes wasps, flies, spiders, and birds were eating the moths, providing the agency with a free extermination treatment. When federal foresters in Oregon's Blue Mountains attacked the moths with pesticides early in the twentieth century, the insect's predators lost out and died too. The moths then bounced back with a vengeance to devour the trees once again.[12]

A dead tree, an obstruction in the eyes of an efficiency-minded forester, was a viable habitat for an insect. Thus, removing fallen trees eliminated a food source for thousands of carpenter ants, preventing them from carrying out their duties on the forest floor of decomposing dead wood and returning it to the soil. The Forest Service ended up interfering with the cycle of death and decomposition on which the future health of the woods rested.[13]

Pinchot's brand of conservation did even more damage when it came to the issue of fire. Fire had long been a major component of the West's—indeed, of North America's—ecological mosaic, and early foresters were fully aware of this fact. In much of the South as well as large parts of California, people set fire to the woods to reduce brush and encourage the growth of pasturage. In 1910, one timberman went so far as to call on the government to make burning mandatory in the Golden State. But it was not an auspicious year for such views, not with fires in the northern Rockies raging out of control. The spring of 1910 was the driest month on record in the northwestern United States. That fact, combined with the buildup of slash as logging increased and Indian burning of the land declined, led to one of the greatest wildfire disasters in American history. Conflagrations raged across Idaho, Montana, Washington, and Oregon, sending smoke as far east as New England.

The 1910 fires turned fire suppression into a veritable religion at the Forest Service. Pinchot laid the intellectual groundwork for such a policy change. "I recall very well indeed," he wrote in 1910, "how, in the early days of forest fires, they were considered simply and solely as acts of God, against which any opposition was hopeless and any attempt to control them not merely hopeless but childish. It was assumed that they came in the natural order of things, as inevitably as the seasons or the rising and setting of the sun. To-day we understand that forest fires are wholly within the control of men."[14]

In 1910, at precisely the same time that Pinchot argued for suppression, ecologist Frederic Clements confirmed the views of foresters like Fernow, who viewed fire as a creative and positive environmental force. But Pinchot and those who came after him in the Forest Service remained unimpressed with such thinking. In keeping with his guiding spirit of efficiency and control, Pinchot feared the threat that fire posed not just to a steady supply of raw material, but to the system of private property on which capitalism rested. In 1898, he wrote, "Forest fires encourage a spirit of lawlessness and a disregard of property rights." Those who burned the forest, for whatever reason, were no better than criminals, outlaws engaged in what federal foresters would soon call "incendiarism" or "woods arson."[15]

In the year following the 1910 calamity, Congress passed the Weeks Act, which allowed the federal government to purchase as much as 75 million acres of land and led to a consensus among federal and state officials on the need for fire suppression. Suppressing forest fires—a major preoccupation of the Forest Service for the bulk of the twentieth century—proved in the end both misguided and self-defeating. Fires aid the decomposition of forest litter and help recycle nutrients through an ecosystem. Without them growth slows down. And by suppressing fires, the Forest Service allowed fuels to build up, increasing the possibility that fires, when they did come, could take the form of catastrophic conflagrations. Pinchot's brand of conservation, centered on maximizing profits, had trumped an earlier, more broadminded concern with the forest's noneconomic functions. Nature, however, had the last laugh.[16]

REVENGE OF THE VARMINTS

There is a dark, cold-blooded side to conservation, although it is rarely acknowledged. Because the philosophy was founded on the most productive use of the land, it sometimes ventured into the realm of death and destruction. It is no coincidence that the most destructive period in the nation's wildlife history— replete with the ruthless and systematic annihilation of some entire animal species—coincided with the decades when conservation gripped the nation's political imagination. Efficiency and extermination went hand in hand.

Taking their cue from Pinchot's philosophy of making trees over into harvestable crops, game managers in the early twentieth century tried to do the same for animals, cultivating those species favored by sport hunters and tourists, such as elk, bison, waterfowl, and especially deer. By the 1880s, overhunting and habitat loss had caused the populations of these animal groups to plummet. To revitalize them, federal and state wildlife managers pushed for laws regulating hunting and setting up refuges. In 1903, Roosevelt designated Pelican Island in Florida as the first federal wildlife preserve. Five years later came the National Bison Range in Montana, located on an old Indian reservation. Tourists queued up to see the pathetic remnants of the once abundant and glorious species.

Conserving some species, however, meant killing others. In 1915, Congress set up a new division within the Department of Agriculture's Bureau of Biological Survey (founded in 1905), the arm of the government responsible for game management. It had an ominous title: Predatory Animal and Rodent Control Service. Its mission was to exterminate those creatures that preyed on the rancher's cattle and sheep and the sport hunter's elk and deer: mountain lions, wolves, coyotes, and bobcats. "Large predatory mammals destructive to livestock and game no longer have a place in our advancing civilization," explained one biologist at the bureau.[17]

There were 40 million sheep in the West by the last decade of the nineteenth century and a vast number of cattle. All were defenseless before the predators that roamed the plains looking for some substitute fare now that the buffalo had been driven off the land. Wolves proved especially destructive to livestock; it would be hard to overestimate the hatred ranchers had for them. Cowboys were known to string a captured wolf between two horses to tear it apart. But poison, mainly strychnine, was the preferred method of dispatching them.[18]

Bounties, established by a number of western states during the late nineteenth century, spurred hunters to kill predatory animals. But it took the intervention of the federal government to put an end to the predator problem. The ruthlessness

PINCHOT WITH SCOUTS

A man concerned with law and order, Gifford Pinchot aggressively pursued the policy of total fire suppression. By interfering with the natural fire cycle, this approach increased the risk of calamitous conflagrations and, ironically, led to more loss of life. (Library of Congress)

of the subsequent extermination campaign—which used steel traps, guns, and strychnine—was breathtaking. An astonishing 40,000 animals were killed in Wyoming alone between 1916 and 1928, including coyotes, wolves, bears, bobcats, lynxes, and mountain lions, plus prairie dogs, gophers, squirrels, and jackrabbits, which had the annoying habit of eating the settlers' crops. "Bring Them in Regardless of How" went the slogan coined by a newsletter for hunters. It was all-out war, and when it was over—by 1926, no wolves existed in Arizona—the West's ranchers, farmers, and sport hunters could rest easier at night.[19]

Life in western America seemed to be moving along swimmingly in the post-predatory age—until it became apparent that wolves, coyotes, and mountain lions actually served a purpose. An object lesson on the importance of predators unfolded on Arizona's Kaibab Plateau. In 1906, Roosevelt set aside a portion of the plateau as a wildlife refuge known as the Grand Canyon National Game Preserve. Roughly 4,000 deer lived there when it was founded. Enter the federal hunters, who between 1916 and 1931 killed 4,889 coyotes, 781 mountain lions, and 554 bobcats. The hunters claimed victory as the deer proliferated, swelling to perhaps as many as 100,000 by 1924, a gain in productivity to end all gains. But two winters later, the deer population crashed, reduced by 60 percent, as the animals starved for lack of forage. With the coyotes and mountain lions not around to hold down their numbers, the deer reproduced almost endlessly, populating the habitat beyond what it could bear and dying off.[20]

While deer overran the Kaibab Plateau, hordes of mice marched on the town of Taft, California. In 1924, the Bureau of Biological Survey had launched, to the glee of farmers, an all-out effort to eradicate coyotes, hawks, and other predators from Kern County. Two years later, the rodents, their numbers now unchecked, descended en masse. "The mice," one report declared, "invaded beds and nibbled the hair of horrified sleepers, chewed through the sides of wooden storehouses to get at food supplies, and crawled boldly into children's desks at Conley School." Passing cars crushed the mice, making some highways too slick for safe travel. Farmers resorted to mechanical harvesters to fend off the rodents. Eventually the Bureau of Biological Survey was called in to exterminate the varmints it had poisoned into existence in the first place. The history of conservation includes more than a few such ironic moments.[21]

KAIBAB NATIONAL FOREST
Deer in the middle of an overgrazed portion of the range. (U.S. Forest Service)

PARK RULES

Managing game was one thing, but administering parks to attract thousands of big game–loving tourists was something else entirely. The setting aside of national parks in the late nineteenth century raised a host of problems for the nation's conservationists. Chief among these was how to rationalize game in the interests of tourism—that is, to create and preserve a wilderness experience in which visitors could be sure to find elk, bison, and other large animals. In carrying out their mission, wildlife managers ran up against a number of obstacles. Native Americans and rural whites—inclined to view the creatures more as a food source than as curiosities—did not appreciate the restrictions the managers imposed on hunting. Complicating matters further, delineating an arbitrary park boundary and using it to contain wild species with biological needs for food that sent them outside the park left government officials forever playing the role of traffic cop.

The national park movement stemmed, in part, from a change in American attitudes toward wilderness. Back in the colonial period, the word "wilderness" referred to desolate, wild places untouched as yet by civilization. There was little, if anything, positive about wilderness areas in the minds of the first settlers, who diligently set about improving—fencing and farming—the raw material of nature. By the late nineteenth century, however, the meaning of the word had undergone a sea change. No longer thought to be worthless, wilderness areas came to be viewed as places of virginal natural beauty in need of zealous care.

Not that the capitalist economic impulse that informed the early idea of wilderness disappeared completely. In setting aside the first national parks, Congress made a point of looking for lands possessed of monumental grandeur but of no value for wealth formation—regions with limited agricultural and ranching prospects and no sign of valuable minerals. Unlike European countries, the United States, a much younger nation by comparison, had few cultural icons to match the castles and cathedrals that gave Old World states unique national identities. With the country emerging from the divisive Civil War, its status as a unified nation still quite fragile, congressmen searched the landscape for awe-inspiring physical features—stunning mountain scenery, vast and colorful canyons, spectacular geysers—around which citizens could rally.[22]

In 1872, Congress settled on 2 million acres where Wyoming, Idaho, and Montana now come together, an improbable place for agriculture averaging 6,000 feet in altitude and prone to frost but containing hundreds of geysers, mudpots, and other geothermal wonders. Here was a picture-perfect spot to knit together the fledgling nation, a place so majestic and so capable of uniting the country under God that Congress purchased a painting of it by artist Thomas Moran to hang in the Capitol. "This will be the grandest park in the world—the grand, instructive museum of the grandest Government on Earth," proclaimed the *Nevada Territorial Enterprise*. To congressmen such as Henry Dawes of Massachusetts, who worked to establish the park, Yellowstone, as the site was named, represented nature in its most pristine state, a beautiful but harsh wilderness environment so formidable that not even Indians, he asserted, could live there, a place seemingly without history.[23]

The establishment of Yellowstone, the nation's first national park, was not simply an idea cooked up in Congress. The railroads also played a major role through the lobbying of Jay Cooke and Frederick Billings, whose Northern Pacific Railway stood to gain immensely from the passenger traffic that the park would bring. As Billings once remarked, "Commerce could serve the cause of conservation by bringing visitors to a site worthy of preservation." In 1883, the Northern Pacific completed its route across the country, becoming the second transcontinental railroad in the nation's history and putting Yellowstone within reach of tourists nationwide. That same year, to accommodate the railroad industry, the nation went on standard time, a key development in the contractual relations necessary for free trade. No wonder there was such fascination with the scheduled eruptions of Yellowstone's most famous geyser, Old Faithful, which, as one observer remarked, "played by the clock."[24]

Advocates for Yellowstone may have thought they were preserving a wilderness area. But it is more accurate to say that they were inventing it. In Yellowstone's case, creating wilderness meant rendering the Native Americans who laid claim to the area invisible, when, in fact, they had long used it for hunting, fishing, and other means of survival. Preservation of the country's national parks and Indian removal proceeded in lock-step motion. Treaties and executive orders signed between 1855 and 1875 effectively consigned the Bannock, Shoshone, Blackfeet, and Crow Indians to reservations, where they would be less likely to interfere with tourists headed for Yellowstone. Park supporters rationalized the removal of Indians by relying on a time-tested strategy first used in the colonial period. The Indians, they pointed out, had made no agricultural improvements to the area; use it or lose it, went the boosters' logic. The rugged physical environment of the park, inhospitable to farming and other economic uses, helped support this supposition, as did the view of park officials such as Philetus Norris, who explained that Indians avoided the Yellowstone area because they held its geothermal features in "superstitious awe."[25]

As late as 1962, one historian claimed that only "deteriorating, half-miserable-animal, half-miserable-man" types inhabited the park prior to its creation. This was little more than park and railroad propaganda. Park officials were quite aware of the Native Americans in Yellowstone and their potential to frighten tourists. As Superintendent Moses Harris explained in 1888, "The mere rumor of the presence of Indians in the park is sufficient to cause much excitement and anxiety." The Northern Pacific Railroad did what it could to allay such fears. It recommended that tourists visit the site of the Battle of Little Big Horn (where George Armstrong Custer went down to defeat in 1876) en route to Yellowstone to reinforce that though Custer lost that fight, the threat posed by the Plains Indians had been consigned to history.[26]

YELLOWSTONE PARK ROUTE

Major supporters of national parks, railroads drummed up riders by capitalizing on Yellowstone's spectacular natural phenomena. (Library of Congress)

The year following Custer's defeat, the U.S. Army waged war against the Nez Perce Indians, at one point chasing them straight through Yellowstone National Park. The Nez Perce, according to accounts written at the time, were lost and frightened by the park's geothermal sites. But as the warrior Yellow Wolf recalled years after the battle, the Indians "knew that country well before passing through there in 1877. The hot smoking springs and high-shooting water were nothing new to us."[27]

A number of Native American groups were intimately familiar with the park and its offerings. The Shoshone, for example, hunted buffalo, fished, and gathered various plants, activities that depending on the season could lead them into what came to be parkland. Aided by horses, even more distant Indian groups descended on the park to trap beaver and hunt elk. Perhaps not surprisingly, the decline of the buffalo beginning in the 1870s only made Indians more dependent on the park's wildlife. And in an ironic turn of events, the displacement of Native Americans onto reservations may actually have increased their visits to the park. Denied adequate rations in the government camps, the Crow and Shoshone set off to hunt on unoccupied public lands, a right granted in an 1868 treaty. As the agent for Idaho's Fort Hall Reservation explained, "Being short-rationed and far from self-supporting according to the white man's methods, they [Bannock and Shoshone] simply follow their custom and hunt for the purpose of obtaining sustenance."[28]

The prospect of Indians taking game within the confines of Yellowstone was long a bone of contention between native groups and park officials. In 1889, Superintendent Moses Harris called Indian hunting an "unmitigated evil" and lamented that it would be impossible to protect the park's remaining game if Yellowstone continued "to afford summer amusement and winter sustenance to a band of savage Indians." Locals who acted as guides to well-off hunters from the East also resented Indian poaching of game because it frightened clients while decreasing the likelihood of a successful outing.[29]

In 1896, the U.S. Supreme Court in the leading case of *Ward v. Race Horse* overturned the protection the 1868 treaty had granted Indians to hunt on unoccupied government land. Even though it was common knowledge that the Shoshone and Bannock Indians pursued game to feed themselves and, moreover, that insufficient rations on the Fort Hall Reservation left many malnourished and more inclined to hunt, Justice Edward White asserted that hunting was a privilege "given" to the tribes by the U.S. government, one that could be revoked when called for by "the necessities of civilization." In his dissenting opinion, Justice Henry Brown pointed out that "the right to hunt on the unoccupied lands of the United States was a matter of supreme importance to them [the Indians]. . . . It is now proposed to take it away from them, not because they have violated a treaty, but because the State of Wyoming desires to preserve its game." The case effectively upheld an 1895 Wyoming law that made it illegal for Indians to hunt on public land during seasons closed to hunting, thereby undermining the centuries-old subsistence practices of the Native American groups. But unlike the well-known *Plessy v. Ferguson* case decided in the same year (establishing "separate but equal" segregation), *Ward*, although heavily criticized then and since, has not been systematically overturned, remaining to this day a legally influential opinion.[30]

The only thing as annoying to park officials as an Indian taking down one of Yellowstone's grand four-legged creatures was the sight of a rural white doing so. The founding of Gardiner, Montana, in 1883, on Yellowstone's northern border gave whites seeking game a base from which to launch forays into the park. "In the town of Gardiner there are a number of men, armed with rifles, who toward game have the gray-wolf quality of mercy," wrote conservationist William Hornaday.[31] Whites also gathered wood from the park and grazed cattle there, prompting the U.S. government to call on the military to restore order. In 1886, the cavalry moved in and stayed more than 30 years, until 1916, when the National Park Service took over the administration of Yellowstone.

The military put the park in order, gratifying those like John Muir who were interested in safeguarding the nation's natural wonders. "Uncle Sam's soldiers," exclaimed Muir, were "the most effective forest police." The military restricted entry into the park, forcing visitors to use one of four main entrances instead of entering willy-nilly along the many surreptitious trails that Indians and rural whites had bushwhacked. It suppressed fires, favored by Indians for killing game and managing the landscape. It erected fences to prevent cattle and other stray animals owned by whites from venturing within park boundaries. And it sought to prevent the poaching of game, which Congress in 1894 had elevated into a federal offense. Conservation, as it played out in the national parks, transformed such ingrained and acceptable behaviors as hunting, collecting, and fire setting into the crimes of trespassing, poaching, and arson. It functioned, in other words, as a form of social control that further divorced the common people from direct interactions with the earth.[32]

The motivation behind this strand of conservation thinking again stemmed from a concern with lawless behavior. Just as Gifford Pinchot feared the chaos and threat to property rights posed by fire setting, wildlife advocates like William Hornaday voiced similar concerns over poaching. Hornaday, who was born in Plainfield, Indiana, in 1854, moved with his family to Wapello County, Iowa, as a young child. Living on the edge of an extensive and sparsely settled stretch of prairie, Hornaday witnessed huge flocks of passenger pigeons. He later went on to become a taxidermist and, in 1896, was chosen to head the New York Zoological Park, familiarly known as the Bronx Zoo. As director of the zoo, he spoke out in favor of wildlife conservation and against the reckless slaughter of game. He was particularly rankled by those, mainly immigrants and blacks, who killed wildlife for food. "The Italian is a born pot-hunter, and he has grown up in the fixed belief that killing song-birds for food is right!" he wrote in 1913. In the West especially, he noted, violators of game laws were often set free by sympathetic juries on the pretext that the suspect needed the meat to survive. Hornaday could not have disagreed more. "Any community which tolerates contempt for law, and law-defying judges, is in a degenerate state, bordering on barbarism; and in the United States there are literally *thousands* of such communities!" he railed. Whatever his love for animals, there is no denying Hornaday's abiding concern for social control or his anti-immigrant rhetoric, which reflected the racialized state of American politics at a time when the United States had embarked on imperialist ventures to dominate "inferior" nonwhite people abroad.[33]

For their part, rural whites took game within the park for several reasons. First, the market in elk teeth boomed after the founding in 1868 of the Elks Club, a New York City fraternal order, which used them for everything from rings to cuff links. Whites also sold hides for cash or traded them in return for coffee and sugar not easily obtained in the Yellowstone area. Second, these locals depended on game as a source of food, especially during economic downturns. One unemployed worker arrested in 1914 for poaching game in the park claimed that being "broke all the time" had driven him to transgress. As one park official noted in 1912, elk wandering out of Yellowstone were often killed by "families that otherwise might have had a slim meat ration for the winter due to dull times for workingmen in this section of country." And third, poaching offered an alternative to the discipline of wage work. As one newspaper put it, "Some men would rather spend a month or more time in trapping a beaver or two, or killing an elk at the risk of fine and imprisonment, than earn a few honest dollars by manual labor."[34]

If it was hard to get rural whites to obey the law, it was even harder to force the park's animals to cooperate with the authorities. The source of the problem was severalfold. To begin with, the boundaries of the park did not conform to a discrete ecosystem. The park was huge, to be sure, but not big enough to support and protect all the species of wildlife that roamed it, a fact recognized by Gen. Philip Sheridan. After years spent trying to annihilate the buffalo and the Indians who depended on it, Sheridan had a second career as a conservationist. Following a tour of Yellowstone in 1881, he suggested that the park be doubled in size in order to encompass the full range of migrating species of wildlife. That never happened, mainly because much of the land Sheridan had in mind ended up as part of a national forest instead.

As it turned out, the arbitrary confines of the park proved considerably troublesome when it came to preserving the tourist-friendly elk. Elk stayed in the park's higher elevations during the summer and early fall, but when winter hit, with its snow and severe cold, the animals drifted into the lower-elevation river valleys farther north. Much of that winter range lay outside of Yellowstone's boundaries. But when the erection of fences and the establishment of communities north of Yellowstone forced the elk to winter inside the park, the animals gobbled up much of the available plant cover and degraded the habitat.

Climate also shaped the prospects for the park managers' beloved big game. A sharp plunge in winter temperatures occurred between 1885 and 1900. Meanwhile, the years from 1877 to 1890 proved the greatest in terms of winter precipitation. Thus, the harshest winters on record in Yellowstone occurred during the latter part of the 1880s, with snow and cold limiting the access of such large herbivores as elk to forage. Climate combined with unregulated hunting depressed wildlife populations and may have spurred the calls for military intervention in the park's affairs.[35]

In the century following 1900, winters in Yellowstone grew increasingly mild, expanding forage prospects and creating more favorable conditions for herbivore populations to expand. This trend toward more mild weather coincided, as it happened, with the advent of predator control in the park. Federal hunters were sent to the park in 1915 after an official from the Bureau of Biological Survey visited and recommended the extermination of coyotes and wolves before they devoured Yellowstone's elk. Debate has continued to swirl over the number of elk in the park at this time, but one estimate places 1,500 animals there in the late 1870s, rising to between 20,000 and 30,000 by 1919. In the latter year, drought gripped the area in the summer, followed by a severe winter. By early 1920, very little forage remained, and, according to Park Service estimates, 6,000 animals starved to death. "The range was in deplorable condition when we first saw it," reported biologists who visited in 1929, "and its deterioration has been progressing steadily since then."[36]

If controversy rages over the park's exact elk count, changes in its vegetation seem indisputable. Communities of willow shrubs once graced Yellowstone's northern range, but over the course of the twentieth century they vanished. The evidence suggests strongly that the elk were to blame, although climate change and fire suppression may also have played a role. However the willow disappeared, the change had effects that extended up and down the food chain. Beavers relied on willow for building dams and for food. Thought to be common in the park in the early nineteenth century, beavers vanished by the 1930s. Wetland habitat declined with the beavers no longer around to maintain it, making the park drier overall. As river habitats dried up, white-tailed deer disappeared, becoming extinct in the park by 1930. Birds and even grizzly bears may have suffered as well.[37]

Despite Yellowstone's vastness, separating the region from the larger ecosystem and packaging it for sale to tourists—chiefly by encouraging the proliferation of big-game species—had unintended consequences. Elk and bison came to rule this world at the expense of beavers, deer, wolves, and coyotes. Conservation of the few came at the expense of the many.

CONCLUSION

"The natural resources of the Nation," Gifford Pinchot wrote in 1910, "exist not for any small group, not for any individual, but for all the people."[38] For most of the nineteenth century, the federal government occupied itself with disposing of the nation's natural riches, often to the benefit of railroad, mining, and timber companies, which then claimed the land as private property and incorporated it into their business plans. With the birth of conservation, however, the federal government shifted roles from gift giver to expert overseer, assuming control over large sections of the continent and seeking to manage them, but hardly in the interests of all the people as a whole.

"The national parks must be maintained in absolutely unimpaired form for the use of future generations," said Secretary of the Interior Franklin Lane in 1918.[39] What he really meant was that the national parks had to be administered to suit the needs of the middle-class tourists streaming into them. Compared to other unprotected lands, the parks were certainly less subject to human intervention. But to view them as untouched or "unimpaired" was to deny all the many attempts by government officials to shape them, especially the efforts by game managers to conserve those animals that appealed to the parks' better-off white tourist clientele.

In getting back to nature in the national parks, tourists actually bore witness to an engineered environment, and a fragile one at that. By the late nineteenth century, Yellowstone was one of only two places in North America where small numbers of buffalo still existed (the other was Canada's Wood Buffalo National Park). Market hunters, however, decimated this remaining herd between 1889 and 1894. A concessionaire by the name of E. C. Waters then imported a handful of bison from a ranch and shipped them off to Dot Island in Yellowstone Lake, where a steamboat shuttled tourists out to see them. Meanwhile, the U.S. military launched its own effort to restore the bison, setting up an enclosure and dragging in bales of hay to lure the animals in for a dose of domestication. The buffalo failed to show. The hay the military cut also destroyed the bison's habitat in the Hayden Valley, spurring them to move on rather than accept the cavalry's offer.[40]

Far more lasting success was obtained beginning in 1902, when President Roosevelt hired Charles "Buffalo" Jones, a bison expert, to maintain Yellowstone's herd. Jones purchased animals from private ranchers and set up a corral near one of the park's main entrances, although it was later moved to the Lamar Valley, where it flourished for half a century. The bison gave the tourists something to see and the railroads a new selling angle. A 1904 advertisement trumpeted: "BISON once roamed the country now traversed by the North Pacific. The remnant of these Noble Beasts is now found in Yellowstone Park reached directly only by this line."[41]

Not only were the nearly exterminated bison monetized, so were the embattled Indians. The Northern Pacific recruited a small group of Blackfeet Indians to advertise the scenic beauty of Glacier National Park, another destination serviced by the line. In 1912, the railroad's president, Louis Hill, arranged to have 10 Indians set up tepees on the roof of a New York City hotel to attract publicity for this new western attraction. The national parks were virgin territory, devoid of Indians, congressmen had said when setting up the parks. Now the railroads, having profited from the expropriation of Indian land, shamelessly objectified the Native Americans in their quest for material gain.[42]

10

DEATH OF THE ORGANIC CITY

Before 1881 it was not the least bit unusual to walk out into the streets of Atlanta and find cows. Then the city's political leaders decided that bovines were no longer welcome. The cows could come home, as the saying goes, but not to the streets of Atlanta—not after the city council passed a law making it illegal for cattle to roam the town. Apparently a large number of working people, who depended on the animals as a source of milk and meat, objected to the 1881 ordinance. One man denounced the law as thinly veiled class warfare. "I speak the feelings of every man when I say this is the dictation of a codfish aristocracy," he said. "It is an issue between flowers and milk—between the front yard of the rich man and the sustenance of the poor family."[1]

While conservationists put the countryside in order, another group of reformers targeted urban areas. In 1869, only 9 cities had populations exceeding 100,000; by 1890, 28 had reached that mark, with a third of all Americans now living in such places. New York, Chicago, Philadelphia, St. Louis, Boston, and Baltimore, in that order, were the nation's largest population centers, filled with immigrants who worked producing apparel, forging steel, and packing meat. Crammed with people and factories in addition to pigs, horses, mules, cattle, and goats, the city by the late nineteenth century was brimming with filth. Muckraker Upton Sinclair captured the enormity of the problem in his novel *The Jungle*, describing the "strange, pungent odor" people smelled as they approached Chicago's stockyards as a stench "you could literally taste" and the chimneys belching out smoke as "thick, oily, and black as night."[2]

Progressive Era reformers such as Jane Addams, Robert Woods, and Florence Kelley aspired to a clean and healthful environment. Taking a page from the British, they formed settlement houses, most famously Hull House, established by Addams in Chicago in 1889—the model for 400 such community institutions nationwide. The settlement houses tried to improve the lives of slum dwellers, setting up kindergartens and sponsoring everything from health clinics to music studios to playgrounds. In 1894, Addams, determined to lower the mortality rate in one city ward, led a group of immigrant women from Hull House on a nightly inspection designed to check up on the work of the city's garbage collectors.

MORTON STREET, NEW YORK CITY

Progressive Era reformers such as New York's street-cleaning commissioner George E.Waring,Jr.,modernized sanitation services. Waring increased both pay and morale among the city's street-cleaning crew, with significant results, as demonstrated in these two photographs, one taken in 1893, and the other in 1895, after Waring assumed his post. (George Waring, Street-Cleaning and the Disposal of a City's Wastes [New York: Doubleday and McClure, 1897])

Underlying these urban reforms was the growing importance in the latter part of the nineteenth century of the market in real estate, along with the belief that cities, in order to compete, had to pursue limitless economic growth and development.[3] The sanitary reforms rationalized urban growth by improving water and sewer systems and contributing to a decline in disease. But they came at a cost. All dirt is not equally bad; cleaner cities are not necessarily better for everyone. Indeed, filth had some virtues. Life in the "organic city," a place swarming with pigs and horses and steeped in mountains of manure, was dirty, but it also had a certain social and environmental logic.

In the nineteenth century, before municipal trash collection, working-class women fed their families with pigs that fattened on city garbage. Horses carried people and goods, hauled pumps to help put out fires, and even produced power for some manufacturing. Nor did horse manure go to waste. It streamed into surrounding vegetable farms, where it bolstered soil fertility. Even a good deal of human waste, which piled up in privies and cesspools in the days before sanitary sewers, found its way to the rural hinterlands. City dwellers and their animals played an integral role in the regional soil cycle, supplying nutrients for growing food that was then trucked back into town. In the organic city, vegetables and hay flowed one way and waste the other.

In the late nineteenth century, reformers bent on sanitation put an end to the city in its down-to-earth form. They drove the pigs out, forcing the working class to rely more on the cash economy for food, and substituted municipal garbage collectors for the hogs. They replaced horses with electric streetcars, ending the city's role as a manure factory and stimulating nearby vegetable farmers to turn to artificial fertilizers. New sewerage systems that harmed lakes, rivers, and harbors, eliminated the privies and the "night soil" men who had delivered the excrement to the countryside, and distanced urbanites from the land they had once helped to enrich. Overall, public health improved. But the poor were left to fend for themselves in the wage economy as the urban commons—akin to the open range of the South and West—vanished. Public health indeed had its virtues, but it also had some important social and ecological tradeoffs.

WALKING SEWERS

No animal loomed larger in the European image of U.S. urban areas than the pig. "I have not yet found any city, county, or town where I have not seen these lovable animals wandering about peacefully in huge herds," wrote Ole Munch Ræder, a Norwegian lawyer who visited America in 1847. Swine kept the streets clean by "eating up all kinds of refuse," he recorded. "And then, when these walking sewers are properly filled up they are butchered and provide a real treat for the dinner-table."[4]

Working-class women set pigs loose to scavenge the urban commons for garbage. While rural hogs fed on the forest's acorns, city pigs fed on the waste that people threw away, converting it into protein for the working poor. But what was a food source to some proved a nuisance to others. So many pigs wandered the streets of Little Rock, Arkansas, at midcentury that they had come "to dispute the side walks with *other persons.*"[5] These creatures were not the sedate porkers encountered today in children's books; as seen by their critics they were wild animals that injured and occasionally killed children, copulated in public, and sometimes even defecated on people.

The authorities in New York City had sought to criminalize pig-keeping in 1816, but public outcry led to the ordinance's repeal. In 1818, however, a grand jury indicted two men for the misdemeanor of "keeping and permitting to run hogs at large in the city of New York." The first of the accused was convicted after failing to mount a defense, and he paid a small fee. The second man, a butcher named Christian Harriet, decided to fight the charge. "The dandies, who are too delicate to endure the sight, or even the idea of so odious a creature," might welcome a conviction, Harriet's lawyers argued. "But many poor families might experience far different sensations, and be driven to beggary or the Alms House for a portion of that subsistence of which a conviction in this case would deprive them." Closing the urban commons, in other words, would take food out of the mouths of the poor.[6]

Weighing in on the matter, Mayor Cadwallader Colden observed, "It is said, that if we restrain swine from running in the street, we shall injure the poor.

PIG ROUNDUP

On August 13, 1859, Frank Leslie's Illustrated Newspaper published this picture of police pursuing hogs. By the following decade the animals had been banished from the area below 86th Street in Manhattan. (Kelvin Smith Library, Case Western Reserve University)

Why, gentlemen! must we feed the poor at the expense of human flesh?" Eliminate the commons and the poor would be forced to find jobs to pay for food, instead of subsisting at the expense of the city's more refined residents, he argued. As for swine playing a useful part in cleaning up the city's streets, Colden intoned, "I think our corporation will not employ brutal agency for that object when men can be got to do it."[7]

In the end, Harriet was convicted, and setting pigs free to scavenge the city was criminalized. But in 1821, when city authorities went to war against the pigs, Irish and black women resisted, banding together to defend the animals. Other significant pig-related conflicts erupted in 1825, 1826, 1830, and 1832. Pigs played a central role in the lives of the poor, who did what they could to save them.[8]

In 1849, however, the urban commons experienced a fatal blow. Cholera broke out in New York, and health officials linked the outbreak to the city's filthy conditions. No animal symbolized dirt more clearly than the pig. Police, armed with clubs, drove thousands of swine out of cellars and garrets, banishing them uptown. By 1860, the area below 86th Street had been secured as a pig-free zone. But in the uptown wards, the pigs still ruled. So many hogs roamed the area around 125th Street in Harlem at midcentury that the area came to be known as Pig's Alley. City authorities in New York and other urban areas continued to tolerate pigsties as late as the 1870s, with some tenement residents even boarding them in their rooms, so important were pigs to the poor.[9]

By the last decades of the nineteenth century, the urban commons was drawing to a close not just in New York, but in cities throughout America. Mayor Colden's wish for a pig-free city, one where women could walk the streets "without encountering the most disgusting spectacles of these animals indulging the propensities of nature," seemed well within reach.[10] The urban pig was ultimately exiled to the farmyard, clearing the way for market-driven real estate development to emerge with full force.

CITY AS MANURE FACTORY

Like the pig, the horse played an important, if somewhat hidden, role in urban ecology, one overshadowed by its far more obvious place at the heart of economic life. No animal, with the possible exception of the mule (important only in the South), did more to serve the transportation needs of urban areas.

In the early days of cities, horse-drawn buses (omnibuses) operated on cobblestone streets at speeds hardly faster than a walking pace. In the period just before the Civil War, however, the so-called horse car spread to cities across the nation. Faster and more efficient than the older omnibuses, these teams of horses hitched to passenger vehicles transported people and goods up and down iron tracks. By 1890, more than 32 million passengers had climbed aboard New York City's horse car lines.

The number of urban horses doubled to nearly 3 million over the course of the last third of the nineteenth century. The adoption of the horse car contributed to the rise, as did the expansion of railroad transportation. As trains shipped more goods from point to point, more horses were needed to haul the freight from terminals to its ultimate destination.

The horse's importance to urban life was made amply apparent in 1872 when a fire scorched Boston's business district. Normally used to pull fire equipment, the city's horses, stricken by a flu-like disease, could not answer the call for help as the fire destroyed over 700 buildings. Equines in other cities ultimately also felt the effect of the outbreak (in Detroit, delivery companies made do with handcarts), which killed about 5 percent of all the urban horses in the Northeast and Canada.[11]

Horses generated power for transportation (and manufacturing too), but they also produced staggering amounts of manure, somewhere between 15 and 30 pounds per animal every day. In 1900, one health officer in Rochester, New York (apparently with nothing better to do), calculated that the city's 15,000 horses contributed enough dung each year to completely cover an acre to a height of 175 feet. However it was piled, the manure attracted countless flies, which harbored typhoid fever and other diseases. Then there was the dust to contend with. Horse turds dried up in the heat, only to be pulverized by the creatures themselves as their hooves made contact with the pavement. Ground horse excrement was the nineteenth-century equivalent of auto pollution and was just as irritating to people's respiratory systems.[12]

The problems created by horse dung would have been even worse but for an ingenious ecological move on the part of farmers living on the outskirts of cities. They purchased the horse manure and used it to fertilize hay and vegetable crops. The hay then went to feed the urban horse population and the vegetables to enhance the dinner tables of the city's better-off residents. As a truck farmer from New Jersey explained: "In our large commercial and manufacturing cities where wealth has concentrated, and where abound families who live regardless of expenditures, fabulous prices are freely paid for vegetables and fruits to please the palate or adorn the table." By the mid-nineteenth century, a reciprocal system, with manure passing one way and vegetables and hay the other, had arisen in New York, Baltimore, Philadelphia, and Boston.[13]

New Yorkers perfected the system. The opening of the Erie Canal in 1825 and the discovery of a new, deeper channel into the port 10 years later propelled the city's economic rise. Farmers within striking distance of the city gave up grain production in favor of potatoes, cucumbers, cabbages, onions, and sweet corn, all of which commanded good prices in the city's market. In 1879, Brooklyn and Queens, today the very essence of urbanity, led the nation in market gardening. One source described Brooklyn as an "immense garden" serving the "vast and increasing demand of the city of New York for vegetables and fruits of a perishable nature."[14]

The soil in Brooklyn and Queens is shallow, limiting root growth, and is not well adapted to the storage of moisture. Normally a farmer would need to keep plenty of hay on hand to feed the livestock that produced the soil-fortifying manure. But with Manhattan dairies and stables located nearby, it made economic sense for farmers to sell their hay and purchase horse manure in return. Manure from all over the New York City area formed the ecological lifeblood of Brooklyn and Queens farming. Many Brooklynites, one newspaper surmised, "are, no doubt, glad to get rid of their filth (and the Board of Health will compel them to do so) [but] our farmers are glad to obtain means with which to enrich their lands, and to pay a fair price for such materials." Horse manure was so critical to farming that one Kings County landowner even made a provision in his will to ensure that his son would receive "all manure on the farm at the time of my decease."[15]

This ingenious recycling system, however, proved short-lived. By the end of the nineteenth century, improvements in refrigeration and railroad transportation had enabled farms in the South and California to outcompete Brooklyn and Queens for New York City's booming vegetable and fruit trade. Another blow came in the late 1880s when the advent of electrified streetcars drove the horse and its manure out of cities. Automobiles soon followed: in 1912, a traffic count revealed, for the first time, more cars than horses in New York. By the following year, so little evidence remained of the manure-based truck farms that the Brooklyn Botanic Garden found itself weighing the educational potential of putting vegetables on exhibit. It was the museum's sense that "innumerable children and young people . . . have never seen . . . beans and peas growing on the plants that produce them."[16] And with the land in cities no longer employed to grow food, it could be put to so-called higher uses as a form of speculative investment, setting the stage for the skyscrapers and towers so common today.

FLUSH AND FORGET

Before the rise of the "flush and forget" mentality, human waste actually served a purpose in life. To understand its role we must, as it were, follow the shit. Generally speaking, mid-nineteenth-century city dwellers relieved themselves in outhouses or privies. From that point, the excrement found its way into privy vaults and cesspools, essentially holes in the ground. Some waste seeped into the surrounding soil. Some of it invariably drained into the street when the vaults backed up and overflowed. And some fell to so-called necessary tubmen (a "necessary" being another name for a privy) to deal with. The tubmen—many of whom were African American—used buckets, casks, and ultimately carts to haul away the night soil, referred to as such because the men did their dirty work under the darkness of night. Predictably, some of the slop ended up spilled in the streets. Some was dumped into nearby rivers and lakes. But a good deal of it, at least by the late nineteenth century (when reliable figures became available), journeyed in good biblical fashion back onto the earth.

PRIVY

Night soil from privies such as this one on Thompson Street in New York City was often shipped to the countryside for use on farms or sold to dealers who made it into fertilizer. (Library of Congress)

In 1880, nearly half of the more than 200 U.S. cities surveyed in one study deposited night soil on the land or sold it to fertilizer dealers. As late as 1912, tubmen in Baltimore, which still lacked a sewer system, cleaned out roughly 70,000 privy vaults and cesspools regularly. Barges then shipped the waste to the outskirts of town, where farmers bought it in 1,000-gallon quantities. They used it to grow tomatoes, cabbages, and other vegetables for urban consumption.[17]

Of course the vast majority of human excrement produced in cities did not resurface on farms. Nevertheless, a viable system for recycling human waste existed in nineteenth-century America. What forces combined to cause its downfall? How did urban populations across the nation find themselves cut off from the soil and bereft of the role they once played in maintaining it?

The story begins with water. In the early nineteenth century, most urbanites depended on cisterns and wells; those who could afford to purchase water bought it from petty proprietors who went from door to door. As urban populations surged, however, and leaking privies contaminated the underground supply, however, the demand for fresh water rose. In response, cities established public water systems. Philadelphia led the way, and New York, Boston, Detroit, and Cincinnati soon fell into step. On the eve of the Civil War, the nation's 16 largest cities all had municipal waterworks in operation. By 1880, nearly 600 public water systems existed, complex networks that brought water, often from many miles away, to urban areas.[18]

CREATIVE DESTRUCTION

East Main Street in West Boylston, Massachusetts, pictured here in 1896, was flooded and destroyed to make way for the Wachusett Reservoir, which supplied Boston with water. (Metropolitan District Commission Archives, Boston, Massachusetts)

In 1842, New York City opened its Croton Aqueduct, which transported water over 40 miles from Westchester County. The city would eventually also draw on the Catskill watershed, 100 miles north. In 1848, Boston tapped Lake Cochituate, 15 miles to the west of the city, and early the following century went even farther afield to dam the waters of the Nashua River to create the Wachusett Reservoir. The water brought life to the city but doomed parts of the rural towns of West Boylston and Clinton, Massachusetts, where residents were sent packing to support population growth in a faraway city. Meanwhile, clear across the continent, Los Angeles was concocting its own imperial plan for draining off the natural riches of the countryside. In 1906, the city obtained the necessary rights of way from the federal government to build a 235-mile aqueduct that would bring water from the Owens River directly into the metropolis. In perfecting the plan, city officials secured the help of the nation's foremost conservationist, President Theodore Roosevelt. "It is a hundred or thousandfold more important to the State and more valuable to the people as a whole," he remarked, "if [this water is] used by the city than if used by the people of the Owens Valley."[19]

As supply increased, demand boomed, especially as rich families installed water closets, the forerunner of the modern toilet. A mere seven years after completion of the Cochituate Aqueduct in 1848, some 18,000 Boston households had water connections. Farther west, Cleveland commandeered Lake Erie in 1856. One year later, Clevelanders were using 8 gallons of water per person each day; a number that soared to 55 by 1872. The cesspools and privy vaults, it turned out, could not handle all the waste. Although an alternative existed in the earth closet (a device consisting of a seat placed over a container of dirt, which "flushed" dirt over the excrement and thereby produced fertilizer), waste removal by water eventually ruled the day. Persuaded by the convenience of water, residents in some cities lobbied governments to allow them to hook up drains directly to existing sewers. These sewers had a grade only steep enough to handle free-flowing rainwater and broke down when used to transport glutinous torrents of human waste. As sewers backed up and cesspools oozed, cities began to drown in filth.

To deal with the problem, engineers, city officials, and sanitary experts rallied around the idea of more underground plumbing. Eventually, cities laid thousands of miles of sewer pipe, and human waste went flushing into rivers, lakes, and harbors. Common wisdom at the time held that running water purified itself, which is true as long as the amount of waste does not exceed the ability of bacteria to break it down into harmless substances. Unaware of the fine points involved in wastewater disposal but attracted to its convenience, major cities built nearly 25,000 miles of sewer lines by 1909. But whereas water supplies tended to be paid for out of public funds, sewers went in only at the request of property owners, who were assessed accordingly. In other words, only those who could afford better public health received it. In 1857,

New York City had installed just 138 miles of sewers along its 500 miles of paved streets, circumnavigating the city's poorest sections. One New York landlord, desperate to hold down his expenses, protested having to pay a sewer assessment. Sewers, he remarked, "are an unhealthy arrangement and should be avoided at all times if possible."[20]

Other opponents, however, seem to have been less driven by mercenary motives than by practicality in objecting to turning the underground into a huge wastewater superhighway. In 1853, one farmer from Ulster County, situated along the Hudson River, lamented that New York City annually wasted enough human excrement to grow 180 million pounds of wheat. Engineer and sewer expert George Waring, Jr., believed New Yorkers flushed away five million dollars' worth of valuable fertilizer each year. Prominent New Yorker and journalist Horace Greeley labeled the city's wasteful practice an "inexplicable stupidity" and observed that ancient societies had been undermined by "the exhaustion of the soil through the loss of such manures in their capitals." It was ridiculous, he wrote in 1871, to pay for guano when New York "annually poisons its own atmosphere and adjacent waters with excretions which science and capital might combine to utilize at less than half the cost."[21]

Although efforts emerged to use urban sewage on farms, especially in the West, a region desperate for water no matter what its source, U.S. cities had by the 1920s severed the connection between human waste and the soil. Seduced by the convenience of water, urban areas, packed with people and water closets, launched one of the largest aquatic experiments in the nation's history.[22]

By 1933, the western end of Lake Erie, one observer remarked, "looked as if it were coated with green paint." That paint was algae—to be more precise, an algal bloom. Algae are microscopic plants normally present in lakes. In Lake Erie's healthier days algae existed in sparse numbers, in part because the lake's limited supply of phosphorus kept them from flourishing. But when the cities around the lake—Buffalo, Cleveland, and Toledo—started discharging untreated sewage into it, the algae had a field day. Human waste contains large amounts of phosphorus, and with city dwellers flushing a growing number of water closets, more of it ended up in the lake, where it made the algae thrive. Eventually, as the algae died, the resulting green slime sank to the bottom, where bacteria set to work decomposing it—using lots of oxygen to carry out the job. Beginning in the late nineteenth century, oxygen decline (in conjunction with overfishing) changed the species makeup of Lake Erie and the rest of the Great Lakes. Whitefish, herring, trout, and sturgeon, the major commercial fish, depend on clear, oxygen-rich water. With the decline in lake conditions, however, fish that were more adapted to the new aquatic environment, such as yellow perch, catfish, and pickerel, began replacing them.[23]

Urban sewage had an even more devastating effect on fish in the lower part of the Delaware River. As late as the 1890s, the Delaware watershed's shad fishery was the nation's largest, supplying places as far away as Cleveland, Chicago, and areas farther west with a fish that was enormously popular in the Gilded Age. A catch of 16.5 million pounds in 1899, however, plummeted to just 210,000 pounds in 1921. A number of factors probably contributed to the decline, including overfishing and changes in precipitation. But the primary blame rested with Philadelphia's quest for limitless growth in population and development, which resulted in an enormous amount of waste-laden water being flushed out into the Delaware. Starting in the late nineteenth century, water use in the city skyrocketed, increasing from 58 million gallons per day in 1880 to an astounding 319 million 30 years later. All that water, of course, once used, had to go somewhere. The sewage entering the river smelled so foul that by the early twentieth century sailors often jumped ship rather than spend the night breathing in the noxious fumes. By the 1910s, dissolved oxygen in the river near Philadelphia registered just two to zero parts per million. With shad requiring at least five parts per million to survive, the fish—headed upstream to spawning grounds—suffocated and died.[24]

One could point to other examples of the harmful effects of sewage on aquatic life, such as oyster contamination in San Francisco Bay, Newark Bay, or Staten Island Sound. The point is that the installation of sewers, although hailed as a victory for public health, also had important ecological consequences. Human waste was discharged into lakes and streams, at times polluting the water supplies of towns downstream. Instead of having social value in maintaining a region's agroecology, it became just crap. By the turn of the century, city dwellers knew little about where their food came from and perhaps even less about where their bodily waste went, as sewers helped obscure from view the very real ecological impact of biological necessity.

THE GARBAGE PROBLEM

Before the 1870s, urbanites took care of garbage themselves. Some people just left it outside for pigs to devour. Others gave it to "swill children," who collected it in carts and sold it for fertilizer or hog feed. It would be wrong to romanticize this system of waste removal: one account from Milwaukee in the 1870s describes the "little garbage gatherers" leaving the alleys "reeking with filth, smelling to heaven."[25] But this approach did have the virtue of giving social value to garbage, recycling it for human good, as well as providing a much-needed source of income for working-class families struggling to survive in the city's Dickensian economy.

Whatever the virtues of this ad hoc approach to disposal, it had broken down by the late nineteenth century. Consider the problem of dead horses. In 1880, New York City carted away 15,000 of them, with an average weight of 1,300 pounds each. In 1912, when cars were beginning to dominate, Chicago still had to send scavengers out to take care of 10,000 horse carcasses.[26]

Surveys conducted between 1903 and 1918 show that a single city dweller produced a half-ton to a ton of refuse each year. Ashes from the burning of wood and coal remained the single largest item on the list of disposals, at least in the colder climates of the Midwest and the North. In the South, the warmer weather and longer growing season meant more organic waste, which required attention before it rotted. Watermelon rinds alone made up 20 percent of the summer garbage of Savannah, Georgia, in 1915. And with the capitalist economy increasingly organized around consumer spending, generating a vast array of new packaged items, the amount of garbage increased dramatically. Between 1903 and 1907, trash collected in Cincinnati rose by nearly one-third, a trend that was becoming apparent in most U.S. cities.[27]

In the 1880s, along came the sanitary reformers to tackle the stinking piles of refuse. Women especially championed the cause. In New York, 15 women from the wealthy Beekman Hill area, incensed by the dirt and dust that soiled clothing and ruined homes, complained to the city board of health about a pile of manure they claimed had mounted to 25 feet. The owner of the pile, Martin Kane, employed approximately 100 men to remove manure from stables that held 12,000 to 13,000 horses, selling the dung as fertilizer to nearby farmers

CAROLINE BARTLETT CRANE

Known nationally for her work in the municipal housekeeping movement, Crane is shown here inspecting a Seattle garbage incinerator. (Western Michigan University)

and stockpiling it until prices rose to his satisfaction. Kane was eventually ordered to remove the nuisance, but he was later allowed to reopen his operation
as long as he promised to keep the pile of horse droppings at a minimum.[28]

Freed by servants from many household chores, middle-class women took
to the streets to join the municipal housekeeping movement. In 1884, women
banded together to form the Ladies' Health Protective Association, an organization dedicated to street cleaning and municipal garbage reform. There followed
the Women's Health Protective Association of Brooklyn, the Municipal Order
League in Chicago, the Women's Civic Association in Louisville, and the Neighborhood Union in Atlanta, the latter comprising a group of African American
women who prevailed on the city to provide black residents with trash collection. Entering the traditionally male domain of civic life, women activists, led
by the legendary Jane Addams and other Progressive reformers, succeeded in
expanding their public authority but ultimately had only limited success in improving sanitary conditions.[29]

Municipal garbage collection put the swill children out of work, although
it took some time. In Milwaukee, aldermen let each ward decide whether it
wanted contractors, hired by the city, to pick up its trash. But the new service
failed when residents, still loyal to the swill children, refused to turn over their
garbage. "Most of the garbage . . . is removed by boys and girls and women,
mostly of Polish nationality, who use the material collected to feed hogs,"
a health department report noted. In 1878, a new health commissioner finally convinced officials to establish one garbage contract for the entire city.
New restrictions on both children and pigs accompanied the contract. As one
working-class newspaper put it, "It is a great pity if [our] stomachs must suffer
to save the noses of the rich."[30]

Once collected, where did city garbage go? Incinerators, a technology invented by the British, proved popular in the southern states, where the warm
climate and large quantities of organic waste made immediate disposal imperative. Northern cities, in contrast, had more ash and disposed of it on the land or
at sea. Chicago unloaded its waste into Lake Michigan, while St. Louis and New
Orleans both turned to the Mississippi River. The city of New York dumped its
garbage in the Atlantic, with garbage scows in 1886 pitching 80 percent of the
city's 1.3 million cartloads of refuse into the sea. From there it drifted south to
New Jersey, where swimmers commonly encountered it—old mattresses and
shoes bobbing along in the waves. By 1896, the city was dumping 760,000
cubic yards of refuse into the ocean.[31]

Smaller cities often sold garbage as hog feed or set up pig farms. (Large cities
could not partake in such an enterprise because it would have required costly
additional collections to keep the refuse from rotting.) City-owned piggeries
flourished, especially in New England, where temperatures cooperated in keeping the garbage edible. In the early twentieth century, 61 cities and towns in
Massachusetts operated some kind of swine-feeding program. Grand Rapids,

St. Paul, Denver, and Los Angeles also used pigs as garbage disposals. During World War I, the U.S. government, anxious to conserve food, encouraged more cities to feed their refuse to hogs. The practice, however, called for the careful separation of edible organic matter from glass and other hazardous items. "Surely very few phonograph needles would find their way into the garbage pail," one government report opined, "if the householders could imagine the tortures suffered by the unfortunate animals."[32]

Although pigs gave garbage a role in the food cycle, by the turn of the century, the vast majority of urban refuse was either buried, dumped at sea, or burned—in short, wasted. Before the evolution of capitalism toward a more consumer orientation in the late nineteenth century, Americans as a whole generated little in the way of trash. Swill children salvaged scattered pieces of food, which mothers incorporated into meals, and sold metal, bones, and bottles to junk dealers. Ragmen scoured city streets for old clothes that could be used for making paper. Women fed leftover food scraps to chickens and pigs. The recycling of waste, in other words, played a role in producing goods and bolstering living standards. Then municipal trash collection eliminated the swill children, while the invention of wood pulp did away with the need for ragmen. The recycling networks disappeared, and a social system dedicated to clean homes and cities superseded them. That move simply shifted waste outside the immediate food and soil cycles to downstream and downwind regions, spelling the end of the organic city.[33]

CONCLUSION

The great cleanup had many virtues: a decline in diseases, especially water-borne ones like typhoid fever, and an improved and more aesthetically pleasing urban environment, plus no more pigs to contend with on the streets. But tidying up the metropolis meant compromising life in other quarters. A whiter and brighter life came at the cost of fish kills, algal blooms, and garbage-strewn beaches. The cleaning compulsion also hurt the poor, who once put filth to work in the service of the family economy. Meanwhile, the increasing power of corporations combined with the rise of advertising and marketing to produce a torrent of packaging and products planned, on purpose, to go obsolete. These developments made it even more difficult for U.S. cities to keep pace with what their citizens no longer wanted.

PART THREE

CONSUMING NATURE

11

MOVEABLE FEAST

The age of the "3,000-mile Caesar salad" began a century ago when a farmer named Mose Hutchings planted a few acres of lettuce along the central coast of California.[1] Columbus is thought to have first brought lettuce to North America, yet commercial farmers in Hutchings's time still grew only crops such as wheat, sugar beets, and beans that required no refrigeration. Hutchings sparked a revolution, and by the mid-1920s hundreds of refrigerated railroad cars full of lettuce left the depot in Watsonville every year. The nearby Salinas Valley, stretching 60 miles across the length of Monterey County, went on to become the "Salad Capital of the World."

The era of long-distance food travel coincided with major changes in daily life. Self-sufficiency at home gave way to the consumption of factory-made items. Railroad track tripled between 1880 and 1920 to create a truly national market for brand-name products like Crisco shortening and Ivory soap. In the 1880s, hundreds of electric lamps installed in New York City lit up the streets, allowing masses of people to crowd establishments after dark. By 1919, electricity powered roughly half of American factories; flashing signs in cities advertised consumer goods such as Heinz pickles. A new and radically different system of distribution also developed, bringing chain stores like Woolworth's and A & P. to the fore and imprinting brand names on the public mind through heavy advertising. This consumer culture helped catapult the United States and its capitalism-based socioecological order into the greatest power on the face of the earth.

The culture of consumption brought equally significant changes to the environment. A new relationship with the land developed as the growth of specialized, one-crop industrial agriculture brought the commercialization of farming, pioneered in the South, to a higher level. This industrial land ethic rested on an extreme vision of nature as little more than a means to maximize economic profits. Markets for farm products grew apace, as railroads—and eventually trucks and ships—brought them all across the nation and soon the globe.

Agribusiness, as this form of farming came to be called, reached its purest form in California. There, factory farms founded on irrigation, monoculture, and cheap immigrant labor sprawled across the landscape. Capitalizing on a favorable

climate and on the virtues of speedy, refrigerated train travel, California's growers became the richest farmers in the nation.

LAND OF SUNSHINE

In the late nineteenth century, boosters tried to lure people to the Golden State
by selling them on the climate. And no one did more to market the image of
California as a sun-drenched oasis than journalist Charles Fletcher Lummis. In
1885, Lummis, recovering from a bout of malaria, decided to walk from his
home in Cincinnati, Ohio, 3,000 miles to Los Angeles. After 143 days of trekking, Lummis arrived in Southern California, tan, fit, and eager to testify to
the virtues of the West Coast's magnificent climate. In 1895, Lummis assumed
the editorship of a magazine aptly named Land of Sunshine. In it he argued that
California's sunny climate made people healthier and fostered their intellectual and creative talents. It was no coincidence, he argued, that some of the
world's greatest minds, from Plato to Jesus to Michelangelo, came from lands
blessed with a great deal of sun. In the United States, he deduced, all roads led
to Los Angeles.[2]

Much of what Lummis told his readers was hype. But there is little question that
California's cloudless skies—putting aside for the moment the agricultural implications of too little rain—gave it an edge over the East when it came to growing
food. Indeed, California is one of only five places on the planet blessed with such a
sun-rich temperate climate (the others are central Chile, southern Africa, southern
Australia, and the Mediterranean basin). In Fresno, California, the heart of raisin
country, average precipitation in May is just one-third of an inch. Barely one-tenth
of an inch of rain falls in June, and essentially none in July and August. Virtually
all of the area's 10 inches of annual precipitation occurs between November and
April. The rest of the year is sunny, amazingly so, with sunshine favoring the city
on average more than 90 percent of the time in the summer months.

Californians have something known as the Pacific High to thank for all the
sunny weather. This zone of high pressure lies stationed off the coast of the central
part of the state, deflecting all precipitation north to the Pacific Northwest. From
late March until October the high pressure stands watch over the Golden State's
sunny skies, before drifting south to Mexico in the fall and allowing rain to slip in.
As regular as clockwork, the Pacific High returns north in the spring, and with it
sunshine beats down on the land, creating perfect conditions for photosynthesis.

With respect to solar radiation, California has struck it rich. And the state's
good fortune does not end there. It extends into the realm of geology as well.
One of the largest river valleys on earth, the Central Valley, an area nearly the
size of England, stretches more than 400 miles through the center of the state.
Drained by the Sacramento River in the north and the San Joaquin in the south,
the valley is, in the words of one environmental scientist, "the richest agricultural region in the history of the world."[3]

In the 1860s, wheat rose to dominance in this valley. Hundreds of square miles of land were planted with the crop, forming fields so colossal that it was not uncommon for a team of plows to work their way across an expanse and then camp out for the night before rising the following day and forging back. A generation later, California emerged as the nation's leader in wheat production. The bulk of the crop, produced with the help of horse-drawn plows and huge steam combines, was exported across the world. But wheat's reign was brief. Beginning in 1883, wheat prices declined, bottoming out in 1894 as Argentina, Russia, Canada, India, and Australia began growing large quantities of the grain and flooded the market. Meanwhile, California wheat growers, eager to cash in on the bonanza, began to deplete the fertility of the soil. When they sought new land to exploit, however, they found that prices were high, especially relative to such places as Kansas and elsewhere on the Great Plains, where land could be bought for little more than a filing fee. Hemmed in by the ocean and with no-where else to turn, California wheat farmers would have to find higher-paying crops to grow if they wanted to prosper.[4]

This is where produce and transportation came in. As long as farmers depended on local markets in the West to sell fruit, they would face overproduction and low prices for their oranges, plums, grapes, and peaches. If only a way could be found to ship the produce—which unlike wheat was bulky and perishable—to markets in the Midwest and East, then California farmers might realize fabulous wealth. Although a transcontinental rail link had been built by 1869, it was not until the 1880s, when competition brought down rates, that orchards turned to the railroads for help. But growers still had to be able to ship the fruit east without it spoiling. It took the meat industry's perfection of the refrigerated railroad car in the 1880s to truly launch the California fruit market, which depended on such transcontinental shipment. In 1888, cherries and apricots left the Golden State aboard a refrigerated train for the very first time. Firms such as Armour and Swift sent meat to California and loaded up on fruit for the return trip. By the turn of the century, consumers in New York City and other urban areas could buy fruits and vegetables out of season.[5]

Apart from being more perishable and bulkier than wheat, fruit also required more water, which was a scarce commodity, especially in California's drier southern reaches. Irrigation offered an answer, but many grape growers initially resisted, believing that irrigating a crop led to a reduction in its quality. California's passage of the Wright Act in 1887—which sanctioned the creation of government units to oversee the collective control of irrigation—coupled with droughts in 1889, 1890, and 1893, helped to convert the skeptical. By 1890, California had emerged as the nation's leader in irrigated acreage. "But for irrigation," one orchard owner explained, "much of our best fruit lands necessarily would be still a desert waste, and some of the special productions of the irrigated regions would be almost unknown in the great markets of the East."[6]

Instead of expanding onto fresh soil—the basis for most agriculture in land-rich America up until this time—California fruit growers increased yields by turning to such capital-intensive technologies as railroads and irrigation works. Instead of moving the frontier, they poured money and technology into the land to maximize output and profits. This new industrial form of agriculture focused exclusively on the efficient production of crops for national and international markets, using large amounts of capital and wage labor.[7]

By the turn of the century, a sweeping 800-mile fruit belt stretched down the length of the state. Apple, pear, cherry, plum, and apricot orchards dominated in coastal areas. Inland in the Santa Clara Valley—known today as Silicon Valley—plum trees yielding hundreds of pounds of fruit spread out across the landscape long before anyone had even heard of high technology. By 1886, the state as a whole produced 40 million pounds of prunes annually, the bulk of which were sent via railroads to the East. In the Central Valley, peaches and pears flourished, crops that ripened before the onset of the long, hot summer weather. Raisins put Fresno County on the map, with growers capitalizing on the hot August sun to dry out the grapes.

New York farmers lost significant ground to the California factory farms, especially during the winter season when the northeastern climate made agriculture impossible. But when the weather turned warmer, New Yorkers still bought fresh locally grown produce, as they had done for generations. The farms that once spread out across Brooklyn and Queens succumbed by the 1920s, but not because the California growers undersold them. Instead, superior marketing by competitors across the continent put them out of business.[8]

SUN KISSED

Before the late nineteenth century, few Americans believed, as many do today, in the value of a diet rich in fruits and vegetables. In fact, many urbanites worried that eating fresh produce might actually harm them, bringing on such dread diseases as cholera or dysentery. Aside from the nuts and raisins consumed once or twice a year at holiday time, the diet of most Americans centered on foods full of fat, starch, and salt.[9]

Although truck farms had sprung up outside of major cities by this time, introducing residents to a variety of fresh produce, it took a self-conscious effort on the part of California orchards to sell consumers on the idea that fruits and vegetables ought to play a part in everyone's daily fare. By the turn of the century, the campaign appeared to be paying off. "The old prejudices against fruit are fast passing away," observed one grower in 1893. "Fruit has become a necessity rather than a luxury." In 1910, a housewife put it this way: "When I first began to keep house, ten years ago, we ate cereal, eggs and coffee for breakfast, with fruit occasionally instead of cereal; but now we must have grapefruit every morning. . . . [T]hen, when I go to market and see fresh beans,

BROOKLYN FARMS

Now a byword for urban life, the Flatbush section of Brooklyn, New York, shown here in the 1870s, once hosted some of the most productive vegetable farms in the nation. (Library of Congress)

cucumbers and spinach, I buy them without really stopping to think; so easily tempted are we." As the reference to fresh produce suggests, marketing by California growers initially increased the demand for locally grown produce.[10]

Earlier, fruit had passed into eastern markets with little concern for quality. But in a clever move, California orchards sought to capture market share through standardization. Growers and shippers joined in establishing formal sets of rules for packing fruit, specifying uniform box sizes and shapes. The fruit was classified into various grades—fancy, choice, and standard. "We must be guided by the experience and adopt the practices of other successful manufacturers, and so arrange and classify our products that each purchaser may secure the identical commodity he orders in the most convenient form," explained one grower. The state government of California, spurred on by a freeze in 1912 that left many growers with little choice but to ship damaged fruit east, also stepped in and passed the Fresh Fruit, Nut, and Vegetable Standardization Act of 1917 to regulate quality.[11]

Growers chose to specialize in those fruits that best met market imperatives. Some 60 different varieties of pears—Bosc, Giffard, Joan of Arc, Vicar, and Wilder Early, among others—once grew on this continent. But California farmers eventually zeroed in on the Bartlett, a pear that was easy to grow, can, and ship, and thus suitable for commercial harvesting. By the early twentieth century, Bartletts made up roughly 80 to 90 percent of the pears raised in California.[12]

Standardization helped orchards sell fruit in eastern markets, but to transform raisins and oranges into year-round staples, growers had to become more aggressive. New marketing organizations formed to oversee the harvesting, processing, and shipping of fruit, as well as brand-name advertising. California raisin growers, centered in sunny Fresno County, produced record-setting yields in the 1890s but found that demand did not keep up with supply, forcing down prices. To solve the problem of underconsumption, the growers founded a cooperative organization, but it soon failed. Then, in 1912, the California Associated Raisin Company, a group uniting over 1,000 orchards, was formed. In one of the new company's very first moves, it created the "Sun-Maid" brand name. Using one part feminine mystique and one part raw natural power, the company tried to sell Americans on the idea that they could get back in touch with nature and improve their health by buying raisins. The Sun-Maid label, showing a girl in a red bonnet with the sun in the background, grew to be one of the most successful trademarks in food history. Then the growers launched an advertising campaign, pitching the raisins in newspapers and women's magazines. Sales agents went from grocer to grocer in major cities hawking the product. In the 1920s, the growers marketed raisins in little nickel packages, the perfect size to fit into a school lunch sack. In six months' time, the company sold 17,000 tons of five-cent boxes valued at 18 million dollars. As consumption boomed, raisins went from being a luxury item eaten only on holidays to an expected and ordinary part of daily fare.[13]

Oranges also remained a luxury item in the late nineteenth century, more a Christmas stocking stuffer than a dietary staple. Since the end of the Civil War, growers in Florida had shipped oranges north by boat during the holiday season. By the mid-1880s, improved railroad transportation had allowed Florida orchards to control the eastern market. One New Jersey vegetable farmer marveled at the way that farmers in Florida "with their evergreen productiveness, have been able to revolutionize the old conditions, by sending to the northern cities, even when snow clad and ice bound, the fruits of balmy summer." Then, in 1895, a freeze pummeled the Sunshine State. The year before the cold, Florida had outstripped California by roughly a million boxes. The onset of the freeze, however, caused Florida production to plummet. By 1909, nearly three-quarters of all the citrus consumed in the United States came from California.[14]

More than just a cold spell accounted for California's lock on the national orange market. In 1885, Americans consumed almost no citrus fruit; in 1914, they were eating roughly 40 oranges per year. Credit for that change must go to the California Fruit Growers Exchange, founded in 1893 (eight years after Florida established a similar organization). The exchange united growers and packing associations around the processing and marketing of citrus. At one time, 200 different brand-name oranges existed. The fruit exchange, however, sought to streamline marketing by creating the Sunkist (originally Sun Kissed) trademark and stamping it on every orange its members produced. During the early decades of the twentieth century, Sunkist's marketers blanketed the nation with images of its product.

They created picturesque labels to stick on tens of millions of citrus crates. They advertised in newspapers and magazines, set up billboards, helped grocers and especially chain stores to create elaborate window displays, and ran promotional spots on the radio. By the early 1930s, the organization had over 1,000 billboards in 11 metropolitan markets, including one in New York's Times Square.[15]

The invention of the electric juicer and the discovery that ascorbic acid (vitamin C) prevents scurvy bolstered Sunkist's marketing prospects. By the middle of the 1930s, one-fifth of all Sunkist oranges went to make juice. In the early years of the twentieth century, middle-class Americans often worried that the advent of modern, urban life had cut them off from the natural world, especially the sunlight that had formerly fostered good mental and physical health. Advertisers capitalized on this yearning for nature, turning it into a commodity by warning mothers to make sure that their children received food in its natural form. And what could be more wholesome than a sun-kissed orange? Oranges soon became an essential part of a normal, healthy diet. Per capita consumption shot up during the first two decades of the twentieth century. "The public may remember the slogan, 'An apple a day keeps the doctor away,'" wrote one observer in 1928, "but it possesses much more specific and convincing information concerning the health value of oranges." Hailed as an antidote to the ills of modern living, the orange soon surpassed the apple as the key to health in the public mind, a means of putting a little sun into everyone's day.[16]

Prune and apricot growers also adopted the solar motif, forming the Sunsweet brand in 1917. Growers tapped the sun's energy and then turned around and marketed the fruit by convincing consumers of the wholesomeness of the product. It was a perfect strategy for reaching sun-starved city dwellers. Advertisements of women proffering the fruits of the land conveyed the impression that what consumers bought came straight from nature to their kitchen table. Capitalism had broken people's direct interactions with the earth and then, under the guiding hand of marketers, sold them a commodity that masked the human energy—indeed, the rank exploitation of workers—involved in putting flawless oranges and plump raisins on the table.[17]

COPING WITH PESTS

The first step in producing perfect-looking plums and oranges was to find the right plant for a particular growing environment. Luther Burbank, a Massachusetts-born plant breeder, probably had more impact in this regard than any other individual. In the 1870s, Burbank, seeking to improve the vegetable varieties available in New England, invented a potato well adapted to the region's stony soil. He then headed west to the Golden State, where he continued to cross-fertilize and graft plants with an eye toward material gain. "Only by growing the most perfect fruit possible could a profit be made," he told a group gathered in Sacramento in 1899. "The fruit grower of to-day is strictly a manufacturer, and should have the latest and best improvements." By this he meant

SUNKIST DISPLAY

Before the early twentieth century, Americans purchased food from neighborhood grocers, who stood behind counters and took orders. The Piggly Wiggly chain, first opened in 1916, pioneered self-service grocery shopping, allowing customers to choose fruit, often artfully displayed, and other items for themselves. (Library of Congress)

fruit engineered to grow rapidly, such as the plums—large, rich in sugar, and easy to ship—he introduced into California in the 1880s.[18]

Although one newspaper called him "the Edison of horticultural mysteries," Burbank is scarcely remembered today because he never received legal recognition for his work. Edison had over 1,000 patents to his name; Burbank had not a single one. The originator of Idaho's now-famous Russet Burbank potato, he garnered just 150 dollars for his efforts. "A man can patent a mouse trap or copyright a nasty song," he once wrote, "but if he gives to the world a new fruit that will add millions to the value of earth's annual harvests he will be fortunate if he is rewarded by so much as having his name connected with the result." Not until the passage of the Plant Patent Act in 1930 was it possible for breeders to transform living things such as fruit trees into intellectual property. The legislation extended the reach of private property rights over an element of the natural world once available to all and cleared the way for capitalists to accumulate considerable wealth.[19]

Growing varieties tailor-made for sale on the national market was one thing. But orchards had to overcome a number of other obstacles to profit, including the threat posed to perfect-looking fruit by a variety of agricultural pests. When California's growers replaced the region's natural vegetation—its sweeping expanses of tule, a grass much like a bulrush, and perennial species of bunchgrass—with domesticated plants, they literally opened a can of worms. Insect infestation, a problem for all farmers who simplify an ecosystem, was made considerably worse by the untold numbers of plants imported into the state in the 60 years after 1860: not only exotic varieties of apple, plum, and cherry trees, but also hundreds of other shrubs and vines. With the new plants came insects, buried in the fruit and hidden under the bark.[20]

Numerous such pests existed, including the pear slug, apricot shot hole, peach blight, red scale, purple scale, citrus mealy-bug, and red spider mite. Perhaps the most troublesome insect was the cottony cushion scale, a bug that attacked California's orange groves beginning in the 1880s. It is hard to say how the scale arrived. One theory is that it first appeared back in 1868, accompanying a shipment of Australian lemon trees to San Mateo County. The scale then worked its way south. Growers first tried oil soaps, liquid sprays, and hydrocyanic gas to combat the pest. But none of the remedies worked. Eventually, the thought dawned that since growers in Australia did not suffer from the scale, a predator must have kept the insect in check. After a visit to Australia in 1888, an American delegation returned with a promising kind of ladybug. The beetle flitted from tree to tree preying on the immobile scale fixed on leaves and branches. Liberated from the pest, California's citrus industry boomed in the last decade of the nineteenth century.[21]

It was a novel solution to an intractable problem, but using bugs to fight bugs—a method known as biological control—proved a short-lived solution. It was impossible to find predators to deal with all the insects that threatened California's fruit and vegetable crops. And not all predators survived when transported out of their original habitat. Chemicals offered what many growers saw as a more workable solution, and orchards eventually turned to new synthetic poisons such as arsenate of lead. Supported by the research of scientists at the University of California at Berkeley, fruit growers sprayed and fumigated away as yields per acre marched upward early in the twentieth century.[22]

California eventually went on to lead the nation in pesticide use. The quest to deliver delicate fruit to market in pristine condition in part explains the state's obsession with insecticides. Like drunks addicted to alcohol, farmers found it hard to stop spraying, especially as chemical corporations hawking pesticides testified to the increased productivity and profits to be gained by employing the products. As pests developed resistance to one poison, another had to be found in the ceaseless effort to keep California's landscape from reverting back to its ecologically complex and diverse ancestral state.[23]

Apart from its harmful environmental effects, increasing pesticide use damaged the health of farmworkers who handled the chemicals directly. They experienced headache, nausea, shortness of breath, and in some cases death. Between 1950 and 1961, 3,000 California farmworkers fell victim to pesticide poisoning, including 63 children who died.[24]

WATER AND POWER

By the 1920s, California had overtaken Iowa as the nation's leading agricultural state. Roughly 9 million orange trees and 73 million grapevines gripped its landscape, not to mention alfalfa, rice, peaches, lemons, plums, prunes, beans, walnuts, cotton, beets, and apricots. These were just some of the more than 200 commercially grown crops produced in the Golden State. Most of them had no business being grown on arid lands and would never have survived but for irrigation.[25]

At the outset, California farmers relied on surface water. But in the 1890s, the perfection of the centrifugal pump brought a vast reserve of underground water—perhaps as much as 750 million acre-feet (an acre-foot is equal to about 326,000 gallons)—within reach. The pump, in other words, put growers in touch with enough water to flood the entire state of California to a depth of seven feet. Tulare County, a major agricultural center, had 739 pumps as of 1910, and 9 years later it had 3,758.[26]

Beginning in 1918 and lasting until early in the next decade, droughts caused growers to run pumps with abandon. The result was predictable. In the upper San Joaquin Valley, the average groundwater level plummeted nearly 40 feet between 1921 and 1939. As the water table dropped, great numbers of ancient oak trees and other native plants died, and thousands of acres of farmland, dependent on the water wealth stored underground, went out of production. By the 1930s, vast expanses of some of the richest agricultural land in the nation were in jeopardy.[27]

Growers could have limited water use and submitted to government control over pumping. But they feared these steps would interfere too much with profitability. Thus a new source of water had to be found if California was to retain its position as the fruit basket of the nation. It had long been known that the northern reaches of the long Central Valley had two-thirds of the state's water but only one-third of its land fit for cultivation. Bringing the water south, as broached by the state in 1933, would be a massive plumbing project. But with the nation mired in a depression, insufficient private money existed to finance such an ambitious scheme. So the state of California turned instead to the federal government to underwrite private wealth accumulation.

In 1937, Congress authorized the engineers and planners at the U.S. Bureau of Reclamation to begin the Central Valley Project, a monumental scheme that, after nearly two decades of work, resulted in four major dams, four elaborate canal systems, and a lot of federally subsidized water for California's growers. The bureau had been created earlier in the century subsequent to the passage of the National Reclamation Act of 1902. Established to fight monopolies and encourage family farms, the legislation set up a system whereby money from the sale of public lands would be used to reclaim patches of soil from the clutches of the desert. Under the law, a landowner was entitled to only enough federal water to irrigate 160 acres—Jefferson's magic number and a figure pushed by the railroads. When the Central Valley Project came under federal control, it too had to live up to this requirement, meaning that big-time growers with land above the 160-acre limit would have to divest themselves of property.[28]

California's great Central Valley was certainly a place ripe for land redistribution, which, on the surface at least, is what the new federal water project would mean. In the mid-1940s, 60 percent of all the landholdings in the southern part of the valley exceeded the federal limit. Just 3 percent of the region's growers controlled 40 percent of the cropland. "This degree of concentration of land ownership," wrote the authors of one 1940s study, "is rarely encountered in the United States." In 1946, the Standard Oil Company alone owned nearly 80,000 acres in the area slated to receive federal water.[29]

But what should have been a means of redistributing land more fairly instead ended up as a huge federal giveaway as the U.S. state continued its tradition of stimulating economic development. First, a group of economists in the Franklin Roosevelt administration argued that the 160-acre figure was a minimum, not a ceiling. Caving to the big growers, they proposed a maximum farm size of 640 acres instead. Then the Truman administration and its new Bureau of Reclamation chief, Michael Straus, came into office calling for "technical compliance" with the reclamation law. This language was a wink and a nod to giant corporate growers to sign land away to their employees and then lease it back, giving them the right to receive subsidized federal water in the process. By requiring growers to comply with only the letter and not the spirit of the law, the bureau reinforced the valley's pattern of unequal land distribution.[30]

Did the completion of the giant Central Valley Project alleviate California's water woes, the intent of the plan? In fact, the project actually accelerated depletion of the aquifers. Indeed, the federal government's generosity even led farmers to plant more acreage. The inexpensive government water, in other words, spawned agricultural expansion. Federal irrigation projects, however, could never keep up with the demand, leaving farmers with no choice but to dig deeper wells. In the 1940s, Kern County farmers had to reach down 275 feet to tap underground water. In 1965, they had to travel nearly 200 feet deeper to reach the much-depleted supply.[31]

The Central Valley Project, which spelled more ecological trouble for California, left agriculture largely in the hands of corporate growers—the main beneficiaries of federal intervention. Now, of course, the growers had to contend with the Bureau of Reclamation, which meant compromising somewhat their jealously guarded autonomy. But by the 1940s, California growers and federal engineers had teamed up to dominate the state's water resources on an unheralded scale in the pursuit of endless economic growth and profits. Whatever democratic pretensions remained from the 1902 reclamation act had dried up like an old irrigation ditch.[32]

THE RISE OF FACTORY FARMING

Turn-of-the-century California stood at the cutting edge of business farming. Like the cotton South, California emerged as a region founded on specialization—first wheat, then produce, and by the 1920s cotton, known in the San Joaquin Valley as "white gold." Southern planters specialized in cotton, but they also produced plenty of corn for personal consumption. Not the California growers. They crammed produce destined for national and international markets onto nearly every square inch of land, perfecting the industrial paradigm. California's approach to business farming rested on two precepts: an industrial land ethic that treated the soil as a vehicle for producing maximum profits and a vision of social relations wedded to cheap labor. Whatever connection between rural life and the natural world had once existed in California faded before the growing embrace of an instrumental understanding of land and soil. What historian Donald Worster calls an "economic culture" founded on "the alienation of man from the land, its commercialization, and its consequent abuse" constituted the essence of this new, aggressive relationship with nature.[33]

Alongside this adoption of a new land ethic, a tendency emerged within the industrial mode toward routinized labor. Growers needed many field hands to bring in the summer harvest, but during the rest of the year the demand for labor remained relatively low. Diversified farms, like those in early New England, which planted a variety of different crops, employed family members year-round. One-crop farming, however, was a seasonal enterprise. In other words, the orchards wanted temporary and cheap workers who would arrive just in time to pick the crops and then disappear down the road, relieving growers of any additional financial burden.

The makeup of the migrant labor force changed over time. Growers first relied on Chinese immigrants, but the Chinese Exclusion Act of 1882 halted their entry into the United States. Japanese workers filled the void, but they evinced a great deal of interest in owning property themselves and escaping wage labor altogether. California orchards then turned to immigrants from Mexico to do the tedious stooping and heavy hauling. When the Mexican government, after a revolution in 1911, failed to live up to the expectations of workers, many headed

DUST BOWL REFUGEES

These refugees, photographed in 1937, fled the effects of capitalist agriculture on the plains for Tracy, California. (Library of Congress)

north in search of jobs. Nothing could have made California growers happier than a cheap and docile labor force willing to hike back across the border when work became scarce. By 1930, some 368,000 Mexicans lived in California. Growers rationalized the brutal working conditions by arguing that Mexicans were naturally suited to work in the blistering hot weather. The Mexican, explained one apologist, "is fitted by natural environment to withstand our climatic conditions . . . and able to perform work which demands hard physical exertion."[34]

By the 1930s, the ranks of California's rural proletariat had expanded yet again with the introduction of refugees fleeing the Dust Bowl. The roots of that disaster resided less in the drought that descended on the Great Plains than in some of the same business practices found in California, especially the treatment of land as a tool for accumulating wealth. Plains farmers broke the sod and stripped the land of its native grass to grow wheat for distant markets. Life became tied to economic imperatives in remote places as the soil wealth of the plains was skimmed off to feed people across the globe. Prosperity ruled the plains until drought and wind in the 1930s combined to cause the dried-out soil to take flight, causing the worst dust storms in the known history of the world. The disaster compelled the so-called Okies and exodusters, immortalized in John Steinbeck's *The Grapes of Wrath* (1939), to head for California. But there was no escaping the dominant industrial paradigm that would now rule agriculture in the United States.[35]

CONCLUSION

In the 1950s, the word "agribusiness" was coined to describe the approach to farming pioneered in California. This new form of capitalist agriculture underwrote considerable demographic growth and urban development, while distancing people from the land and mediating their relations with the natural world through complex corporate organizations that relied on novel technologies to push the earth to its maximum limit—indeed, beyond that limit when it came to exploiting groundwater in an arid land. Genetic diversity declined as growers streamlined crop production, cultivating only those plant varieties best suited to market imperatives, such as square tomatoes that shipped well. Ecology suffered, and so too did direct democracy, as corporate enterprises with large amounts of capital and a yen for cheap labor came to lord over the agricultural social structure. Even nutrition paid a price. Although California marketers championed the health benefits of eating more fruits and vegetables, the long distances the produce had to travel to market reduced its nutritional value and increased its ecological cost.

THE SECRET HISTORY OF MEAT

In 1954, a 52-year-old struggling salesman named Ray Kroc, who had sold everything from paper cups to Florida real estate, traveled to San Bernadino, California, to hawk his latest item, the Multimixer milkshake machine. He headed for a restaurant owned by two brothers named Mac and Dick McDonald. Kroc sat outside the octagonal building, transfixed by the sight of customers queuing up to buy sacks of hamburgers. The restaurant appealed to him on a number of levels. He liked the stripped-down, simple menu centered around the hamburger. He admired the preparation process, which resembled a kind of assembly line for food. Even the building with its arches impressed him. And the name McDonald's seemed to have a nice ring to it. "I had a feeling," he later wrote, "that it would be one of those promotable names that would catch the public fancy."[1]

No food is more closely associated with American consumer culture than the hamburger. Only the invention of the automobile rivals fast food meat eating in impact on nature and social relations. Behind the Golden Arches lay a set of profound changes in the land and in agriculture itself. To support the masses of new consumers eager for beef, raising livestock evolved into a factory enterprise. Beef led the way, but in the years after World War II poultry and pork production perfected the industrial form. Thousands of animals, confined to feedlots, were fed corn, soybeans, and fishmeal, plus vitamins, hormones, and antibiotics. Such a diet relied on formidable amounts of water and energy to grow the feed; water the cattle, pigs, and chickens; and produce the fertilizers that farmers depended on more than ever before. With crops and animals raised in separate places, manure lost its role as a vehicle for transporting nutrients back to the soil; instead it degenerated into a major source of water pollution. Munching a hamburger may have seemed innocent enough, but Americans' burgeoning love affair with meat had enormous consequences for people and ecosystems across the continent.

THE DEBUT OF BEEF

Before the late nineteenth century, pork, not beef, dominated the national palate. The popularity of pork is not surprising in light of all the advantages of raising pigs. To begin with, swine are terrific reproducers. Where cows take nine months to give birth to just one calf, pigs take barely half as long to produce multi-piglet litters. In 1539, when explorer Hernando de Soto came to Florida, he brought 13 pigs with him; a mere three years later he had 700. Pigs will eat just about anything, from acorns to garbage. When it comes to converting plant matter into animal protein, they are more than three times as efficient as cattle. Pigs also love corn, long a popular American crop. And finally, in the days before refrigeration staved off decomposition, pig meat took much better than beef to salting and smoking. For all these reasons, pork played a far larger role than beef in the American diet up until the end of the nineteenth century.[2]

Despite all these virtues, however, the pig did have one main disadvantage that initially limited its full incorporation into industrial capitalism: unlike cattle, swine cannot be driven long distances. Hogs were thus slaughtered in many small-scale packinghouses scattered across mid-nineteenth-century America. The pork plants in Cincinnati were the only exception. Situated near the junctions of several smaller rivers with the Ohio and benefiting from the Miami and Erie Canal, opened in 1827, Cincinnati emerged by the 1830s as the nation's leader in pork packing. The city managed to tap the rich agricultural resources of the Ohio Valley so successfully that it was dubbed Porkopolis.[3]

Cincinnati's pork packers took the first steps in streamlining meat production. Long before Henry Ford employed the assembly line for mass-producing cars, Porkopolis packers pioneered a method for slaughtering animals in large numbers. By hanging pigs from a rotating wheel, workers could efficiently gut the animal before sending it on to the chopping table, where butchers would finish the job of cutting the meat and packing it off to market. "No iron cog-wheels could work with more regular motion," wrote landscape architect Frederick Law Olmsted on a visit to the city in the 1850s. "Plump falls the hog upon the table, chop, chop; chop chop; chop, chop, fall the cleavers. All is over." Thus was born the "disassembly line" for the mass slaughtering of livestock.[4]

Exactly how much pork Americans produced in the nineteenth century is difficult to say. A conservative estimate places production in 1849 at 139 pounds per capita, declining to 119 pounds 40 years later. By that time, the grasslands of the Great Plains had been opened for settlement, and beef had begun to take on a larger role in the American diet. In the 1850s, the stretch west of the Mississippi River was largely free of cattle. Once the buffalo had been driven to the brink of extinction, however, cattle filed into their former eco-niches.[5]

The perishability of beef, which, unlike pork, did not lend itself as well to salting or smoking, meant that the animals had to be slaughtered near where they would be consumed. The advent of refrigeration, however, revolutionized the beef-packing industry. In the 1860s, a refrigerated railroad car successfully carried a load of dressed beef (cleaned animal carcasses) from Chicago to Boston. Corporate titan Gustavus F. Swift later hired an engineer to improve the refrigerated railroad car, introducing enhancements that made his cars the most popular among the nation's major beef producers.[6]

By the 1880s, the slaughter and marketing of beef had evolved from a local business handled by neighborhood butchers into a national industry dominated by major meatpacking centers in Chicago, Kansas City, and St. Louis. A handful of companies, of which Swift and Armour were the most prominent, industrialized the meatpacking trade. In the 1880s, these companies began building branch houses, cold-storage facilities that received the dressed beef from packinghouses and distributed it to grocers, who marketed it to consumers. In 1887, the five largest packinghouses had just a few branch houses in operation; ten years later, the companies had 20 plants and roughly 600 branch houses. Meat now traveled in refrigerated railroad cars from the Midwest as far as California.[7]

The national trade in dressed beef did have its critics. Railroads that had invested heavily in building stock cars for transporting animals, which would lose money as the lighter dressed beef replaced the considerably heavier live cattle, were among the first to object. Meanwhile, butchers feared for their jobs as the new meatpacking industry took over the role of slaughtering, improving on the disassembly line originally developed for pork. In 1886, meat cutters assembled to form the Butcher's National Protective Association, an organization that tried to undermine consumer confidence in dressed beef by calling it unsanitary.[8]

The most prominent critic of meatpacking was journalist Upton Sinclair, whose 1906 novel The Jungle included horrific descriptions of meatpacking plants. "It was too dark in these storage places to see well, but a man could run his hand over these piles of meat and sweep off handfuls of the dried dung of rats," one passage reported. "These rats were nuisances, and the packers would put poisoned bread out for them; they would die, and then rats, bread, and meat would go into the hoppers together." President Theodore Roosevelt read the book and dispatched federal investigators to Chicago to learn more about the industry's filthy conditions, information that helped pressure Congress into passing the 1906 Meat Inspection Act mandating sanitary workplace conditions for the interstate meat trade.[9]

Sinclair's book upset people accustomed to purchasing meat from trusted local butchers. But if they were disgusted by conditions at the faraway packinghouses, consumers nevertheless must have found it hard to resist the lower prices that the meat-packers offered. Only a little more than half of a slaughtered steer's live weight could be cut up into merchantable meat. The other 45 percent was wasted, as was the cost of shipping it. With dressed meat, however, packers could transport a far higher percentage of usable beef, lowering

MARKET ROOM

Cattle carcasses, also known as dressed beef, were stored in large rooms cooled with ice, like the one shown in this late-nineteenth-century Chicago packinghouse. The meat was then shipped to butchers, who cut it up for sale to consumers. (Library of Congress)

transportation costs and passing some of the savings on to consumers. Meat-packers also encouraged distributors to slice the dressed beef up into a variety of cuts to enhance its appearance in order to lure consumers into buying more on impulse.[10]

By World War I, meatpacking had diffused across the Great Plains. Chicago still led the nation in production, followed by Kansas City, Omaha, and St. Louis, and the so-called Big Five companies accounted for roughly half of all red meat produced in the nation. These giants controlled about 90 percent of all the branch houses, assuming almost complete dominance in some markets. Nearly all the beef distributed in New York City, for example, came from the Big Five.[11]

Sinclair's novel, by drawing attention to the unsanitary environment in the factories and sparking a legislative initiative, helped to restore the public's confidence in meat and thus laid the groundwork for the industry's eventual success. Sinclair actually set out not to indict meat but to alert people to the brutal labor conditions present in the plants. What mainly concerned him was the plight of immigrant laborers, who worked at high speeds and with new technologies that he compared to "the thumbscrew of the medieval torture chamber." The new corporate slaughterhouses dehumanized workers and made them indifferent to the fast-paced killing of living creatures. As Sinclair wrote, "It was like some horrible crime committed in a dungeon, all unseen and unheeded, buried out of sight and of memory."[12]

FAT IS KING

Before a steer made its trip from the plains grasslands to the stockyard for slaughter, it made one last stop. After grazing on the western range for a period of years, cattle journeyed to Iowa or Illinois. There a stock feeder purchased them and briefly fattened the animals on corn before shipping them off to the meat-packers. A symbiotic relationship emerged between the grasslands and the Corn Belt. The former reared cattle; the latter fattened them in preparation for slaughter. Grasslands and feedlots combined to produce the fat-laced beef that meat-packers found easiest to sell.[13]

Prior to the Civil War, stock feeders waited until steers were five or six years old before finishing them on grain and shipping them to market. But by the latter part of the nineteenth century, they could no longer be bothered with the five-year wait. Land was expensive in Iowa, Indiana, and Illinois, where the feedlot came to reign; to make the land pay, stock feeders felt pressured to purchase young steers—two years old—and to fatten them quickly on corn. The speedup resulted in a far more intensive and profitable use of property.[14]

By the late nineteenth century, feedlots were gaining in popularity in the Midwest, in the process allowing the meatpacking industry to further indulge consumers with fat-laden beef. When slaughtered, cattle finished on feedlot corn were fatter than animals raised on grass alone. But it took large amounts of grain to produce relatively small amounts of protein.

When the U.S. Department of Agriculture (USDA, established in 1862) created its beef grading system in 1927, it further solidified the grip that fatty meat had on the American diet. Under the USDA guidelines, the higher the fat content, the better the beef quality. By giving marbled beef its stamp of approval, the government increased pressure on stockmen to feed cattle as much grain as possible to yield the most profitable product. The new quality grades also helped to institutionalize the feedlot and made raising livestock a more factory-oriented enterprise.

Feedlots took off after World War II, when the development of aluminum irrigation pipe and hybrid varieties of sorghum transformed the southern plains into the nation's major feed grain region. The genetic enhancement of sorghum, a main source of animal feed, allowed the crop to tolerate the closely spaced plantings of irrigated farms. It also helped the crop adapt nicely to the high doses of synthetic fertilizer widely employed after the war.

Using knowledge gained from the wartime production of explosives, manufacturers made an inexpensive new breed of fertilizer that vastly increased crop yields by liberating farming from the constraints imposed by nature. Farmers formerly had relied on bacteria found on the roots of legumes to capture nitrogen from the air and restore this key soil nutrient. They grew clover and alfalfa hay, fed it to livestock, and then spread the manure over fields to supply the nitrogen that the crops had depleted from the soil. Early in the twentieth century, however, German chemist Fritz Haber and others discovered a way to produce nitrogen artificially in a laboratory. It was a stunning scientific breakthrough, and Haber went on to win a Nobel Prize. With the advent of synthetic fertilizers made from fossil fuels, farmers had access to a nitrogen source independent of soil bacteria.[15] This development further industrialized agriculture by giving farmers the freedom to specialize in either the crop or the animal end of the business.

Cattle once played a role in a diversified farming regime that integrated animals and crops. Stock produced the manure for carrying nutrients back to soils depleted by raising corn or wheat. But as occurred earlier in the city, the feedlot broke the manure and crop cycle and instead transformed cattle into virtual machines for channeling grain into fat. Cattle went from being valuable carriers of nutrients, the lifeblood of the farm system, to half-ton fat factories.

SPEEDUP

Despite these innovations at the packing plant and feedlot, it took time for beef to outdistance pork in the race to command the national palate. As late as 1950, pork still had the edge, with Americans consuming about six pounds more pig than cow per person annually. What happened to make beef the centerpiece of the U.S. diet?[16]

To begin with, a number of important changes on feedlots further streamlined beef production. In 1935, only about 5 percent of the nation's more than 40 million beef cattle were fed grain. But after World War II, giant feedlots sprung up to capitalize on the demand for high-quality cuts of meat. Grocery chains such as Safeway Store, sought prime cuts to cater to more affluent and discriminating consumers. Since cattle fed only on grass could not make the grade, massive feedlots stepped in. Some of these operations, such as the Texas County Feedlot, built in Oklahoma in 1965, handled as many as 50,000 animals a year.[17]

The giant new feedlots sprung up on the high plains to capitalize on the region's vast water reserves. Beneath the land gurgled a 174,000-square-mile underground reservoir known as the Ogallala aquifer that once contained a few billion acre-feet of water. Seeking to tap this source, thousands of high plains farmers petitioned for irrigation permits in the 1960s; 30 years later, these farmers had sucked more than half a billion acre-feet of water out of the ground. The plains underwent a facelift as the dry-land farming of wheat gave way to the irrigated cultivation of sorghum for cattle feed. Trucks now hauled the cattle to feedlots anywhere from Nebraska south to Texas. The animals came in such numbers that by 1970 a lane dedicated just to cattle traffic had to be added to a highway near Greeley, Colorado.[18]

For much of their lives the cattle, instead of roaming the range and eating grass, received a steady diet of grain. They would arrive at a feedlot weighing 400 pounds and double in weight within four months—a big improvement over the time it once took to finish cattle for slaughter. A number of factors helped to shorten the fattening process. First, beginning in the 1950s, stock raisers began using feeds laced with antibiotics. The steady dose of medicine promoted growth and also gave farmers the ability to confine massive numbers of animals—not just cattle, but pigs and chickens as well—in close quarters without the risk of contagious disease. The use of antibiotic feed additives skyrocketed. By the 1990s, animals consumed 30 times the amount of antibiotics used by human beings.[19]

A second factor that helped to propel weight gain was the development of the synthetic hormone DES (diethylstilbestrol). Discovered in the 1930s, DES, an artificial form of estrogen, promoted growth, increasing the weight of steers by between 15 and 19 percent. By the 1950s, DES was commonly employed in feedlots. Feedlot managers had grown so attached to the drug that when its use was finally banned in 1979 because of the dangers it posed to human health, they ignored the prohibition and continued to implant animals—some 427,275 cattle alone—with it.[20]

While antibiotics and hormone therapy shortened the time cattle spent on the feedlot, another set of changes hastened the slaughtering process. Technologically speaking, there had been relatively little change on the killing floors of packing plants between 1930 and 1960. Then, in the 1960s, a host of new instruments—stunners, hide skinners, electric knives, and power saws—increased productivity in meatpacking by nearly 50 percent.[21]

With the old Big Five hobbled by federal antitrust actions, a new generation of firms arose to take advantage of the technological changes revolutionizing beef production. Chicago, Kansas City, and St. Louis, once the nation's major packing centers, gave way to new plants built in Denison, Iowa; Dakota City, Nebraska; Holcomb, Kansas; and elsewhere on the Great Plains near the giant feedlots, thereby reducing transportation costs. Iowa Beef Packers (IBP), founded in 1960, proved the most innovative of the new generation of firms. Over the course of the next 20 years, the company constructed factories in Iowa, Nebraska, Minnesota, Texas, and Kansas. In 1981, it built a 14-acre meat plant in Holcomb, a state-of-the-art facility that ranked as the largest slaughterhouse in the world.[22]

IBP's greatest innovation was "boxed beef." In 1967, the company took the earlier dressed beef idea one step further: it began wrapping beef in individual packages instead of shipping entire carcasses. If it was more efficient to ship sides of beef, as opposed to live animals, it was even more profitable to load trucks and railroad cars with tightly fitting boxes. "A side of beef has an awkward shape—it can't be neatly packed, and a side has a lot of bone and trim that will never go into the meat case," explained one IBP executive. "It was logical to move to boxed beef"—logical, that is, under a system bent on endless accumulation of capital. It was not long before the operators of feedlots insisted on buying cattle with a uniform size, weight, and genetic stock so that when cut they would fit nicely into a box. Boxed beef saved on transportation costs and also allowed supermarkets to rid themselves of many highly paid butchers, with IBP shipping a product cut specifically for the retail trade.[23]

In 1970, the company changed its name from Iowa Beef Packers to Iowa Beef Processors to reflect the streamlining of its slaughtering operation. By using capital-intensive technology to simplify and speed up the killing and cutting of animals, IBP was able to employ cheap immigrant labor, often Mexicans or Laotians. As IBP's chief executive officer put it in 1980, "We're proud of our workers, but basically we can teach anybody to do a job in our plant in 30 days or less—they don't need the skills of an old-time butcher who had to know how to cut up a whole carcass." The disassembly line, with its chutes, chains, and conveyor belts, moved so quickly that in one IBP plant workers were denied bathroom breaks. Others resorted to taking methamphetamines to stay alert. The pace of the line made meatpacking one of America's most dangerous trades. The fact that states hosting the nation's largest feedlots also tended to be solidly anti-union did not help.[24]

By 1980, IBP had become the leading boxed beef processor in the nation, slaughtering 5.7 million cattle in its 10 plants annually. Behind it lurked giants such as Cargill and ConAgra, which also championed the new, neater trend in packaging. In 1976, Americans consumed nearly 130 pounds of beef per person, more than double the amount they had eaten in 1950. The sudden and enormous rise in beef eating, however, was not simply the result of developments in feedlots and packinghouses.[25]

TWO ALL-BEEF PATTIES

More than anything else, it was the rise in popularity of the fast food hamburger that launched Americans on a bovine extravaganza. The hamburger's origins are obscure. As far back as the 1830s, something called a hamburg steak was served at Delmonico's restaurant in New York City. White Castle, founded in 1921 in Wichita, Kansas, was the first company to promote the hamburger as a form of fast food. Spreading from Kansas to cities across the Midwest and then to markets in the East, White Castle sold its burgers for five cents apiece and catered mainly to a working-class clientele, often building locations near factories. In one banner week in 1925, the company sold over 84,000 burgers, stuffed into insulated bags printed with the slogan "Buy 'em by the Sack."[26]

Not until the 1950s did fast food restaurants assume their dominant role in American culture, in large part because of the work of McDonald's founder Ray Kroc. After his visit to the famed San Bernardino hamburger bar, Kroc bought the franchise rights from the two McDonald brothers. In 1955, Kroc opened his first restaurant in a suburb of Chicago.

Kroc realized that if he made his hamburgers bland enough, holding off on seasonings and spicy sauces, he could sell them to a wide segment of the American population, even to children. Indeed, Kroc set out to target the unsophisticated palates of children, creating the Ronald McDonald clown as a way of pitching his burgers. According to one poll conducted in 1986, 96 percent of children surveyed could identify Ronald; only Santa Claus scored higher.[27]

Kroc also seemed to have a knack for locating his restaurants. In 1959, having opened 100 stores to date, Kroc hired an airplane to help him identify the best sites for future stores. He singled out shopping centers and large intersections as he sought to tap into the nation's suburban, highway-oriented culture. Clever placement near housing developments helped him attract overworked mothers. "You Deserve a Break Today," the company sloganeered. As one foreign observer marveled, "A family of four can save Mother two hours in the kitchen, eat and drink for about $5 and get back into their station wagon in fifteen minutes flat." On less hectic days, a family might choose to linger at one of the playgrounds that soon became fixtures at McDonald's and other fast food restaurants, allowing the chains to capitalize on the decline in open space endemic to heavily developed suburban areas.[28]

Everything in McDonald's was planned, right down to the size of the hamburger patty itself: 3.785 inches across, weighing 1.6 ounces and containing no more than 19 percent fat. Kroc put earlier efficiency experts such as Frederick Taylor to shame. He sought total control, taking apart each and every step in the food preparation and service processes and detailing exactly how it was to be accomplished in a company operations manual. The first manual was 75 pages, spelling out such trivial details as the order in which to flip rows of hamburgers (third row first). Over the years, the manual grew to more than 600 pages.[29]

The assembly-line production of hamburgers was the retail counterpart to the equally efficient cattle disassembly line. In both cases, the introduction of machines and precise instructions drove down labor costs. By the late twentieth century, McDonald's was training more people than the entire U.S. Army, primarily young adults, ages 15 to 19. Like the new generation of meat-packers, McDonald's was fiercely anti-union. In the 1970s, the company staved off more than 400 unionization efforts, using lie detector tests in at least one instance to intimidate employees.[30]

McDonald's experienced extraordinary success. In 1972, the company became the largest meal-serving organization in the nation. In 1976, when beef eating in the United States peaked (it has since declined because of worries about its health effects), McDonald's sold more than 6 million hamburgers a day. By the late 1990s, one in seven visits out to eat found the American consumer headed for its Golden Arches. The orgy of hamburger eating has helped make McDonald's the world's largest beef buyer, relying on the slaughter of 3 million cattle each year in the United States alone.[31]

The rise in hamburger eating was of course good news for America's beef industry. Clever marketing by fast food companies helped the industry's market share, but so did earlier initiatives by Washington. In 1946, the USDA legally defined what a hamburger could be: under its definition, a "hamburger" could contain nothing but ground beef and beef fat. Although any kind of fat would do the job of binding together a burger to keep it from falling apart on the grill, the agency, by decreeing that only cattle fat could be used, gave the beef industry a veritable patent on perhaps the only food product more American than apple pie. Because cattle set free on open pastures and fed on grass alone do not have enough fat, the fast food companies turned to the sedentary feedlot cattle, which had a thick layer of fat that could be carved off at slaughter. In the end, the fast food companies received the ingredients for making inexpensive hamburgers, while the beef industry received a monopoly on the nation's most popular food item.[32]

The beef industry exerted tremendous clout in Washington. Beginning in the mid-1950s, at precisely the time when Americans sat poised to go on a beef-eating splurge, scientists uncovered a relationship between diets high in fat and heart disease. With evidence of fat's harmful effects mounting, the liberal senator George McGovern opened hearings in 1977 on the relationship between food and chronic diseases. His committee's report recommended that Americans "decrease consumption of meat." The National Cattlemen's Association objected to the government's advice. Shying away from doing battle with the powerful beef lobby, McGovern's committee revised its recommendation. Instead of issuing a blanket statement advising citizens to eat less meat, the committee weakened its position, counseling consumers to decrease the consumption of "animal fat, and [to] choose meats, poultry, and fish which will reduce saturated fat intake."[33]

In the early 1990s, when the USDA determined that American consumers needed more guidance in choosing healthy food, the beef industry again intervened. This time the agency came up with a food pyramid. Grains and cereals occupied the longest band at the base, vegetables and fruits occupied the layer above, and meat and dairy products the next layer up, with fats and sugary items capping off the chart. The National Cattlemen's Association cried out that the guide unfairly stigmatized beef. Its protests caused the USDA to backpedal and ultimately to postpone publication of the pyramid. When it finally released the guide, the USDA had revised its accompanying recommendations to urge consumers to eat two to three portions of meat and dairy each day, the same advice it had been giving Americans since as far back as 1958. But what really pleased the industry was the agency's modification of its stance on the upper limits of meat eating. In 1990, it had advised Americans to consume on a daily basis no more than six ounces of meat per day. Under the revised food pyramid, the upper limit was bumped up to seven ounces—yet another triumph for the beef lobby.[34]

OIL, WATER, GRASS

Oil is one of the main building blocks of the modern American steer. Raising cattle on feedlots is an immensely energy-intensive enterprise. Where some of the energy goes is readily apparent, such as the fuel needed to run farm equipment. But other energy use is less evident, such as in producing the fertilizer that farmers use to grow corn, which in the United States mainly fattens livestock. In 1990, America's cornfields accounted for roughly 40 percent of the nitrogen fertilizer consumed in the nation. One 1980 study demonstrated that it took 17,000 kilocalories of energy to produce a kilogram of beef. That is roughly equivalent to the energy in a half-gallon of gasoline, all for just 2.2 pounds of meat.[35]

Apart from being a heavy drain on the nation's energy supply, beef production requires large quantities of water. When you add together all the water it takes to produce a pound of beef—to irrigate grain, water the stock, and process the cattle—the total comes to 360 gallons. This demand for water is especially problematic on the Great Plains, home to the nation's feedlots and beef processors. By the 1990s, IBP's Holcomb, Kansas, plant used an average of 400 gallons of water to slaughter and process just one animal. That translated into 600 million gallons of water every year to process 1 million head of cattle.[36]

Cattle raising also impacted the vast landholdings of the federal government, both in national forests and in other prime pasture areas. In 1934, Congress enacted the Taylor Grazing Act to bring some semblance of order to the public domain. The act set up a system for leasing the land to ranchers and established the National Grazing Service (which later became the U.S. Bureau of Land Management) to supervise the cowboys. Although explicitly set up as a rental arrangement, the system has led permit holders to treat the leases as a form of private property, to be disposed of as the leaseholder saw fit. In other words, ranchers have at times sold something that was not theirs to sell, the right to use government-owned land to graze cattle.[37]

The low price charged ranchers for grazing permits has long been a bone of contention. The price has often been just a fraction of what the land would lease for if it were privately owned. And the government's intricate pricing formula gives ranchers an economic incentive to overstock the public range. The grazing program is yet another example of how the American state has advanced the cause of private accumulation—"cowboy welfare," in the words of radical environmentalist Edward Abbey.[38]

The predictable result has been rampant overgrazing, especially along streams, where cattle congregate to access water and to forage on level ground. A 1990 study by the Bureau of Land Management and the U.S. Forest Service (the other organization that oversees public grazing lands) revealed that only one-third of the bureau's nearly 58 million acres of holdings were in either good or excellent ecological condition.[39]

In the intermountain West—the area between the Rockies and the Sierras and Cascades—cattle have had some unforeseen consequences. Cattle are heavy, exerting on the order of 24 pounds per square inch of land. Their sheer weight, combined with their constant grazing of the native bunchgrasses, has severely disrupted the soil in vast stretches of the public range. Into this environment in the 1890s came an Old World plant that westerners called cheatgrass, a species so pernicious that it robbed farmers of their livelihood. Stockmen initially welcomed the nonnative plant, which thrives in disturbed soils. It soon became clear, however, that cheatgrass had limited value as forage. It dies quickly, and the dead grass has little nutritional content. The plant, in part because it does not stay green for long, also promotes the spread of wildfires. Cheatgrass is now the single most common plant species in this region.[40]

THE CONFINEMENT

Despite all the changes outlined here, there was one aspect of the steer's existence that did not change all that much: it still spent nearly all its life outside grazing, save for the last three months, which it spent on feedlots. The lives of chickens and pigs, however, changed far more dramatically. Beginning in the 1950s, the industrial paradigm was applied even more thoroughly to poultry and hog farming. The quaint image of Old MacDonald's farm, a peaceful scene in which roosters followed cows around the barnyard, gave way to large-scale operations founded on the confinement of colossal numbers of chickens and hogs in indoor quarters. The animals were closely monitored and controlled from birth to death. And with hog and poultry production concentrated in the hands of just a few large corporations, modern animal agriculture presented a set of formidable environmental challenges.

Back before the 1930s, chicken was considerably less popular than it is today. The meat, which was thought to be dry and unappetizing, came primarily from sterile old hens. It was the development of the broiler industry in the Delmarva Peninsula (where Delaware, Maryland, and Virginia come together) that introduced Americans to modern chicken eating as we know it. Broilers were tender, young roosters suitable, as the name suggests, for broiling (the old chickens were normally fried). The market for broilers boomed during World War II as the government's "Food for Freedom" program urged Americans to eat more chicken and leave the beef and pork for the troops.[41]

In the 1950s, when antibiotics became widely available, farmers began moving chickens from the barnyard into indoor facilities. By early the following decade, large, vertically integrated firms controlled all aspects of chicken production—hatching, feeding, and ultimately slaughtering. By the 1960s, large corporations controlled all phases of broiler production, marketing individualized brands sold directly to consumers. In 1968, Frank Perdue, whose father had entered the Delmarva broiler business during the 1930s, went on television himself to attest to the quality of his birds. "It takes a tough man to make tender chicken," he intoned, marketing his birds as a brand-name product. The Perdue company fed its birds xanthophyll, derived from marigold petals, to turn their skins from white to yellow, making them better looking and tastier. By 1970, Perdue controlled more than 15 percent of New York City's broiler market.[42]

Perdue started out processing about 18 birds per minute. Workers hung the birds by their feet, stunned them, and then slit their throats, severed the heads and feet, and vacuumed out the lungs. After that, they cut them up and wrapped them in plastic. By 1979, production had increased to 300 birds per minute. For the disassembly line to run at maximum efficiency, all the birds had to have the same body shape, driving Perdue and the other major poultry companies to take control all aspects of the growth and production process, beginning with the bird's genetic stock. The broilers were genetically engineered to grow larger thighs and breasts than wild chickens. Programmed to grow quickly, the birds reached a weight ripe for slaughter in half the time (just seven weeks) it had once taken. Capitalism encourages precisely this kind of faster growth so that profits can be invested more quickly in the name of more wealth creation.[43]

Broiler companies concentrated in the South, where the warm climate cut down on barn heating costs. In Arkansas, packing plants sprouted near where farmers, under contract with the companies, raised the birds in large confinement barns. By locating in anti-union states such as Arkansas, the companies also held down labor costs. The rise of large-scale broiler companies almost completely eliminated the small chicken farmer. Between 1974 and 1992, the percentage of sales by broiler producers selling 100,000 or more birds increased from 70 to 97 percent of the chicken sales nationally. The rise of the chicken nugget—a boneless creation perfectly suited to a society increasingly taking its meals on the run—bolstered industrial poultry still further. Today, the chicken has taken the place of the passenger pigeon as the continent's most populous bird.[44]

Likewise, antibiotic use allowed farmers to confine pigs in football field–sized buildings containing concrete and steel pens. The creatures were genetically identical and programmed to produce a leaner meat that could compete with chicken in both fat and cholesterol content. After a breeding sow delivered piglets (about every five months), workers ushered them off to a nursery and eventually to a finishing farm, where they reached a marketable weight of 250 pounds in only six months.

The man generally credited with industrializing hog farming is a North Carolinian named Wendell Murphy. Beginning in 1969, after an epidemic of cholera caused state officials to quarantine his pig herd, Murphy convinced his neighbors to take on the risk of raising hogs. He provided the pigs and feed; the farmers put up the land and labor. Murphy agreed to pay the farmers a specified price for each pig they raised to market weight. If hog prices shot up, Murphy gained; if they went down, he took a loss. But by only paying for live pigs—it was too bad for the farmers if the pigs died—Murphy shifted the risk of hog raising to others. To contract with Murphy, farmers had to build large confinement barns, structures that became more automated and expensive over time. Predictably, the number of hog farms nationwide declined precipitously (from 600,000 to 157,000 between 1984 and 1999) as fewer, larger indoor settings corralled the animals.[45]

In the year 2000, Smithfield Foods acquired Murphy Family Farms, making it the largest hog raiser and pork producer in the world. Taking its cue from the giant chicken firms, Smithfield employed vertical integration, controlling all aspects of pork production from the pig's birth to its conversion into bacon and other products. "There's only one way to get consistency—that's to have common genetics, feed the animals the same way and process them the same way," remarked Smithfield chief executive officer Joseph Luter.[46]

In the early 2000s, Smithfield operated a nearly 1 million–square-foot plant in Tar Heel, North Carolina, that dispatched 32,000 hogs in an average day. The concentration of hog farms and meatpacking plants in North Carolina over the last 20 years is no accident. Anti-union sentiment, low wages, and lax environmental regulations, some of which were advanced by none other than Wendell Murphy himself (who served as a state senator in the 1980s and early 1990s) account for the trend. By the 1990s, North Carolina was home to almost twice as many hogs as people, with 10 million creatures crammed into the state.[47]

Immense confinement barns stocking thousands of animals posed a new and daunting set of environmental problems. Chief among these was the question of what to do with the millions of tons of animal waste. By some estimates, in the late twentieth century almost 130 times more animal waste than human waste was produced in the United States each year. It amounted to approximately five tons of manure for every citizen.[48]

Back in the days when manure was integrated into the crop and nutrient cycle, animal waste posed few problems. That changed with the advent of megafarms and feedlots for producing livestock. As one environmentalist explained, "The problem is that nature never intended for 80,000 hogs to shit in the same place."[49]

To save on labor costs, workers flushed away pig manure with hoses into holes in barn floors. From there it was channeled into giant lagoons. In 1995, approximately 25 million gallons of hog waste from a 12,000-animal "barn" in North Carolina—more than twice the volume of pollutants involved in the notorious 1989 *Exxon Valdez* oil spill—overflowed out of one such lagoon. The waste eventually flowed into the New River, where it wreaked havoc on aquatic life in a 17-mile stretch. In this instance, and in all others, the high ecological costs associated with factory-style animal farms were left for the public to bear.[50] Together, vast amounts of hog and chicken waste, laden with nitrogen and phosphorus, coursed into coastal waters. In 1991, North Carolina's Pamlico Sound was the scene of a fish kill so massive that bulldozers had to be called in to bury the dead. Although the exact cause of this massive die-off and other more limited fish kills in Chesapeake Bay is not known, some scientists suspect that hog and chicken manure was the culprit. The animal waste, they surmise, set off algal blooms that depleted oxygen from the water and put stress on fish populations. The algae also helped to feed a microscopic organism named pfiesteria—dubbed "the cell from hell"—which released a toxin lethal to fish. Manure, once a vital and integral aspect of farm life, disappeared from the barnyard into the nation's waters to surface as one of the most serious environmental quandaries in modern America.[51]

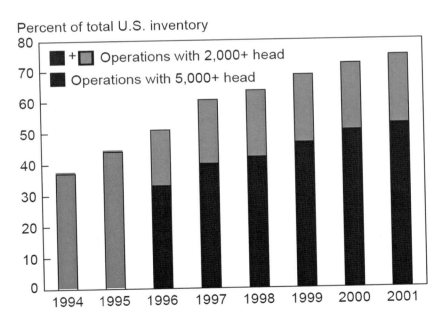

Operations with 5,000+ head were not reported prior to 1996.

INVENTORY OF LARGEST U.S. HOG FARMS

Concentrated animal feeding operations increased in size in the last half of the 1990s. (William D. McBride and Nigel Key, Economic and Structural Relationships in U.S. Hog Production, USDA Agricultural Economic Report No. 818 [2003], 5)

CONCLUSION

This chapter has tried to bring historical consciousness to bear on meat eating under advanced capitalism. Once, farm cattle fed on grass and hay; pigs ate garbage, including waste produced in some of America's largest cities; and chickens trailed cattle around the barnyard pecking grass seeds out of dung. The animals converted matter unsuitable for human consumption into a much-valued source of protein. The rise of factory-style livestock production, especially in the decades after World War II, transformed these farm animals into eating machines requiring large quantities of corn and soybeans. Livestock guzzled energy and water, shedding their old role as garbage collectors and assuming a new one as waste producers and a leading source of water pollution. Old MacDonald must have been turning over in his grave.

AMERICA IN BLACK AND GREEN

On November 14, 1956, near Topeka, Kansas, the political leadership of the state gathered to dedicate eight miles of freshly poured concrete. In time, that little stretch of pavement would evolve to link up with over 40,000 miles of what has become the greatest public works project ever carried out on the planet, an interstate highway system so vast and all-encompassing that it can even be seen from outer space. "More than any single action by the government since the end of the war," wrote President Dwight D. Eisenhower, who signed the legislation authorizing the construction of this system, "this one would change the face of America."[1]

Critics like novelist John Steinbeck, writing in 1962, claimed the freeways meant Americans could traverse the nation but not see anything, barreling down the road oblivious to any sense of place. A blander, more standardized landscape took shape in the postwar years as subdivisions, shopping centers, and fast food restaurants organized around the new highway culture. Fast food hamburger outfits remained so wedded to freeways that it took over a decade after opening in the 1950s for McDonald's to even bother to install seats and tables. A generation after Steinbeck, another critic summed up the entire postwar U.S. landscape as "the geography of nowhere."[2]

A new, literally national landscape blossomed. No longer did local plant and animal life or even contrasting agroecologies dominate the continent. Now a much more uniform American landscape unfurled based not only on highways but on the ubiquitous lawn as well. Cut off from any direct relationship with the food supply, Americans now had the luxury of planting turf grass, spending billions of dollars cultivating flawless emerald green lawns. As late as the 1930s, working-class suburbanites grew fruits and vegetables and even raised chickens and geese in their yards. Even those higher up the social scale had lawns that fell far short of the weed-free, super-green expanses that would later flourish in suburbia. Only in the period following World War II did the idea of a perfect grass monoculture materialize as garden companies tried to profit by selling Americans increasing amounts of chemical inputs as part of the elusive quest for lawn perfection.[3]

It required a lot of money to achieve a good lawn because Kentucky bluegrass and most other turf species are nonnative; growing them in North America is largely an uphill ecological battle requiring untold amounts of water, fertilizer, and pesticides. The perfect-lawn aesthetic thus meshed nicely with the needs of an economic system founded on selling consumers more and more things. By the early twenty-first century, turf covered more than 63,000 square miles of the nation—an area about the size of Florida. The lawn had become one of the nation's leading "crops." To channel German philosopher Max Horkheimer, who believed that the domination of nature was central to capitalism, landscape had descended into "landscaping" as the perfect-lawn aesthetic alienated people still further from the earth.[4]

LIVE FREE AND DRIVE

The rise of the automobile is a well-known chapter in the American past. First built in the 1890s as a luxury item for the well-to-do, the car soon underwent mass production. The man chiefly responsible for this momentous change was Henry Ford, who pioneered the use of the assembly line. In 1914, concerned that the market for cars would remain limited as long as even autoworkers themselves could not afford them, Ford began paying some of his employees five dollars per day, at the time a relatively high wage. By 1929, nearly 50 percent of all U.S. families owned automobiles, a milestone not reached in England until four decades later.

Although some opposed the automobile—early in the century, a group of Minnesota farmers, for instance, plowed up roads and strung barbed wire between trees—most Americans embraced the car with enormous enthusiasm. The automobile succeeded because it met the real, legitimate needs of people for transportation. Consumerism had reorganized people's relationship with the land in a way that transformed the car from a luxury to a necessity. Food and clothing once produced in the home, especially by women, were by the 1920s largely bought in towns and villages. By the 1930s, 66 percent of rural families and 90 percent of urban families purchased store-bought bread instead of making it themselves. More shopping meant that people spent more time in cars headed to stores. People's priorities quickly changed. In the 1920s, an inspector from the USDA asked a farmwoman why she bought a Model T before installing indoor plumbing. "Why you can't go to town in a bathtub!" she exclaimed.[5]

The impact of the car transcended its role as a convenient means of transportation. It also helped to stimulate suburbanization. The suburbs began to appear as far back as the 1840s with the advent of railroad travel, proliferating after the Civil War with the introduction of streetcar lines. By the late nineteenth century, New York, Chicago, and Philadelphia, which embraced factory production, were turning increasingly toward finance. Now, after World War I, with real estate developers far more interested in constructing office buildings than new housing, many middle-class residents left the city for the suburbs, relying on cars to shuttle them back and forth to work. By 1940, 13 million Americans lived in auto-centered communities not serviced by public transportation.[6]

If the automobile met the genuine need for transportation, especially in the more decentralized suburban environment, it also brought with it a vast amount of social baggage. Tellingly, the French term *automobile* and not the British phrase *motorcar* prevailed in the United States. *Motorcar* focused attention on the engine, the driving force behind the new form of transportation. But *automobile* suggested something far more complex: literally, self-movement. The autonomy that cars created—freeing people from train and streetcar schedules—resonated with the American ideals of freedom, individuality, and democracy.[7]

Automobiles were sold to Americans with precisely this notion of freedom and liberation in mind. A 1924 advertisement by the Ford Motor Company shows a woman persevering in the face of inclement weather. Snuggled in behind the wheel in her Ford's heated cabin, the woman sets off without worrying that snow or rain might impede her trip. Complete independence from the forces of nature is the message conveyed.

The freedom of movement that the automobile made possible came at a price, however, which people at the time recognized. "Our streets smell badly enough without the addition to the atmosphere of vast quantities of unburned gasoline," declared one observer in a 1910 issue of the magazine *Horseless Age*. Gasoline not only caused pollution, but its status as a nonrenewable resource even led some engineers and industry analysts to worry about whether an adequate supply would always remain available. As early as 1905, engineer Thomas J. Fay foresaw that "one of the great problems of the near future in connection with the popularization of the automobile will be that of an adequate and suitable fuel supply."[8]

Alternative fuels such as grain alcohol existed. But relative to gasoline, alcohol was more expensive, about double the price per gallon at the turn of the century. And that price did not include a federal excise tax placed on alcohol beginning in 1862 to help defray the Union's costs in the Civil War. In 1907, the tax was repealed. Nevertheless, the process of denaturing alcohol to render it undrinkable and help with sobriety added to its price and gave gasoline the edge. It took more alcohol than gas to cover the same distance, compounding gasoline's advantage. Added to this was the political muscle of John D. Rockefeller and his Standard Oil Company, which by the 1880s had come to dominate the U.S. oil market. Together these factors combined with the nation's long-standing concern with temperance to produce a terrible dependency of another kind.[9]

GET THE LEAD IN

Henry Ford pioneered mass production, but it was Alfred P. Sloan, Jr., the president of General Motors (GM), who figured out a way of selling everyone on the need for all these new cars. In 1927, Sloan introduced the annual model change as a way to "keep the consumer dissatisfied." He reasoned that if people saw neighbors driving around in a new car with features their own vehicle did not have, they too would soon be heading off to the showroom. Under Sloan's leadership, GM surpassed Ford as the nation's number one auto producer. The company succeeded not by offering consumers a basic, durable means of transportation—Ford's stock in trade—but by holding out the prospect of faster cars that grew more stylish, more colorful (with the advent in the 1920s of lacquer-based paints), and larger with every passing year. It was a stroke of genius that set the stage for GM's decades-long dominance within the industry.[10]

Leaded gasoline was the key to fulfilling Sloan's ambitions for GM. Early on, cars had to be cranked by hand to start. But in 1911, the invention of the self-starter eliminated the laborious task of hand cranking, allowing more people to take to the roads. Automakers could now produce cars with larger, easy-to-start engines. The electrical breakthrough had one drawback: customers noted a knocking sound coming from the engine.[11]

Not long after the invention of the self-starter, the staff at Dayton Engineering Laboratories Company (DELCO) discovered that ethanol, or grain alcohol, when burned in a car's engine, helped to remedy the problem of the "knock." The problem with grain alcohol, however, at least as the oil companies saw it, was that anyone, even ordinary people, could make it. In 1921 research chemist Thomas Midgley, who was working at DELCO, now owned by GM, discovered that tetraethyl lead also functioned as an excellent antiknock agent. The oil and lead interests rejoiced. (Later, Midgley went on to invent Freon, the first chlorofluorocarbon. Americans received better air conditioners, deodorants, and hair sprays as a result, but future generations would pay the price for them in the form of skin cancer as the compounds damaged the ozone layer, which shields the earth from the harmful effects of ultraviolet radiation. Midgley, in the words of historian J. R. McNeill, "had more impact on the atmosphere than any other single organism in earth history.")[12]

In early 1923, the first gallon of leaded gas was pumped in Dayton, Ohio. The following year, GM, the Du Pont Chemical Company (which controlled roughly one-third of GM's stock), and Standard Oil of New Jersey, combining various patents, manufactured leaded gasoline under the "Ethyl" brand name. A few months before Ethyl went on sale, William Mansfield Clark at the U.S. Public Health Service came forward to explain that tetraethyl lead—considered a neurotoxin today—was exceedingly poisonous and a danger to public health.[13]

In 1922, U.S. Surgeon General H. S. Cumming wrote a letter to Pierre du Pont, chairman of the board of the chemical company, inquiring about the health hazard posed by leaded gasoline. The public health effect of leaded gasoline received "serious consideration," Midgley wrote, but "no actual experimental data has been taken." Despite the lack of evidence, Midgley believed that "the average street will probably be so free from lead that it will be impossible to detect it or its absorption." With no studies to draw on, how could Midgley have been so sure of its safety? That remains a mystery, and a doubly curious one given that shortly before responding to Cumming, Midgley had come down with lead poisoning.[14]

In 1923, General Motors, reasoning that an in-house scientific study would be viewed skeptically, agreed to finance the U.S. Bureau of Mines to study the safety of tetraethyl lead. The following year, the newly formed Ethyl Gasoline Corporation negotiated a new research contract with the bureau that required the government agency to submit its results to the company for "comment, criticism, and approval." This was not going to be a disinterested piece of research. The bureau soon issued a report downplaying leaded gasoline's potential adverse impact on public health. The report prompted one rival car manufacturer to ask whether the bureau existed "for the benefit of Ford and the GM Corporation and the Standard Oil Co. of New Jersey, . . . or is the Bureau supposed to be for the public benefit and in protection of life and health?"[15]

The bureau's one-sidedness caused some in the scientific community to object. Alice Hamilton, a physician who studied the industrial use of lead and its medical effects (and the first woman faculty member of Harvard Medical School), doubted the safety of leaded gasoline. In 1925, Yandell Henderson, a physiologist from Yale University, predicted that if the industry had its way, lead poisoning would emerge slowly but "insidiously . . . before the public and the government awaken to the situation."[16] He turned out to be right. With the burning of huge quantities of gasoline (especially in the three decades after 1950), lead was deposited on the soil and, unknowingly, tracked into houses across the nation. There, it was ingested by infants crawling on the floor, interfering with nervous system development and contributing to hyperactivity and hearing loss, although it would be decades, as Henderson had surmised, before the full scope of the problem surfaced.

In 1926, another federal study again found "no good grounds for prohibiting the use of ethyl gasoline." The authors did note that widespread use of leaded gasoline at some point might present a health hazard and urged additional follow-up studies, but none were conducted. Instead, the manufacturers of the product financed all the research into leaded gasoline's safety. Although Midgley and others in the auto, oil, and chemical industries knew about other more benign alternative additives (ethyl alcohol blends, for example), they pushed the use of lead, probably because of the profits corporations gained from its sale.[17]

Leaded gasoline allowed Detroit to boost performance and sell more automobiles, but at a high biological price. Even something as pernicious as radioactive waste breaks down over the long run, but not lead. In the United States alone, automobiles released 7 million tons of lead between the 1920s and 1986, when it was phased out as automakers switched over to catalytic converters. Ethyl is gone, but the lead remains, having insinuated itself into the air, water, and soil.[18]

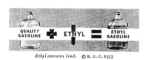

RAIN STORMS will play tricks on you. And so will an old motor—unless it has Ethyl.

But stop beside the pump that bears the Ethyl emblem every time you need gas and then you *know* what your car will do.

It will run its best all the time!

You don't always want top speed—or flashing pick-up—or the extra power it takes to zoom over hills in high. But when you do, you *want 'em!* And when you're driving at moderate speed, Ethyl makes the difference between real pleasure and just going somewhere. It brings back the *fun* you used to get from your car.

Stop at an Ethyl pump and discover what millions of others know today: *The next best thing to a brand-new car is your present car with Ethyl.* With oil companies selling Ethyl at only 2c a gallon over the price of regular, you can't afford not to use it. The savings Ethyl makes in repairs and upkeep more than offset this new low premium. Ethyl Gasoline Corporation, New York City.

NOW

SOLD BY OIL COMPANIES AT

only **2**c PER GALLON

over "regular"

Ethyl contains lead. © E. G. C. 1933

NEXT TIME STOP AT THE ETHYL PUMP

"THIS CAR NEEDS ETHYL"

The makers of Ethyl gasoline touted the power and pickup that came with the use of their product but chose not to highlight the lead that was one of its main ingredients. (Time, November 20, 1933)

MASS TRANSIT MELTDOWN

It would take more than speed and style to ensure the auto's dominance over mass transit. Rising numbers of automobiles in the 1910s and 1920s did not spell the end of public transportation. In fact, if the figures on mass transit are broken down, some cities—including St. Louis, New York, and Chicago—actually showed an increase in ridership between 1918 and 1927. *population increase* GM's effort to spur consumption through model changes and the introduction of faster, more stylish cars was partly a response to the continued vitality of public transportation. But even these changes failed to give the industry the boost in sales it longed for. The situation, GM concluded, called for stronger measures.[19]

Not that public transportation was without problems. Streetcar companies throughout the nation were buckling under debt. Municipal regulations saddled them with low fares and often prevented the elimination of unprofitable routes. And some evidence points to significant dissatisfaction among riders. All these trends placed the industry in jeopardy before 1920 but did not themselves lead to its demise. It would take the auto, truck, tire, and oil companies, in league with the federal government, to help accomplish that.[20]

In 1932, GM launched a plan to buy up urban transit systems throughout the nation and replace the trolleys with buses, another one of its product lines. One theory has it that the company did this not so much to destroy mass transit as to create a market for its diesel buses. Joining forces through a complex interlocking directorate with a group of jitney companies—the streetcar's competition—GM spent 18 months in the mid-1930s putting New York City's trolley system, one of the world's largest, out of business, substituting buses in the process.[21]

In 1936, GM formed National City Lines, a consortium made up of Firestone Tire and Rubber, Phillips Petroleum, Standard Oil of California, and Mack Manufacturing, the truck company. Over the course of the next decade, the group took control of almost 40 transit companies located in 14 states. It also acquired a controlling interest in a number of other companies located in four additional states.[22]

Eventually the federal government caught on to the National City scheme, and in 1947 a grand jury indicted the company and its affiliates—GM, Firestone, and others. Prosecutors brought suit against the consortium for violating the Sherman Antitrust Act (1890), which prohibits companies from conspiring to restrain trade. The government argued that the National City group required the streetcar companies to pledge never to use electric trolleys and forced them to buy supplies—buses, tires, and so on—exclusively from the consortium. The case dragged on for eight years; in the end the government triumphed. Although acquitted of the more serious charge of conspiring to restrain trade, the group was found guilty of having entered into a "collusive agreement" to monopolize the transit market. It was, however, a hollow victory. GM alone sold buses to National City worth roughly 25 million dollars, and yet it and the other guilty companies walked away with fines of 5,000 dollars each, the convicted executives with just a one-dollar penalty.[23]

Meanwhile, Franklin Roosevelt's New Deal was funneling huge amounts of money into building roads but little into mass transit. As far back as 1916, the Federal Road Act had made funds available to states to establish highway departments. Legislation passed in 1921 set up the federal Bureau of Public Roads and outlined a plan for a network of highways linking cities with populations of more than 50,000. Under the New Deal road building began in earnest: nearly half of the 2 million people employed in New Deal programs worked constructing roads and highways. During the decade of the 1930s, the nation's total amount of surfaced roads doubled, to more than 1.3 million miles, while mass transportation languished. Public transit commanded just a tenth of the funds that the Works Progress Administration expended on pavement.[24]

America was well on its way to becoming what one critic has termed an "asphalt nation," as a variety of forces—serious weaknesses in the streetcar industry, GM's quest to sell buses, and the state-sponsored building of roads during the Depression—limited the choices available to consumers. No outright conspiracy worked to defraud the American public; people had a certain measure of control over the auto-centric decisions they made. Many no doubt enjoyed the pleasures that came with driving a car. But that said, all the freedoms that accompanied automobile culture often distracted people from the role corporate capitalism played in shaping their lives.

TO BUILD IS HUMAN?

If not for World War II, the automobile's rise no doubt would have continued unabated. The war, however, put a dent in American auto culture. The production of cars for civilian use ended temporarily, and gas rationing began. Posted highway signs read "Victory Speed 35 Miles Per Hour" to save both oil and rubber in order to aid the Allied cause. Mass transit ridership increased, while the number of miles Americans traveled in cars fell from 334 billion to 213 billion between 1941 and 1944.[25]

The war years represented a moment of ecological and social possibility, a brief period of innovation that bucked the trend toward more automobiles and more roads. In the Los Angeles area, a place now known for its love affair with the car, there arose a housing development that shunted the automobile to the periphery. Completed in 1942, Baldwin Hills Village consisted of garden apartments built around inviting expanses of open space. This pedestrian-friendly community turned out to be one of the city's most vibrant neighborhoods.[26]

But when the war ended, the nation's romance with the car reemerged to take command of the American landscape. On July 3, 1945, the Ford Motor Company, which had suspended civilian production in 1942, built its first new sedan for domestic use. It took just a month for the assembly lines to raise production to 25,000 cars per day. Soon thereafter the nation's roads and streets became choked with traffic. "AVENUE TRAFFIC IS TIED UP BY CROSS-STREET CONGESTION," proclaimed one New York newspaper, a headline that would seem silly today.[27]

Even before the war, city planners had discovered that building more roads to solve traffic problems did not always work. In fact, under some circumstances adding a new road to relieve congestion actually made the traffic move even more slowly—a condition known as Braess's paradox, after the German mathematician, Dietrich Braess, who first explained the problem in 1968. Although the theory behind the paradox was still unformulated in the 1940s, New York City planners watched firsthand as new bridges and roads went in only to find that they worsened traffic on both the new and the old routes.[28]

Such complexities were lost on Robert Moses, a road builder to match any in history. Born in 1888, Moses held a long list of public appointments, including stints as the head of New York City's Park Commission and the Triborough Bridge and Tunnel Authority. For four decades, Moses wielded power in one capacity or another in New York, using his influence to help reshape the city and the surrounding areas into the megalopolis that it is today. Just about every major highway that exists in the New York City area was a Moses creation: the Van Wyck, the Bruckner, the Major Deegan, the Whitestone, the Clearview, the Cross-Bronx, the Staten Island, the Brooklyn-Queens, and the Long Island expressways. He also was responsible for building 416 miles of parkways, roads that barred trucks and stretched out into the surrounding Long Island suburbs. The major bridges that he planned included the Triborough, the Verrazano, the Bronx-Whitestone, and the Throgs Neck.

Before Moses came along, rarely was a highway built within the confines of an American city. There were roads that connected one city with another, roads that existed on the outskirts of urban areas, but few roads barreled straight through the heart of a metropolis. Under his leadership, that changed. The expressway was Moses's stock in trade. To the question of what to do with the people and buildings in the way of such roads, Moses had a simple answer: "You can draw any kind of picture you like on a clean slate and indulge your every whim in the wilderness . . . but when you operate in an overbuilt metropolis, you have to hack your way with a meat ax." Moses dislocated an estimated 250,000 people from their homes in his road-building exploits. "You can't make an omelet without breaking eggs," he was fond of saying.[29]

But Moses did more than just uproot a quarter-million people. His environmental legacy has been even more profound. The roads he built, with nary a thought given to mass transit, brought suburbanization, at a furious pace, in their wake. And because the suburbs had fewer people per given unit of space than higher-density cities, they would be unable, until far into the future, to support mass transportation systems. This made roads a self-fulfilling

RIDE TOGETHER

WORK TOGETHER

SAVE RUBBER

FOR VICTORY

PHILADELPHIA METROPOLITAN WAR TRANSPORTATION COMMITTEE
MAYOR BERNARD SAMUEL   ROBERT A MITCHELL, ADMINISTRATOR WP A

"RIDE TOGETHER, WORK TOGETHER"

In 1942, the Japanese blocked American access to Asian rubber, stimulating a call for carpooling to conserve this precious resource. (Library of Congress)

prophecy. As a result, Long Island became a giant parking lot, with commuters inching back and forth between suburban homes and jobs in New York City.

No road did more to transform Long Island into a suburban auto-centered sprawl than the Long Island Expressway (LIE). In 1955, the year workers fired up bulldozers to make way for the LIE, approximately 90,000 drivers made the commute from the island into the city. In the next 30 years, went the prediction, population growth would double the number of commuters.

The LIE was originally designed as a six-lane road—three lanes in each direction. A single lane could handle roughly 1,500 automobiles per hour, giving the road a capacity of 4,500 cars in each direction. The road, in other words, would be able to handle just 5 percent of the island's 1955 commuter population.[30]

Recognizing that the numbers did not add up, some foresighted planners advised setting aside the center of the expressway for mass transit. That system would be able to accommodate 40,000 people each hour, nearly 10 times what the road could carry. One study estimated the cost of the mass transit option at 21 million dollars, minuscule compared to the 500 million dollars earmarked for the expressway. Moses would hear none of it. He forged ahead with the expressway before the mass transit study was even completed, making it impossible to add the track without spoiling the work already accomplished. Moreover, by failing to acquire the rights of way (the space necessary to build such a mass transit system), Moses foreclosed it as a future option. Whenever planners returned to study the feasibility of increasing public transportation, they discovered that acquiring the land on either side of the expressway—now densely packed with homes and businesses—was prohibitively expensive. Moses built his road, and commuters to this day are paying the price. (Although the Long Island Rail Road predated Moses, by the time he left office in 1968, it had declined to such a degree that one reporter described it as "the kind of train that, if smaller, would make your little boy cry if he found it under his Christmas tree.") Ironically, Moses never learned to drive.[31]

What happened in New York was hardly unique. Beginning in the 1950s, planners nationwide began ramming highways through cities, linking urban centers with surrounding suburbs and shortchanging mass transit in the process. The driving force behind all the road building and suburban expansion was a set of federal programs that had one thing in common: they conceived of cities as outmoded and sought to help residents—or at least white residents— escape them.[32]

Nothing encouraged the flight to the suburbs more than the Federal-Aid Highway Act of 1956. By the 1950s, a number of special interest groups— the automobile industry, truckers, bus operators, oil companies, the asphalt and construction industries, plus various labor unions—had lined up to support federal funding of more roads. And if this coalition of powerful lobbying groups was not enough, the Cold War gave legislators another reason to support an elaborate road network. The reasoning went as follows. The threat of a nuclear attack made it imperative for the nation's population not to congregate in large urban agglomerations. Small-scale cities and low-density suburban communities connected by a vast network of superhighways would thus help ward off the Red Menace.[33]

In 1954, President Dwight Eisenhower formed a committee to explore the nation's need for roads. Its chairman was Lucius Clay, who held a seat on

ROBERT MOSES

Robert Moses, pictured here in 1938, probably did more than any other single individual to transform the landscape of the New York metropolitan area. (Getty Images)

the General Motors board of directors. The committee recommended a massive road-building program that formed the basis for nearly all the suburban sprawl that has come to define the geography of modern America. Championed in the Senate by Albert Gore, Sr., the final bill gained congressional approval by requiring that more than 2,000 miles of interstate highways be built in cities. That change gave representatives from urban areas something tangible to show constituents and ensured the act's passage. The Federal-Aid Highway Act, as the legislation was called, provided 25 billion dollars over 12 years to build thousands of miles of interstate highways. The federal government would assume 90 percent of the cost, with individual states making up the balance.[34]

Federal highway legislation boosted the bottom lines of America's automakers and the other special interests, from oil to asphalt, that lobbied for its passage. Mass transit continued on its relentless downward spiral, while expressways stretched out toward the horizon. People thronged the new roads. Annual vehicle miles increased to 587 billion in 1960—roughly equal to 62 trips to Pluto and back. Not only did the 1956 legislation earmark billions for roads, but it also set up the Highway Trust Fund, which allowed the government to tax gasoline and tires for use in building more roads. A paltry sum went to support mass transit. Is it any wonder that, as early as 1970, an automobile-centered city like Los Angeles managed to devote a third of its total land surface to roads, parking lots, and driveways?[35]

Never did the prospects for suburban expansion look brighter than in the postwar period. Not only did the federal government provide funds for roads, but it also established an entire host of programs and policies that inspired the building of homes in auto-dependent suburbs. The postwar baby boom provided the impetus for this move. To deal with the strain on the housing supply, the U.S. government, prompted by builders, guaranteed low-interest Veterans Administration and Federal Housing Administration mortgages. Just as important, changes to the federal tax code in the 1940s allowed homeowners to deduct both mortgage interest and property taxes. Renters—the vast majority of big-city dwellers—received no such deduction. The tax break amounted to a huge federal giveaway that fostered suburban real estate development at the expense of low-income renters in urban areas.[36]

In 1950, America's suburban population stood at 36 million. Twenty years later, the number had more than doubled to 74 million. In 1970, suburbanites outnumbered city dwellers and rural people. The rush to the suburbs came largely as a result of the U.S. government and its highway and housing programs. The price of suburban life has been amortized by taxpayers across the nation, with the benefits going mainly to those affluent enough to buy cars and live amidst the sprawl, not the poor and minorities left behind. Urban decay and suburban sprawl remain two sides of the same coin.[37]

THE PERILS OF SPRAWL

In 1946, the Levitt family purchased 4,000 acres of potato farms on Long Island and turned them into a town with over 17,000 houses. They named their creation Levittown. The Levitts did for housing what Henry Ford did for cars. They figured out how to mass-produce homes and bring them within reach of the multitudes, especially working-class and newly married couples. Time magazine dubbed their company, Levitt and Sons, "the General Motors" of housing.[38]

First they brought in bulldozers, a technology advanced during World War II, to level the landscape and remove whatever tree cover remained.

INTERSTATE HIGHWAY DEDICATION
The dedication of a new section of interstate highway in Wisconsin. (*Wisconsin Historical Society, photo by* Milwaukee Journal Sentinel)

Then the Levitts divvied up the production process into 27 separate steps, from the laying of the concrete foundation to the landscaping of the home. The Levitts eventually branched out to colonize old spinach and broccoli farms outside of Philadelphia. They also constructed tract housing in Willingboro, New Jersey, and ultimately inspired similar residential developments across the nation.

During each year of the 1950s, developers encroached on an area 1 million acres in extent—larger than the size of Rhode Island. On a quest to maximize profits from the land, builders left very little open space. In the New York metropolitan area, subdivisions built after World War II had just one-tenth the amount of open space reserved for parks in communities developed before the war. As early as the 1960s, planners predicted that Los Angeles County would confront a 100,000-acre shortage of recreational open space by 1975.[39]

Eager for more fresh land, developers entertained the idea of building on marshlands, floodplains, and even hillsides. "With level land near cities getting scarce and costly," *House and Home* magazine disclosed in 1953, "many builders are taking to the hills. Big islands of rolling land left high and dry in the first waves of expansion are getting a second look for development. New earth-moving equipment and techniques are making hill building possible as never before." Split-level homes, developed in the 1950s to accommodate steep grades, proliferated. In the foothills and more mountainous areas of Los Angeles County

Dear Mr. President
We Have no Place
to go when we
want to go out
in the canyon
Because there
ar going to Build
houses So could you
Set aside some
land where we could
Play? thank you four listenig
love SCOtt

BACKYARD BLUES

Suburbanization led to a major decline in open space, a trend that especially affected children. In 1962, Scott Turner, age seven, sent this letter to President John F. Kennedy. (U.S. Department of Interior, The Race for Inner Space [Washington, DC: Division of Information, 1964])

bulldozers made way for more than 60,000 houses. Suburban expansion in Southern California, however, entailed significant risks. As Los Angeles developers pressed ever harder against the San Gabriel Mountains, residents paid the price. In 1969 and 1978, the geologically active mountain chain released a torrent of debris—tons of mud and boulders, some the size of cars—that turned quiet suburban life into a nightmare.[40]

Tortilla Curtain

Wildfire posed an even more persistent menace. The foothills of the San Gabriels are covered with chaparral, a dense thicket of evergreen shrubs that flourish in a climate defined by hot, dry summers and moist, cool winters. Chaparral is extremely prone to fire; the flames actually help nurture the growth of the various small trees and shrubs in the region. When developers descended on the foothills of Los Angeles, they were building in the midst of one of North America's most flammable environments.

In a sense, suburbanites and developers conspired to bring disaster upon themselves. The rich in such places as Malibu enjoyed the beauty of the brush and the privacy it offered, even though it significantly increased the risk of fire, a point borne out in a devastating 1956 blaze. The proliferation of fire-prone wooden roofs in the postwar period boosted that hazard even further. Tragically, fashionable Southern California homeowners opposed the one strategy that experts believe could have helped ward off disaster: prescriptive burning. Setting fire to the land every five years or so reduces both the fuel load and the possibility of more serious conflagrations. Residents of toney neighborhoods objected that such a strategy would blacken the countryside and reduce property values. Instead, they relied on state and federal

MALIBU FIRE, 1956

Firefighters, who once focused on controlling outbreaks in wilderness areas, found that the Malibu disaster marked the start of a new breed of conflagration that occurred on the border between the backcountry and built-up suburban developments. (Regional History Collection, University of Southern California)

firefighters and disaster relief to bail them out when self-inflicted calamity hit. The scale of the subsidy given suburban development was simply staggering, especially when one considers that in the 1980s alone, 10,000 wildfires struck the Golden State.[41]

Ultimately, the risk of fire was divorced from the place in which it occurred, spread out for each and every American to bear. Postwar capitalism amounted to one huge exercise in risk sharing, one monstrous gift from the U.S. state to the suburbs. Without such sharing, life in suburbia would have been impossible.

HOME AND GARDEN

Just about everything we associate with the suburban home—the car, the lawn, the house—devours nonrenewable fossil fuels. For 25 years following the end of World War II, American homes consumed rising amounts of energy. In the 1960s alone, energy use per house rose an unprecedented 30 percent.[42]

But the high-energy home was not the inevitable outcome of suburban expansion. It might surprise some to learn, for instance, that in the 1940s even such mainstream magazines as *Newsweek* touted the virtues of solar design. These innovative homes were oriented toward the south to capitalize on the sun's heat in the winter and had overhangs to fend off the scorching summer sun. They saved on precious natural resources and appealed to America's wartime conservation mentality. Even into the late 1940s and early 1950s, solar homes commanded serious attention from architects, builders, and the popular press. Once again, the World War II era represented a moment of ecological possibility. As the 1950s unfolded, however, the availability of cheap heating fuels like oil and natural gas dimmed the attraction of the sun. Before too long, the federal government retreated from investing in solar research. "Our descendants 1,000 years hence may curse us for using coal, oil, and gas to heat our homes, when we might as well have used the sun," declared one solar researcher in 1954.[43]

With solar design waning in popularity, the stage was set for an orgy of suburban home energy use. In 1945, very few American homes had air conditioning, a technology available since the 1930s. But the development of cheaper and more compact units in the late 1940s caused sales to rise. Even more important, once the wartime housing shortage ended in the mid-1950s, builders had to figure out how to continue to stimulate demand for new homes. Air conditioning provided the answer. Builders found themselves in the same position as the auto industry, which responded to a saturated market by selling people on the virtues of a second car by offering station wagons and convertibles.[44]

The addition of air conditioning to new homes tempted buyers to trade up. Women who stayed at home while their husbands left for air-conditioned offices helped fuel the market for central air. The National Weather Bureau also worked to further sensitize people to heat. In 1959, the bureau issued a "Discomfort Index," a composite measure of both heat and humidity. The air conditioning industry seized on the index to stimulate sales.[45]

Between 1960 and 1970, the number of air-conditioned houses went from 1 million to almost 8 million. The energy-intensive machines added comfort to the home and unquestionably made life more bearable in the South. They also helped to lengthen the lives of those suffering from heart or respiratory disease.[46]

The suburban home's drain on energy resources also had some less obvious causes. When the Levitts and other builders cleared the land of trees, they exposed the new homes to more heat and cold, increasing the energy that had to be expended to keep the temperature comfortable inside. With the trees gone, developers then planted grass to cover up the scarred earth left behind in the building process. A quick and simple means of sprucing up the terrain, however, soon turned into a major-league obsession. Whatever complexity existed in the agricultural ecosystems that preceded suburbia gave way to a homogenous sea of green, a mass-produced landscape to accompany the mass-produced homes. Homeowners broke out lawnmowers, pesticides, fertilizers, and sprinklers and set about furiously transforming the landscape into a lush green carpet that was dependent on rampant fossil fuel use.

Landscape architect Frederick Law Olmsted pioneered the lawn in its suburban incarnation. In the 1860s, Olmsted designed a community outside of Chicago with houses set back far enough from the street to make room for a nice swath of grass. "A smooth, closely shaven surface of grass is by far the most essential element of beauty on the grounds of a suburban house," wrote lawn advocate Frank J. Scott in 1870.

Lawns may have been closely cropped ever since people gained access to reel lawn mowers, invented in the 1830s. But whatever lawns existed on the outskirts of cities—and working-class people still commonly grew vegetables and raised chickens and geese in their yards into the 1930s—were hardly the weed-free, super-green monocultures that we associate today with modern American lawn culture. Before World War II, plenty of clover and other "weeds" could be found in these expanses, because weeding was commonly accomplished by hand, if it was performed at all.[47]

During the war companies such as O. M. Scott & Sons tried to turn the lawn into a means of cultivating national unity and moral uplift. "Your lawn is the symbol of peace at home and its proper maintenance a vital factor in keeping up morale," read a 1942 advertisement for the seed company. Tending lawns may have evolved into a patriotic duty, but the idea of *perfection* in lawn care is actually a very recent invention. As late as 1950, Abraham Levitt, a founder of the iconic

American suburb, argued that there was no need to become "a slave to the lawn." Abe had no problem with clover. "Even our lowly weeds, which are just other native grasses, if kept cut to not more than two inches, help to green carpet the ground," he wrote.[48]

It turns out that the perennial species of grass that form the basis of the perfect lawn are not native to North America. Kentucky bluegrass, for example, is found naturally in the moist, cool regions of Europe and only arrived in America with the colonists. Growing bluegrass in the United States, especially in arid regions, is thus a struggle that requires significant inputs of chemicals, water, and energy, especially if a homeowner is questing after perfection, the dominant trend beginning in the 1950s.

In that decade, the Scotts Company, which grew out of O. M. Scott & Sons, began marketing the idea of perfect lawns to the American public in order to sell more of its products. As Scotts chairman Charles B. Mills put it, "Here at Scotts we refuse to recognize the virtue in weeds." The company concocted an ingenious step-by-step program designed to deliver a perfect lawn and provided retailers with reminder cards to send out to customers as spring approached. It also tapped into the postwar surge in interest in family togetherness and even marketed a grass seed that it dubbed "Family," packaged in a box that featured a happy couple and kids gathered around a barbeque surrounded by a nice big lawn.[49]

Scotts benefited financially from advances in fertilizer, herbicides, and pesticides that grew out of the military economy organized to fight World War II. Although considered a dangerous insecticide today, DDT (dichlorodiphenyltrichloroethane), first tested in the United States in 1942, saved the lives of countless U.S. soldiers and millions of others across the globe at risk of malaria. In light of its success abroad, when the war ended, DDT was deployed at home on American soil to eliminate sod webworms, chinch bugs, and other lawn pests.[50]

Likewise, the selective herbicide 2,4-D was developed by the military during the war as a chemical warfare agent. After the war, Scotts and other companies marketed it to homeowners to deal with broadleaf weeds such as dandelions and chickweed while sparing the grass plants that made up the perfect lawn. In 1947, Scotts incorporated the herbicide into a product that became the stock-in-trade of lawn perfection: Lawn Food Plus Weed Control, later renamed Weed & Feed. It is certainly true that lawns require regular fertilization, but by adding 2,4-D to the mix, homeowners were now spreading a toxin around the yard as a matter of course, whether there was a problem with so-called weeds or not. Predictably, production of 2,4-D surged to 53 million pounds by 1964. We now know that 2,4-D is persuasively linked to cancer, reproductive harm, and neurological impairment, meaning that Scotts and other chemical formulators had unwittingly launched a giant nationwide medical experiment.[51]

Another problem with 2,4-D is that it killed the clover in the lawn. Though now often thought of as a weed, clover (which is in the pea plant family) has the ability to transform nitrogen in the air and add it to the soil. In short, clover creates its own food supply. Scotts even capitalized on the evolutionary connection between clover and bluegrass by selling a product into the 1950s called Clovex. Nevertheless, chemical formulators soured on clover because it tamped down the need for consumers to purchase chemical inputs. Eliminate clover and homeowners would have to return repeatedly to the store to buy more fertilizer, which is used in lawn care not to increase yields, as in farming, but to enhance the color of the grass plants. The perfect lawn was the perfect instrument for selling more products in a capitalist economic system contending with challenges such as market saturation.[52]

By the mid-1980s, saturated markets had emerged as an even more dire problem for the producers of chemical inputs. A farm crisis brought on by a food surplus (aggravated by the U.S. grain embargo against the Soviet Union) caused crop prices to fall. Demand for chemicals declined as a result. (In any case, by this point nearly all the cropland in the United States was already being treated with pesticides.) Agrochemical companies now looked to the lawn as a potential savior, hoping that more U.S. homeowners who applied no chemicals to their yards could be seduced into either buying bags of chemicals or hiring a company such as Chemlawn (founded in 1968) to apply the inputs for them. The Scotts Company turned to more aggressive advertising, akin to the approach taken in pharmaceuticals: they urged consumers to "ask your lawn doctor" *before* detecting problems with insects or weeds so that the experts could recommend products to ward them off. The goal was to generate more consumer demand for chemicals.[53]

The result was rampant chemical overtreatment. Prior to 1940, one pound of nitrogen fertilizer per 1,000 square feet of lawn was all the experts recommended; by the 1970s, the figure had risen to eight pounds. In the early 1980s, Americans spread more fertilizer on their lawns than the entire nation of India used to grow food for its people. Excessive use of fertilizer fostered algal blooms: the nutrients ran off into rivers, only to emerge in coastal waters where they harmed aquatic life. Fertilizer also contaminated groundwater supplies and may have played a role in causing cancer, birth defects, and "blue baby syndrome," in which an infant's blood is deprived of oxygen. The profits of chemical companies, formulators, and applicators were built on the externalization of costs to the environment, consumers, and the workers who handled the toxins.[54]

The lawn has become an ideal vehicle for promoting economic growth under capitalism, luring Americans into a war they cannot win. Much of the nation's climate and geography stands in the way of triumph. But from the standpoint of those in the lawn-care industry, the fact that total victory remains elusive is, of course, a source of great profits. The unattainable quest for perfection has allowed suppliers to sell Americans on the need for an arsenal of high-energy pesticides, herbicides, and lawn tools for use in a battle that is essentially over before it starts. What Alfred Sloan accomplished with his yearly model change and postwar builders accomplished by promoting air conditioning, the nation's lawn-care industry arrived at by virtue of ecological misfortune. Turf grass species developed in colder European climes simply cannot flourish easily in this country. Consumer capitalism, a system of socioecological relations predicated on people's inability to satisfy their insatiable needs, easily took root in the American lawn.

CONCLUSION

Suburban development profoundly affected ecosystems across the continent. Taken together, lawns and automobiles redefined the American landscape, knitting the nation together in swaths of green and ribbons of black. Locking into auto-centered suburbanization has also imperiled the nation's ability to respond to future environmental challenges. Whether auto-centered suburban expansion has mortgaged the future is debatable. But there is no question that it has foreclosed, to a major extent, on the nation's ability to adapt to the ecological changes ahead.[55]

The reduction of meadow, prairie, desert, and forest habitats into a perfect-lawn monoculture is one of the singular ecological developments of modern American history, a shift that has affected not just plant life, but various birds, insects, butterflies, and small mammals. True, simplified lawn ecosystems attract large numbers of birds. But whereas the native vegetation allowed for a range of avian life, the lawn has drawn only those species—house sparrows and starlings, for example—that feed on the seeds and insects commonly found on the streamlined green expanses. From the loss of species diversity to fertilizer-induced groundwater contamination to carbon emissions from leaf blowers and mowers, the quest for lawn perfection continues to exact a high environmental toll.

Compared to the lawn, the ecological impact of the car seems far more glaring. The tendency to evaluate technology narrowly has historically focused attention on the automobile's obvious by-products: its role in generating petroleum dependence, air pollution, toxic waste, and global warming—all major effects of the nation's shift to cars as the primary means of transportation. But if we consider not just the car but the system of highways, a fuller and less recognized understanding of auto culture's impact on nature becomes evident. The creation of a national interstate highway system, like the making of a national lawnscape, has had significant effects on local habitats. When Interstate 75 slashed through Florida's Big Cypress Swamp, it split the habitat of the

Sunshine State's panther population and caused its numbers to decline. In the Northeast, road salt caused oak trees to dwindle and salt-tolerant sycamores to grow instead. The ubiquitous ragweed also dominates the roadside because it thrives on salt.[56]

The eclipse of regional ecologies by a national landscape founded on perfect lawns and interstates is one of the defining features of modern U.S. environmental history. It could never have happened as it did but for the strong support and intervention of the American state, which underwrote the infrastructure that facilitated the rise to power of modern automobile, chemical, and oil corporations.

$$14$$

THROWAWAY SOCIETY

The garbage wars began in the 1990s when New York City began running out of room for trash. At first it may have seemed like a simple problem, nothing that could not be solved by a fleet of tractor trailers carrying garbage to open spaces farther south and west. If only Virginia Gov. James S. Gilmore had not spoken up. "The home state of Washington, Jefferson and Madison has no intention of becoming New York's dumping grounds," he declared.[1] New York City Mayor Rudolph W. Giuliani responded that accepting some trash was a small price to pay for the enormous cultural benefits that tourists experienced when they came to town on vacation.

Culture in exchange for garbage seemed like a reasonable deal, unless you found yourself living in one of the unlucky places now playing host to what the city no longer wanted. "It may be out of sight, out of mind" for New Yorkers, remarked one resident of Old Forge, Pennsylvania, home to a landfill that received trash originating in Brooklyn and Queens. "But in our neck of the woods, we are the ones feeling the impact, we have the hundreds of tractor trailers every day with the New York license plates and a landfill that is tearing apart the side of a mountain." Not everyone was so negative. Charles City County, Virginia, received 3.4 million dollars in 2000 from Waste Management, Inc., for the privilege of operating a 1,000-acre landfill, the ultimate destination of waste produced in Brooklyn. "Our elementary, middle and high schools are all new and they were built from landfill dollars," the chairman of the county's board of supervisors explained. "That is a very concrete benefit." The trash-financed schools certainly gave the term *recycling* new meaning.[2]

"The important thing to remember about landfills," one scholar has noted, "is that they're not just an unfortunate byproduct of capitalism; they actually represent the success of capitalism."[3] New York's Fresh Kills landfill, opened in 1948 and closed in 2001—its piles of detritus so monumental that together they rank among the largest man-made structures in the world—was just one measure of the triumph of postwar free enterprise. What explains all this so-called success?

The answer is that marketers and industrial designers figured out ways to create continued demand for all the goods being pumped out of factories by building obsolescence into consumer products. Trash evolved into the engine of consumer capitalism. It was no accident that by 1956, Americans were junking cars roughly three years earlier than they had in the 1940s. Nor did happenstance explain how in 1969, the streets of New York City were temporary home to 57,000 abandoned automobiles , or that Americans in the 1980s began throwing out turntables to make way for compact disc players. "At the time we developed the compact disk," explained Norio Ohga of Sony Corporation, "the LP market was saturated, and the cassette market was beginning to slow down. We knew that we needed a new carrier." Profits, not sound quality, drove the compact disc revolution. In solving the problem of underconsumption, however, manufacturers created another—the trash crisis.[4]

PLANNED OBSOLESCENCE

Automakers employed annual stylistic changes like the tail fins shown here on a 1956 Cadillac Eldorado Seville to help entice consumers into trading in old vehicles for new ones. (General Motors Corp. Used with permission, GM Media Archives)

Derelict cars and old turntables made up just one small part of the solid waste stream produced by the culture of consumption, a stream that turned into a torrent as the baby boomers came of age during the 1960s and 1970s. Before the war, plastic played a very limited role in material life, incorporated mainly into radios and some furniture. After the war, with the U.S. economy organized around oil, plastics (which are made from petroleum) became ubiquitous, used in everything from dry cleaning bags and disposable pens to Styrofoam and shrink-wrap. Meanwhile, an array of disposable products from plastic silverware to paper cups enshrined cleanliness and convenience as the dominant selling points of postwar consumerism. Even the advent of computers, initially hailed as a step toward the paperless office, resulted in more wasted reams as Americans ran off multiple drafts of documents formerly produced just once on a typewriter. "People said paper would shrink with the computer—just the opposite is happening," explained the vice president of a Canadian paper mill in 2000. "Office paper is the fastest growing segment. People print out everything they see—Web sites, e-mail."[5]

THE RISE OF PLANNED OBSOLESCENCE

A consumer concerned about durability would have done well to buy a 1920s Ford Model T. The cars lasted two years longer, on average, than other passenger vehicles, a full eight years in all. "We want the man who buys one of our cars never to have to buy another," Henry Ford explained in 1922. "We never make an improvement that renders any previous model obsolete."[6]

Unfortunately, durability was bad for business, a point eventually recognized by Ford's competitor, Alfred Sloan of General Motors. In the early 1920s, GM sought competitive advantage by adopting small design changes, such as producing longer hoods to make it appear as if a more powerful engine rested underneath. Soon, however, GM was setting its sights higher with annual model changes in style and color to help compel consumers to trade up for something better. Sloan realized that he was competing not just with Ford, but with the durability of his very own cars.[7]

Sloan was a visionary ahead of his time, as the Great Depression of the following decade would soon prove. The length and intensity of the economic downturn have in part been traced to American industry's inability to manufacture the perfect consumer. Such a person would routinely opt for buying more things, returning to the showroom repeatedly. But in the auto industry at least, improvements in the durability of cars and tires in the 1920s combined with better road conditions to undercut demand. Customers did not keep returning because their former purchases proved too durable, a trend that eventually undermined the economy.[8]

"People everywhere are today disobeying the law of obsolescence," wrote a New York real estate man named Bernard London in a book titled Ending the Depression Through Planned Obsolescence (1932). London proposed that the government step in and mandate when a consumer item became "legally 'dead.'" That way "new products would constantly be pouring forth from the factories and marketplaces, to take the place of the obsolete." By the 1930s, General Electric had begun experimenting with technical changes that made lightbulbs wear out more quickly.[9]

The resource demands of World War II slowed the momentum building among business leaders for planned obsolescence. Rationing led the federal government to advise: "If you don't need it, DON'T BUY IT!" Then pent-up demand following the war gave way to an economic recession in 1957. The downturn so unnerved manufacturers that planned obsolescence soon gravitated back onto their radar. As Ford design specialist George Walker put it, "We design a car to make a man unhappy with his 1957 Ford 'long about the end of 1958." To help further this trend, GM, rather than making small stylistic changes, undertook the costly step of completely refurbishing its auto bodies every new model year.[10]

When Vice President Richard Nixon went to Moscow in 1959 to promote the virtues of capitalism over communism in the famous "kitchen debate" with Premier Nikita Khrushchev, he bragged about the tens of thousands of cars, televisions, and radios owned by Americans. Nixon tied freedom in a "classless society" to the right to consume, free from government intervention or restraint.[11] But the free enterprise symbolized by the modern American kitchen with its refrigerators and electric stoves involved some significant planning on the part of U.S. manufacturers. Ultimately, building planned obsolescence into the mass production of goods allowed companies to engineer better consumers while shifting the cost of disposing of the old products onto the environment and municipalities.

DON'T POLLUTE

No one knows who threw the first glass beverage bottle into a Vermont cow pasture. "Farmers, who comprise nearly one-third of the House membership," the New York Times reported in 1953 about a session of the Vermont legislature, "say that bottles are sometimes thrown into hay mows and that there is need to prevent loss of cows from swallowing them in fodder." The furor ended with a state ban on the containers.[12]

Packaging exploded in importance in the postwar years, though the origins of the trend are rooted in the earlier emergence of consumerism. In the nineteenth century, everything from pickles to flour to toothbrushes was sold in bulk. The move toward packaging consumer items began in the late nineteenth century. In 1899, the National Biscuit Company patented a cardboard and wax paper carton for selling crackers, once sold out of a barrel. The new In-Er-Seal carton, the company informed consumers, shielded the biscuits from moisture, keeping them fresh. Prophylactic Tooth Brushes even went so far as to sell buyers on the very package itself, not simply what it contained. Packages, went the sales pitch, worked to protect consumers from germs spread as people rummaged through piles of loose brushes.[13]

Plastic packaging later became ubiquitous as oil, the building block of plastic, emerged as the driving force behind the postwar economy. Everything from meat to toys to green beans came wrapped in plastic. By 1964, every American consumed a staggering 2,000 packages on average per year. The title of a 1957 article in *Better Homes and Gardens* epitomized the trend: "Wastebaskets—Do You Have Enough?"[14]

An entire industry soon emerged to service the packaging needs of consumer products manufacturers. In response to a 1953 Vermont ban on non-refillable bottles, the American Can Company and the Owens-Illinois Glass Company, pioneers of throwaway cans and glass bottles, formed a trade group called Keep America Beautiful. (Even through the 1960s, companies typically sold beverages in thick glass bottles and collected, washed, and reused them.) Joined by Coca-Cola and other companies with a stake in promoting convenient throwaway containers, the group enlisted schools and churches in a media campaign that focused on the misbegotten behavior of individual "litterbugs" as a way to forestall any more industry regulation. Instead the group supported fines and jail terms for littering and even succeeded in persuading Vermont legislators to eliminate the state's bottle ban in 1957.[15]

Keep America Beautiful produced one of the most successful public service announcements in history. The 1971 commercial featured actor Iron Eyes Cody playing a Native American who cries at the sight of litter tossed onto the road. "People start pollution," the advertisement declared. "People can stop it." No mention was made of the corporations that had a stake in the nation's solid waste woes. The commercial located responsibility at the individual level, drawing attention away from the major role that industry itself played—through its relentless efforts at increasing consumption—in perpetuating waste.

In the 1970s, with the environmental movement in full swing, a battle erupted between industry and those opposed to the throwaway ethic. Plastic had come to symbolize the nation's materialistic impulse. In a famous scene from the 1968 movie *The Graduate*, a family friend tells Dustin Hoffman: "I just want to say one word to you. Just one word . . . Plastics. . . . There's a great future in plastics." Beverage companies first began using plastic bottles two years after the film's release. In 1976, more plastic was manufactured, in terms of cubic volume, than all steel, copper, and aluminum combined. Seeking to stem the flood of disposable items, Oregon in 1971 established a five-cent refundable deposit for bottles to give people a financial incentive to return the containers for reuse or recycling. Vermont later followed suit. The following year, Minnesota passed an even stronger measure that tried to restrict the amount of packaging used by industry. "Recycling of solid waste materials is one alternative for the conservation of material and energy resources," read the law, "but it is also in the public interest to reduce the amount of materials requiring recycling or disposal."[16]

By 1976, states and communities were considering measures to restrict the growth of packaging. Calling proponents of such measures "Communists," William May of the American Can Company mobilized Keep America Beautiful and challenged these moves in court, succeeding in large part by decade's end. Industry triumphed because it cleverly tied the reform measures to the loss of jobs. The group also recruited the power of consumer freedom to its cause. In an effort to forestall a national beverage deposit law, Donald Kendall, president of Pepsi, wrote the Environmental Protection Agency in the 1970s to complain. "Your position defies and denies the free will of the people expressed by their free choice of containers," he declared.[17] The postwar American dream rested on a seductive vision of material abundance, free expression, and individual responsibility for the waste that kept the nation's landfills growing.

SOME THINGS ARE FOREVER

Corporate capitalism rested on convenience and disposability, but durability too has had important ecological consequences. On the one hand, modern consumer culture has broken the local recycling systems of the past, and on the other, it has turned out products so durable that they threaten never to go away.

Consider plastics, which, measured by weight, have gone from composing a mere 0.5 percent of total solid waste in 1960 to 8.5 percent in 1990, a steady, although hardly explosive, increase. These figures, however, are by weight, which is why they are commonly cited by the plastics industry. In terms of volume, the impact is far greater, with the substance making up anywhere from 16 to 25 percent of the waste stream.[18]

In recent years, plastics have been "light-weighted," somewhat reducing their impact. Plastic grocery bags were 40 percent thinner in the early 1990s than in the mid-1970s. While plastics take up less room in landfills, they can take hundreds of years to degrade. Although it is possible to make the substance break down more quickly, it requires a complex and expensive production process. The "greener" plastic also takes up as much if not more room than the nonbiodegradable kind. Indeed, the entire idea of biodegradable plastic may be little more than a scheme to allow corporations to falsely market green products. "Degradability is just a marketing tool," a representative of the Mobil Chemical Corporation once admitted. "We're talking out of both sides of our mouths because we want to sell bags. I don't think the average consumer even knows what degradability means. Customers don't care if it solves the solid waste problem. It makes them feel good." And besides, most manufacturers choose plastic precisely because it is so durable and resistant to decay.[19]

Plastics may well represent a greater ecological threat at sea than on land. In the 1980s, commercial fleets jettisoned an estimated 52 million pounds of packaging into the ocean every year, in addition to 300 million pounds of plastic fishing nets. Tens of thousands of sea mammals, birds, and fish died in a plastic tidal wave. One estimate placed the number of fish with plastic lodged in their stomachs, interfering with digestion, at 30 percent of the total population.[20]

With respect to disposal, rubber, a material every bit as important as plastic to the culture of consumption, has posed an even greater environmental challenge. The problems with rubber derive from modern society's love affair with the road. Early in the century, rubber was extracted from Brazil—where workers went from tree to tree making cuts and capturing the latex within—in order to meet the rising demand for tires. By the end of World War I, however, major plantations built on Asia's Malay Peninsula had eclipsed the Amazon as the world's leading rubber source.

In the years after World War II, as the automobile rose to dominance, America's stockpile of used tires began to grow. At first the increase was slow because the discarded rubber could be reused for making new tires. Beginning in the 1960s, however, tire manufacturers began to reject recycled rubber. The advent of the steel-belted radial, increasing concern with tire safety, and a surplus of synthetic rubber all contributed to the downfall of tire reprocessing. Nor did it help that the new generation of steel-belted radial tires proved harder to recycle.[21]

The result was predictable: a massive buildup of used tires. By the 1980s, Americans junked roughly one tire for every man, woman, and child, some 200

TIRE DUMP

Piles of discarded tires, like these in Kilgore, Texas, littered the American landscape as early as the 1930s. (Library of Congress)

to 250 million, each year. Of that amount, an estimated 168 million entered either landfills or junkyards.[22]

The problem with tires is that like old ghosts, they have a way of returning to haunt us. Bury them with a bulldozer and they will eventually resurface as they expand back to their original shape. So the operators of dumps routinely collected them and put them in piles. Soon the piles grew into mountains. By 1990, somewhere between 2 and 3 billion scrap tires existed nationwide. California, with its affinity for auto transport, led the country in such refuse in the 1990s, with roughly 28 million tires located at 140 sites.[23]

What harm is there in tire mountains? Unexpected biological consequences have been one result. Beginning in the 1970s, a market arose in the United States for used tires imported from Japan and other Asian countries. (Japanese drivers are apparently more finicky than their American counterparts, who are untroubled by buying slightly worn tires.) The tires made the trip overseas and so, evidently, did the Asian tiger mosquito (*Aedes albopictus*), which can transmit a number of diseases to humans, including malaria and some forms of encephalitis. Tires retain water and provide ideal breeding environments for mosquitoes. In 1984, the Asian mosquito surfaced in several Houston tire dumps. By 1997, the insect, hitching a ride in tires hauled around the vast interstate highway system, had expanded into 25 states, although no evidence linked the mosquito to the onset of disease in the United States.[24]

Of more concern is the fire threat. Since the 1980s, a number of blazes have broken out at tire dumps around the country (and in Canada) as lightning, arson, and spontaneous combustion have ignited huge stockpiles of rubber. In 1983, a fire at a Virginia tire dump blazed for a full nine months. Somewhere between 5 million and 7 million tires burned to produce 250,000 million gallons of toxic sludge. "You don't know what Hell's going to look like," said one volunteer firefighter, "but you had that feeling about it."[25] A 1998 California tire fire smoldered for more than a year because officials feared that suppressing it might contaminate groundwater. And in 1999, what has been described as the West's largest tire pile, near Westley, California, went up in smoke after a lightning strike, igniting a blaze so fierce it required the state to hire a crew of professional firefighters from Texas to extinguish the inferno.

The fire threat has helped to spur recycling, which increased markedly in the 1990s. Scrap tires are used to make roadways, to cover landfills, and in place of rock as a substitute drainage material. They are also burned to make cement. But market imperatives undercut such efforts. The demand for recycled rubber simply cannot keep pace with the millions of tires Americans heave onto their trash heaps each year. As one scrap tire expert put it, "Tires, like diamonds, are forever."[26]

DUMPED ON

Between 1940 and 1968, Americans doubled the amount of solid waste, per capita, they produced each day, from two to four pounds. To deal with the garbage, cities built sanitary landfills. Earlier in the century, municipalities had relied on incinerators. But they were expensive to build, and burning garbage severely compromised air quality. In the years following World War II, the number of municipal incinerators fell from 300 to just 67 in 1979. Landfills took up the slack. A dump involved ditching garbage willy-nilly. A landfill, thought to be a concept invented by the British in the 1920s, involved burying the detritus with dirt on a daily basis, a practice designed to eliminate the foul smell of decomposing organic matter. The idea left open the possibility that the landfill might be landscaped and transformed into real estate when its capacity for garbage had been exhausted. Although landfills may have appeared in America early in the twentieth century, they sprang up in great numbers after 1945. Roughly 100 landfills existed when the war ended and 1,400 a decade and a half later.[27]

The notorious Fresh Kills landfill in Staten Island, New York, opened in 1948. Robert Moses planned to fill the area with garbage for about two decades and then turn the site into viable real estate suitable for homes, parks, and light industry. Before its reinvention as a dumping ground for New York City's trash, Fresh Kills was a tidal wetland. Indeed, the word kill is Dutch for creek. In the 1940s, scientists had yet to realize that wetlands (a term ecologists only first employed in the 1950s to replace the pejorative *swamp*) serve an important ecological role. They absorb and filter water and thus help prevent floods while preserving water quality. Unaware of this information, planners believed that wetlands made perfect landfill sites. In fact, moist environments, where trash and soil are in direct contact, aid biodegradation, contaminating the surrounding water and soil with toxins.[28]

In the 1980s, the growing ecological impact of toxic waste in landfills spurred the federal government to more stringently regulate them. The price of disposing of trash rose considerably; many landfills closed, unable to comply with the stiffer regulatory framework. Roughly 3,500 landfills shut down between 1979 and 1986 alone. In 1993, the federal government required new landfills to protect land and water with plastic liners and install systems for handling the collection of leachate, a toxic sludge that oozed from the compressed waste.[29]

The regulations ironically had two other results. First, they led to increasing corporate dominance of waste disposal because only large companies could comply with the tougher environmental and safety standards. By 1998, nearly two-thirds of all waste destined for a landfill went to a private facility, many owned by large multinational corporations such as Waste Management. Second, the regulations also hastened the interstate movement of waste—especially as cities turned increasingly to rural areas as a solution to their dumping needs—and its transformation into a commodity.[30]

A new legal framework underwrote the commodification of trash. The U.S. Supreme Court had long allowed states to regulate imported goods that compromised human health. Then, in a landmark 1978 decision involving the city of Philadelphia and the state of New Jersey, the court overturned that precedent, holding that state laws attempting to bar interstate trash shipment violated the commerce clause of the Constitution and giving Congress the right to oversee trade among the states. As a result, garbage evolved into a commodity that moved, unfettered by state laws, according to the market's invisible hand.[31]

The interstate movement of trash increased in the 1980s, with New York, New Jersey, and Pennsylvania exporting 8 million tons, mostly to the Midwest. By 1995, every single state, even Alaska and Hawaii, either imported or exported garbage. More than 17 million tons circulated in an intricate web of movements.[32] But that movement wasn't always smooth. In the summer of 1992, 80 boxcars of New York City trash left the South Bronx headed for a landfill in Libory, Illinois—only the landfill's permit had expired by the time the trash train arrived. The load of putrefying waste changed course and made stops in Sauget and Fairmont City, Illinois; Kansas City, Kansas; Medille, Missouri; Fort Madison, Iowa; and Streator, Illinois. No one seemed to want it. Eventually the entire smelly mess had to be hauled back east—the sides of the cars buckling as the heat swelled the size of the load—and buried in the Fresh Kills landfill.[33]

That same summer, another "poo-poo choo-choo" pulled out of New York and again chugged west toward Sauget, Illinois. This time residents protested the dumping of out-of-state garbage by organizing a sit-in. "The people here have dictated they don't want any part of it," the town's mayor remarked. "If it was from Illinois, it might not be near as bad. But being from New York, they frown on that."[34]

THE FINAL BURIAL

The last load of New York City garbage destined for the notorious Fresh Kills site on Staten Island arrived on March 22, 2001. The landfill, now closed, is being turned into a 2,200-acre New York City park. (Mary Chapman)

The rise of a free market in trash may not have proceeded as smoothly as some economists would have liked, but it seems to have produced some social consequences nonetheless. One study of garbage movement uncovered three important trends. First, trash seemed to move from states with high population densities to those with lower ones. Second, the waste gravitated from states with high per capita incomes to poorer ones. And third, the trash apparently flowed from states with relatively little air and water pollution to those with more of it.[35] Garbage, driven out of sight and out of mind, now circulated the country just like any other commodity, before being dumped wherever the free market dictated.

IS RECYCLING A LOAD OF GARBAGE?

It is within the context of an evolving capitalist system that the modern recycling movement—with its curbside pickups—is best understood. Such programs go back to the 1960s, but even as late as the end of the 1980s only a few hundred municipalities operated them. Nothing did more to galvanize the proponents of recycling than the travails of a barge named the Mobro 4000. In 1987, the barge, loaded with trash from Long Island, began cruising the high seas for weeks looking for a spot to deposit its load, which was rumored to contain medical waste. According to Newsweek, the plight of the Mobro was "to the trash crisis what the sinking of the Lusitania was to World War I." A surge of interest in recycling soon followed. Municipalities pledged to recycle a given percentage of trash by some specified date. Nine thousand recycling programs, with their now-familiar plastic containers, existed nationwide by 2003.[36]

The rise of this individuated response to waste rested on a set of market imperatives. First, recycling operated not by restricting U.S. manufacturers, but by burdening individuals with the responsibility of separating-out recyclable materials. Second, recycling presumed that companies would want the reclaimed material. Yet without a demand for recycled paper—often used to make fresh newsprint, wallboard, and insulation—collection is pointless and even potentially counterproductive. By the early 1990s, a glut had developed in the United States—too many old newspapers and not enough demand—leading some companies to dump the paper abroad.[37] In other words, recycling unfolded within a capitalist system founded on the endless accumulation of wealth and an abject dependence on markets.

Household trash makes up an infinitesimal 2 percent of the total national waste stream, which also includes industrial, agricultural, and mining waste. With industry responsible for 98 percent of the problem, municipal recycling is obviously not likely to have much impact on the nation's, much less the planet's, waste problems.[38]

Recycling is often viewed as a liberal reform brought about in the late 1960s by rising awareness among consumers of the environmental impact of modern life. In fact, new research is beginning to uncover a darker story of industry intervention. As the environmental movement grew, paper corporations and other industrial enterprises began shaping the meaning of recycling, describing it as akin to a natural process and thereby directing attention away from the unnatural quest for endless accumulation that made recycling necessary in the first place. Consumers, in other words, were given the impression that recycling under an increasingly globalized form of capitalism was roughly equivalent to the old closed-loop system that once characterized agriculture. That was a fairy tale that corporations were eager to encourage in a system that compelled them to compete to sell more goods and services to accumulate wealth in order to accumulate still more wealth. One sociologist has described this process as akin to "white mice on a treadmill, running ever faster in order to run still faster." The limitations of recycling in such a system are painfully evident.[39]

NOT IN UNCLE SAM'S BACKYARD

Beginning in 1986, a ship named the *Khian Sea* spent more than two years searching the world for a place to deep-six toxic ash from incinerators in Philadelphia, Pennsylvania. It eventually deposited some of its load in Haiti, falsely representing it as fertilizer. The crew pitched the rest overboard somewhere in the waters between Egypt and Singapore.

The travails of the *Khian Sea* dramatized the growing problem of rich countries dumping their waste on poor ones. In 1991, economist Lawrence Summers, who went on to become president of Harvard University, stunned the world with a frank comment that revealed the free-market assumptions behind the global trash nexus. Summers observed that Africa was "vastly underpolluted," pointing out that "the economic logic behind dumping a load of toxic waste in the lowest-wage country is impeccable." Economists like Summers measure human life in terms of its ability to produce present and future wages. As they reason, why saddle high-wage earners in rich nations with hazardous waste when it is more economically efficient to just lay it at the doorsteps of the poor, who are not contributing to economic growth anyway?[40]

Currently, the most significant and hazardous component of the export market in trash is electronic waste, or e-waste. The virtual world of high-tech consumer electronics might seem cleaner and less resource intense than the old smokestack industries of the Rust Belt. But California's Santa Clara County—home to Silicon Valley—as of 1998 hosted no fewer than 31 toxic Superfund sites. Chemical solvents used in the production of semiconductors and stored in leaking underground storage tanks caused Silicon Valley's ecological troubles. E-waste represents an even more serious environmental problem. Over the last generation, the amount of discarded electronics—containing lead, arsenic, cadmium, and other toxins harmful to living organisms—has ballooned.[41]

The profusion of e-waste can be traced back to 1965, when the age of disposable electronics was born. That year, Gordon Moore, one of the founders of Intel, made a stunningly accurate prediction. He held that the power of a microchip would double about every 18 months, quickly rendering all new computers and other electronic devices obsolete. His prediction was borne out: instead of repairing broken electronics, consumers simply bought new equipment and abandoned the old stuff. A steady stream of old computers, calculators, watches, and cell phones headed to the garbage bin courtesy of what came to be known as Moore's Law.[42]

The ecological consequences of Moore's revelation probably began showing up on foreign shores by the 1980s. E-waste brokers in the United States and other industrialized nations began shipping discarded electronic equipment to China, India, and Pakistan for recycling and disposal. There it was disassembled by workers with crude tools and no safety gear. Using screwdrivers and open flames, the workers coaxed small pieces of copper, gold, and other valuable metals from circuit boards, hard disks, and monitors. Ecological consequences ramified across the landscape. A recycling hub in the village of Guiyu, China, epitomized the dark side of the information age. Water samples taken from the Lianjiang River in 2000 revealed lead at 2,400 times the recommended safe level.[43]

In 1989, moral outrage over the transfer of waste from industrialized nations to developing countries led the United Nations Environment Program to draft the Basel Convention, an international agreement established to lessen the amount of waste produced and to require disposal near the source that generated it. Some 186 countries are now party to the agreement, but not the United States. In 1995, the convention agreement was amended with the so-called Basel Ban prohibiting nations that had ratified the earlier convention from exporting hazardous waste. These landmark agreements tried to rein in the free market in garbage. Although the United States leads the world in waste generation—producing

E-WASTE

A child in Hunan province perches on a pile of imported computer waste. (Copyright: *Basel Action Network*)

twice the amount of trash per capita as France, Britain, and Japan—it is the only industrialized nation that has yet to ratify the Basel Convention, choosing instead to externalize the cost of doing business onto the rest of world.[44]

CONCLUSION

In 2009, the Federal Communications Commission required television broadcasters to switch from analog to digital television technology. It was one of the largest instances of technological obsolescence ever. Millions of old analog televisions, each containing as much as eight pounds of toxic lead, began piling up in attics, landfills, and recycling warehouses. They could even be found abandoned on roadsides. There was once a profitable market for the leaded glass in these products, which was recycled into cathode ray tubes for new televisions and computer monitors. The shift to flat-panel displays, however, caused the bottom to fall out of the lead market. The new television technology had no need for the metal. With no viable recycling market, the old televisions just sat around burdening municipalities and recycling companies; in California, televisions covered an area the size of a football field stacked to a height of nine feet, decomposing to cover the floor in a layer of lead dust.[45]

The current e-waste problem is the product of a set of forces dating back to the emergence of corporate capitalism in the late nineteenth century. Over the course of the last 100 years, the corporations driving this socioecological order have produced a seemingly endless array of things made to break down or go obsolete, with the economic cost of the remains of the old family room falling onto the ledger books of state and local municipalities, which have had to deal with the environmental impact. More recently, the cost of a trip to the mall was shuffled across the globe as container ships sailed for poor countries with capitalism's leftovers.

15

SHADES OF GREEN

Spontaneous combustion is not supposed to happen to a river, unless it's the Cuyahoga, which cuts through the center of Cleveland, Ohio. The worst fire on the Cuyahoga raged through a shipyard, seriously burned three tugboats, and caused more than a half-million dollars in damage. Exactly what caused the river to ignite is not clear, though oil likely played a role. "We have photographs that show nearly six inches of oil on the river," Bernard Mulcahy, a fire prevention expert, said after the blaze.[1]

That was 1952 and Dwight D. Eisenhower was poised to win the presidency in a landslide victory. Meanwhile, the Cuyahoga was merely repeating itself. A half-century earlier, on December 31, 1899, two men operating a Cleveland railroad bridge noticed "a great volume of smoke intermingled with flame rising from the river."[2]

So when fire broke out on the river on June 22, 1969, no one in Cleveland could have been surprised. Although a photograph of the fire appeared on the front page of the city's main newspaper, the actual story lay buried deep inside. "It was strictly a run of the mill fire," said Chief William Barry of the Cleveland Fire Department. Later that summer, however, the fire became a poster child for the ills of modern America when Time magazine unveiled a new "Environment" section with a report on the sorry state of the Cuyahoga. "Chocolate-brown, oily, bubbling with sub-surface gases, it oozes rather than flows," Time reported. A routine event in a gritty industrial city had now become an environmental cause célèbre?[3]

What had changed? The answer is ecology-based environmentalism, which grew to be one of the most dramatic and significant reform movements in American history. The movement questioned capitalism's tendency to view nature solely as an instrument in the service of economic gain. It helped inspire the push for a vast set of new environmental regulations. It even brought a whole new field of law into existence. Within the space of just two decades, it created a concern for nature that penetrated the fabric of everyday life. A 1990 Gallup poll found that three-quarters of those Americans surveyed fashioned themselves environmentalists.[4] Even the very corporations targeted by the environmental movement began to project a greener image. Since the late 1960s, environmentalism has evolved into a diverse, multifaceted phenomenon—broad enough to

CUYAHOGA FIRE, 1952

Although most people recall only the 1969 fire that helped marshal support for the environmental movement, the Cuyahoga River, on the banks of which sat a large number of oil refineries by the latter part of the nineteenth century, often ignited, as it did here in 1952. (Special Collections, Cleveland State University Library)

include within its spectrum everyone from CEOs advocating for "natural capitalism" to ecowarriors and student activists seeking to drive a spike through the heart of some of the world's largest corporations.

SAVING THE WILD KINGDOM

Long before there was an environmental movement, there was wilderness preservation. The automobile brought rising numbers of Americans to the doorstep of wilderness. By the early 1920s, perhaps as many as 10 million to 15 million people were piling into cars and heading off on summer vacations away from the hectic pace of urban life. Millions more set off on Sunday afternoon trips to nearby lakes and woods that were now within easy reach. Under the leadership of Stephen Mather, the National Park Service embraced automobile tourism. In 1913, Yosemite National Park opened its gates to cars. Four years later, Yellowstone did the same. The number of visitors leaped from 356,000 to 1.3 million in just seven years (1916–1923), in response to a massive publicity campaign, replete with photographs, postcards, and magazine articles. As the parks became tourist attractions, nature came to be seen as a separate and faraway locale packaged up for human consumption. "Yellowstone is like an aquarium," observed writer E. B. White on a visit in 1922, "all sorts of queer specimens, with thousands of people pressing in to get a glimpse. . . . [I]t is so obviously 'on exhibition' all the time."[5]

This commercialized approach to nature drew a backlash in the form of the first calls for preservation. After World War I, preservationists lobbied for setting aside undeveloped "wilderness areas." A wildlife biologist named Aldo Leopold played a leading role in the effort. Born in 1887 in Burlington, Iowa, Leopold went on to study at Yale University's School of Forestry. After receiving his master's degree in 1909, Leopold took a job with the Forest Service, where his influence on public policy grew. In the 1920s, he succeeded in getting the agency to establish wilderness locales within its holdings—places off-limits to automobiles, roads, and other forms of development. Leopold is best known, however, for his book *A Sand County Almanac*, published in 1949, a year after he collapsed and died while fighting a fire that broke out near his home in central Wisconsin. "We abuse land because we regard it as a commodity belonging to us," he wrote in this book. "When we see land as a community to which we belong, we may begin to use it with love and respect." He argued that planners must transcend narrow economic considerations in making decisions over land use and instead adopt a broader ethical interest in preserving trees, insects, and other living organisms. Adopting such a "land ethic," he believed, meant resisting the temptation of preserving individual wildlife species—the focus of most conservation efforts to that point—at the cost of upholding the health of the larger ecosystem. "A thing is right," he concluded, "when it tends to preserve the integrity, stability, and beauty of the biotic community. It is wrong when it tends otherwise."[6]

During the 1930s, the packaging of the natural world as a recreational resource gained momentum as the New Deal, through organizations such as the Civilian Conservation Corps, added roads and campgrounds to the country's national parks and forests. In 1935, plans to build a parkway across the Appalachian Mountains galvanized preservation advocates and led Leopold, forester Robert Marshall, and several others to form the Wilderness Society, a group dedicated to opposing the commercialization of nature represented by auto-centered tourism.[7]

Whatever threat tourism posed to wilderness, it was far outweighed by postwar suburban development and economic growth. By the 1940s, private forest holdings in the Pacific Northwest, the country's last lumber frontier (with the Midwest and South already logged out), were edging toward exhaustion. This trend, combined with the postwar suburban building boom, drove the timber industry to call on Washington to open up the federal forests to logging. Logging required roads, and the Forest Service dutifully complied. Between 1940 and 1960, road mileage in national forests doubled to more than three times the extent of the present-day interstate highway system. The amount of timber harvested between

1950 and 1966 amounted to twice what had been cut in the prior four and a half decades from the national forest system. And as road building and timber cutting increased, they fragmented wilderness and opened it to abuse.[8]

The Wilderness Society pressed legislators to protect the nation's forests in the face of this mounting assault. In 1964, Congress complied by passing the Wilderness Act. This legislation gave the Forest Service the power to sequester 9 million acres of land from development. The act made the preservation of wilderness into national policy and—enacted within a system that glorified limitless economic expansion—represented one of the best examples of restraint the world has ever seen. Still, the legislation also had some significant flaws. It set aside just 9 million of the 14 million acres that the Forest Service had designated as wilderness and allowed mining in such areas until 1983, a move that sped up development in some of the very places Congress sought to "preserve."[9]

Meanwhile, more than four decades' worth of efforts to tame western rivers reached a zenith. In 1911, the first major dam went up across the Colorado River. Twenty-five years later, Hoover Dam, a 726-foot-high structure, plugged the Colorado valley. By 1964, 19 large dams impeded this one river's journey to the sea.

Leading the charge for dams was the U.S. Bureau of Reclamation. In the 1940s, the bureau began building what it called "cash register" dams, profit-making structures for generating valuable electricity. The proceeds went to subsidize the bureau's irrigation projects, which sold water cheaply and thus bolstered agribusiness. One early such project proposed by the Bureau was a dam on the Colorado in Echo Park, one of Utah's most scenic canyons and a part of the Dinosaur National Monument.[10]

Wilderness advocates cried out, and no one more than David Brower. As a child growing up in Berkeley, California, Brower had heard about the famed controversy over the Hetch Hetchy Valley, where the Tuolumne River was dammed in 1913, despite the efforts of preservationist John Muir, to serve the imperial dreams of San Francisco's business community. Now, Brower was determined not to let history repeat itself. As executive director of the Sierra Club, he joined with other wilderness advocates to mount a massive publicity effort. They launched a direct mail campaign that asked, "Will You DAM the Scenic Wildlands of Our National Park System?" They also produced a color movie on the issue; New York publisher Alfred Knopf put out a slick book of photographs titled *This Is Dinosaur*. All the attention created such a stir that tourists descended in droves on the canyon, 45,000 in the summer of 1955 alone. In the end, Brower and the conservationists prevailed. There would be no Echo Park Dam. But to save Dinosaur, the wilderness advocates agreed to a dam at Glen Canyon, also on the Colorado. Brower considered the Glen Canyon Dam, completed in 1963, one of the biggest mistakes of his life; as the dam filled, some of his friends worried that he might even kill himself.[11]

BLACK CANYON, COLORADO RIVER

Black Canyon before and after the construction of Hoover Dam, a 726-foot-high concrete structure completed in 1936. (U.S. Bureau of Reclamation)

SIERRA CLUB FLOAT TRIP

Wilderness advocates flocked to remote sections of the Colorado River in the mid-1950s as conflict erupted over plans to build the Echo Park Dam. (National Park Service, Harpers Ferry, West Virginia)

Never again, Brower said. In 1966, when the Bureau of Reclamation an-nounced that it would build two dams and flood the Grand Canyon, Brower and the Sierra Club flew into action. When the bureau suggested that the dams might actually afford tourists better access to the area (because of the lake they would create), the wilderness advocates took out full-page advertisements that blared: "SHOULD WE ALSO FLOOD THE SISTINE CHAPEL SO TOURISTS CAN GET NEARER THE CEILING?"[12] They succeeded: no dams went up along that stretch of the Colorado.

To Brower goes the credit for transforming environmental issues into the focus of a national campaign. Sierra Club membership alone grew from 7,000 in 1952 to over 77,000 in 1969. Brower succeeded in large part because of his media savvy. He also prevailed because his brand of pull-out-all-the-plugs environmentalism struck a chord among those Americans fed up with life in an affluent, materialistic society in which economic logic trumped everything else. "Objectivity," Brower once said, "is the greatest threat to the United States today." Brower opposed objectivity because he was for moral absolutes, for the position that being "reasonable" about building dams and other environmental issues was simply another way of saying, "Let's compromise for the sake of more economic growth."[13]

Ironically, Brower and his colleagues saved Dinosaur by transforming it into a tourist attraction, advertising its virtues in print and on film. Glen Canyon, meanwhile, a place unknown to most, took on water because no such campaign ensued. Brower was for moral reason, but to garner support he felt compelled to engage in the same sales techniques employed by Madison Avenue. The success of his publicity campaign attracted flocks of tourists, placing stress on the very wilderness—Dinosaur National Monument—that he was trying to save.

Brower also succeeded because he was able to tap into some fertile cultural terrain. Postwar America was a world where nature had increasingly come to be seen as an amenity, an object of leisure-time pursuit, not simply as something employed in the service of production. Nature films are a case in point. In the 1950s, Walt Disney Studios produced a series of films shot in open prairies and ancient forests, perceived by many as pristine wilderness removed from both urban and suburban life. The Vanishing Prairie (1954), for instance, was set "before civilization left its mark upon the land." Disney packaged nature for mass audiences, transforming wilderness into a commodity that anyone able to afford the price of a movie ticket could enjoy. Wilderness advocates, in turn, capitalized on the public's evident fascination with unsullied nature. In 1955, the Audubon Society even awarded Walt Disney a conservation medal.[14]

Disney's version of the wilderness experience resonated in postwar suburbia, where the homogeneity of the lawn replaced indigenous plant life. With the advent of television—Americans bought more than 40 million sets between 1946 and 1955 alone—nature shows such as Wild Kingdom (which premiered in 1963) offered suburbanites an avenue of escape from the tedious landscape outside their picture windows. A widespread hunger seemed to be growing for a refuge from the buzz of the lawn mower and the resinous smell of freshly laid asphalt.[15]

DECLARATION OF INTERDEPENDENCE

It took the work of a marine biologist named Rachel Carson to change the terms of the debate over environmental reform. Wilderness was at the heart of Leopold's and Brower's environmentalism. Carson, however, took ecology as her main point of departure. By making this leap, she showed that human beings not only affected ecosystems but also existed within them. Our own biological destinies, in other words, were bound up with the fate of the natural world.

Carson breathed new life into a very old intellectual tradition dating back at least to John Muir (1838–1914). Muir believed that the natural world existed in a complex, interdependent harmony. Any disturbance by human beings to this smoothly functioning relationship threatened to send out dangerous ripple effects, potentially undermining all semblance of natural order. In the 1950s, ecologist Eugene Odum provided a scientific defense of much the same view. Odum held that ecosystems—all plant and animal organisms plus the habitat in which they resided—always evolved toward, if they had not already achieved, a state of order, or "homeostasis." Interfere with the ecosystem in some fundamental way, and this intricate interrelation of species and habitat might unravel.

Carson took these views and popularized them in her 1962 book *Silent Spring*, a stinging critique of chemical dependency. She embraced the idea that all of nature was bound up in an interdependent web of life, which humankind had the potential to destroy. She then took this concern and tapped into the Cold War political climate, arguing that the threat from pesticide use, her main concern in the book, was no different from the danger that radioactive fallout posed to human life. Pesticides, touted by industry as nothing short of miraculous, were riding high with their use increasing steeply in the years after 1949. Carson called attention to the ways in which pesticides upset nature's balance. "We spray our elms and the following springs are silent of robin song," she wrote, "not because we sprayed the robins directly but because the poison traveled, step by step, through the now familiar elm leaf-earthworm-robin cycle." Such a sequence of events reflected "the web of life—or death—that scientists know as ecology."[16]

Although she used the word sparingly in her book, Carson helped to transform *ecology* into the rallying cry of the environmental movement. Unlike *wilderness*, conceived as a world apart, *ecology* suggested the reverse—a world in which all life was bound up in an intricate, interconnected web. Human beings, she believed, were thus part of the balance of nature, not divorced from it in the way that some wilderness advocates implied.

The pesticide industry mounted a massive attack against Carson, at one point threatening to sue her publisher. They dismissed her as a hysterical woman with a "mystical attachment to the balance of nature," even going so far as to brand her a Communist. But the assault did little to undermine the popularity of her book, which remained on the *New York Times* best-seller list for 31 weeks. In fact, the book probably did more to galvanize the modern environmental movement than any other single publication. One historian has called it "the *Uncle Tom's Cabin* of modern environmentalism."[17]

The book motivated the administration of John F. Kennedy to form a task force to examine the federal government's policies on pesticides and pollution. The latter was understood before the 1960s to be primarily the responsibility of local governments. President Dwight Eisenhower vetoed federal water pollution legislation in his last year in office invoking precisely this rationale. The liberal administrations of John F. Kennedy and Lyndon B. Johnson, however, articulated the need for federal intervention in the struggle for clean water and air. They created new bureaucratic organizations, such as the Federal Water Pollution Control Administration, to put this principle into action.[18]

In the mid-1960s, Americans received an object lesson in the meaning of ecological interdependence. A massive drought began in the year Carson published her book, the worst dry spell since the 1930s, battering an area from Maine south to Virginia and west to Ohio and Michigan. The drought lasted four years, focusing increasing public attention on the nation's supply of water, especially in the Great Lakes, the world's largest aggregation of fresh water. Lake Erie alone contains nearly 10,000 square miles of water—more than six times the size of Rhode Island.[19]

As the lake level fell during the drought, residents living near Lake Erie learned that they drew their water from what amounted to one huge cesspool. Detroit and Buffalo were allowing tens of thousands of tons of untreated sewage to drain into it. But it was soapsuds—skeins of foam 300 feet long in places, clinging to the shore like so much cotton on Santa Claus's cheeks—that really captured the public's attention. The use of oil-based synthetic detergent had ballooned in the 1950s and early 1960s as more households installed automatic washing machines. The suds that washed up on the shores of Lake Erie, turning the lake into what Time magazine called "a North American Dead Sea," came from something as simple as doing the laundry.[20]

In truth, the suds highlighted a far more serious problem. Detergents contained phosphates, a nutrient that causes algae to bloom like mad, only to die, decay, and drain oxygen from the water—oxygen that other life forms need to live. In 1969, one scientist involved in assessing the lake's ecology spoke for many when he said: "In this day and age, in a society which is so affluent—to have to paddle in its own sewage is just disgusting."[21]

The flames that lapped the banks of the Cuyahoga River that same year confirmed for many the nation's environmental problems. After all, a body of water had been turned into a fire hazard. Even California, once looked on as the land of hopes, dreams, and untrammeled natural beauty, was feeling the impact of petroleum-based life. Several months before the Cuyahoga went up in flames, an oil spill occurred off the coast near the affluent community of Santa Barbara. A year later, Roderick Nash, a professor of history at the University of California at Santa Barbara, appeared on television to lecture on the ecological ills of life in modern America, calling his message a "declaration of interdependence."[22]

The tumultuous political context of the late 1960s drew even more attention to the ecological concerns raised by Carson and others. As the Vietnam War escalated, widespread suspicion of the federal government and corporations like Dow Chemical, makers of napalm, dovetailed with Carson's warnings about pesticides. The feminist press also took to criticizing the "male-feasance" of American agribusiness, focusing on the perils of DDT, a chemical Carson singled out as especially troubling. One feminist publication lampooned the high levels of DDT found in the bodies of new mothers with a cartoon showing a woman squirting a fly with breast milk. In 1969, the *Rat*, a radical underground newspaper, observed that "the word 'ecology' had been lifted from the dusty academic shelves of abstract scientific definition." It was now "a powerful breathing consciousness . . . that no radical could avoid." In 1970, economist Robert Heilbroner declared simply, "Ecology has become the Thing."[23]

Neighborhood activism surged in response to the radical political climate and the growing media attention devoted to ecological problems. In Santa Barbara, environmental activists formed Get Oil Out (GOO) to put an end to the drilling off the coast. In Chicago, Paul Booth, a founder of the radical New Left organization Students for a Democratic Society, helped to form the Citizens Action Program (CAP) to protest the pollution spewed by the coal-hungry Commonwealth Edison electricity company. "Think Globally, Act Locally" went the cry of these activists as they protested everything from air pollution to new superhighways.[24]

Together, Carson's eloquent book, an extraordinary drought, a superheated political climate, and a series of made-for-TV ecological disasters dramatized the elemental interdependence of life on the planet. The social and ecological underpinnings of modern capitalism, often masked by distance or suppressed by corporations, briefly made themselves seen. Many no doubt realized the impact that turning on the washer could have for a distant lake. A sharpening of the links between everyday life and its ecological consequences laid the groundwork for the emergence of a new moral framework, one that for the most part urged individual Americans to take responsibility for their actions with respect to nonhuman nature. Call it the environmental movement.

THE MAINSTREAM

Although his motives were far from pure, Richard Nixon was arguably one of the greenest presidents ever to occupy the White House. In the tumultuous political atmosphere of the 1960s, it was far safer for establishment politicians to support the environment than the more threatening antiwar agenda proposed by campus radicals. No one recognized this better than Nixon. Some of the most important environmental legislation ever passed became law with his signature, beginning with the National Environmental Policy Act, which he signed—live on television—on January 1, 1970. Discussion of major federal undertakings, from building a dam to constructing a highway, would no longer take place behind closed doors, but in public, where people could debate the potential ecological fallout.[25]

The act marked the start of a veritable torrent of federal legislation, transforming such issues as air and water pollution, hitherto considered state or local problems, into matters of national policy. There was the Clean Air Act (1970); the Water Pollution Control Act (1972); the Federal Insecticide,

Rodenticide, and Fungicide Act (1972); the Coastal Zone Management Act (1972); the Marine Mammals Protection Act (1972); the Endangered Species Act (1973); and the Energy Policy and Conservation Act (1975), which set federal fuel economy standards. To deal with industrial waste, Congress passed the Toxic Substances Control Act (1976); the Resource Conservation and Recovery Act (1976); and the Comprehensive Environmental Response, Compensation, and Liability Act (1980), better known as the Superfund law. The Environmental Protection Agency (EPA), established in 1970, served as the government's watchdog on pollution issues, maturing into one of the nation's largest federal agencies.

The legislation read like a gigantic handbook on how to counter the ills of corporate capitalism. It dealt with everything from limiting industrial pollutants to protecting endangered species to cleaning up the synthetic detergent problem. Although none of the legislation interfered, to any major extent, with the corporation's systematic commodification of nature, the gains were real nonetheless.

The Clean Air Act of 1970, for example, set air quality standards for pollutants such as carbon monoxide and lead—standards based not on what they would cost industry to attain but on a scientific determination of the risk such substances posed to human health. The result proved positive for people's lungs. By the 1990s, smoke pollution had fallen nearly 80 percent from its level in the 1970s, while lead emissions had plummeted by 98 percent. Still, the legislation had some significant flaws. New air pollution sources received vigorous policing, but preexisting sources were "grandfathered" in under the law. Because monitoring took place close to the factories producing the pollution, businesses opted for tall smokestacks so emissions would miss the sensors and instead drift downwind. Nor did the initial legislation place any cap on the total amount of emissions allowed in the nation's air, although later legislation regulating lead and sulfur did so.[26]

The Water Pollution Control Act of 1972 was a tougher measure, mandating permits for all businesses discharging pollutants—no grandfathering allowed. It led to major improvements in water quality. According to one 1982 estimate, the required pollution control devices had by then been installed on 96 percent of all industrial sources of wastewater. But because the EPA, charged with overseeing the legislation, had no authority to regulate pollution coming from stormwater runoff or hog farms, some bodies of water declined in quality.[27]

In putting forth such environmental reforms, Congress took its cue from the American public. Never before had people shown such overwhelming concern for the planet as they did in the 1970s. The decade opened with Earth Day, the brainchild of Gaylord Nelson, a liberal Wisconsin senator who believed in the essential goodness of government. Nelson proposed a teach-in on the

BAD AIR

Scenes like this one from 1953, showing New York City's Chrysler Building obscured by smog, were common in U.S. cities before the beginning of clean air regulations in 1970. (Library of Congress)

environment modeled on the antiwar protests popular in the 1960s. He hired some graduate students from Harvard University to pursue the project. On April 22, 1970, some 12,000 demonstrations, parades, and rallies in support of ecological issues took place, the clearest evidence to date of environmentalism's status as a mass movement. Students at the University of Minnesota staged a mock funeral for the automobile by burying an internal combustion engine. Activists charged onto the corporate campus of Standard Oil of California and dumped oil into its reflecting pools. Political and business leaders "are talking about filters on smokestacks," said Denis Hayes, a Stanford graduate hired to coordinate the nationwide protests, "while we are challenging corporate irresponsibility."[28]

Although they had little or nothing to do with Earth Day, mainstream environmental organizations benefited from the surge in interest immensely. Audubon Society membership rose from 120,000 in 1970 to 400,000 in 1980. Sierra Club membership swelled more than 46 percent over the same period. In the 15 years after 1970, total participation in environmental organizations went from 500,000 to 2.5 million—powerful evidence of the public's growing interest in the environment.[29]

These organizations turned increasingly to the law, especially now that the entire environmental regulatory system was open to public scrutiny. The new legislation passed in the 1970s gave environmental organizations the opportunity to affect the debate over matters of wide-ranging ecological importance. Now the federal government had the Sierra Club and the Natural Resources Defense Council looking over its shoulders, making sure it enforced what Congress intended.

Then the 1980 election of Ronald Reagan threatened to bring the reforms of the past decade to a screeching halt. In response to declining corporate profits and stagnating economic growth, Reagan pushed for the deregulation of industry. He appointed Anne Gorsuch, a staunch foe of government regulation of business (and mother of a future conservative Supreme Court justice), to head the EPA. She reduced the agency's budget sharply and boasted of cutting the six-inch-thick handbook on clean water rules, for example, to just half an inch. Over at the Department of the Interior, Reagan drafted James Watt, a strident champion of private property rights, to sell off federal lands. Such blatant anti-environmentalism fired up people to join the Sierra Club and the rest of the opposition. In 1980, only four environmental organizations had 100,000 or more members; 10 years later 15 groups boasted that many, and seven had more than half a million recruits.[30]

At the same time, the main-line environmental groups lost a certain radical edge as they swelled their membership rolls. They employed larger professional staffs and even engaged in niche marketing in order to boost their memberships still further. Before long donations were arriving from the very corporations they had been criticizing. The National Wildlife Federation under Jay Hair's leadership in the 1980s established a "corporate conservation council" and charged the likes of Du Pont, Conoco, Dow Chemical, and Weyerhauser a 10,000-dollar fee to join. A 1990 study of the boards of seven major environmental groups uncovered the presence of executives from Exxon, Monsanto, and Union Carbide, all notorious polluters.[31]

Even the annual Earth Day celebrations became more tied to corporations. *Fortune* magazine in the months leading up to the twentieth anniversary of the protest in 1990 called the impending event "a veritable biz-fest." As a public affairs director at Monsanto put it, "There's a mad scramble for many companies to project an 'I am greener than thou' attitude. The fact of the matter is that Earth Day is the best way to get news coverage." The *Wall Street Journal* simply reported: "Earth Day could easily be renamed Marketing Day." Meanwhile, critics of Earth Day such as radical environmentalist Kirkpatrick Sale called attention not only to the increasing corporate involvement but also to the overarching emphasis on individual responsibility for environmental ills. "Earth Day's primary emphasis," he wrote, "is on individual responses: 'what you can do' to stop ozone depletion or rain forest destruction." Focusing on personal responsibility, he argued, diverted attention from the systemic forces—the decisions of corporations to externalize costs—that explained the more fundamental roots of environmental problems.[32]

Increasing corporate involvement in environmentalism brought with it a more general acceptance by mainstream groups of so-called win-win solutions. Such solutions involved an approach to regulation that employed market incentives, as opposed to new rules or taxes, to compel corporate compliance. "A new environmentalism has emerged that embraces . . . market-oriented environmental protection policies," explained Robert Stavins, formerly a staff economist with the Environmental Defense Fund, in 1989.[33]

The Clean Air Act of 1990 epitomized this new environmentalism. A complex piece of legislation, it tried to address some of the polluting effects of coal-fired power plants including smog, toxic emissions, ozone, and acid rain. As fossil fuels go, coal is dirty: when burned, it releases carbon, nitrogen oxide, mercury, and sulfur. Nitrogen oxide emissions contribute to smog, an important cause of summertime respiratory illness. Mercury released into the air settles in lakes and accumulates in fish, which, if eaten, can lead to brain damage in human beings. And sulfur dioxide can lower the pH of rainfall. First diagnosed in the 1970s, so-called acid rain resulted in the decline of forests, especially in the eastern United States. To address some of these issues, President George H. W. Bush appointed William Reilly, administrator of the EPA and a former head of the Environmental Defense Fund, to put together a legislative package. The ultimate legislation passed by Congress mandated a 50 percent reduction in sulfur dioxide emissions to 8.9 million tons per year and, in addition, capped future emissions at that level. Utilities supported the legislation because the law also included a mechanism for "emissions trading," a system dreamed up by the Environmental Defense Fund. The idea allowed power plants that curbed emissions to sell their unused pollution allowances to other less conservation-minded plants to use. The logic embraced by Reilly was as follows. Since the market is smarter and more powerful than the human mind, the solution to a failure of the market—in this case, pollution—is simply recourse to more reliance on the market. In other words, as one economist has explained, the solution to "market failures is always more markets."[34]

The acid rain provision of the 1990 Clean Air Act had by 2006 helped to reduce sulfur dioxide emissions by 66 percent from the 1980 level. But Germany's experience offers an illuminating comparison. Confronting a similar acid rain problem, Germany used stringent industry regulation, as opposed to market incentives, and managed to reduce sulfur dioxide emissions by roughly 90 percent in just six years. Other critics of emissions trading have pointed out that taxes—fiercely resisted by U.S. corporations—are a more efficient way of getting utilities to internalize air pollution costs. And still others have criticized emissions trading for shifting the harmful effects of pollution from relatively better-off regions with fewer health issues to poorer places—Appalachia, for example—with more health problems.[35]

William Reilly and his colleagues at the Environmental Defense Fund, in devising such an emissions trading scheme, managed to win over the hearts of industry and secure passage of the 1990 law. They thus helped to significantly reduce sulfur dioxide pollution. Turning even pollution into a commodity, however, created a false sense of security in market solutions. In 2005, the EPA instituted a "cap and trade" program for mercury emissions from coal-fired power plants. The problem is that, unlike sulfur dioxide, mercury does not disperse widely but instead settles near where it is initially released, causing neurological impairment as it works its way up the food chain. Mercury trading has allowed polluting power plants to buy emissions allowances that have aggravated the mercury problem in already embattled areas. Such market-based approaches are based on a view of nature as a limitless resource and are a long way from the ideals and no-holds-barred methods of early environmentalists like David Brower.[36]

THE RADICALS

Grassroots community groups aspired to a far more ambitious agenda than the mainstream environmental movement, seeking both ecological justice and social empowerment. Unlike the largely white, male-dominated big green organizations, these activist groups included many working-class women and people of color. They were also less interested in wilderness, a concept that cultivates an image of nature as existing at some distance from the experiences of ordinary people. Instead, they sought to build decent places to live by liberating their communities from the grip of corporations. As a result, they were far less compromising.

Working-class environmental concerns emerged in the late 1970s with the Love Canal disaster. Located in Niagara Falls, New York, the Love Canal community was built during the 1950s on a landfill once owned by the Hooker Chemical and Plastics Corporation. Some 100,000 drums of chemical contaminants lay buried at the site. In the early 1970s, Lois Gibbs moved to a bungalow in the development, thinking she was buying into the American Dream. She soon learned differently. Her children fell ill with epilepsy, asthma, and blood disorders.

In 1978, a reporter wrote a story on the dangers of the buried chemicals at Love Canal. Gibbs was not alone in her troubles; other residents suffered from chronic illnesses, birth defects, and miscarriages. Banding together, they organized the Love Canal Homeowners Association. State and federal officials responded slowly to their plight, so slowly that at one point Gibbs and 500 others took two EPA officials hostage for five hours. Jimmy Carter eventually declared Love Canal a disaster area, and the government paid for its evacuation. Gibbs moved to Virginia and founded the Citizens Clearing House for Hazardous Wastes, an organization that by the late 1980s provided support to more than 5,000 grassroots groups concerned with toxic waste.[37]

Love Canal evolved into a symbol of reckless corporate behavior, but even more importantly, it galvanized women around the issue of environmental justice. One of the most successful Love Canal protests was a Mother's Day Die-In, in which women called attention to the relationship between corporate-generated toxins and reproductive health. In the wake of the New York disaster, other groups arose, including Mothers of East Los Angeles and Mothers Air Watch of Texarkana, Arkansas. These activists tended to forgo litigation and lobbying in favor of aggressive protests and publicity campaigns. The mainstream environmental organizations, Gibbs explained, ask: "'What can we support to achieve a legislative victory?' Our approach is to ask: 'What is morally correct?'"[38]

Love Canal victimized primarily white working-class people. Then, in 1982, when an EPA-sponsored toxic waste dump was slated for Warren County, North Carolina, a poor and largely African American area, residents rose up in protest. With dump trucks loaded with contaminated soil set to roll, protesters, including many women and children, threw themselves in the way. Police arrested more than 500 people, including several civil rights leaders.

The protest sparked inquiries into the relationship between race and hazardous waste siting. Were people of color literally being dumped on? The evidence, found by both government and other studies, strongly suggested yes. One 1987 study found that three out of five blacks lived in places with abandoned toxic waste dumps.[39] Toxic waste landfills lowered surrounding land values, drawing in those who lacked the means to live elsewhere. A 1992 study pointed out that fines imposed on polluters in white areas were, on average, more than five times the fines leveled on those operating in minority communities.[40]

American Indian communities also had to confront toxic waste problems. Indian reservations often sat atop rich uranium deposits, making them repositories of the nation's industrial poisons. Uranium mining in the Southwest began in the 1940s with the advent of nuclear energy. By 1960, 6 million tons of uranium ore had been mined on Navajo lands, generating serious water and soil contamination. Teenage reproductive organ cancer rates in Navajo quarry areas eventually registered 17 times the national average. In 1979, shortly after the well-known nuclear reactor disaster at Three Mile Island in Pennsylvania, a dam at the Church Rock mine in New Mexico ruptured,

LOVE CANAL

Love Canal, New York, 1981. (*Special Collections, University of Buffalo*)

sending radioactive tailings spilling into the Rio Puerco River. To this day, radiation levels around the spill remain high; however, the EPA did not even begin testing radiation levels at the Navajo reservation until 1998. Mainstream environmental organizations largely ignored the uranium issue, leaving it to small grassroots groups such as the Eastern Navajo Diné Against Uranium Mining to wage the battle.[41]

William Ruckelshaus, the EPA's first administrator, once called the grassroots environmental movement one of "the most radicalized groups I've seen since Vietnam." The grassroots community groups were one example; Earth First!

provided another. In 1980, Dave Foreman, an ex-Marine and Wilderness Society staffer, along with several others, founded Earth First! on the premise that "in *any* decision consideration for the health of the earth must come first." Taking a page out of the work of Norwegian philosopher Arne Naess, the group rejected the view that human needs should form the basis of our relationship with nature, opting instead for what Naess called "deep ecology," the view that all living organisms, both human and nonhuman, have equal claims on the earth. Philosophically speaking, they argued, human beings are no more important or valuable to life on the planet than lichens, trees, grizzly bears, or wolves.[42]

Earth First! endured its harshest test in the old-growth forests of the Pacific Northwest. Located between the Pacific Ocean and the Cascade Mountains and reaching from California north into Canada, these ancient woodlands offer a storybook picture of wilderness. (The Disney company set many of its nature films in them.) These majestic forests contain tremendous biodiversity and prior to human settlement may have covered 15 million to 24 million acres.[43] In the 1980s a body of new ecological knowledge was slowly developing that revealed the perils of timber harvests for the animal world. But in 1980, the election of Ronald Reagan led to the appointment of federal officials who did everything they could to increase timber cutting on national forestlands. The timber industry trained its sights on the old growth not to meet domestic needs but to make large profits by shipping unprocessed logs to foreign markets in Asia. In 1987, corporations carved a record-breaking 5.6 billion board feet of timber out of the old growth of Washington and Oregon.[44]

In 1983, Earth First!—fed up with the discreet legalisms of the major environmental groups—hammered nails into trees in Oregon's Siskiyou Mountains. They reasoned that tree spiking, as it came to be called, would pose such a threat to safety—given the risk of serious injury when a saw blade struck a nail—that timber companies would place the affected areas off-limits. But since the people making the decision to proceed would not bear the safety risk, the cutting continued. In 1987, George Alexander, a worker at Louisiana Pacific's mill in Cloverdale, California, plunged his band saw into a spiked log. Shrapnel sliced through his protective facemask, breaking his jaw and knocking out his teeth. No evidence surfaced linking Earth First! to the accident, but the group's indifference angered critics.

By the early 1990s, Earth First! had begun to fracture under the stress placed on the organization by its extreme nature-centered views. Dave Foreman left the group as some members questioned whether the philosophy of deep ecology made any sense in a capitalist system riven by class conflict. Could social justice for workers and ecological balance in the forest be made to work together? Judi Bari, the daughter of two socialists and a former union organizer who opposed tree spiking and the more general indifference to the rights of workers, thought that they could. In the wake of the George Alexander tragedy, Bari tried to interest women and workers in Earth First! by focusing on workplace concerns such as mill closings and safety. To advance her cause, she organized Redwood Summer in 1990, a nonviolent protest for both ecological and social justice modeled on Martin Luther King's civil rights demonstrations.

Bari tried to widen the focus of environmentalism and make it a more inclusive movement. By the twenty-first century, the radicalism of people such as Bari and Gibbs had begun to have an impact on some mainstream groups. In 2005, the National Wildlife Federation—historically a largely apolitical organization—chose a union organizer and environmental justice activist named Jerome Ringo as chairman of its board. Ringo was the first African American to lead a major U.S. conservation group. Raised in Louisiana's bayou country in the 1950s, Ringo watched the region's ecology decline with the rise of the petrochemical industry. Explaining why the dispossessed have eschewed environmentalism, he pointed out that the bulk of the green groups "were founded by people who fished to put fish on the wall, not by people who fished to put fish on the table. And for poor people, issues like ozone depletion have not been a priority, compared with next month's rent."[45]

CAN CAPITALISM SAVE THE PLANET?

In the 1990s, corporations began burnishing their environmental bona fides. In 1989, Du Pont CEO Edgar Woolard coined the phrase "corporate environmentalism" after the Exxon Valdez oil spill, which released 250,000 barrels of petroleum into Alaska's Prince William Sound. The disaster—often blamed wholly on the ship's drunken captain—highlighted the ecological perils of business as usual in a corporation. Exxon had only a small crew on board the ship to save on labor costs; its emergency response plan did little to limit the spill. Thousands of sea otters, loons, and cormorants died. Instead of calling for the dismantling of the Trans-Alaska Pipeline, an 800-mile pipe that beginning in the 1970s brought oil from the North Slope to Valdez, Alaska, or demanding substantive corporate reform, mainstream environmental groups responded by simply asking Exxon to clean up the mess. For his part, Woolard argued that environmental organizations could not solve the world's ecological problems, and neither could government. "Corporations have to do it," he said.[46]

The poster child for corporate environmental responsibility was Paul Hawken, a founder of the garden supply company Smith & Hawken. Hawken and his collaborators, Amory and L. Hunter Lovins, championed "natural capitalism." Not content simply to call on industry to reform, they argued for "a new type of industrialism," a more ecologically sensitive form of production. More intelligently designed products, they believed, such as lighter cars that use composite material instead of steel, would lead to a radical increase in "resource productivity." In order to combat planned obsolescence, they advocated for a more service-oriented form of consumerism. People would not purchase a washing machine, but a washing machine *service*; the machine would remain the property of the manufacturer, who would be responsible for fixing or replacing it. That would give manufacturers a built-in incentive to produce more durable products.[47]

Architect William McDonough and chemist Michael Braungart proposed an even more imaginative effort to reform capitalism. They sought a return to the "cradle-to-cradle" world that existed before industrial capitalism, in which people recycled nutrients back into production through the husbanding of manure. Born in 1951 in Tokyo, McDonough recalled people coming with ox carts for the night soil, depositing it as fertilizer on farms, and returning to the city in the morning with vegetables in a cycle that preserved the local ecology. It was quite unlike the "cradle-to-grave" ethos that followed and that continues to govern the manufacturing of products designed eventually to wind up in a landfill. Rather than seeking to dominate and control the natural world, McDonough and Braungart wanted to imitate nature in their designs—producing plastic books, for instance, that can be endlessly recycled. They aspired to make reincarnation the guiding principle of business and thus "eliminate the concept of waste." McDonough, Braungart, and Hawken tried to spur environmental reform from within the capitalist system.[48]

In the 1990s, a carpet manufacturing executive named Ray Anderson read one of Hawken's books and experienced a conversion. "I am a plunderer of the earth and a thief," Anderson wrote. And yet, "by our civilization's definition, I am a captain of industry . . . a modern day hero, an entrepreneur." Anderson decided to overhaul his company, the Atlanta-based Interface. It was a difficult challenge. The production of carpeting uses copious amounts of petroleum; when the carpet wears out it can languish in a landfill for tens of thousands of years. By 2006, however, the company used significantly less energy and water than it once did; it even had a leasing program in which the company replaced threadbare carpet tiles overnight. This approach vastly reduced the amount of carpeting produced because the unworn carpet remained in place. Anderson became the personification of natural capitalism, though he proved a lone voice in the corporate wilderness. As environmentalist Bill McKibben asked in 2006, "Why is there still only one Ray Anderson?"[49]

The answer has largely to do with the legal and institutional framework that structures how corporations conduct business. One of the central principles of the corporate form is that it exists to pursue what is in the best financial interests of its shareholders. As economist Milton Friedman once explained: "A corporation is the property of its stockholders. Its interests are the interests of its stockholders. Now, beyond that should it spend the stockholders' money for purposes which it regards as socially responsible but which it cannot connect to its bottom line? The answer I would say is no." That same financial logic drives CEOs to externalize costs onto the environment and the public, improving a company's short-term economic prospects, regardless of its collateral damage.[50]

If environmentalism fits into a company's business plan, gains can and have been made. In the 1990s, Du Pont began cutting emissions and saving six dollars for each ton of carbon it eliminated. No company, however, is likely to betray its shareholders in the name of sustainability. No company will foreclose on growth for the sake of a greener planet. No company will embrace environmentalism at the expense of a bad profit-and-loss statement. Corporate environmentalism, in other words, does not address the fundamental quest for the endless accumulation of capital that is at the core of the capitalist system.[51]

That point is driven home by the recent history of the Scotts Company, the retailer of lawn and garden chemicals and the current owner of Paul Hawken's old garden supply company. In 2007, a shareholder initiative called on Scotts to disclose its lobbying aimed at defeating state and local attempts to restrict fertilizer and pesticides that arose from scientific concern about these chemicals' health and environmental effects. Some shareholders worried that by working surreptitiously against pesticide reform the company might tarnish its image among green consumers. The Scotts board, however, fought the corporate disclosure initiative, which ultimately went down to defeat. Scotts, of course, would argue that it hopes to make the world a greener place. But it makes money by selling Americans more chemical applications while passing along the health and environmental risks of lawn treatments. This fundamental contradiction stands, like a large mountain, in the way of the success of natural capitalism.[52]

WHEN BRANDS BITE BACK

By the mid-1990s, the ghastly evidence of socially irresponsible corporate behavior had reached a prime-time audience. Gap, Nike, and even Disney came under fire for profiting from sweatshops located in developing nations. Some consumers began to think twice about brand-name products, perhaps wondering what poor Latin American child had stitched together their shirt. Environmentalists too, it turned out, capitalized on the revenge of the brand.[53]

Disgruntled by corporate-dominated recycling efforts, activists in the United States launched the so-called zero-waste movement. While natural capitalists called on corporations to reform, activists in the zero-waste movement saw a more important role for state intervention in healing the ecological ills of capitalism. If the zero-waste activists had their way, government would force industry not only to reform but also to retool the manufacturing process and thereby produce radically less waste.[54]

Building on ideas circulating in Germany—where an innovative packaging law went into effect in 1991—U.S. zero-waste proponents began advocating for "extended producer responsibility." Under this system, industry would be accountable for waste throughout a product's entire life span, from its manufacture through its consumption and eventual disposal. Putting extended producer responsibility into law would thus give industry an incentive to retool and generate less waste. It would also cause companies to better manage their waste, since they would bear ultimate responsibility for it. Extended producer responsibility is a way, in other words, to persuade companies to internalize the environmental costs of their products.[55]

In the United States, the GrassRoots Recycling Network, an activist organization formed in the mid-1990s, spearheaded the zero-waste charge. An early campaign targeted the Coca-Cola Company for reneging on a pledge to use more recycled plastic in its bottles. The company turned instead to cheaper virgin plastic and, to make matters worse, also introduced its 20-ounce single-serving container. The activists at the network realized that Coke's powerful brand image also made it vulnerable to attack. The group called on consumers to tell the company to "Do the Real Thing!" It asked people to mail two-liter Coke bottles back to the company with the message, "Take it back and use it again." It recruited students, urging them to lobby for vending machines that sold containers using only recycled material. In 2001, Coke agreed to include a small amount of recycled material in every soda bottle, but the group, unsatisfied, pressed on, constructing two 25-foot Coke and Pepsi bottles and hauling them to Washington, DC, where it asked people to wager on which company did more recycling. They called their campaign "The New Pepsi-Coke Challenge."[56]

The network next moved on to tackle consumer electronics. It teamed up with the Silicon Valley Toxics Coalition, organized in 1982 as an environmental justice group concerned with leaching at semiconductor factories from storage tanks into groundwater supplies. In 2001, the two groups in league with the Texas Campaign for the Environment, Clean Water Action, Basel Action Network, and other nonprofit groups launched the Computer Take Back Campaign (CTBC). The CTBC targeted the Dell corporation, at the time the dominant force in the personal computer business.[57]

The CTBC chose Dell for reasons other than simply its large market share. Founded in the 1980s by Michael Dell, the company came of age at the same time as a new corporate management theory. Companies began to move out of the business of manufacturing things and into the business of manufacturing brands. They outsourced production and instead focused on their corporate image. "There is no value in making things any more," explained Nike's Phil Knight. "The value is added by careful research, by innovation and by marketing." Dell followed in Nike's footsteps. It began assembling its computers to order using components produced elsewhere and then simply branded the result with its distinctive logo. The success of its brand, however, also made it vulnerable to precisely the kind of attack planned by the CTBC.[58]

Dell had succeeded in capturing buying contracts with universities, so the CTBC focused on generating campus support for its efforts. It was a savvy move in part because it capitalized on the burgeoning green campus movement brewing since 1990. Campuses had undertaken various environmental initiatives. Oberlin erected green buildings with photovoltaic panels and native plantings, Tufts University required "ecological literacy" of its students, and the University of Kansas hired an ombudsman to spot opportunities for making the campus more energy efficient. The CTBC had found the perfect audience for its message.

In 2001, the group issued a "computer report card," terminology immediately recognizable to any student, for evaluating the environmental, health, and safety records of the major electronics companies. Dell earned a poor grade, lagging behind its main competitor, Hewlett Packard. Then the group took on the company's "Steven the Dell Dude" advertising pitch. "Dude, why won't they take back my old Dell?" the CTBC asked.[59]

The group also organized showings of the documentary *Exporting Harm*, a powerful look at the afterlife of consumer electronics. The film showed computers being dismantled in Guiyu, China, by people wearing no safety gear, with the resulting toxic compounds moving on to degrade the water supply. The gripping images of poor people breaking apart computer components with ball-peen hammers brought home the unvarnished consequences of corporate capitalism. As one college student put it after seeing the film, "When they zoomed in on all that junk, it made me think, What if that was my printer that I just threw away last year?"[60]

Dell eventually ameliorated its environmental record to the point that the CTBC deemed it the most improved computer company of 2004. The company even ended its use of prison labor. When first called on to recycle, Dell recruited prisoners to do the dirty work to save on labor costs and boost corporate profits. The CTBC responded by simply increasing the political costs of doing business. For Dell the question became: How do we preserve the asset value of our brand name in the face of CTBC activists, dressed up in prison garb and hauling old computers around the country in a stunt called the "high-tech chain gang"? Dell found an answer in reform.[61]

Given trends in Europe, further reform of global capitalism may be in the offing. Over the last 15 years, the European Union (EU) has put forward laws that compel electronics companies to become less reliant on hazardous materials in production and more responsible for e-waste. The driving force behind these European initiatives is the "precautionary principle." The idea was pioneered in Germany back in the 1970s to deal with the threat of air pollution. It involves intervening to protect the environment when there is substantial—even if not conclusive—evidence of harm. The precautionary principle was invoked in 1987 at the Second International Conference on the Protection of the North Sea, which sought protection from chemical threats "even before a causal link has been established by absolutely clear scientific evidence." The principle has since found its way into municipal ordinances in Canada banning the cosmetic use of lawn-care pesticides and the EU's legislation on hazardous substances used in electrical equipment.[62]

COMPUTER TAKE BACK CAMPAIGN

The Computer Take Back Campaign called attention to Apple Computer's mounting e-waste contribution at the 2005 MacWorld convention in San Francisco. (Silicon Valley Toxics Coalition, "Challenging the Chip")

CONCLUSION

The environmental movement has succeeded to some extent in unmasking the ecological consequences of modern capitalism, fighting to subvert the corporation's conventional arithmetic by exposing the serious but often hidden price of the culture of consumption. And as journalist Alexander Cockburn has written, "If you know what's happening you're in a position to figure out how to do something about it, and that's always uplifting."[63]

16

CAPITALISM VERSUS THE EARTH

In the aftermath of World War II, capitalism mushroomed under the stewardship of an American empire into an international system with a planetary impact so profound that it has called into question the earth's very capacity to support life as we have come to know it.

Capitalism is a system founded on economic growth, on the never-ending accumulation of *capital*, that is, "accumulated wealth reproductively employed," as the dictionary puts it. No such economic growth, however, can be created without the transformation of nature. The natural world is, in other words, one of the building blocks of capital. To play that role it has to be reshaped in a way that fits some human purposes but not others. It is hardly an accident that the nation with the largest economy in the world has contributed more carbon dioxide to the atmosphere than any other country on the planet.[1]

Three developments made the era following World War II stand out in the history of capitalism. The first was a boom in capital accumulation unlike anything that had happened over the last five centuries. The second was the emergence of an American empire as the United States, now the richest, most powerful country in the world, took over where the British Empire had left off and, indeed, went the British one better (since the United States could reinforce its financial might with the ability to bomb any place on the planet).[2] And the third was that the capitalist system expanded to encompass virtually all the earth's people and natural resources. In short, capitalism under U.S. supervision had gone global.

The development of global capitalism under the guiding hand of the American state, which worked to enhance the opportunities of capitalists across the world to make profits, was a phenomenon of unprecedented planetary importance. Evidence of accelerating ecological impacts has abounded during the postwar period: urban development, often in biologically productive estuaries; increasing numbers of automobiles; the construction of large dams with consequent flooding; mass deforestation, especially in the tropics; vast mounds of non-decomposing trash; rising global temperatures from omnipresent fossil fuels. As some scientists have concluded, the last half-century has witnessed "the most rapid transformation of the human relationship with the natural world in the history of humankind."[3]

Interpretations of the planet's ecological woes that eschew an examination of capitalism and instead single out "human action" fall short. To point a finger at diverse aspects of postwar life such as population growth, cities, and fossil fuels without looking for the driving force behind the individual changes ignores the systemic factors structuring human interactions with the planet.[4]

For capitalism is, above all else, a system with coercive mechanisms built into it that allow it to reproduce itself. Those deprived of access to the land and the means of production, for example, have no choice but to work to make money to survive. Those with the power and means to be capitalists, for their part, arise each day knowing that if they do not figure out ways of successfully investing their money, other sharper entrepreneurs will beat them to the punch. This endless quest to accumulate and maximize wealth, to view labor and nature as commodities, has, unquestionably, produced a vast amount of material goods. It has also proved—so far—decisive in determining the fate of the earth.

DESTINATION UNLIMITED

One thing about capitalism is indisputable: it is prone to crisis. In the twentieth century, the worst was the Great Depression, an event that ended up playing a crucial role in shaping global ecology. It was viewed by many as the result of underconsumption, a state of affairs in which consumers were either unable or unwilling to buy all the material goods churned out by the economy. Even though the United States led the world in 1929 in automobile ownership—with more than three-quarters of all the globe's cars—that was still somehow not enough to ward off the worst economic catastrophe of the twentieth century.[5]

In response to the Depression and subsequent war, American society was reorganized around mass consumption, the idea that people should buy things en masse not simply to satisfy their individual needs but to advance the interests of the nation as a whole. The idea found expression at the 1939 New York World's Fair in an exhibit that highlighted the virtues of a "New Age of Abundance" destined to supersede the "Dark Ages of Scarcity." Even the architecture of the fair, epitomized by the 620-foot gleaming, modernist Trylon reaching toward the sky, suggested a yearning to transcend all limits. What that meant back on earth was driven home by General Motors' *Futurama* exhibit, which anticipated the emergence and spread of an interstate highway system plowing through suburbs.[6]

What the historian Lizabeth Cohen has dubbed a "consumers' republic" had emerged by the 1940s, introducing a new political culture that combined economic abundance with the American penchant for political freedom. An agreement had been worked out between capital, labor, and government to work together to grow the economic pie. In other words, the concern was not with redistributing wealth, but with producing more of it so that everyone could have a larger slice. The passage of the Employment Act of 1946 epitomized the maximizing imperatives at the heart of this new approach to economic affairs. The act obligated the federal government to promote "maximum employment, production, and purchasing power," with *maximum* being the operative word. To chart the progress of this newly maximizing culture, economists popularized the concepts of "gross national product" (GNP) and, almost the same thing, "gross domestic product" (GDP). Eventually both were expressed in constant dollars so that everyone could put the course of progress in perspective. Not expressed in these figures nor accounted for in any way was the ecological impact of spiraling economic growth.[7]

One resource in particular stood at the heart of the consumers' republic and literally fueled global capitalism. Oil underwrote not just growth but *faster* growth. Concentrated animal feeding operations are a case in point. Petroleum was integral to these animal factories, in which livestock, after a few months of grazing, were fed grain shipped to the site, allowing the less active animals to gain weight more quickly. Petroleum was also a *global* resource, something coal never was. Generally speaking, coal was mined and used on the same continent. Oil was much more mobile and could be pumped into pipelines and shipped across the world, eventually accounting (in 1970) for nearly two-thirds of the cargo crossing the seas.[8]

The United States played a key role in the globalization of this crucial fossil fuel. In the 1930s, the Franklin D. Roosevelt (FDR) administration elevated petroleum into an issue of national importance. It intervened to stabilize the oil market with government regulation under the Bureau of Mines so that wildcatters did not cause the price of oil and industry profits to plummet. The stabilized market in oil rested on the assumption that demand for the product would forever soar. Meanwhile, Standard Oil of California was busy halfway across the globe working out an oil concession with Saudi Arabia. Although the FDR administration tried to gain government ownership over the concession, a hybrid arrangement was achieved in which the United States would oversee investment and protection of the oil fields while U.S. companies drilled and shipped the petroleum to satisfy worldwide demand.[9]

Until 1945, the United States was self-sufficient in oil. It even supplied the vast majority of the petroleum needs of its allies in World War II. Thus, when the war ended, the United States was left with a monumental infrastructure for refining petroleum into everything from gasoline to jet fuel to asphalt. Petroleum insinuated itself into nearly every aspect of mass consumption, from plastics for toys to pesticides and fertilizer for the perfect lawns now sprawling across the burgeoning suburbs. Oil was the lifeblood of the postwar consumer economy, not only in North America but increasingly overseas, as the United States tried to re-create the world in its own image.[10]

The Marshall Plan, an economic aid program named for U.S. Secretary of State George Marshall and designed to rebuild postwar Europe along capitalist lines, was a means to this end. Europe had a choice after the war of how it would define its standard of living. Ideas for reform emanating from the European Left centered on social guarantees, but the Marshall Plan first addressed the shortage of dollars that kept Europeans from buying U.S. goods. It then evolved into a plan for economic reform that pulled Europe down the same path the United States had taken: toward generating a larger economic pie, with all its attendant ecological consequences. Economic growth, not the redistribution of wealth, was the order of the day.[11]

And, again, oil would be the lubricant that greased the way forward. The single largest expenditure under the plan was for Middle Eastern oil, a move that swelled the profits of oil companies. The Marshall Plan helped orchestrate a shift from coal to oil, in part to circumvent Communist-led miners' unions. The recovery plan also provided money for the purchase of U.S. vehicles and encouraged road building. Europeans watched as U.S. consumerism, with its automobiles, interstate highways, and suburbs, boomed. In Germany, Volkswagen emulated the U.S. automakers in its advertising and marketing.[12] Europe, in short, took a page out of the U.S. economic handbook.

The overall U.S. strategy was to tear down barriers to trade and capital in the name of economic growth. And by the 1950s, the strategy was paying off for corporations such as Unilever, Procter & Gamble, and Colgate-Palmolive. These companies set off to compete in Europe's nascent detergent market. Again, petroleum was at the center of the story. Europeans had cleaned with ashes and soaps for centuries. But in a mere generation, U.S. corporations had managed to sell Europeans on the need for a higher level of cleanliness that could only be achieved, they argued, with petroleum-based detergents, a market that one historian has described as "practically limitless." Of course the phosphates in the formula contributed to the same damaging algal blooms in Europe that happened in the United States.[13]

Through its actions in rehabilitating Europe—indeed, in its conduct throughout the world—the United States created a system of global capitalism in which endless accumulation of wealth could proceed apace. Oil was the engine driving this new form of capitalism, and no region figured more centrally in the rise of this international order than the Middle East.

U.S. Persian Gulf policy was based on two pillars. The first centered on Saudi Arabia, where U.S. oil companies and the Saudi monarchy collaborated to form a petroleum consortium named Aramco in the 1940s. The consortium cooperated with U.S. intelligence to help unlock the underground riches of the kingdom, while the American military proceeded apace to build bases throughout the region. The second pillar was Iran. In 1953, the United States and Britain conspired to overthrow the democratically elected government of Mohammad Mosaddegh, who had led the charge to nationalize and expel a British oil company operating in the country. The coup brought to power the country's hereditary "shah," Mohammad Reza Pahlavi, who helped U.S. oil companies receive a 40 percent share in the nation's oil concessions in return for supporting his rise to power. With friendly governments in place in Saudi Arabia and Iran, Western companies further exploited the Middle Eastern oil fields. Though it is true that the United States was becoming increasingly dependent on foreign oil imports, U.S. policy in the Middle East was not actually a resource grab for the benefit of American consumers. Rather, the goal of American empire in this region was (and remains) to help guarantee global trade, the free movement of capital, and thereby grow the economic pie.[14]

This preoccupation with economic growth rested on a sky's-the-limit approach to the natural world, a point underscored by an animated cartoon titled *Destination Earth* produced in 1954 by the American Petroleum Institute. In the film, Mars and Earth face off, the former led by a communist dictatorship, the latter by prosperous freedom-lovers smitten with automobiles powered by oil, which, conveniently, does quadruple duty as an input in asphalt, tires, weed killer, and heating fuel. When a Martian explorer returns with news about the virtues of the auto-loving free world, the citizens of Mars revolt in the name of capitalism and mass consumption. Together oil and capitalism can make any dream come true and pave the way for what the film calls "destination unlimited."[15]

BANKING ON NATURE

If the transformation of capitalism into a truly global system had its start in any one place, it was in the halls of the U.S. Department of the Treasury. By the 1930s, as the world struggled through the Great Depression and many nations devalued their currencies, the Treasury Department focused on one main issue: figuring out how to ensure the health of U.S. exports and thereby surpass Britain in dominating international trade.

The goal of Treasury officials was to stabilize currencies and put in place a world economic order in which trade and investment could flourish as investors moved money across the globe. The first step in making the world safe for the free movement of capital occurred in 1944 in the little town of Bretton Woods, New Hampshire, where world leaders gathered to enshrine the U.S. dollar and thereby allow the United States to preside over the health of the global economy. To advance this goal, the Bretton Woods agreement established a system of fixed exchange rates based on the link between the dollar and gold at a time when the United States controlled the bulk of the world's gold. The agreement also gave birth to the International Monetary Fund (IMF) and the World Bank. Led by the United States, the largest financial contributor to both, these institutions liberalized the conditions for trade in goods and the investment of capital. (It is important to realize that, with memories of the Great Depression still fresh, countries could still impose some tariffs and restrict the flow of capital to protect their citizens from the dangers of unrestrained capitalism.)[16]

U.S. Secretary of the Treasury Henry Morgenthau, who presided over the Bretton Woods meeting, nicely summed up the assumptions behind this new international economic order. In his view, limitless economic expansion was the key to world peace and stability. He urged the Bretton Woods delegates to seize the opportunity for increasing "material progress on an earth infinitely blessed with natural riches." He believed that growth was a limitless proposition, that "prosperity has no fixed limits"[17] If Morgenthau had any doubts about whether the planet could support this perpetual economic development under U.S. empire, he withheld them.

Although some might quarrel with the use of the term *empire* in discussing the United States' role in the making of global capitalism, without the intervention of the United States the entire planet could never have come to embrace the postwar economic order.

Consider Indonesia, which won its independence from the Dutch after World War II. Independence required the newly formed nation to pay off large debts to the Netherlands. By the 1960s, with the price of rubber—a major export— falling, the country entered a crisis. President Sukarno operated under the assumption that the world owed the Indonesian people a minimum standard of living, especially in light of the horrors of Dutch colonialism and Japanese wartime occupation. Sukarno borrowed money but also began veering to the left by supporting the Communist Party and eventually pulled out of the IMF and the World Bank. The U.S. intelligence establishment subsequently backed procapitalist military forces in a coup led by a general named Suharto and then abetted the slaughter of hundreds of thousands of people in the coup's aftermath.[18]

The Suharto regime was firmly in the capitalist camp. It opened its arms to foreign investment in oil and timber, creating profits and increasing the revenue of the Indonesian government but doing little to lift the economic prospects of the people as a whole. Timber exports stood at 10 million dollars annually when Suharto took over in 1966. Five years later that number had skyrocketed 16 times, as logging companies based in the United States, Japan, and the Philippines, profiting from a currency reform imposed by the IMF, denuded forestland and compromised water quality.[19]

The intensive exploitation of the natural resources of poor countries evolved into a cornerstone of global capitalism. The U.S.-dominated IMF aided this process with its heavily conditioned loans to governments and so did the World Bank, which underwrote and guaranteed the loans of private capital. These loans helped construct large-scale infrastructure that stimulated economic growth by mortgaging the natural environment of the country in question. The model worked particularly well under authoritarian governments such as Suharto's in Indonesia. The World Bank had denied his predecessor (Sukarno) funding, but Suharto, whose government embraced capitalism, was another story. In the 20 years following 1968, the World Bank approved hundreds of millions of dollars in loans for more than 20 large dams in Indonesia, not to mention hundreds of smaller water control projects. When protests arose because of these large, technocratic endeavors, which fragmented watersheds and limited the movement of species, Suharto's government quashed them.[20]

The model for large-scale, top-down projects like those in Indonesia had been pioneered by the United States. In 1933, the federal government embarked on an immense plan for rescuing the Tennessee River Valley, an expanse of flood- and erosion-prone land mired in poverty in the heart of Appalachia. A federal agency, the Tennessee Valley Authority (TVA), oversaw an elaborate scheme, centered on flood control and inexpensive electricity, for breathing new life into this embattled region. The authority oversaw one of the most extraordinary outbursts of dam building ever recorded, constructing 16 imposing concrete structures between 1933 and 1944, as well as coal-fired power plants designed to provide electricity to the poor. Never before in American history had a federal agency been formed to manage the economic destiny of such a vast region, making it the perfect model for the new international order symbolized by the World Bank. Although the undertaking had some positive economic implications for the valley, it caused immense ecological and social dislocation. The building of dams flooded many areas and forced thousands off the land (15,000 in Tennessee's Norris River basin alone), while the strip-mining of coal ransacked the landscape and led to serious pollution and erosion.[21]

TVA'S CHICKAMAUGA DAM AND POWERHOUSE RECEPTION ROOM

Completed in 1940, the modernist Chickamauga Dam was one of 16 dams built between 1933 and 1944 that, in President Truman's words, "put . . . under the control of man a whole vast river." (Library of Congress)

With the TVA model in mind, the World Bank set off to transform watersheds around the world. The bank's environmental footprint has been stunning: in the 50 years after 1944, it lent tens of billions of dollars for more than 600 dams located in 93 countries. The bank seemed to prefer authoritarian governments. For example, it largely ignored Brazil under João Goulart, who advocated state intervention to benefit the poor. But in 1964, after a U.S.-supported military coup replaced Goulart with a dictatorship, the World Bank poured money into the country to support monumental dams. These included the largest hydropower scheme in the world, jointly constructed by Brazil and Paraguay, a project that displaced 42,000 people and flooded an area—including forest ecosystems— about 50 percent larger than the entire state of Texas.[22] The resulting electric power hardly put a dent in Brazil's poverty problem.

In Thailand, the World Bank spent years helping the government focus on the export of timber, rubber, palm oil, and sugarcane. Loans subsidized the creation of plantations dedicated to such export-oriented agriculture. The consequent breakneck economic development had at least two important consequences. First, as more land was cleared for agriculture, forests declined dramatically— from 53 percent to 28 percent of the total land area between 1961 and the late 1980s. Deforestation, in turn, played a role in catastrophic floods that tore through the nation in 1988. Second, the transformation of the countryside into large agricultural enterprises left millions with no land at all. Evicted in the name of more efficient, capitalist development, landless farmers, families in tow, flooded into cities. The vast majority of Bangkok's prostitutes, one study has shown, came from such poor rural areas.[23]

Likewise, in Ecuador, aid from the U.S. government and the World Bank financed highways so that banana production could thrive. Virgin rain forest succumbed to chemical-intensive agriculture as Dow Chemical and Monsanto penetrated the country's tropics. Across the world, the deforestation of tropical regions accelerated beginning in the 1940s as poor countries, drawn into the orbit of a pulsating global capitalist system, shifted toward the production of export crops such as bananas, coffee, and sugar.[24]

Local, direct interactions with the natural world among peoples who seemed to know how to live in a world of limits—from rice farmers in Burma (now Myanmar) to pastoralists in Afghanistan—were replaced by roundabout dealings with nature orchestrated by bureaucratic institutions. National economic planning schemes that relied on outside corporations, technology, and complex economic calculations necessitated by the rise of global capitalism operated as if the natural world were an inexhaustible source of "factors of production."

The wrenching social and ecological consequences of postwar development stand in marked contrast to the local irrigation agriculture that once dominated the countryside. Rice farmers had long been accustomed to banding together to build simple irrigation systems using mud, bamboo, and logs to channel the water. This method prevented sediment from building up, a problem caused by large dams, which often completely sealed off a river. These local committees also protected upland forest areas to ensure that the watershed functioned in an ecologically sustainable way.[25]

THE GREEN REVOLUTION

The actions of the World Bank, the IMF, and other U.S.-dominated global financial institutions unfolded against the backdrop of decolonization. From the desert and savanna of Africa to the plains of India and Pakistan to the rain forests of Indonesia and Papua New Guinea, colonial empires, the product of decades of European imperialism, collapsed in the postwar years. And as Western Europe's empires broke apart, U.S. policymakers saw an opportunity not to rectify past injustices but to absorb decolonized people into the global capitalist system.

The Americans had in mind their own kind of revolution, a green one. Beginning in the 1940s and accelerating in the 1960s, what became known (in 1968) as the green revolution swept across many poor parts of the globe, transforming them with the introduction of high-yielding strains of crops—wheat and rice especially—that depended on large amounts of chemical inputs, machinery, and water. The idea was to mount a green revolution, address hunger, and thereby preempt a red revolution, a turn toward communism.[26]

The United States had gone through its own green revolution beginning in the 1930s. Previously, farmers growing corn had depended on the natural process of pollination to produce seeds—in the case of corn, the actual kernels. When the wind blew, pollen from different varieties of corn plants went airborne and fertilized the same or other corn plants. A diverse gene pool resulted. Then, in the early part of the twentieth century, scientists took the seed from two hybrid varieties of corn—each bringing with it different genetic stock—to produce a "double-cross" hybrid. The move dramatically increased corn yields. In the 1930s, companies sold the new and improved seeds to farmers throughout the Midwest's Corn Belt. World War II siphoned manpower from farms and made high crop yields increasingly important, spurring the sale of hybrid seeds. By the 1960s, the new generation of corn had almost completely overtaken America's fields.[27]

Although these varieties boosted yields, they also narrowed the gene pool (as company-bred seed eclipsed pollination) and led to the further intrusion of corporate enterprise into agriculture. Traditional corn seeds could be replanted from one year to the next without diminishing yields, but not the new varieties. Replanting led to a reduced harvest. Each year, farmers had to buy more from seed companies, which patented the parent stock and breeding sequence for the double-cross hybrid corn. Instead of producing their own corn seed or trading for it with a neighbor, farmers now grew more dependent than ever on outside companies for agricultural germ plasm. Seeds had made the leap from a public good to a sheer commodity.

One of the first people to realize the commercial value of the high-yield hybrid corn seeds was Henry Wallace, a prominent Iowa farmer who went on to become secretary of agriculture in the FDR administration. In the 1940s, Wallace convinced the Rockefeller Foundation—a corporate philanthropy endowed by the founder of the Standard Oil Company in 1913—to set up an agricultural research center in Mexico. The Mexican government's populist reforms in the 1930s had led to the expropriation of many farm holdings and oil fields owned by U.S. companies. Given Mexico's proximity to the United States, the Rockefeller Foundation was eager to head off any further movement in a left-wing direction. The foundation recruited plant scientist Norman Borlaug to work on developing a more productive breed of wheat to boost Mexican harvests. Eventually, Borlaug, who in 1970 won the Nobel Peace Prize, succeeded in breeding a set of high-yielding semidwarf wheat varieties. The new strains of wheat required heavy doses of nitrogen and focused photosynthetic activity on the production of grain, as opposed to the stem of the plant. Shorter stalks also kept the wheat heads—now much larger—from toppling over.[28]

Between 1956 and 1966, the productivity of Mexican agriculture boomed in response to the changes. Large landowners mainly benefited—these substantial commercial farms could afford the herbicides, fertilizer, and water control measures necessary to grow the new crops. It was these enterprises that generated the money to finance imports of consumer goods, while the peasants working communal lands found that the green revolution had passed them by. Many migrated to the United States to find work.[29]

From its origins in Mexico, the green revolution—with the aid of the Rockefeller and Ford foundations, the United Nations, and the U.S. Agency for International Development—spread around the globe. If the green revolution played a positive role in the tripling of harvests worldwide between 1950 and 1990, overall, there was nothing revolutionary about it in any traditional sense. It was a technocratic reform founded on the idea that enough economic growth would lift all boats. It did not address unequal land distribution and worsened life at the bottom of rural societies: by substituting technology for labor, it created a surplus population that could no longer survive on the land.[30]

Just as had happened to U.S. farmers, those who worked the soil in foreign lands lost control over the agricultural gene pool, as seeds went from being a free good to a commodity that had to be purchased. Farmers who had once saved seeds and exchanged them freely now had to figure out how to pay for the expensive new varieties sold by corporations.[31]

The new generation of higher-yielding seeds also undermined the nutrient cycle. In India, for instance, rice was traditionally raised not only for food but also to produce fodder. Stalks fed to livestock generated valuable manure that was used to maintain soil fertility. The new green revolution varieties—containing less stalk and more grain—broke up this endless loop of nutrient transmission and substituted a costly and ecologically destructive one-way production system.

Basic agricultural inputs such as seeds, fertilizer, and pesticides now had to be purchased to produce a single commercially viable product: grain. Nitrogen-based fertilizer was especially crucial to the success of the new dwarf species. "If I were a member of your parliament," Nobel laureate Borlaug told Indian politicians in 1967, "I would leap from my seat every fifteen minutes and yell at the top of my voice, 'Fertilizers! . . . Give the farmers more fertilizers!'" By 1980, India imported 600 percent more fertilizer than it had in the late 1960s. Nearby lakes and rivers suffered increased nutrient pollution as some of the chemicals missed their mark.[32]

The green revolution also dramatically reduced genetic diversity. Untold numbers of ecologically adapted, locally grown species of wheat and rice disappeared, replaced by a mere handful of varieties. By the mid-1980s, for example, the thousands of different kinds of rice once grown in the Philippines had given way to just two green revolution species.[33]

Another problem was monoculture. Single-crop farming led, as it almost always does, to increased problems with pests. Beginning in the late 1960s, bacterial blights followed by the tungro virus, struck the new dwarf rice in Southeast Asia. Infestation, in turn, produced greater reliance on pesticides. In the Philippines, pesticide imports quadrupled between 1972 and 1978. Ultimately, the green revolution forced Third World nations down the path of chemical dependency. The revolution ended when the economic downturn of the 1970s and a spike in oil prices raised the costs of agricultural inputs.[34]

Increased grain yields, many have argued, justified the ecological price. By the 1970s, peasants in Malaysia, who for centuries had lived under the specter of famine, had enough rice to last the entire year. In the Philippines, grain harvests improved so much that by the late 1970s the country was actually exporting rice. The benefits of the increased yields, however, bypassed the Philippine people, who remained one of the most poorly fed populations in all of Asia. Similarly, in India, wheat yields in the Punjab soared in the 1960s while, at the same time, the number of people living in poverty actually increased. Even in Malaysia, a supposed success story, the results of the revolution proved far more mixed. The greatest profits from the revolution went to those with the means to afford large amounts of land and capital, contributing to increased social inequality. In the final analysis, those countries that benefited most, as it were, from the green revolution—Mexico, India, Pakistan, the Philippines, and Indonesia—have ended up as some of the most malnourished nations on the globe.[35]

CAPITALISM GOES GLOBAL

Even into the 1970s, international capitalism was a work in progress and had yet to penetrate all four corners of the globe. There were still important restraints on capital, with economic nationalists in poor countries bent on bettering the lives of their own citizens rather than caving in to the wishes of foreign investors for profit. This was expressed through various nationalizations (transfers of assets from private to government control) in petroleum-rich countries in the mid-1970s. In 1974, the United Nations gave its imprimatur to such activity by resolving that every country had a legal right to expropriate foreign property. Even in the United States—the capital of capitalism—there were restraints in place. Political leaders felt compelled to compromise with labor—understandable in light of the 5,716 work stoppages in 1970—and manage the money supply with the aim of full employment. In addition, Richard Nixon signed an impressive list of environmental and occupational health and safety reforms that constrained the behavior of corporations.[36] What happened to remove these checks and set capitalism free to conquer the globe?

The short answer is that capitalism entered into one of its perennial crises in the 1970s, a crisis of profitability linked to a decline in economic growth. One theory is that all the class and environmental conflict caused a shock to the system. Nevertheless, it is agreed that a crisis related to stagnating labor productivity and a decline in profits presented the most serious threat to capitalism since the Great Depression. The postwar economic order—managing demand by underwriting mass consumption with high-wage jobs and government benefits—proved unable to address the decline in economic growth and the harsh 1974 recession that grew out of it. While some advocated for even more liberal government intervention and coordination with business and labor, others cried out for a new form of liberalism: *neoliberalism*, an ideology that threw all restraint to the wind.[37]

In the 1930s, Franklin D. Roosevelt appropriated the word *liberalism* and associated it with an activist state founded on reforms such as welfare and social security. Neoliberals, however, built on the neoclassical tradition in economics, which placed its faith in people's ability to maximize utility and profits under competitive markets. Where they differed from this tradition was that they saw a need for state intervention to establish a framework of strong private property rights and free trade and markets in which capitalists would rule the roost. Within that framework, the market with its price mechanism could function as the all-knowing arbiter of life on earth—all limits and restraints with respect to both social and ecological relations be damned.[38]

Early proponents of this new ideology included economists such as Austrian Friedrich A. von Hayek and University of Chicago professor Milton Friedman. That both men won the Nobel Prize in Economics in the mid-1970s testifies to the power of this new philosophy. In that same era, Freidman and like-minded economists from the University of Chicago ("the Chicago Boys") were enlisted to help the military dictator of Chile, Augusto Pinochet (installed with CIA help in a 1973 coup against the elected left-wing government), to privatize formerly public services and to repress labor unions. Export-oriented agriculture expanded at the expense of the Chilean people and the natural environment. Forests soon suffered from overexploitation.[39]

Although operating in a democratic framework, Ronald Reagan in the United States (president 1981–1989) and Margaret Thatcher in Britain (prime minister 1979–1990) shared a Pinochet-like reverence for the free market, unfettered by governmental regulation and labor unions. Their version of neoliberalism helped grease the way, in other words, for the flourishing of global capitalism. The new view of the economic world, as one French commentator presciently put it, "accepts no self-limitation in the name of the collective interest, or of the right of future generations to the common heritage of humanity—a planet where they can live."[40]

At precisely the moment when some scientists were warning that compound economic growth on a finite planet could not go on forever, those pushing the neoliberal worldview moved in exactly the opposite direction: toward a trust that markets, more than democratic governance, would set people free. They contended that unlike shortsighted politicians whose vision of the future did not extend beyond the next election, markets in natural resources such as oil operated as vast processors of information. Stand back, they urged, and let the market work its magic. Yet even those economists promoting this point of view had to admit that the invisible hand tended to overlook "the welfare of future inhabitants of the planet," as one Nobel laureate infatuated with economic growth wrote in 1974.[41]

For capitalism to encompass the globe, this obsession with market discipline had to expand well beyond the musty world of economics journals. Before that could happen, the United States had to get its own house in order. To deal with rampant inflation—an economic ill that eats away at the value of money—and tame the unruly working class, the U.S. Federal Reserve raised interest rates and put in place a monetary policy that caused unemployment to rise to double digits by the early 1980s. Inflation declined, but at the expense of the working class. Under neoliberalism, the individual, not collective action or the well-being of society, was what mattered. People were not supposed to worry about the welfare of the old widow down the street. And if people could not be concerned with widows, they certainly could not be allowed to care about the natural world, a point underscored by a 1979 study by one prominent business group that recommended lower standards for air quality and tried to shore up industry profits by floating the idea of "acceptable risk."[42]

At roughly the same time, some Arab states, seeking to draw the world's attention to the problem of Israel's occupation of Palestine, cut back on the production of oil. Oil prices rose considerably in the 1970s as a result. Oil-exporting countries now had lots of dollars to channel into U.S. banks. And with poor countries struggling to stay afloat and pay back Western creditors during a global recession—an event precipitated in part by the Federal Reserve's hike in interest rates—banks such as Chase Manhattan seized a golden opportunity to peddle loans to Third World countries, eventually hastening a debt crisis as interest rates ballooned throughout the decade.[43] From the U.S. Treasury came word to Third World nations: reduce imports, produce more exports, and subject your nation to austerity—tighten your belts, in other words, regardless of what it might mean for your people or the environment.

What it meant for the environment crystallized soon enough as the Third World debt problem assumed crisis proportions. Between 1982 and 1990, poor countries paid a staggering 1.3 trillion dollars to creditor nations, and many still failed to meet their repayment obligations. Under the old economic approach, lenders would simply be forced to accept the consequences of making bad loans. Under neoliberalism, however, the borrowing countries had to repay the debt regardless of the impact. So the World Bank and the IMF lent these nations more money, but in exchange, the banks forced the debtor nations to remove government subsidies and barriers to trade, bringing market discipline to bear as these countries were forced to embrace "structural adjustment," a euphemism that masked the pillaging of the environment that took place as poor nations, stuck on a debt treadmill, became even more dependent on the export of commodities—timber, fish, minerals—to pay back their loans. Some 70 countries underwent structural adjustment between 1978 and 1992.[44]

One study of the 24 largest debtor nations found that two-thirds of them experienced major deforestation in the 1980s. Brazil, for example, the largest debtor nation, had to come up with 12 billion to 14 billion dollars in interest payments each year by the late 1980s. To raise that kind of money, the country turned to soybeans, a cash crop used in animal feeds. To grow soybeans on the necessary scale, a significant amount of land in the agriculturally rich southern part of the country had to be dedicated to commercial farming. And before that could happen, the peasants living there had to be driven off. Thus the Brazilian government, with loans from the World Bank for a road-building venture, urged farmers to migrate north to the Amazon, where land was plentiful but covered with trees. By the mid-1980s, the forests of the Brazilian Amazon had come under attack. The fires set to clear them could be seen from outer space.[45]

Brazil was not alone in its debt and deforestation woes. Costa Rica, Ghana, and the Philippines also liquidated their woodlands to generate greater foreign exchange earnings. Tropical forests, one of the most biologically diverse areas on the planet, declined by one-third between 1960 and 1990. One study has estimated that reducing a nation's debt by 1 billion dollars could decrease deforestation by anywhere from 20 to 385 square miles. A blind faith in market imperatives had in 30 years' time transformed tropical forests in Asia, Africa, and Latin America—forests with a combined area the size of India—into pulp.[46]

The globalization of capitalism involved more than just the traditional liquidation of natural resources for sale on markets. As export production expanded—a process driven by the liberalization of trade, the imposition of structural adjustment, and greater freedom for capital—it inspired new, more industrial forms of agriculture that incorporated the natural environment in innovative ways beyond the simple absorption of nature into the world of market exchange.

In Latin America, exotic fruits, vegetables, and flowers, all heavily dependent on industrial inputs that had to be purchased from multinational corporations, took command of the landscape. In Chile, table grapes and avocados supplanted more mundane exports such as beans and wool. In Ecuador and Colombia, cut flowers, sent north for Valentine's and Mother's Day, proliferated. (One report on Ecuadorian floriculture noted that chemical runoff from the fields had led to the extinction of some plants and animals.) Governments and international financial institutions invested in "cool chains," energy-hungry logistics systems that preserved produce and flowers from production to distribution.[47]

Meanwhile, in Asia, global capitalism brought about yet another form of industrial agriculture: so-called aquaculture, or fish farming, on a scale previously unheard of in world history, a blue revolution that followed the green one. Aquaculture had been practiced in Asia on a small scale for thousands of years, but after World War II, as demand in the global north for shrimp and salmon increased, it evolved into an industrial enterprise, though it accounted for less than 4 percent of world fish production in 1970. Thirty years later, as trade liberalization and export markets continued to grow relentlessly, it represented more than 27 percent of the world total. Shrimp farming in Southeast Asia surged beginning in the 1980s. Estuaries and mangrove forests, some of the most biologically productive environments on the planet, gave way to ponds managed with chemicals, feeds, and machines for quickly freezing the shrimp for shipment. The new ecosystem, said one critic, "no more mimics the mangrove forest or the coastal estuary in which it is situated than would a parking lot." In some instances, corporations carved shrimp farms into spots along government land, locations that had long been vital to the success of local communities. Thus the ramped-up fish farming ultimately meant enclosure and dispossession. And ecological impacts abounded, including excessive exploitation of groundwater supplies, nutrient pollution, and, unsurprisingly, given shrimp farming's status as a form of monoculture, the outbreak of serious disease that led production to crash periodically.[48]

The commodification of nature had evolved into the production of true commodities, or commodities that would not exist were it not for the production process itself. Take tree plantations, another industry that has thrived in Southeast Asia, Brazil, and Chile over the last 30 years. We have seen how the United States shifted its logging operations across the country with the depletion of old-growth forest. But with the exhaustion of forest cover across the globe, an entirely new form of industrial production arose to cater to the market in wood products. In this case, the living organisms—the trees—would not exist were it not for the intervention of foreign capital and workers. The trees are bred to grow rapidly and, again, depend on large amounts of chemical inputs. The advent of these plantations led to the eviction of the locals and their replacement with industrial forests. As one critic put it, "Trees eat people."[49] It is more accurate, however, to say that global capitalism ate the natural forest and those who depended on it not just to cut trees for market, but for firewood and fodder. We are a long way from the world of some bundled-up New England colonists with axes heading into the seventeenth-century forest and shipping the timber off to market in Boston.

LIFE'S ESSENTIALS

If global capitalism ratcheted up the commodification of nature, it also cast its shadow across the essentials of life, capitalizing on the earth's biodiversity as well as its supply of freshwater in ways never dreamed of before.

In 1973, two U.S. biologists, Stanley Cohen and Herbert Boyer, combined genetic material from two different living organisms that, on their own, would not normally reproduce with each other. The new biotechnology, as it was called, allowed scientists to manipulate genes and to introduce new and potentially valuable traits into plants and animals.

Not until the 1980s did the commercial value of biotechnology—which some have compared to the discovery of fire—begin to be realized. Investors awaited the development of a brave new legal world, one in which living organisms could be patented, giving corporations an incentive to finance research and development in this promising field. At the time of Cohen and Boyer's discovery, patents could be secured for fruit trees and strawberries (under federal legislation passed in 1930) and for crops bred with seeds such as wheat and soybeans (under the 1970 Plant Variety Protection Act). In 1972, a General Electric scientist had tried to expand the reach of the law by patenting a microscopic organism, a type of bacteria that broke down crude oil and was used to mop up tanker spills. The U.S. Patent and Trademark Office had rejected his request. In 1980, however, the U.S. Supreme Court ruled the oil-eating bacterium "patentable subject matter." Wall Street was elated. New public offerings of biotechnology stocks surged.[50]

Armed with the necessary legal tools, biotechnology firms set about researching and developing new plants and animals. They claimed to be solving world hunger. With the green revolution having run its course, they argued, an opportunity existed to boost agricultural yields and help impoverished children. "Worrying about starving future generations won't feed them. Food biotechnology will," read one Monsanto advertisement.[51]

Feeding the malnourished was never the driving force behind biotechnology. Profits from chemical sales, not human welfare, motivated this bold new science. Multinational corporations such as Monsanto and Du Pont make money selling chemicals. Monsanto introduced an entire line of crops designed to tolerate heavy doses of the company's most popular pesticide product. Farmers could funnel the pesticide into sprinkler systems and spray it far and wide, killing weeds without worrying about harming their crops. In return, the company required customers to sign an agreement forbidding them from saving any genetically modified seeds produced for replanting, from sharing the company's patented seeds with neighbors, and from using any pesticide except the one sold by the company. It even hired muscle to handle those who broke the rules.[52]

Trade agreements also created a legal environment that permitted multinational corporations to profit from plant life found in the Third World. In 1995, intellectual property law was codified in the agreements of the World Trade Organization (WTO), newly founded to oversee global trade rules. The WTO obligated over 100 nations to abide by legal norms hatched in an Anglo-American context, which now applied to everything from software to living organisms.[53]

Consider, for example, the neem tree found in India. Various parts of the tree had been used there to treat medical ailments and insect problems. In the early 1970s, a U.S. citizen imported neem extract to help develop a pesticide. He eventually sold his patents on the tree extract to the multinational corporation W. R. Grace; it went on to patent a number of solutions derived from the tree's seeds. Although Indian farmers had long been aware of the tree's valuable uses, one Grace executive characterized such local, nonscientific knowledge as "folk medicine."[54]

A corporate perspective views Third World genetic material as part of the "common heritage of mankind," a gift of nature. In reality, these thousands of plant species did not evolve by chance; countless hours of labor, much of it conducted by peasant women who used kitchen gardens to breed and manage plant and animal life for domestic uses, produced them. "God didn't give us 'rice' or 'wheat' or 'potato,'" Suman Sahai, an Indian opponent of bioprospecting, observed. Peasants did, developing domesticated plants from wild ones.[55]

In 1984, a Du Pont biotechnology executive called for "international conventions that would provide greater uniformity with respect to patentability." In the 1990s, a world trade agreement made this wish a dream come true, compelling nations to grant at least some protection to patented plants. Vandana Shiva, a prominent Indian environmental activist, pointed out that the word *patent* derived from the letters patent granted to Columbus and other explorers as they set off to conquer and colonize the Western Hemisphere. Recall that the European colonists found what they took to be vast stretches of empty lands when they first settled North America. That assumption allowed them to justify the conquest of Native American soil as a mission to improve an untouched wilderness. Such a view overlooked the ways in which native peoples made use of these lands. Now multinational companies sought to colonize Third World genetic material—the product of considerable time and effort—by defining it as just another wasted resource in need of improvement. International conventions confirming this outlook, according to Shiva, amounted to little more than what she called biopiracy.[56]

Multinational corporations have also tried to profit from privatizing water. Freshwater is a scarce resource, with only 2.5 percent of the blue planet's water free from salt. Seeking to capitalize on this scarcity, multinationals including

Vivendi Universal, Suez, Bechtel, and Enron entered the water services market. Four billion dollars in water megadeals occurred between 1994 and 1998 alone. As *Fortune* magazine reported in 2000, "Water promises to be to the 21st century what oil was to the 20th century: the precious commodity that determines the wealth of nations."[57]

The World Bank and the IMF encouraged the corporate takeover of water. These institutions commonly required the privatization of local water supplies as a condition for loans. Then, at the 2000 World Water Forum held at The Hague, government leaders, World Bank officials, executives, and nongovernmental groups endorsed the idea of water as a "basic human need." For centuries, drinking water had been viewed as a shared, common resource and access to it tacitly understood as a *right*. (The word for Islamic law, *shari'a*, means "the sharing of water.") If water is a *need*, then it makes perfect sense for the World Bank to support dams and other projects that will yield profits for some instead of safe drinking water for all. To call water a need implies that it must be paid for by those who want it.[58]

That was precisely the logic of Bechtel and its subsidiary in Cochabamba, Bolivia. In 1999, the company struck a 40-year deal with the Bolivian government to improve the city's water supply and to enrich itself with a return of 16 percent per year. The water flowed and water bills increased. It was not simply the price rise alone that outraged Cochabambinos. What also upset them was the assault on customary rights to the resource, in particular, the expropriation of cooperative wells—built by local residents without any government help—and the installation of company water meters. As some peasants put it, Bechtel was trying to "lease the rain." Residents organized protests and battled the Bolivian government to force it to end the agreement with Bechtel. The violence escalated as the government cracked down on the protestors, killing a teenager. With the prospect of increased tensions, the Bolivian government ended its contract with the company. "We have proved that the water is ours," said Oscar Olivera, a shoe worker who led the opposition to Bechtel. "We the people own it. Not private companies or even the government."[59] After all, everyone on the planet should have a legitimate right to the wealth of nature.

A COLOSSAL MARKET FAILURE

By the end of the twentieth century, the United States used more energy per capita than any other nation in the world: twice the rate of Sweden, roughly three times that of Japan or Italy. As of 1988, the United States, with just 5 percent of the earth's population, consumed 25 percent of all the world's oil and released roughly a quarter of all global carbon emissions. More recently, the pattern of emissions has shifted. In 2014, the top emitters of carbon dioxide were China, the United States, the European Union, India, the Russian Federation, and Japan. But the rampant energy use that has characterized life in the capital of capitalism has meant that the United States has contributed more than any other nation in the world to the global carbon dioxide problem. "In cumulative terms," U.S. political scientist David Victor recently explained, "we certainly own this problem more than anybody else does."[60]

Back about 4.5 billion years ago, when the earth was formed, roughly 95 percent of the atmosphere consisted of carbon dioxide. The emergence of plant life, however, changed the planet's atmospheric composition because plants, through the process of photosynthesis, absorb carbon dioxide. Carbon was drawn out of the atmosphere and settled in the earth's vegetation, which eventually died, decomposed, and in some areas formed coal and oil. As a result, the carbon dioxide load declined dramatically.

With the onset of industrial capitalism and the burning of fossil fuels, the earth's previous atmospheric history was sent into reverse. Instead of being drawn out of the air, carbon was now extracted from the ground and launched into the sky once again. In the United States, the largest surge in energy consumption occurred between the late 1930s and the 1970s, ballooning by 350 percent. Americans began using more oil and natural gas to meet their industrial, agricultural, and everyday needs for transportation and housing. Oil and natural gas contain less carbon than coal or wood, but this small piece of good news was more than outweighed by the huge increase in demand for electricity and fuel as the nation's economy became more consumption-oriented. In 1950, Americans drove three-quarters of all the world's automobiles. They lived in high-energy suburban homes with inefficient electric heaters and air conditioners. A 1970s color television, left on for the four hours a day that a household on average watched, was the energy equivalent of a week's worth of work for a team of horses. U.S. energy consumption slowed in the 1970s and 1980s, as manufacturers introduced more efficient appliances. Nevertheless, even in the late 1980s, Americans consumed more petroleum than Germany, Japan, France, Italy, Canada, and the United Kingdom did together.[61]

Burgeoning fossil fuel use in the twentieth century left its mark on the carbon history of the earth. Deforestation also added to the atmosphere's carbon load. Forests normally serve as vast "carbon sinks," producing oxygen while keeping carbon dioxide in check. The massive clearing of forests in the United States early in the century, however, combined with the huge increase in postwar tropical deforestation, has helped to reshape atmospheric conditions. In 1900, carbon dioxide levels measured about 295 parts per million (ppm). By 1950, that figure had increased to 310 to 315 ppm, rising to 378 ppm in 2005, courtesy of the double punch provided by fossil fuel consumption and deforestation. As of this writing, the average concentration of carbon dioxide in the earth's atmosphere, as measured by the National Oceanic and Atmospheric Administration at its observatory in Hawaii, has reached 408 ppm.[62]

Carbon dioxide, in combination with its fellow greenhouse gases methane and ozone, traps the sun's heat. Without these greenhouse gases, life on earth would be frigid. Human beings need them, but not in the amounts currently being pumped into the atmosphere. And the downside is becoming more and more evident. Most of the warming of the earth's surface temperatures has occurred during the past 35 years. In a stunning development, 16 of the 17 warmest years on record (from data extending back to 1880) have occurred since 2001.[63]

The consequences of global warming are showing up all across the planet. Glaciers throughout the world are receding. In 1979, Arctic sea ice spread across 1.7 billion acres. Recent NASA investigations, however, have detected a substantial sea-ice decline of 250 million acres. Plant life is coming into bloom earlier than it once did. Even the world's oceans, a vast resource covering 70 percent of the earth's surface, are feeling the effects. The water is becoming not just warmer but more acidic, endangering coral reefs and the millions of species that reside on them. Coastal areas are beginning to feel the effects of rising sea levels, threatening not only low-lying islands but some of the world's largest cities.[64]

If history is any guide, the warming could precipitate an era of "megadrought," as happened in the American West during the so-called Medieval Warm Period from A.D. 800 to 1300. The potential exists for such droughts to cause enormous human suffering, especially in light of the 20 to 30 million people who died worldwide during El Niño–driven droughts and famines in the late nineteenth century. Already there is evidence that in the second half of the twentieth century the majority of changes in the hydrological cycle of the American West resulted from climate change caused by greenhouse gases. The changing hydrology will negatively impact the region's embattled water supply. "Our results," the authors of one major study ominously conclude, "are not good news for those living in the western United States." In short, a giant, potentially devastating global experiment is now underway.[65]

Scientists first expressed concern about the perils of increasing carbon emissions and their link to global climate change back in the 1960s. In 1965, President Lyndon Johnson even saw fit to make a brief mention of the matter to Congress. But the issue was quickly obscured by the Vietnam War and the racial unrest that came to define LBJ's presidency. And in any case, since the world's climate is prone to change, it remained unclear at that time whether rising temperature readings had resulted from human or natural causes.[66]

Increasingly, however, scientific opinion crystallized into an acceptance that global warming was a long-term trend, reflecting above all the steeply increasing consumption of fossil fuels since the mid-twentieth century. In the late 1980s the World Meteorological Organization and the United Nations Environment Program formed the Intergovernmental Panel on Climate Change (IPCC). The group of over 1,000 scientists has periodically assessed the peer-reviewed scientific literature on global warming and synthesized the findings. "It is *extremely likely*," the IPCC's most recent assessment (2013) explains, "that human influence has been the dominant cause of the observed warming since the mid-20th century."[67]

Variations of the Earth's surface temperature for:

(a) the past 140 years

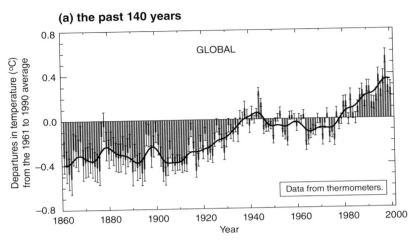

(b) the past 1,000 years

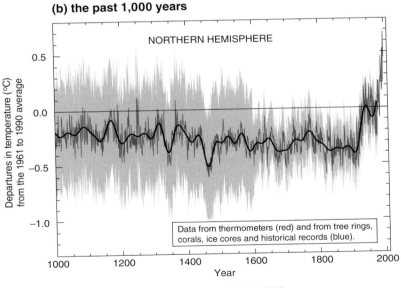

HOCKEY STICK GRAPH

Using data collected from tree rings, lake sediment, and ice core analyses, this graph, which dates from 1999, shows that for 900 years surface temperatures remained fairly stable before rising sharply. (Working Group I to the Third Assessment Report of the Intergovernmental Panel on Climate Change, Figure 1 of the "Summary for Policymakers," in Climate Change 2001: The Scientific Basis [Cambridge University Press, 2001])

In a 2006 report for the British government, Nicholas Stern, a former economist with the World Bank, warned that the untoward economic impact of global warming could perhaps approach the magnitude of the Great Depression. Stern portrayed climate change as the "greatest and widest-ranging market failure ever seen."[68]

LONG LIVE THE HOLOCENE!

It has become fashionable of late to argue that human control of nature has precipitated a new geological era called the Anthropocene, a word coined by the Dutch chemist Paul Crutzen.

And, indeed, a fair case can be made that for virtually all of human history, even acknowledging whatever damage and extinctions occurred, the natural world—climate especially—influenced people more than the reverse. After World War II, however, the world changed. Atmospheric carbon dioxide increased steeply, the concentration propelled to a level not witnessed in 870,000 years. More nitrogen is now made available through the production of synthetic fertilizer and the combustion of fossil fuel than is assimilated naturally by microorganisms. Species extinction rates have increased dramatically since 1950 on a planet where it is likely that somewhere between 39 and 50 percent of the land has been transformed by human action and more than half of all the available freshwater has been appropriated. These developments unfolded over a period when the population more than doubled to 7 billion people, when the number of those people living in cities surged from 30 to 50 percent, and when the number of motor vehicles shot up more than 20 times to 850 million pollution-spewing cars, buses, and trucks. As the historians J. R. McNeill and Peter Engelke have written, "Only after 1945 did human actions become genuine driving forces behind crucial Earth systems." Only then did a "Great Acceleration," they argue, lead to a human-dominated planet.[69]

There is, of course, no way that a single cause can account for all of the global ecological change that has occurred in recent years. But there is also danger in resisting a larger interpretation by focusing on such obvious proximate causes as increased automobile use, population growth, and urbanization. The explosion in fossil fuel consumption is often taken as a driving force behind global ecological change by advocates of the Anthropocene. And, indeed, global energy use has increased fivefold since 1950. But to focus on "the creation and spread of fossil fuel society" is to give up on a deeper analysis.[70] Surely there must be something happening here beyond more copulation, more drivers, and more people attracted to life in the big city.

In terms of carbon dioxide emissions, the key turning point actually occurred in the mid-1980s. Half of all the emissions between 1751 and 2010 have occurred since 1986. Driving the boom in emissions was the realization of global capitalism. In response to the 1970s crisis of profitability, the U.S. auto industry, for instance, shifted its product line from cars to trucks and SUVs as a way of fending off foreign competitors. Light trucks remained exempt from fuel economy legislation, passed in 1975, because, legislators argued, farmers and construction workers used them for business. In fact, the trucks functioned in the same capacity as cars. When Chrysler rolled out its first minivan in the 1980s, it also took advantage of this loophole to evade fuel economy standards. Despite

President George H. W. Bush's signing of a global warming treaty at the 1992 Earth Summit in Brazil, the federal government did not force the auto industry to ramp up fuel economy. Instead, it settled for more research and development, and, even worse, it continued to subsidize the oil industry. U.S. automakers with help from the federal government returned to profitability in the 1990s, but at the expense of the planet.[71]

China's recent dependence on carbon-based fuels is also singled out by those advocating for the Anthropocene as a crucial element in the formation of a human-dominated planet. Left unsaid, however, is that China's turn toward the rampant burning of coal did not just happen. It was the product of China's absorption into global capitalism beginning in 1978 under Deng Xiaoping, who brought the country into the capitalist fold by such actions as opening village- and state-owned enterprises to foreign ownership. China took an even larger step in the direction of capitalism when it negotiated with U.S. policymakers to enter the World Trade Organization in 2001. Under the WTO, China agreed to respect the property rights of foreign companies and not to engage in discriminatory economic treatment. U.S. multinational corporations were increasingly drawn to China because of the profits to be made by exploiting its vast, low-wage labor force, an investment trend that gathered additional steam as the country built the necessary infrastructure, especially along its coast, to support such foreign direct investment. China also created a good climate for business by eliminating regulations on the mining of coal and embracing other market-oriented reforms. Export production based on the proliferation of low-wage work has garnered China the unenviable designation as Chimney of the World, with the country's carbon emissions surging after it joined the WTO.[72]

Nor is it an accident that, though global warming has been recognized as a problem since at least the 1980s, efforts to address the planetary threat have proved sorely deficient. We can trace the failure of reform to the power of neoliberalism, which allowed the supposed superior abilities of the market to oversee human relations with the earth.

Economist Philip Mirowski has argued that the neoliberal approach to global warming has consisted of a tripartite set of tactics—science denialism, carbon trading permits, and geoengineering—all designed "to leave the entire problem to be solved, ultimately not by the state, but rather by the market." Thus far, denial has had the most impact on the U.S. approach to the problem, as industrial interests have papered over the areas of scientific agreement and misled the American public. By the 1990s scientists were not debating whether global warming had occurred; that was widely accepted. What divided them was the cause of the warming and future projections about how much the earth would heat up. Using the same strategy employed by the tobacco industry to cast doubt on the hazards of cigarette smoking, a group of scientists with strong ties to industry obfuscated the science of global warming. Indeed, some of the very same people involved in confusing the American public about tobacco went on to

tenthingstodo

Want to do something to help stop global warming?
Here are 10 simple things you can do and how much carbon dioxide you'll save doing them.

Change a light
Replacing one regular light bulb with a compact fluorescent light bulb will save 150 pounds of carbon dioxide a year.

Drive less
Walk, bike, carpool or take mass transit more often. You'll save one pound of carbon dioxide for every mile you don't drive!

Recycle more
You can save 2,400 pounds of carbon dioxide per year by recycling just half of your household waste.

Check your tires
Keeping your tires inflated properly can improve gas mileage by more than 3%.
Every gallon of gasoline saved keeps 20 pounds of carbon dioxide out of the atmosphere!

Use less hot water
It takes a lot of energy to heat water. Use less hot water by installing a low flow showerhead
(350 pounds of CO2 saved per year) and washing your clothes in cold or warm water (500 pounds saved per year).

Avoid products with a lot of packaging
You can save 1,200 pounds of carbon dioxide if you cut down your garbage by 10%.

Adjust your thermostat
Moving your thermostat just 2 degrees in winter and up 2 degrees in summer
You could save about 2,000 pounds of carbon dioxide a year with this simple adjustment.

Plant a tree
A single tree will absorb one ton of carbon dioxide over its lifetime.

Turn off electronic devices
Simply turning off your television, DVD player, stereo, and computer when you're
not using them will save you thousands of pounds of carbon dioxide a year.

Spread the word! Encourage your friends to buy An Inconvenient Truth

aninconvenienttruth
available on DVD
November 21
www.climatecrisis.net

"TEN THINGS TO DO"

A flier promoting Al Gore's An Inconvenient Truth *urges individual action, not corporate reform or other structural changes. (Paramount Vantage)*

make careers out of denying global warming. Sowing seeds of doubt grew into a cottage industry as rogue scientists financed with money from foundations and the fossil fuel industry took on the science of global warming. In the early 1990s, the Information Council on the Environment, a group made up of coal and utility companies, hired a public relations firm to, in its own words, "reposition global warming as theory rather than fact."[73] Thus, to argue that "human actions" caused the carbon cycle woes, when the evidence supports the view that profit-maximizing business interests are to blame, is misleading.

Likewise, to focus on the impact of urbanization as a driving force behind the Great Acceleration does not get us very far. Yes, there has been significant population growth in postwar cities, especially in the Third World. But to imagine that people flocked there in search of employment or "social services" or to unite with families or because they were somehow influenced by "economic, political, and military developments" is to offer a superficially rational, commonsense explanation that does not explain much.[74] A more compelling explanation emerges if we consider the problem as one of urbanization under the conditions of global capitalism. Capitalism has been incredibly successful at producing mountains of material goods. It has failed, however, at distributing that wealth equally. Virtually the entire planet is now under the thumb of a system that treats people as "human capital" and nature as a commodity. What kinds of cities has such a system produced?

To speak of urbanization and cities without also discussing slums is to overlook the harsh reality of postwar urban development. A United Nations report determined that in the early twenty-first century nearly 1 billion people, or one-third of the world's urban population, lived in slums, that is, in places that were overcrowded, hazardous, and lacking in adequate water and sanitation. The slums in large part have their roots in structural adjustment programs put in place by the IMF and the World Bank. By forcing governments to agree to eliminate food subsidies, these policies worked to drive small landholders off the land. Neoliberal reforms, in other words, laid the groundwork for burgeoning urbanization. In Mexico, for example, which was driven into bankruptcy in 1982 (in part by the high interest rates established by the U.S. Federal Reserve and the ensuing recession that undermined demand for imports), a financial bailout was arranged by the United States in exchange for the country's agreement to austerity and privatization measures congenial to foreign capital. Peasants suffered as a result. By the early 1990s, the Mexican government was allowing communal lands that protected indigenous peoples to be privatized, laying the groundwork for foreign ownership. Faced with liberalized trade agreements that permitted inexpensive U.S. crops (the product of government-subsidized agribusiness) to enter the country, struggling peasants had few other choices but to leave the land for cities that were already suffering from too many people and inadequate employment.[75]

A similar story unfolded in China, whose hundreds of cities bulging at the seams make it the world capital of urbanization. Deng Xiaoping and the Communist Party in the late 1970s put in place market reforms that broke with a tradition that prioritized equality and communes and instead encouraged personal responsibility and capitalist enterprises. Economic growth followed, and although many people benefited from the capitalist turn, it also produced a polarization of wealth. While we can debate the social impact of the neoliberal reforms, the ecological consequences of Chinese urbanization have been devastating. Much of the urban growth has occurred in cities such as Shenzhen and

Dongguan, which are located in delicate estuarine environments now subject to eutrophication and flood hazards made worse by the rising sea level that is the fruit of global warming.[76]

CONCLUSION

To place the focus on *human* transformations of nature, as the Anthropocene concept does, ignores the fact that some institutions and the people who run them—corporations, global governance organizations, and the U.S. Treasury—have more power to influence the planet's ecological destiny than others. Ordinary people, while they may collectively transform the natural world by driving to work or eating fast food, do not set the terms under which history unfolds.

People, powerful or not, are making history, but they are doing so within the confines set by a system that, unlike any before it, rests on the relentless pursuit of economic growth, that requires the transformation of the earth into commodities in order to create wealth, that has alienated people from the natural world and from each other, and that has expanded to encompass virtually the entire planet over the last 65 years.

There is a saying these days that it is easier to imagine the end of the world than the end of capitalism.[77] Many people take capitalism for granted and have trouble imagining an alternative. But capitalism, as any historian can tell you, had a beginning and a middle, and it will have an end. For what it is worth, a 2016 Harvard University opinion poll of 18- to 29-year-olds found that 51 percent rejected capitalism (almost as many as scorned socialism).[78] These young people have come of age watching the wind blow, the earth heat, and the water rise. They likely see nature as a dynamic force and may be more inclined to face up to its limits. Perhaps someday they will push out the old socioecological system and discover a way of organizing life on earth that is less polarizing in terms of wealth and income, less infatuated with economic growth, more respectful of natural limits, and more humble in its relations with land and sea.

NOTES

PREFACE

1. Donald Worster, *The Wealth of Nature: Environmental History and the Ecological Imagination* (New York, 1993), 58.
2. A nontechnical discussion of the history of the corporation can be found in Joel Bakan, *The Corporation: The Pathological Pursuit of Profit and Power* (New York, 2004). A more detailed discussion of corporation law appears in Morton J. Horwitz, *The Transformation of American Law, 1870–1960: The Crisis of Legal Orthodoxy* (Cambridge, MA, 1992), 65–107.
3. Ellen Meiksins Wood, *The Origins of Capitalism: A Longer View* (London, 2002), 95–121; Spencer Dimmock, *The Origin of Capitalism in England, 1400–1600* (Chicago, 2014), 272–300.
4. Karl Marx, "The Eighteenth Brumaire of Louis Bonaparte," in *The Marx-Engels Reader*, 2d ed., ed. Robert C. Tucker (New York, 1978), 595.

PROLOGUE: ROCKS AND HISTORY

1. Alfred Crosby, *Ecological Imperialism: The Biological Expansion of Europe, 900–1900* (New York, 1986), 305–306.
2. Jeff Goodell, *Big Coal: The Dirty Secret Behind America's Energy Future* (Boston, 2006), xvi, 10–11; Charles B. Hunt, *Natural Regions of the United States and Canada* (San Francisco, 1974), 203.
3. Quoted in Tim Flannery, *The Eternal Frontier: An Ecological History of North America and Its Peoples* (New York, 2001), 267.

CHAPTER 1: WILDERNESS UNDER FIRE

1. Mark Seielstad, Nadira Yuldasheva, Nadia Singh, Peter Underhill, Peter Oefner, Peidong Shen, and R. Spencer Wells, "A Novel Y-Chromosome Variant Puts an Upper Limit on the Timing of First Entry into the Americas," *American Journal of Human Genetics* 73 (2003): 700–705; Charles G. Mann, *1491: New Revelations of the Americas Before Columbus*, 2d ed. (New York, 2011), 19.
2. William M. Denevan, "Charles Mann and Humanized Landscapes," *Geographical Review* 96 (July 2006): 486; Eric R. Wolf, *Europe and the People Without History* (Berkeley, CA, 1982), 24–25; John L. Brooke, *Climate Change and the Course of Global History* (New York, 2014), 8–9.
3. Tim Flannery, *The Eternal Frontier: An Ecological History of North America and Its Peoples* (New York, 2001), 187; Shepard Krech III, *The Ecological Indian: Myth and History* (New York, 1999), 38–39.
4. Jack M. Broughton, "Pre-Columbian Human Impact on California Vertebrates: Evidence from Old Bones and Implications for Wilderness Policy," in *Wilderness and Political Ecology: Aboriginal Influences and the Original State of Nature*, ed. Charles E. Kay and Randy T. Simmons (Salt Lake City, UT, 2002), 67; Charles E. Kay, "Afterword: False Gods, Ecological Myths, and Biological Reality," in ibid., 240, 242; Krech, *Ecological Indian*, 29–30, 40.

5. Jared Diamond, *Guns, Germs, and Steel: The Fates of Human Societies* (New York, 1997), 159, 355; idem, "Why Was Post-Pleistocene Development of Human Societies Slightly More Rapid in the Old World Than in the New World?" in *Americans Before Columbus: Ice Age Origins*, ed. Ronald C. Carlisle (Pittsburgh, PA, 1988), 27.

6. John D. Daniels, "The Indian Population of North America in 1492," *William and Mary Quarterly* 49 (April 1992): 298–299, 300, 306, 310–311, 320.

7. Ibid., 314–315, 317; Roxanne Dunbar-Ortiz, *An Indigenous Peoples' History of the United States* (Boston, 2014), 39–42; Siep Stuurman, *The Invention of Humanity: Equality and Cultural Difference in World History* (Cambridge, MA, 2017), 201.

8. William Cronon, *Changes in the Land: Indians, Colonists, and the Ecology of New England* (New York, 1983), 39–40, 53 (quotation).

9. Timothy Silver, *A New Face on the Countryside: Indians, Colonists, and Slaves in South Atlantic Forests, 1500–1800* (New York, 1990), 46–49.

10. Ibid., 43, 45, 51–52.

11. Richard White, *The Roots of Dependency: Subsistence, Environment, and Social Change Among the Choctaws, Pawnees, and Navajos* (Lincoln, NE, 1983), 160, 165, 167, 170–171.

12. M. Kat Anderson, Michael G. Barbour, and Valerie Whitworth, "A World of Balance and Plenty: Land, Plants, Animals, and Humans in a Pre-European California," in *Contested Eden: California Before the Gold Rush*, ed. Ramón A. Gutiérrez and Richard J. Orsi (Berkeley, CA, 1998), 33; Cronon, *Changes in the Land*, 40–42; William Cronon and Richard White, "Indians in the Land," *American Heritage* 37 (August/September 1986): 21.

13. Quoted in Krech, *Ecological Indian*, 201.

14. Ibid., 164, 165 (quotation), 170–171.

15. Kay, "Afterword: False Gods," 250–256; Michael Williams, *Americans and Their Forests: A Historical Geography* (New York, 1989), 41–42 (1st quotation); Krech, *Ecological Indian*, 103 (2d quotation).

16. Williams, *Americans and Their Forests*, 42, 44 (quotation).

17. Krech, *Ecological Indian*, 104.

18. Quoted in ibid., 104–105.

19. White, *Roots of Dependency*, 184–185.

20. Anderson, Barbour, and Whitworth, "World of Balance," 19–20, 35.

21. White, *Roots of Dependency*, 186; Silver, *New Face on the Countryside*, 61, 62.

22. Williams, *Americans and Their Forests*, 46–48.

23. Colin G. Calloway, *One Vast Winter Count: The Native American West Before Lewis and Clark* (Lincoln, NE, 2003), 78, 83, 84, 99, 102; Daniel K. Richter, *Facing East from Indian Country: A Native History of Early America* (Cambridge, MA, 2001), 3.

24. Calloway, *One Vast Winter Count*, 80, 88, 103.

25. Cronon and White, "Indians in the Land," 20.

CHAPTER 2: A TRULY NEW WORLD

1 David W. Stahle, Malcolm K. Cleaveland, Dennis B. Blanton, Matthew D. Therrell, and David A. Gray, "The Lost Colony and Jamestown Droughts," *Science* 280 (April 24, 1998): 564–567.

2. Ellen Meiksins Wood, *The Origins of Capitalism: A Longer View* (London, 2002), 95–121; Peter Linebaugh, "Enclosures from the Bottom Up," *Radical History Review* 108 (Fall 2010): 13–14.

3. W. Jeffrey Bolster, *The Mortal Sea: Fishing the Atlantic in the Age of Sail* (Cambridge, MA, 2012), 33–34.

4. John L. Brooke, *Climate Change and the Course of Global History* (New York, 2014), 463; Andrea L. Smalley, *Wild by Nature: North American Animals Confront Colonization* (Baltimore, MD, 2017), 88 (quotation); Donald Worster, *Shrinking the Earth: The Rise and Decline of American Abundance* (New York, 2016), 13.

5. Daniel K. Richter, *Facing East from Indian Country: A Native History of Early America* (Cambridge, MA, 2001), 2–3.

6. Quoted in Karen Ordahl Kupperman, "The Puzzle of the American Climate in the Early Colonial Period," *American Historical Review* 87 (December 1982): 1270.

7. Quoted in S. Max Edelson, "Planting the Lowcountry: Agricultural Enterprise and Economic Experience in the Lower South, 1695–1785" (Ph.D. diss., Johns Hopkins University, 1998), 13.

8. Kupperman, "Puzzle of the American Climate," 1266; idem, "Fear of Hot Climates in the Anglo-American Colonial Experience," *William and Mary Quarterly* 41 (April 1984): 227.

9. Quoted in Carville Earle, *Geographical Inquiry and American Historical Problems* (Stanford, CA, 1992), 27.

10. Stahle et al., "Lost Colony," 566.

11. Earle, *Geographical Inquiry*, 32–40.

12. Quoted in H. Roy Merrens and George D. Terry, "Dying in Paradise: Malaria, Mortality, and the Perceptual Environment in Colonial South Carolina," *Journal of Southern History* 50 (November 1984): 549.

13. Quoted in Kupperman, "Puzzle of the American Climate," 1272.

14. Brian Fagan, *The Little Ice Age: How Climate Made History, 1300–1850* (New York, 2000), xiii.

15. Karen Ordahl Kupperman, "Climate and Mastery of the Wilderness in Seventeenth-Century New England," in *Seventeenth-Century New England*, ed. Colonial Society of Massachusetts (Boston, 1984), 31, 32 (quotation), 35–36.

16. Lenore A. Stiffarm and Phil Lane, Jr., "The Demography of Native North America: A Question of American Indian Survival," in *The State of Native America: Genocide, Colonization, and Resistance*, ed. M. Annette Jaimes (Boston, 1992), 37.

17. Elizabeth A. Fenn, "Biological Warfare in Eighteenth-Century North America: Beyond Jeffrey Amherst," *Journal of American History* 86 (March 2000): 1559 (quotation), 1560–1561.

18. Alfred Crosby, *Ecological Imperialism: The Biological Expansion of Europe, 900–1900* (New York, 1986), 202 (1st quotation); Timothy Silver, *A New Face on the Countryside: Indians, Colonists, and Slaves in South Atlantic Forests, 1500–1800* (New York, 1990), 74 (2d quotation).

19. Crosby, *Ecological Imperialism*, 208 (1st quotation); Colin G. Calloway, *New Worlds for All: Indians, Europeans, and the Remaking of Early America* (Baltimore, 1997), 39 (2d quotation).

20. Michael A. McDonnell, *Masters of Empire: Great Lakes Indians and the Making of America* (New York, 2015), 216; Fenn, "Biological Warfare," 1552, 1558, 1573.

21. Paul Kelton, *Epidemics and Enslavement: Biological Catastrophe in the Native Southeast, 1492–1715* (Lincoln, NE, 2007), 101–159.

22. Alfred W. Crosby, Jr., *The Columbian Exchange: Biological and Cultural Consequences of 1492* (Westport, CT, 1972), 66, 107.

23. Judith A. Carney, *Black Rice: The African Origins of Rice Cultivation in the Americas* (Cambridge, MA, 2001), 7, 10–11, 38, 164–168.

24. Quotations in ibid., 52.

25. David Brion Davis, *Inhuman Bondage: The Rise and Fall of Slavery in the New World* (New York, 2006), 86.

26. Quoted in Stephen Innes, "Fulfilling John Smith's Vision: Work and Labor in Early America," in *Work and Labor in Early America*, ed. Stephen Innes (Chapel Hill, NC, 1988), 3.

27. Dorothy V. Jones, *License for Empire: Colonialism by Treaty in Early America* (Chicago, 1982), 84.

28. Quoted in Silver, *New Face on the Countryside*, 190.

29. William Cronon, *Changes in the Land: Indians, Colonists, and the Ecology of New England* (New York, 1983), 65.

30. Nancy Shoemaker, *A Strange Likeness: Becoming Red and White in Eighteenth-Century North America* (New York, 2004), 29; Stuart Banner, *How the Indians Lost Their Land: Law and Power on the Frontier* (Cambridge, MA, 2005), 58.

31. Quoted in Cronon, *Changes in the Land*, 60.

32. Margaret Wickens Pearce, "Native Mapping in Southern New England Indian Deeds," in *Cartographic Encounters: Perspectives on Native American Mapmaking and Map Use*, ed. G. Malcolm Lewis (Chicago, 1998), 174–177.

33. Jean M. O'Brien, *Dispossession by Degrees: Indian Land and Identity in Natick, Massachusetts, 1650–1790* (Lincoln, NE, 1997), 91–92, 104, 111, 151, 168–169, 209.

34. Barry Field, "The Evolution of Individual Property Rights in Massachusetts Agriculture, 17th–19th Centuries," *Northeastern Journal of Agricultural and Resource Economics* 14 (October 1985): 97–109.

35. Calvin Martin, "The European Impact on the Culture of a Northeastern Algonquian Tribe: An Ecological Interpretation," *William and Mary Quarterly* 31 (January 1974): 25.

36. Cronon, *Changes in the Land*, 94–97.

37. Richter, *Facing East from Indian Country*, 178; Silver, *New Face on the Countryside*, 94 (quotation), 97.

38. J. R. McNeill, *Mosquito Empires: Ecology and War in the Greater Caribbean, 1620–1914* (New York, 2010), 23; Sidney W. Mintz, *Sweetness and Power: The Place of Sugar in Modern History* (New York, 1985), 32, 37–39.

39. McNeill, *Mosquito Empires*, 23–24, 27–28 (quotation); Mintz, *Sweetness and Power*, 52; James H. Merrell, *Into the American Woods: Negotiators on the Pennsylvania Frontier* (New York, 1999), 27.

40. McNeill, *Mosquito Empires*, 61.

41. E. L. Jones, *The European Miracle: Environments, Economics and Geopolitics in the History of Europe and Asia* (Cambridge, UK, 1981), 84.

CHAPTER 3: UNFETTERED ACCUMULATION

1. Alan Taylor, *American Colonies: The Settling of North America* (New York, 2001), 364, 368, 397, 406; Colin G. Calloway, *New Worlds for All: Indians, Europeans, and the Remaking of Early America* (Baltimore, 1997), 244–245; Daniel K. Richter, *Facing East from Indian Country: A Native History of Early America* (Cambridge, MA, 2001), 7.

2. Stuart Banner, *How the Indians Lost Their Land: Law and Power on the Frontier* (Cambridge, MA, 2005), 106; Thomas Paine, *Agrarian Justice, Opposed to Agrarian Law, and to Agrarian Monopoly . . .*, 2d ed. (Paris, 1797), 16.

3. Gail D. MacLeitch, "'Red' Labor: Iroquois Participation in the Atlantic Economy," *Labor Studies in Working-Class History of the Americas* 1 (Winter 2004): 74, 75, 76.

4. Ibid., 77.

5. Ibid., 77; Richter, *Facing East from Indian Country*, 179.

6. Richter, *Facing East from Indian Country*, 184 (quotation).

7. MacLeitch, "'Red' Labor," 78–79, 80 (quotation).

8. Richter, *Facing East from Indian Country*, 177; MacLeitch, "'Red' Labor," 89 (quotation).

9. Richter, *Facing East from Indian Country*, 187; Dorothy V. Jones, *License for Empire: Colonialism by Treaty in Early America* (Chicago, 1982), 1 (quotation).

10. Banner, *How the Indians*, 87 (quotation), 88–90.

11. Richter, *Facing East from Indian Country*, 154, 187; Jones, *License for Empire*, 48 (1st quotation), 71 (2d quotation).

12. Richter, *Facing East from Indian Country*, 151–154.

13. Banner, *How the Indians*, 91–93.

14. Ibid., 108–109.

15. Ibid., 98–101, 106.

16. Eric Foner, *The Story of American Freedom* (New York, 1998), 9.

17. Marjoleine Kars, *Breaking Loose Together: The Regulator Rebellion in Pre-Revolutionary North Carolina* (Chapel Hill, NC, 2002), 6; Thomas J. Humphrey, *Land and Liberty: Hudson Valley Riots in the Age of Revolution* (DeKalb, IL, 2004), 12–20.

18. Richter, *Facing East from Indian Country*, 216–217.

19. Banner, *How the Indians*, 112–113.

20. Jones, *License for Empire*, 2 (quotation); Banner, *How the Indians*, 113, 138, 146–148.

21. Richter, *Facing East from Indian Country*, 226.

22. Donald Worster, *The Wealth of Nature: Environmental History and the Ecological Imagination* (New York, 1993), 58; Daniel Vickers, "Competency and Competition: Economic Culture in Early America," *William and Mary Quarterly* 47 (January 1990): 3–29.

23. Brian Donahue, *The Great Meadow: Farmers and the Land in Colonial Concord* (New Haven, CT, 2004), xv, xix, 230.

24. Barbara Clark Smith, *The Freedoms We Lost: Consent and Resistance in Revolutionary America* (New York, 2010), 72.

25. Ibid., 81 (quotation).

26. Alan Taylor, *Liberty Men and Great Proprietors: The Revolutionary Settlement on the Maine Frontier* (Chapel Hill, NC, 1990), 101–105, 112 (quotation).

27. Brian Donahue, "Plowland, Pastureland, Woodland and Meadow: Husbandry in Concord, Massachusetts, 1635–1771" (Ph.D. diss., Brandeis University, 1995), 369.

28. E. L. Jones, "Creative Disruptions in American Agriculture, 1620–1820," *Agricultural History* 48 (October 1974): 519.

29. Pennsylvania Constitution of 1776, art. V (1st quotation), § 43 (2d quotation); Terry Bouton, *Taming Democracy: "The People," the Founders, and the Troubled Ending of the American Revolution* (New York, 2007), 7; Pennsylvania Constitution of 1790.

30. Andrea L. Smalley, *Wild by Nature: North American Animals Confront Colonization* (Baltimore, MD, 2017), 128 (1st quotation), 131 (2d quotation).

31. Paul E. Johnson, "The Modernization of Mayo Greenleaf Patch: Land, Family, and Marginality in New England, 1766–1818," *New England Quarterly* 55 (December 1982): 488–516.

CHAPTER 4: A WORLD OF COMMODITIES

1. Quoted in Alan Taylor, "'The Hungry Year': 1789 on the Northern Border of Revolutionary America," in *Dreadful Visitations: Confronting Natural Catastrophe in the Age of Enlightenment*, ed. Alessa Johns (New York, 1999), 151.

2. Ibid., 153–161.

3. John D. Post, *The Last Great Subsistence Crisis in the Western World* (Baltimore, 1977), 4.

4. John L. Brooke, *Climate Change and the Course of Global History: A Rough Journey* (New York, 2014), 9.

5. Quoted in Leah Hager Cohen, *Glass, Paper, Beans: Revelations on the Nature and Value of Ordinary Things* (New York, 1997), 236.

6. Steven Stoll, "A Metabolism of Society: Capitalism for Environmental Historians," in *The Oxford Handbook of Environmental History*, ed. Andrew C. Isenberg (New York, 2014), 369–397.

7. John T. Cumbler, "The Early Making of an Environmental Consciousness: Fish, Fisheries Commissions, and the Connecticut River," *Environmental History Review* 15 (Winter 1991): 75 (quotation); Theodore Steinberg, *Nature Incorporated: Industrialization and the Waters of New England* (New York, 1991), 170; John T. Cumbler, *Reasonable Use: The People, the Environment, and the State: New England, 1790–1930* (New York, 2001), 15–16.

8. Gary Kulik, "Dams, Fish, and Farmers: Defense of Public Rights in Eighteenth-Century Rhode Island," in *The Countryside in the Age of Capitalist Transformation*, ed. Steven Hahn and Jonathan Prude (Chapel Hill, NC, 1985), 42–43.

9. Steinberg, *Nature Incorporated*, 85, 87.

10. Quoted in ibid., 147.

11. Quoted in Richard Manning, *Grassland: The History, Biology, Politics, and Promise of the American Prairie* (New York, 1995), 94.

12. William Cronon, *Nature's Metropolis: Chicago and the Great West* (New York, 1991), 111, 113, 116, 120, 125, 145.

13. Michael Williams, *Americans and Their Forests: A Historical Geography* (New York, 1989), 160–161.

14. Ibid., 130 (1st quotation); Edwin G. Burrows and Mike Wallace, *Gotham: A History of New York City to 1898* (New York, 1999), 450 (2d quotation).

15. Williams, *Americans and Their Forests*, 132; Thomas R. Cox, Robert S. Maxwell, Phillip Drennon Thomas, and Joseph J. Malone, *This Well-Wooded Land: Americans and Their Forests from Colonial Times to the Present* (Lincoln, NE, 1985), 72; Cronon, *Nature's Metropolis*, 179.

16. Williams, *Americans and Their Forests*, 184–185, 188.

17. Ibid., 193–194; Cox et al., *This Well-Wooded Land*, 125.

18. Cronon, *Nature's Metropolis*, 159; Cox et al., *This Well-Wooded Land*, 158; Williams, *Americans and Their Forests*, 201–202.

19. Williams, *Americans and Their Forests*, 208–209.

20. Ibid., 211–212.

21. Ibid., 221.

22. Ibid., 217–218; James Willard Hurst, *Law and Economic Growth: The Legal History of the Lumber Industry in Wisconsin, 1836–1915*, rev. ed. (Madison, WI, 1984), 140–141.

23. Hurst, *Law and Economic Growth*, 127.

24. Williams, *Americans and Their Forests*, 233–236.

25. Stephen J. Pyne, *Fire in America: A Cultural History of Wildland and Rural Fire*, rev. ed. (Seattle, 1997), 200–201, 204–206.

26. Quoted in ibid., 205.

27. James Fenimore Cooper, *The Pioneers* (New York, [1823] 1959), 250; Jennifer Price, *Flight Maps: Adventures with Nature in Modern America* (New York, 1999), 1.

28. David R. Foster, *Thoreau's Country: Journey Through a Transformed Landscape* (Cambridge, MA, 1999), 167 (quotation), 168, 171; David S. Wilcove, *The Condor's Shadow: The Loss and Recovery of Wildlife in America* (New York, 1999), 29.

29. Quoted in Price, *Flight Maps*, 41.

30. Wilcove, *Condor's Shadow*, 30; Price, *Flight Maps*, 6, 18–19.

31. Wilcove, *Condor's Shadow*, 28, 30.

32. Foster, *Thoreau's Country*, 169, 172.

33. Georg Simmel, *The Sociology of Georg Simmel*, ed. Kurt H. Wolf (Glencoe, IL, [1908] 1950), 414; idem, *The Philosophy of Money*, trans. Tom Bottomore and David Frisby (London, [1900] 1978), 427.

CHAPTER 5: KING CLIMATE IN DIXIE

1. David M. Ludlum, *Early American Winters, 1821–1870* (Boston, 1968), 106, 107 (1st quotation); Robert Croom Aldredge, *Weather Observers and Observations at Charleston, South Carolina, 1670–1871* (Charleston, SC, [1936] 1940), 202 (2d quotation).

2. A. Cash Koeniger, "Climate and Southern Distinctiveness," *Journal of Southern History* 54 (February 1988): 21–44.

3. Albert E. Cowdrey, *This Land, This South: An Environmental History*, rev. ed. (Lexington, KY, 1996), 29, 30.

4. T. H. Breen, *Tobacco Culture: The Mentality of the Great Tidewater Planters on the Eve of Revolution* (Princeton, NJ, 1985), 46–49, 60 (quotation).

5. Quotations in Alan Kulikoff, *Tobacco and Slaves: The Development of Southern Cultures in the Chesapeake, 1680–1800* (Chapel Hill, NC, 1986), 47.

6. Carville Earle, *Geographical Inquiry and American Historical Problems* (Stanford, CA, 1992), 280–282.

7. Ibid., 283; Anthony S. Parent, Jr., *Foul Means: The Formation of a Slave Society in Virginia, 1660–1740* (Chapel Hill, NC, 2003), 60–65.

8. Steven Stoll, *Larding the Lean Earth: Soil and Society in Nineteenth-Century America* (New York, 2002), 131.

9. Parent, *Foul Means*, 53.

10. Quoted in ibid., 125.

11. Henry M. Miller, "Transforming a 'Splendid and Delightsome Land': Colonists and Ecological Change in the Chesapeake, 1607–1820," *Journal of the Washington Academy of Sciences* 76 (September 1986): 183; Stanley Wayne Trimble, *Man-Induced Soil Erosion on the Southern Piedmont, 1700–1970* (Ankeny, IA, 1974), 47 (quotation); Lewis Cecil Gray, *History of Agriculture in the Southern United States to 1860*, 2 vols. (Gloucester, MA, [1932] 1958), 1: 446.

12. Quoted in S. Max Edelson, "Planting the Lowcountry: Agricultural Enterprise and Economic Experience in the Lower South, 1695–1785" (Ph.D. diss., Johns Hopkins University, 1998), 223.

13. Philip D. Morgan, "Work and Culture: The Task System and the World of Lowcountry Blacks, 1700 to 1880," *William and Mary Quarterly* 39 (October 1982): 577 (quotation).

14. Joyce E. Chaplin, "Tidal Rice Cultivation and the Problem of Slavery in South Carolina and Georgia, 1760–1815," *William and Mary Quarterly* 49 (January 1992): 47.

15. Judith A. Carney, *Black Rice: The African Origins of Rice Cultivation in the Americas* (Cambridge, MA, 2001), 91 (quotation), 93–94.

16. Morgan, "Work and Culture," 568–569, 575 (quotation).

17. Quoted in Edelson, "Planting the Lowcountry," 250.

18. Mart A. Stewart, *"What Nature Suffers to Groe": Life, Labor, and Landscape on the Georgia Coast, 1680–1920* (Athens, GA, 1996), 104, 110.

19. Ibid., 161–162.

20. Ibid., 139–140; Chaplin, "Tidal Rice Cultivation," 60 (quotation).

21. Quoted in Stewart, *"What Nature Suffers to Groe,"* 155.

22. Harry L. Watson, "'The Common Rights of Mankind': Subsistence, Shad, and Commerce in the Early Republican South," *Journal of American History* 83 (June 1996): 15 (quotation), 21.

23. Quoted in ibid., 33.

24. Quotations in ibid., 13, 14.

25. Ibid., 19, 41–43.

26. Robin Blackburn, "White Gold, Black Labour," *New Left Review* 95 (September/October 2015): 153.

27. James L. Watkins, *King Cotton: A Historical and Statistical Review, 1790 to 1908* (New York, [1908] 1969), 13.

28. Gray, *History of Agriculture,* 2: 689, 705.

29. Michael Paul Rogin, *Fathers and Children: Andrew Jackson and the Subjugation of the American Indian* (New York, 1975), 180 (quotation); Richard White, *The Roots of Dependency: Subsistence, Environment, and Social Change Among the Choctaws, Pawnees, and Navajos* (Lincoln, NE, 1983), 22–23.

30. Ira Berlin, *Many Thousands Gone: The First Two Centuries of Slavery in North America* (Cambridge, MA, 1998), 359.

31. Earle, *Geographical Inquiry,* 288; Trimble, *Man-Induced Soil Erosion,* 54 (quotation); Charles Reagan Wilson, William Ferris, Ann J. Abadie, and Mary L. Hart, eds., *Encyclopedia of Southern Culture* (Chapel Hill, NC, 1989), 319.

32. Stanley W. Trimble, "Perspectives on the History of Soil Erosion Control in the Eastern United States," *Agricultural History* 59 (April 1985): 174.

33. Gavin Wright, *Old South, New South: Revolutions in the Southern Economy Since the Civil War* (New York, 1986), 17–19, 30–31.

34. Quoted in Eugene D. Genovese, *The Political Economy of Slavery: Studies in the Economy and Society of the Slave South* (New York, 1967), 95.

35. Ibid., 91 (quotation); Julius Rubin, "The Limits of Agricultural Progress in the Nineteenth-Century South," *Agricultural History* 49 (April 1975): 365–366; Tamara Miner Haygood, "Cows, Ticks, and Disease: A Medical Interpretation of the Southern Cattle Industry," *Journal of Southern History* 52 (November 1986): 553, 563.

36. Stoll, *Larding the Lean Earth,* 187–190.

37. Jimmy M. Skaggs, *The Great Guano Rush: Entrepreneurs and American Overseas Expansion* (New York, 1994), 14, 71; Gray, *History of Agriculture,* 2: 805–806; Genovese, *Political Economy of Slavery,* 94; Stoll, *Larding the Lean Earth,* 189.

CHAPTER 6: THE GREAT FOOD FIGHT

1. David Madden, ed., *Beyond the Battlefield: The Ordinary Life and Extraordinary Times of the Civil War Soldier* (New York, 2000), 158 (quotation); James M. McPherson, *Battle Cry of Freedom: The Civil War Era* (New York, 1988), 850.

2. John J. Clegg, "Capitalism and Slavery," *Critical Historical Studies* 2 (Fall 2015): 281–304; Mark Fiege, "Gettysburg and the Organic Nature of the American Civil War," in *Natural Enemy, Natural Ally: Toward an Environmental History of Warfare,* ed. Richard P. Tucker and Edmund Russell (Corvallis, OR, 2004), 103.

3. Quoted in George Brown Tindall and David E. Shi, *America: A Narrative History,* 5th ed., 2 vols. (New York, 1999), 1: 785.

4. Quoted in James M. McPherson, *Ordeal by Fire: The Civil War and Reconstruction* (New York, 1982), 191.

5. McPherson, *Battle Cry of Freedom,* 325.

6. Quoted in David M. Ludlum, *Early American Winters, 1821–1870* (Boston, 1968), 129.

7. Geoffrey C. Ward, *The Civil War* (New York, 1990), 158 (1st quotation), 159 (2d quotation); McPherson, *Battle Cry of Freedom,* 584 (3d quotation).

8. Reprinted in Ludlum, *Early American Winters,* 234.

9. Quotations in Madden, *Beyond the Battlefield,* 147, 158–159.

10. Douglas Southall Freeman, *R. E. Lee: A Biography,* 4 vols. (New York, 1934–1935), 3: 247 (1st quotation); Fiege, "Gettysburg and the Organic Nature," 93 (2d quotation), 102.

11. Freeman, *R. E. Lee,* 3: 252.

12. Ibid., 2: 491; 3: 252–253.

13. Quoted in Madden, *Beyond the Battlefield*, 155–156.

14. Gary B. Nash and Julie Roy Jeffrey, eds., *The American People: Creating a Nation and a Society*, 5th ed. (New York, 2001), 486 (1st quotation); John Solomon Otto, *Southern Agriculture During the Civil War Era, 1860–1880* (Westport, CT, 1994), 30 (2d quotation).

15. Christopher Clark et al., *Who Built America?: Working People and the Nation's Economy, Politics, Culture, and Society*, 2 vols. (New York, 2000), 1: 626 (1st quotation); McPherson, *Ordeal by Fire*, 370 (2d quotation).

16. Fiege, "Gettysburg and the Organic Nature," 104.

17. Paul W. Gates, *Agriculture and the Civil War* (New York, 1965), 38–39.

18. Michael B. Chesson, "Harlots or Heroines? A New Look at the Richmond Bread Riot," *Virginia Magazine of History and Biography* 92 (April 1984): 134–135, 144 (quotations).

19. Quotations in Drew Gilpin Faust, *The Creation of Confederate Nationalism* (Baton Rouge, LA, 1988), 54–55.

20. Otto, *Southern Agriculture*, 23, 32.

21. Gates, *Agriculture and the Civil War*, 86, 116 (quotation).

22. Ibid., 120 (1st quotation); Lisa M. Brady, "The Wilderness of War: Nature and Strategy in the American Civil War," *Environmental History* 10 (July 2005): 431 (2d quotation); Ward, *Civil War*, 197 (3d quotation).

23. Ludlum, *Early American Winters*, 133 (quotation); Gates, *Agriculture and the Civil War*, 86; Freeman, *R. E. Lee*, 3: 247.

24. Gates, *Agriculture and the Civil War*, 16 (quotations), 19.

25. Joseph P. Reidy, *From Slavery to Agrarian Capitalism in the Cotton Plantation South: Central Georgia, 1800–1880* (Chapel Hill, NC, 1992), 115–116 (quotation); Gates, *Agriculture and the Civil War*, 18.

26. Quoted in Reidy, *From Slavery to Agrarian Capitalism*, 117.

27. Eric Foner, *The Story of American Freedom* (New York, 1998), 98; Donald Worster, "The Vulnerable Earth: Toward a Planetary History," in *The Ends of the Earth*, ed. Donald Worster (New York, 1988), 6; Fiege, "Gettysburg and the Organic Nature," 103.

CHAPTER 7: EXTRACTING THE NEW SOUTH

1. Quoted in George Brown Tindall and David E. Shi, *America: A Narrative History*, 5th ed., 2 vols. (New York, 1999), 2: 793.

2. Gavin Wright, *Old South, New South: Revolutions in the Southern Economy Since the Civil War* (New York, 1986), 34; C. Vann Woodward, *Origins of the New South, 1877–1913* (Baton Rouge, LA, 1951), 182 (quotation).

3. Roger L. Ransom and Richard Sutch, *One Kind of Freedom: The Economic Consequences of Emancipation* (Cambridge, UK, 1977), 87, 89, 95, 98; Wright, *Old South, New South*, 91.

4. Steven Hahn, *The Roots of Southern Populism: Yeoman Farmers and the Transformation of the Georgia Upcountry, 1850–1890* (New York, 1983), 145; Gilbert C. Fite, *Cotton Fields No More: Southern Agriculture, 1865–1980* (Lexington, KY, 1984), 10 (quotation).

5. Ransom and Sutch, *One Kind of Freedom*, 101–102.

6. Carville Earle, *Geographical Inquiry and American Historical Problems* (Stanford, CA, 1992), 295; David F. Weiman, "The Economic Emancipation of the Non-Slaveholding Class: Upcountry Farmers in the Georgia Cotton Economy," *Journal of Economic History* 45 (March 1985): 87; Ransom and Sutch, *One Kind of Freedom*, 187.

7. Earle, *Geographical Inquiry*, 295–296 (quotation); Stanley Wayne Trimble, *Man-Induced Soil Erosion on the Southern Piedmont, 1700–1970* (Ankeny, IA, 1974), 69–93.

8. Arvarh E. Strickland, "The Strange Affair of the Boll Weevil: The Pest as Liberator," *Agricultural History* 68 (Spring 1994): 166.

9. James R. Grossman, *Land of Hope: Chicago, Black Southerners, and the Great Migration* (Chicago, 1989), 14, 28–29, 30 (quotation).

10. Strickland, "Strange Affair," 157; Kathryn Holland Braund, "'Hog Wild' and 'Nuts: Billy Boll Weevil Comes to the Alabama Wiregrass," *Agricultural History* 63 (Summer 1989): 32.

11. Quoted in Paul Garon, *Blues and the Poetic Spirit* (New York, [1975] 1979), 117.

12. Fite, *Cotton Fields No More*, 22 (quotations); Albert E. Cowdrey, *This Land, This South: An Environmental History*, rev. ed. (Lexington, KY, 1996), 106; Robert C. McMath, Jr., "Sandy Land and Hogs in the Timber: (Agri)cultural Origins of the Farmers' Alliance in Texas," in *The Countryside in the Age of Capitalist Transformation*, ed. Steven Hahn and Jonathan Prude (Chapel Hill, NC, 1985), 223.

13. Eugene D. Genovese, *Roll, Jordan, Roll: The World the Slaves Made* (New York, 1974), 486 (1st quotation); Charles Joyner, *Down by the Riverside: A South Carolina Slave Community* (Urbana, IL, 1984), 100 (2d quotation), 100–101 (3d quotation); Mart A. Stewart, *"What Nature Suffers to Groe": Life, Labor, and Landscape on the Georgia Coast, 1680–1920* (Athens, GA, 1996), 136.

14. Philip D. Morgan, "The Ownership of Property by Slaves in the Mid-Nineteenth-Century Low Country," *Journal of Southern History* 49 (August 1983): 411 (quotation).

15. Hahn, *Roots of Southern Populism*, 60 (quotations); R. Ben Brown, "The Southern Range: A Study in Nineteenth Century Law and Society" (Ph.D. diss., University of Michigan, 1993), 7.

16. Hahn, *Roots of Southern Populism*, 252 (1st quotation); Mart A. Stewart, "'Whether Wast, Deodand, or Stray': Cattle, Culture, and the Environment in Early Georgia," *Agricultural History* 65 (Summer 1991): 24; Steven Hahn, "Hunting, Fishing, and Foraging: Common Rights and Class Relations in the Postbellum South," *Radical History Review* 26 (October 1982): 42 (2d quotation).

17. Hahn, "Hunting, Fishing, and Foraging," 44 (1st quotation), 39 (2d quotation); idem, *Roots of Southern Populism*, 241 (3d quotation).

18. Hahn, *Roots of Southern Populism*, 242; Brown, "Southern Range," 190.

19. Cowdrey, *This Land, This South*, 115, 117; Jennifer Price, *Flight Maps: Adventures with Nature in Modern America* (New York, 1999), 59.

20. Stuart A. Marks, *Southern Hunting in Black and White: Nature, History, and Ritual in a Carolina Community* (Princeton, NJ, 1991), 48 (quotation).

21. J. Crawford King, Jr., "The Closing of the Southern Range: An Exploratory Study," *Journal of Southern History* 48 (February 1982): 62, 68 (quotation).

22. Hahn, "Hunting, Fishing, and Foraging," 46 (1st quotation); Brown, "Southern Range," 206 (2d quotation).

23. Shawn Everett Kantor and J. Morgan Kousser, "Common Sense or Commonwealth?: The Fence Law and Institutional Change in the Postbellum South," *Journal of Southern History* 59 (May 1993): 208, 215.

24. Claire Strom, "Texas Fever and the Dispossession of the Southern Yeoman Farmer," *Journal of Southern History* 66 (February 2000): 73.

25. McMath, "Sandy Land," 205–229.

26. Michael Williams, *Americans and Their Forests: A Historical Geography* (New York, 1989), 238; Donald Edward Davis, *Where There Are Mountains: An Environmental History of the Southern Appalachians* (Athens, GA, 2000), 168 (quotation), 176.

27. Williams, *Americans and Their Forests*, 240–243.

28. Paul Wallace Gates, "Federal Land Policy in the South, 1866–1888," *Journal of Southern History* 6 (August 1940): 314; Williams, *Americans and Their Forests*, 242.

29. Ibid., 254; Ronald L. Lewis, *Transforming the Appalachian Countryside: Railroads, Deforestation, and Social Change in West Virginia, 1880–1920* (Chapel Hill, NC, 1998), 47 (1st quotation); Thomas R. Cox, Robert S. Maxwell, Phillip Drennon Thomas, and Joseph J. Malone, *This Well-Wooded Land: Americans and Their Forests from Colonial Times to the Present* (Lincoln, NE, 1985), 164 (2d quotation).

30. Davis, *Where There Are Mountains*, 168; Lewis, *Transforming the Appalachian Countryside*, 265.

31. Stephen J. Pyne, *Fire in America: A Cultural History of Wildland and Rural Fire*, rev. ed. (Seattle, 1997), 148, 150, 155.

32. Davis, *Where There Are Mountains*, 176.

33. Quoted in ibid., 179.

34. J. R. McNeill, *Something New Under the Sun: An Environmental History of the Twentieth-Century World* (New York, 2000), 256.

35. Davis, *Where There Are Mountains*, 194 (1st quotation), 195 (2d quotation), 197 (3d quotation).

36. Williams, *Americans and Their Forests*, 238.

37. Wilma A. Dunaway, *The First American Frontier: Transition to Capitalism in Southern Appalachia, 1700–1860* (Chapel Hill, NC, 1996), 56–57, 61, 69, 76, table 3.1.

38. Ibid., 285, 170, 179, 182–183, 185.

39. Barbara Freese, *Coal: A Human History* (New York, 2003), 137.

40. Paul Salstrom, *Appalachia's Path to Dependency: Rethinking a Region's Economic History, 1730–1940* (Lexington, KY, 1994), 21.

CHAPTER 8: THE UNFORGIVING WEST

1. Marc Reisner, *Cadillac Desert: The American West and Its Disappearing Water* (New York, 1986), 37 (1st quotation); John Opie, *Ogallala: Water for a Dry Land* (Lincoln, NE, 1993), 66 (2d quotation).

2. Donald Worster, *A River Running West: The Life of John Wesley Powell* (New York, 2001), 348–349; Reisner, *Cadillac Desert*, 47 (quotation).

3. Gray Brechin, *Imperial San Francisco: Urban Power, Earthly Ruin* (Berkeley, CA, 1999), 29.

4. William Preston, "Serpent in the Garden: Environmental Change in Colonial California," in *Contested Eden: California Before the Gold Rush*, ed. Ramón A. Gutiérrez and Richard J. Orsi (Berkeley, CA, 1998), 265, 273–274, 278.

5. Mary Hill, *Gold: The California Story* (Berkeley, CA, 1999), 18–19, 94–97; Brechin, *Imperial San Francisco*, 31–32.

6. Hill, *Gold*, 72–73.

7. Brechin, *Imperial San Francisco*, 36 (1st quotation); Hill, *Gold*, 116, 118 (2d quotation).

8. Quoted in Brechin, *Imperial San Francisco*, 50.

9. Ibid., 48; Hill, *Gold*, 119–120.

10. Peter L. Reich, "Western Courts and the Privatization of Hispanic Mineral Rights Since 1850: An Alchemy of Title," *Columbia Journal of Environmental Law* 23 (1998): 57, 76 (quotation).

11. Robert Kelley, *Battling the Inland Sea: American Political Culture, Public Policy, and the Sacramento Valley, 1850–1986* (Berkeley, CA, 1989), 74, 77, 107–108; Jed Handelsman Shugerman, "The Floodgates of Strict Liability: Bursting Reservoirs and the Adoption of *Fletcher v. Rylands* in the Gilded Age," *Yale Law Journal* 110 (November 2000): 333.

12. Elliott West, *The Way to the West: Essays on the Central Plains* (Albuquerque, NM, 1995), 30–32; Hill, *Gold*, 48.

13. West, *Way to the West*, 15, 17.

14. Ibid., 21, 24–26, 29 (quotation).

15. Ibid., 38–40; Elliott West, *The Contested Plains: Indians, Goldseekers, and the Rush to Colorado* (Lawrence, KS, 1998), 89.

16. West, *Way to the West*, 43.

17. Ibid., 45–46; West, *Contested Plains*, xv, 233 (quotation).

18. West, *Way to the West*, 47.

19. Quoted in David D. Smits, "The Frontier Army and the Destruction of the Buffalo: 1865–1883," *Western Historical Quarterly* 25 (Autumn 1994): 338.

20. William Cronon, *Nature's Metropolis: Chicago and the Great West* (New York, 1991), 215 (1st quotation); Shepard Krech III, *The Ecological Indian: Myth and History* (New York, 1999), 124 (2d quotation).

21. Andrew C. Isenberg, *The Destruction of the Bison* (New York, 2000), 24–25, 106.

22. Ibid., 39–40, 47; West, *Contested Plains*, 49–53.

23. Krech, *Ecological Indian*, 127, 128 (quotation).

24. Isenberg, *Destruction of the Bison*, 82 (1st quotation), 83; Krech, *Ecological Indian*, 148 (2d quotation), 149.

25. West, *Way to the West*, 61–63.

26. Quoted in Isenberg, *Destruction of the Bison*, 112.

27. Ibid., 99–100, 131; Richard Manning, *Grassland: The History, Biology, Politics, and Promise of the American Prairie* (New York, 1995), 83.

28. Isenberg, *Destruction of the Bison*, 136–137.

29. Smits, "Frontier Army," 316 (1st quotation), 314 (2d quotation); Manning, *Grassland*, 85 (3d quotation).

30. Isenberg, *Destruction of the Bison*, 141–142; Manning, *Grassland*, 87.

31. Quoted in Ernest Staples Osgood, *The Day of the Cattlemen* (Minneapolis, MN, 1929), 83.

32. Richard White, "Animals and Enterprise," in *The Oxford History of the American West*, ed. Clyde A. Milner II, Carol A. O'Connor, and Martha A. Sandweiss (New York, 1994), 252–253; Terry G. Jordan, *North American Cattle-Ranching Frontiers: Origins, Diffusion, and Differentiation* (Albuquerque, NM, 1993), 220.

33. Jordan, *North American Cattle-Ranching Frontiers*, 222.

34. Ibid., 237.

35. Osgood, *Day of the Cattlemen*, 99; Jeremy Rifkin, *Beyond Beef: The Rise and Fall of the Cattle Culture* (New York, 1993), 88–91.

36. Osgood, *Day of the Cattlemen*, 190; David L. Wheeler, "The Blizzard of 1886 and Its Effect on the Range Cattle Industry in the Southern Plains," *Southwestern Historical Quarterly* 94 (1990–1991): 418–419.

37. Thadis W. Box, "Range Deterioration in West Texas," *Southwestern Historical Quarterly* 71 (1967–1968): 41 (1st quotation); Osgood, *Day of the Cattlemen*, 193 (2d quotation).

38. Jordan, *North American Cattle-Ranching Frontiers*, 237, 238 (quotation).

39. Quoted in Box, "Range Deterioration in West Texas," 38.

40. Wheeler, "Blizzard of 1886," 426.

41. Quoted in Edmund Morris, *The Rise of Theodore Roosevelt* (New York, 1979), 364–365.

42. Quoted in ibid., 365.

43. Richard L. Knight, "Ecology of Ranching," in *Ranching West of the 100th Meridian*, ed. R. L. Knight, W. Gilgert, and E. Marston (Washington, DC, 2002).

44. Peter Iverson, *When Indians Became Cowboys: Native Peoples and Cattle Ranching in the American West* (Norman, OK, 1994), 82, 84; Carolyn Gilman and Mary Jane Schneider, *The Way to Independence: Memories of a Hidatsa Indian Family, 1840–1920* (St. Paul, MN, 1987), 242–243.

45. Jeffrey A. Lockwood, *Locust: The Devastating Rise and Mysterious Disappearance of the Insect That Shaped the American Frontier* (New York, 2004), xvii, 26, 51, 78 (quotation), 84.

46. Ibid., 164.

47. Ibid., xviii, 232–254.

48. Opie, *Ogallala*, 67–68 (quotations).

CHAPTER 9: CONSERVATION RECONSIDERED

1. Quotations in Edmund Morris, *The Rise of Theodore Roosevelt* (New York, 1979), 372.

2. Ibid., 382–384.

3. Gail Bederman, *Manliness and Civilization: A Cultural History of Gender and Race in the United States, 1880–1917* (Chicago, 1995), 170–215; Richard W. Judd, *Common Lands, Common People: The Origins of Conservation in Northern New England* (Cambridge, MA, 1997).

4. Samuel P. Hays, *Conservation and the Gospel of Efficiency: The Progressive Conservation Movement, 1890–1920* (Cambridge, MA, 1959), 1–4, 265–266.

5. Donald Worster, *The Wealth of Nature: Environmental History and the Ecological Imagination* (New York, 1993), 190–193 (1st quotation), 194–196; John Mack Faragher, Mari Jo Buhle, Daniel Czitrom, and Susan H. Armitage, *Out of Many: A History of the American People*, 3d ed. (Upper Saddle River, NJ, 2000), 634 (2d quotation).

6. David F. Noble, *America by Design: Science, Technology and the Rise of Corporate Capitalism* (New York, 1977), 262–271.

7. Nancy Langston, *Forest Dreams, Forest Nightmares: The Paradox of Old Growth in the Inland West* (Seattle, 1995), 93, 106, 107 (1st quotation), 108.

8. Gifford Pinchot, *The Fight for Conservation* (New York, 1910), 42–43.

9. Patricia Nelson Limerick, *The Legacy of Conquest: The Unbroken Past of the American West* (New York, 1987), 298 (quotation).

10. Michael Williams, *Americans and Their Forests: A Historical Geography* (New York, 1989), 416, 433, 441 (quotation).

11. Donald Worster, *Nature's Economy: A History of Ecological Ideas* (New York, [1977] 1985), 267 (1st quotation); Langston, *Forest Dreams, Forest Nightmares*, 112 (2d quotation).

12. Langston, *Forest Dreams, Forest Nightmares*, 151, 155.

13. Ibid., 151, 291.

14. Stephen J. Pyne, *Year of the Fires: The Story of the Great Fires of 1910* (New York, 2001), 196–197; Pinchot, *Fight for Conservation*, 44–45.

15. Pyne, *Year of the Fires*, 80 (Pinchot quotation), 237.

16. Ibid., 257–258.

17. Quoted in Mike Davis, *Ecology of Fear: Los Angeles and the Imagination of Disaster* (New York, 1998), 229.

18. Peter Steinhart, *The Company of Wolves* (New York, 1995), 36–37.

19. Donald Worster, *An Unsettled Country: Changing Landscapes of the American West* (Albuquerque, NM, 1994), 79; Steinhart, *Company of Wolves*, 37–38, 39 (quotation).

20. Worster, *Nature's Economy*, 270–271.

21. Thomas R. Dunlap, "Values for Varmints: Predator Control and Environmental Ideas, 1920–1939," *Pacific Historical Review* 53 (May 1984): 151; Davis, *Ecology of Fear*, 234 (quotation), 235–236.

22. Alfred Runte, *National Parks: The American Experience*, rev. ed. (Lincoln, NE, 1987), 11, 48.

23. Chris J. Magoc, *Yellowstone: The Creation and Selling of an American Landscape, 1870–1903* (Albuquerque, NM, 1999), 19 (quotation); Runte, *National Parks*, 53.

24. Mark David Spence, *Dispossessing the Wilderness: Indian Removal and the Making of the National Parks* (New York, 1999), 37 (1st quotation); Magoc, *Yellowstone*, 93 (2d quotation). On standard time, see Michael O'Malley, *Keeping Watch: A History of American Time* (New York, 1990), 130.

25. Spence, *Dispossessing the Wilderness*, 4, 59 (quotation).

26. Magoc, *Yellowstone*, 141 (1st quotation), 146 (2d quotation).

27. Quoted in Spence, *Dispossessing the Wilderness*, 56.

28. Ibid., 45, 48, 50, 63; Karl Jacoby, *Crimes Against Nature: Squatters, Poachers, Thieves, and the Hidden History of American Conservation* (Berkeley, CA, 2001), 88 (quotation).

29. Spence, *Dispossessing the Wilderness*, 63 (quotations), 65.

30. *Ward v. Race Horse*, 163 U.S. 504, 509, 518 (1896); Spence, *Dispossessing the Wilderness*, 67–68; David E. Wilkins, *American Indian Sovereignty and the U.S. Supreme Court: The Masking of Justice* (Austin, TX, 1997), 104.

31. Quoted in Jacoby, *Crimes Against Nature*, 96.

32. Ibid., 2, 99 (quotation), 106–107, 118–119.
33. William T. Hornaday, *Our Vanishing Wild Life: Its Extermination and Preservation* (New York, 1913), 101; William T. Hornaday, *Wild Life Conservation in Theory and Practice* (New Haven, CT, 1914), 189.
34. Jacoby, *Crimes Against Nature*, 134, 137 (1st and 2d quotations), 138 (3d quotation).
35. Mary Meagher and Douglas B. Houston, *Yellowstone and the Biology of Time: Photographs Across a Century* (Norman, OK, 1998), 223–224.
36. David S. Wilcove, *The Condor's Shadow: The Loss and Recovery of Wildlife in America* (New York, 1999), 56; Michael B. Coughenour and Francis J. Singer, "The Concept of Over-grazing and Its Application to Yellowstone's Northern Range," in *The Greater Yellowstone Ecosystem: Redefining America's Wilderness Heritage*, ed. Robert B. Keiter and Mark S. Boyce (New Haven, CT, 1991), 211; Alston Chase, *Playing God in Yellowstone: The Destruction of America's First National Park* (San Diego, CA, 1987), 23 (quotation).
37. Steve W. Chadde and Charles E. Kay, "Tall-Willow Communities on Yellowstone's Northern Range: A Test of the 'Natural-Regulation' Paradigm," in *The Greater Yellowstone Ecosystem* (see n. 36), 236, 253–257.
38. Pinchot, *Fight for Conservation*, 103.
39. Quoted in Chase, *Playing God in Yellowstone*, 125.
40. Andrew C. Isenberg, *The Destruction of the Bison* (New York, 2000), 179–180; Magoc, *Yellowstone*, 161.
41. Quoted in Isenberg, *Destruction of the Bison*, 181.
42. Spence, *Dispossessing the Wilderness*, 69; Louis S. Warren, *The Hunter's Game: Poachers and Conservationists in Twentieth-Century America* (New Haven, CT, 1997), 144–145.

CHAPTER 10: DEATH OF THE ORGANIC CITY

1. R. Ben Brown, "The Southern Range: A Study in Nineteenth Century Law and Society" (Ph.D. diss., University of Michigan, 1993), 280–281 (quotation).
2. Upton Sinclair, *The Jungle* (New York, [1906] 1981), 24–25.
3. For more on this issue as it developed in New York, see Ted Steinberg, *Gotham Unbound: The Ecological History of Greater New York* (New York, 2014), 119–120.
4. Quoted in Oscar Handlin, *This Was America: True Accounts of People and Places, Manners and Customs, as Recorded by European Travelers to the Western Shore in the Eighteenth, Nineteenth, and Twentieth Centuries* (Cambridge, MA, 1949), 217.
5. Quoted in Charles E. Rosenberg, *The Cholera Years: The United States in 1832, 1849, and 1866* (Chicago, 1962), 103.
6. Hendrik Hartog, "Pigs and Positivism," *Wisconsin Law Review* 4 (July/August 1985): 905 (1st quotation), 908 (2d and 3d quotations).
7. Quotations in ibid., 910.
8. Edwin G. Burrows and Mike Wallace, *Gotham: A History of New York City to 1898* (New York, 1999), 477.
9. Ibid., 747, 786; Rosenberg, *Cholera Years*, 113; Susan Strasser, *Waste and Want: A Social History of Trash* (New York, 1999), 30.
10. Quoted in Burrows and Wallace, *Gotham*, 477.
11. Clay McShane and Joel A. Tarr, "The Centrality of the Horse in the Nineteenth-Century American City," in *The Making of Urban America*, 2d ed., ed. Raymond A. Mohl (Wilmington, DE, 1997), 105–106; Silas Farmer, *The History of Detroit and Michigan* (Detroit, 1889), 892.
12. Joel A. Tarr, *The Search for the Ultimate Sink: Urban Pollution in Historical Perspective* (Akron, OH, 1996), 323–324, 326, 331.
13. Marc Linder and Lawrence S. Zacharias, *Of Cabbages and Kings County: Agriculture and the Formation of Modern Brooklyn* (Iowa City, IA, 1999), 35 (quotation); McShane and Tarr, "Centrality of the Horse," 120.

14. Linder and Zacharias, *Of Cabbages and Kings County*, 6 (quotation), 29–31, 306 (table 5).

15. Ibid., 45 (1st quotation), 46 (2d quotation).

16. Quoted in ibid., 4.

17. Tarr, *Search for the Ultimate Sink*, 295, 299.

18. Ibid., 9.

19. Quoted in Norris Hundley, Jr., *The Great Thirst: Californians and Water, 1770s–1990s* (Berkeley, CA, 1992), 153.

20. Tarr, *Search for the Ultimate Sink*, 12; Burrows and Wallace, *Gotham*, 787; Elizabeth Blackmar, "Accountability for Public Health: Regulating the Housing Market in Nineteenth-Century New York City," in *Hives of Sickness: Public Health and Epidemics in New York City*, ed. David Rosner (New Brunswick, NJ, 1995), 52 (quotation), 53.

21. Edward K. Spann, *The New Metropolis: New York City, 1840–1857* (New York, 1981), 130–131 (1st quotation); Richard A. Wines, *Fertilizer in America: From Waste Recycling to Resource Exploitation* (Philadelphia, 1985), 32 (2d quotation).

22. Tarr, *Search for the Ultimate Sink*, 301–303.

23. William Ashworth, *The Late, Great Lakes: An Environmental History* (New York, 1986), 123 (quotation), 132, 134–135; Margaret Beattie Bogue, *Fishing the Great Lakes: An Environmental History, 1783–1933* (Madison, WI, 2000), 169.

24. Charles Hardy, "Fish or Foul: A History of the Delaware River Basin Through the Perspective of the American Shad, 1682 to the Present," *Pennsylvania History* 66 (Autumn 1999): 507, 518, 522–525, 533n.

25. Quoted in Judith Walzer Leavitt, *The Healthiest City: Milwaukee and the Politics of Health Reform* (Princeton, NJ, 1982), 124–125.

26. McShane and Tarr, "Centrality of the Horse," 122; Martin V. Melosi, *The Sanitary City: Urban Infrastructure in America from Colonial Times to the Present* (Baltimore, 2000), 179.

27. Melosi, *Sanitary City*, 176, 177; Strasser, *Waste and Want*, 125.

28. Suellen Hoy, *Chasing Dirt: The American Pursuit of Cleanliness* (New York, 1995), 72–75; Joel Tarr, e-mail with author, April 9, 2001.

29. Strasser, *Waste and Want*, 121–123.

30. Leavitt, *Healthiest City*, 126 (1st quotation), 127 (2d quotation).

31. Benjamin Miller, *Fat of the Land: Garbage of New York the Last Two Hundred Years* (New York, 2000), 73 (photo caption); Martin V. Melosi, *Garbage in the Cities: Refuse, Reform, and the Environment, 1880–1980* (College Station, TX, 1981), 42.

32. Melosi, *Garbage in the Cities*, 169–170; idem, "Refuse Pollution and Municipal Reform: The Waste Problem in America, 1880–1917," in *Pollution and Reform in American Cities, 1870–1930*, ed. Martin V. Melosi (Austin, TX, 1980), 127; Strasser, *Waste and Want*, 129 (quotation).

33. Strasser, *Waste and Want*, 12–15, 73, 91.

CHAPTER 11: MOVEABLE FEAST

1. James Howard Kunstler, "Clusterfuck Nation: A Glimpse into the Future," http://www.kunstler.com/mags_ure.htm (accessed May 11, 2007).

2. Kevin Starr, *Inventing the Dream: California Through the Progressive Era* (New York, 1985), 75–76, 83.

3. Quoted in Stephen Johnson, Robert Dawson, and Gerald Haslam, *The Great Central Valley: California's Heartland* (Berkeley, CA, 1993), 6.

4. Starr, *Inventing the Dream*, 131–132; Steven Stoll, *The Fruits of Natural Advantage: Making the Industrial Countryside in California* (Berkeley, CA, 1998), 28–29; Donald Worster, *Rivers of Empire: Water, Aridity, and the Growth of the American West* (New York, 1985), 99.

5. Ian Tyrrell, *True Gardens of the Gods: Californian-Australian Environmental Reform, 1860–1930* (Berkeley, CA, 1999), 223–224; Stoll, *Fruits of Natural Advantage*, 60; Starr, *Inventing the Dream*, 133.

6. Worster, *Rivers of Empire*, 108–109; Tyrrell, *True Gardens of the Gods*, 106, 108 (quotation).

7. Stoll, *Fruits of Natural Advantage*, xiii–xiv.

8. Marc Linder and Lawrence S. Zacharias, *Of Cabbages and Kings County: Agriculture and the Formation of Modern Brooklyn* (Iowa City, IA, 1999), 69–70.

9. David Vaught, *Cultivating California: Growers, Specialty Crops, and Labor, 1875–1920* (Baltimore, 1999), 49–50; Starr, *Inventing the Dream*, 134.

10. Vaught, *Cultivating California*, 50 (1st quotation); Harold Barger and Hans H. Landsberg, *American Agriculture, 1899–1939: A Study of Output, Employment and Productivity* (New York, 1942), 167–168 (2d quotation); Linder and Zacharias, *Of Cabbages and Kings County*, 71.

11. Vaught, *Cultivating California*, 109; Howard Seftel, "Government Regulation and the Rise of the California Fruit Industry: The Entrepreneurial Attack on Fruit Pests, 1880–1920," *Business History Review* 59 (Autumn 1985): 372; Stoll, *Fruits of Natural Advantage*, 90 (quotation).

12. Stoll, *Fruits of Natural Advantage*, 92–93.

13. Victoria Saker Woeste, *The Farmer's Benevolent Trust: Law and Agricultural Cooperation in Industrial America, 1865–1945* (Chapel Hill, NC, 1998), 30, 78, 81, 112–113, 120–121; Starr, *Inventing the Dream*, 160–161; Charles C. Colby, "The California Raisin Industry—A Study in Geographic Interpretation," *Annals of the Association of American Geographers* 14 (June 1924): 103.

14. Linder and Zacharias, *Of Cabbages and Kings County*, 70 (quotation); Seftel, "Government Regulation," 386–388.

15. Douglas Cazaux Sackman, *Orange Empire: California and the Fruits of Eden* (Berkeley, CA, 2005), 97.

16. Ibid., 101, 104; Stoll, *Fruits of Natural Advantage*, 88 (quotation).

17. Sackman, *Orange Empire*, 123–153.

18. Quotations from ibid., 102.

19. Ibid., 94 (1st quotation); Jack Doyle, *Altered Harvest: Agriculture, Genetics, and the Fate of the World's Food Supply* (New York, 1985), 54 (2d quotation), 56.

20. Stoll, *Fruits of Natural Advantage*, 95–97.

21. Ibid., 98, 104; Seftel, "Government Regulation," 377; Tyrrell, *True Gardens of the Gods*, 179–181, 195–196.

22. Stoll, *Fruits of Natural Advantage*, 106, 108, 121; Seftel, "Government Regulation," 393.

23. Stoll, *Fruits of Natural Advantage*, 123; Worster, *Rivers of Empire*, 317–318.

24. Worster, *Rivers of Empire*, 318.

25. Marc Reisner, *Cadillac Desert: The American West and Its Disappearing Water* (New York, 1986), 348; Worster, *Rivers of Empire*, 214.

26. Worster, *Rivers of Empire*, 234.

27. Ibid., 234–235; Reisner, *Cadillac Desert*, 348; Norris Hundley, Jr., *The Great Thirst: Californians and Water, 1770s–1990s* (Berkeley, CA, 1992), 235.

28. Worster, *Rivers of Empire*, 160–161, 240, 243; Hundley, *Great Thirst*, 237, 252; Reisner, *Cadillac Desert*, 348–349.

29. Worster, *Rivers of Empire*, 246–247 (quotation); Reisner, *Cadillac Desert*, 350.

30. Worster, *Rivers of Empire*, 253–255; Hundley, *Great Thirst*, 265–266.

31. Reisner, *Cadillac Desert*, 353–354.

32. Worster, *Rivers of Empire*, 256.

33. Donald Worster, *Dust Bowl: The Southern Plains in the 1930s* (New York, 1979), 54, 63.

34. Worster, *Rivers of Empire*, 221–222; Don Mitchell, *The Lie of the Land: Migrant Workers and the California Landscape* (Minneapolis, MN, 1996), 91; Sackman, *Orange Empire*, 129 (quotation).

35. Worster, *Dust Bowl*, 4, 42–43.

CHAPTER 12: THE SECRET HISTORY OF MEAT

1. Quoted in John Vidal, *McLibel: Burger Culture on Trial* (New York, 1997), 30.
2. William Cronon, *Nature's Metropolis: Chicago and the Great West* (New York, 1991), 225–226; Marvin Harris and Eric B. Ross, "How Beef Became King," *Psychology Today*, October 1978, 91.
3. Cronon, *Nature's Metropolis*, 228.
4. Ibid., 228, 229 (quotation).
5. Timothy Cuff, "A Weighty Issue Revisited: New Evidence on Commercial Swine Weights and Pork Production in Mid-Nineteenth Century America," *Agricultural History* 66 (Fall 1992): 67, table 1; Alexander Cockburn, "A Short, Meat-Oriented History of the World: From Eden to the Mattole," *New Left Review* 215 (January/February 1996): 24.
6. Robert Aduddell and Louis Cain, "Location and Collusion in the Meat Packing Industry," in *Business Enterprise and Economic Change*, ed. Louis P. Cain and Paul J. Uselding (Kent, OH, 1973), 91, 94–95; Cronon, *Nature's Metropolis*, 233–234.
7. Richard J. Arnould, "Changing Patterns of Concentration in American Meat Packing, 1880–1963," *Business History Review* 45 (Spring 1971): 20.
8. Aduddell and Cain, "Location and Collusion," 95–96.
9. Upton Sinclair, *The Jungle* (New York, [1906] 1981), 134–135.
10. Cronon, *Nature's Metropolis*, 236–237.
11. Arnould, "Changing Patterns of Concentration," 20; Jimmy M. Skaggs, *Prime Cut: Livestock Raising and Meatpacking in the United States, 1607–1983* (College Station, TX, 1986), 98–99.
12. Sinclair, *Jungle*, 35, 109.
13. Cronon, *Nature's Metropolis*, 222–223; Aduddell and Cain, "Location and Collusion," 91–92; Edward Everett Dale, *The Range Cattle Industry: Ranching on the Great Plains from 1865 to 1925* (Norman, OK, 1960), 148.
14. Dale, *Range Cattle Industry*, 153, 156.
15. Jack Doyle, *Altered Harvest: Agriculture, Genetics, and the Fate of the World's Food Supply* (New York, 1985), 120–121; Vaclav Smil, *Enriching the Earth: Fritz Haber, Carl Bosch, and the Transformation of World Food Production* (Cambridge, MA, 2001), xiv–xv.
16. Harris and Ross, "How Beef Became King," 91, table.
17. Skaggs, *Prime Cut*, 179–180.
18. John Opie, *Ogallala: Water for a Dry Land* (Lincoln, NE, 1993), 3; Shane Hamilton, "Trucking Country: Food Politics and the Transformation of Rural Life in Postwar America" (Ph.D. diss., Massachusetts Institute of Technology, 2005), 191–199.
19. Marvin Harris, *The Sacred Cow and the Abominable Pig: Riddles of Food and Culture* (New York, 1987), 119; Orville Schell, *Modern Meat* (New York, 1984), 19, 21–23; J. R. McNeill, *Something New Under the Sun: An Environmental History of the Twentieth-Century World* (New York, 2000), 202n.
20. Schell, *Modern Meat*, 189–190, 252.
21. Jon Lauck, *American Agriculture and the Problem of Monopoly: The Political Economy of Grain Belt Farming, 1953–1980* (Lincoln, NE, 2000), 54.
22. Skaggs, *Prime Cut*, 190–191; Opie, *Ogallala*, 153.
23. Skaggs, *Prime Cut*, 190–191 (quotation); Doyle, *Altered Harvest*, 131.
24. Lauck, *American Agriculture*, 56 (1st quotation); "Inside Big Meat," *CounterPunch* 6 (July 16–30, 1999), 1; Eric Schlosser, *Fast Food Nation: The Dark Side of the All-American Meal* (Boston, 2001), 172, 174; William Greider, "The Last Farm Crisis," *Nation*, November 20, 2000, 16 (2d quotation).
25. Skaggs, *Prime Cut*, 194; Harris and Ross, "How Beef Became King," 91, table.

26. David Gerard Hogan, *Selling 'em by the Sack: White Castle and the Creation of American Food* (New York, 1997), 24, 38–39.

27. Vidal, *McLibel*, 24–25.

28. Ibid., 37 (observer quotation), 46; Schlosser, *Fast Food Nation*, 47.

29. Vidal, *McLibel*, 33.

30. Ibid., 38–40; Schlosser, *Fast Food Nation*, 76.

31. Margaret J. King, "Empires of Popular Culture: McDonald's and Disney," in *Ronald Revisited: The World of Ronald McDonald*, ed. Marshall William Fishwick (Bowling Green, OH, 1983), 107; Vidal, *McLibel*, 44, 183.

32. Harris, *Sacred Cow*, 124–125.

33. Marion Nestle, "Food Lobbies, the Food Pyramid, and U.S. Nutrition Policy," in *The Nation's Health*, 5th ed., ed. Philip R. Lee and Carroll L. Estes (Sudbury, MA, 1997), 212–213, 214 (quotations).

34. Ibid., 217–218.

35. Michael Pollan, *The Omnivore's Dilemma: A Natural History of Four Meals* (New York, 2006), 83–84; Alan B. Durning and Holly B. Brough, *Taking Stock: Animal Farming and the Environment*, Worldwatch Paper 103 (July 1991), 16–17, table 4.

36. Durning and Brough, *Taking Stock*, 17–18; Cockburn, "Short, Meat-Oriented History," 35; Opie, *Ogallala*, 5–6, 153–154.

37. Donald Worster, *Under Western Skies: Nature and History in the American West* (New York, 1992), 43–44.

38. Denzel Ferguson and Nancy Ferguson, *Sacred Cows at the Public Trough* (Bend, OR, 1983), 36; Patricia Nelson Limerick, *The Legacy of Conquest: The Unbroken Past of the American West* (New York, 1987), 157 (quotation).

39. Durning and Brough, *Taking Stock*, 24.

40. Ferguson and Ferguson, *Sacred Cows*, 55, 94; Robert S. Devine, *Alien Invasion: America's Battle with Non-Native Animals and Plants* (Washington, DC, 1998), 52–53, 55, 59, 62.

41. Glen E. Bugos, "Intellectual Property Protection in the American Chicken-Breeding Industry," *Business History Review* 66 (Spring 1992): 136–137, 147–148.

42. Ibid., 150–155; Roger Horowitz, "Making the Chicken of Tomorrow: Reworking Poultry as Commodities and as Creatures, 1945–1990," in *Industrializing Organisms: Introducing Evolutionary History*, ed. Susan R. Schrepfer and Philip Scranton (New York, 2004), 226 (quotation).

43. Bugos, "Intellectual Property Protection," 155–156; Ian Angus, *Facing the Anthropocene: Fossil Capitalism and the Crisis of the Earth System* (New York, 2016), 120–121.

44. U.S. General Accounting Office, *Animal Agriculture: Information on Waste Management and Water Quality Issues*, GAO/RCED-95-200BR (June 1995), 47; Tim Flannery, *The Eternal Frontier: An Ecological History of North America and Its Peoples* (New York, 2001), 324; Pollan, *Omnivore's Dilemma*, 110.

45. Ken Silverstein, "Meat Factories," *Sierra*, January/February 1999, 31.

46. Quoted in Dale Miller, "Straight Talk from Smithfield's Joe Luter," *National Hog Farmer*, May 2000, accessed March 24, 2018, http://www.nationalhogfarmer.com/mag/farming_straight_talk_smithfields.

47. David Barboza, "Goliath of the Hog World," *New York Times*, April 7, 2000; Otis L. Graham, "Again the Backward Region? Environmental History in and of the American South," *Southern Cultures* 6 (Summer 2000): 56.

48. U.S. General Accounting Office, *Animal Agriculture: Waste Management Practices*, GAO/RCED-99-205 (July 1999).

49. Quoted in Silverstein, "Meat Factories," 30.

50. Michael Satchell, "Hog Heaven—and Hell," *U.S. News & World Report*, January 22, 1996, 55.

51. Sharon Guynup, "Cell from Hell," *Sierra*, January/February 1999, 34.

CHAPTER 13: AMERICA IN BLACK AND GREEN

1. Tom Lewis, *Divided Highways: Building the Interstate Highways, Transforming American Life* (New York, 1997), ix, 125; Pete Davies, *American Road: The Story of an Epic Transcontinental Journey at the Dawn of the Motor Age* (New York, 2002), 215 (quotation).

2. John Steinbeck, *Travels with Charley: In Search of America* (New York, 1962); James Howard Kunstler, *The Geography of Nowhere: The Rise and Decline of America's Man-Made Landscape* (New York, 1993), 15.

3. Ted Steinberg, *American Green: The Obsessive Quest for the Perfect Lawn* (New York, 2006), 12–13.

4. Ibid., 4, 32. On Horkheimer and the Frankfurt School of philosophy, see Donald Worster, *Rivers of Empire: Water, Aridity, and the Growth of the American West* (New York, 1985), 53–58.

5. Joseph Interrante, "You Can't Go to Town in a Bathtub: Automobile Movement and the Reorganization of Rural American Space, 1900–1930," *Radical History Review* 21 (Fall 1979): 151, 152 (quotation), 160; idem, "The Road to Autopia: The Automobile and the Spatial Transformation of American Culture," in *The Automobile and American Culture*, ed. David L. Lewis and Laurence Goldstein (Ann Arbor, MI, 1983), 98.

6. Interrante, "Road to Autopia," 93.

7. Joseph Anthony Interrante, "A Moveable Feast: The Automobile and the Spatial Transformation of American Culture, 1890–1940" (Ph.D. diss., Harvard University, 1983), 12.

8. Tom McCarthy, "The Coming Wonder? Foresight and Early Concerns About the Automobile," *Environmental History* 6 (January 2001): 48 (1st quotation), 50 (2d quotation).

9. Ibid., 49–54.

10. Nelson Lichtenstein, Susan Strasser, and Roy Rosenzweig, *Who Built America? Working People and the Nation's Economy, Politics, Culture, and Society*, 2 vols. (New York, 2000), 2: 329, 330 (quotation); Tom McCarthy, *Auto Mania: Cars, Consumers, and the Environment* (New Haven, CT, 2007), 80.

11. Alan P. Loeb, "Birth of the Kettering Doctrine: Fordism, Sloanism and the Discovery of Tetraethyl Lead," *Business and Economic History* 24 (Fall 1995): 77.

12. Ibid., 81; David Rosner and Gerald Markowitz, "A 'Gift of God'? The Public Health Controversy over Leaded Gasoline During the 1920s," *American Journal of Public Health* 75 (April 1985): 344; Jamie Lincoln Kitman, "The Secret History of Lead," *Nation*, March 20, 2000, 16–17, 19–20; J. R. McNeill, *Something New Under the Sun: An Environmental History of the Twentieth-Century World* (New York, 2000), 111.

13. Loeb, "Birth of the Kettering Doctrine," 82.

14. Quotations in Rosner and Markowitz, "A 'Gift of God'?," 345; Kitman, "Secret History of Lead," 20.

15. Rosner and Markowitz, "A 'Gift of God'?," 345 (1st quotation), 346 (2d quotation).

16. Quoted in ibid., 349.

17. Ibid., 350 (quotation), 351; William Joseph Kovarik, "The Ethyl Controversy: The News Media and the Public Health Debate over Leaded Gasoline, 1924–1926" (Ph.D. diss., University of Maryland, College Park, 1993), 80, 91.

18. Kitman, "Secret History of Lead," 14.

19. Glenn Yago, *The Decline of Transit: Urban Transportation in German and U.S. Cities, 1900–1970* (Cambridge, UK, 1984), 56–58.

20. Stephen B. Goddard, *Getting There: The Epic Struggle Between Road and Rail in the American Century* (New York, 1994), 121–122; Martha Janet Bianco, "Private Profit Versus Public Service: Competing Demands in Urban Transportation History and Policy, Portland, Oregon, 1872–1970" (Ph.D. diss., Portland State University, 1994), 27–55; McCarthy, *Auto Mania*, 151–52.

21. Bianco, "Private Profit Versus Public Service," 453–454; Yago, *Decline of Transit*, 58–59.

22. Bianco, "Private Profit Versus Public Service," 441.

23. Ibid., 441–442; Goddard, *Getting There*, 132, 134–135; Yago, *Decline of Transit*, 62.

24. Kenneth T. Jackson, *Crabgrass Frontier: The Suburbanization of the United States* (New York, 1985), 167; Jane Holtz Kay, *Asphalt Nation: How the Automobile Took over America and How We Can Take It Back* (New York, 1998), 199.

25. Kay, *Asphalt Nation*, 222–223; Interrante, "Moveable Feast," 287.

26. Mike Davis, *Ecology of Fear: Los Angeles and the Imagination of Disaster* (New York, 1998), 73–74.

27. Robert A. Caro, *The Power Broker: Robert Moses and the Fall of New York* (New York, 1975), 895 (quotation).

28. Ibid., 897.

29. Ibid., 19, 838, 849 (quotations); Kay, *Asphalt Nation*, 230; Marshall Berman, *All That Is Solid Melts into Air: The Experience of Modernity* (New York, 1982), 294.

30. Caro, *Power Broker*, 940, 943–944.

31. Ibid., 934, 935 (quotation), 944–949.

32. Berman, *All That Is Solid*, 307.

33. Jackson, *Crabgrass Frontier*, 248–249; Kay, *Asphalt Nation*, 232.

34. Jackson, *Crabgrass Frontier*, 249; Kay, *Asphalt Nation*, 231; Lewis, *Divided Highways*, 118, 120–121.

35. Kay, *Asphalt Nation*, 243–244; Deborah Gordon, *Steering a New Course: Transportation, Energy, and the Environment* (Washington, DC, 1991), 12, 37; Davis, *Ecology of Fear*, 80; McCarthy, *Auto Mania*, 152.

36. Jackson, *Crabgrass Frontier*, 232–233, 293–294.

37. Ibid., 283–284.

38. Ibid., 234, 236; Adam Rome, *The Bulldozer in the Countryside: Suburban Sprawl and the Rise of American Environmentalism* (New York, 2001), 16 (quotation).

39. Rome, *Bulldozer in the Countryside*, 120, 122; Eckbo, Dean, Austin, and Williams, *Open Space: The Choices Before California: The Urban Metropolitan Open Space Study* (San Francisco, 1969), 15.

40. Rome, *Bulldozer in the Countryside*, 121, 166 (quotation); John McPhee, *The Control of Nature* (New York, 1989), 203.

41. Stephen J. Pyne, *Fire in America: A Cultural History of Wildland and Rural Fire*, rev. ed. (Seattle, 1997), 405; Davis, *Ecology of Fear*, 141–146.

42. Rome, *Bulldozer in the Countryside*, 46.

43. Ibid., 45–51, 52 (quotation), 53–54.

44. McCarthy, *Auto Mania*, 148–149.

45. Rome, *Bulldozer in the Countryside*, 65–71; Raymond Arsenault, "The End of the Long Hot Summer: The Air Conditioner and Southern Culture," *Journal of Southern History* 50 (November 1984): 615.

46. Arsenault, "End of the Long Hot Summer," 617.

47. Paul Robbins, *Lawn People: How Grasses, Weeds, and Chemicals Make Us Who We Are* (Philadelphia, 2007), 47–48.

48. Virginia Scott Jenkins, "'Fairway Living': Lawncare and Lifestyle from Croquet to the Golf Course," in *The American Lawn*, ed. Georges Teyssot (New York, 1999), 127 (1st quotation); Steinberg, *American Green*, 35 (2d and 3d quotations).

49. Steinberg, *American Green*, 43 (quotation), 44–45.

50. Edmund Russell, *War and Nature: Fighting Humans and Insects with Chemicals from World War I to Silent Spring* (New York, 2001), 95–144; Malcolm Gladwell, "The Mosquito Killer," *New Yorker*, July 2, 2001, 42, 48; Robbins, *Lawn People*, 52.

51. Steinberg, *American Green*, 45–46; Environment and Human Health, Inc., *Risks from Lawn-Care Pesticides* (North Haven, CT, 2003), 13.

52. Steinberg, *American Green*, 46–47.

53. Robbins, *Lawn People*, 78, 90–91; Steinberg, *American Green*, 72–74.

54. Virginia Scott Jenkins, *The Lawn: A History of an American Obsession* (Washington, DC, 1994), 86–87, 142; F. Herbert Bormann, Diana Balmori, and Gordon T. Geballe, *Redesigning the American Lawn: A Search for Environmental Harmony* (New Haven, CT, 1993), 109; Robbins, *Lawn People*, xix.

55. Roy A. Rappaport, "Nature, Culture, and Ecological Anthropology," in *Man, Culture, and Society*, ed. Harry L. Shapiro (London, 1956), 263.

56. Kay, *Asphalt Nation*, 91, 96.

CHAPTER 14: THROWAWAY SOCIETY

1. Quoted in Eric Lipton, "The Long and Winding Road Now Followed by New York City's Trash," *New York Times*, March 24, 2001.

2. Quotations from ibid.

3. Quoted in Heather Rogers, *Gone Tomorrow: The Hidden Life of Garbage* (New York, 2005), 153.

4. Jane Celia Busch, "The Throwaway Ethic in America" (Ph.D. diss., University of Pennsylvania, 1983), 335–336; Martin V. Melosi, *The Sanitary City: Urban Infrastructure in America from Colonial Times to the Present* (Baltimore, 2000), 340; Michael Dawson, *The Consumer Trap: Big Business Marketing in American Life* (Urbana, IL, 2003), 89 (quotation).

5. James Brooke, "That Secure Feeling of a Printed Document," *New York Times*, April 21, 2000 (quotation).

6. Giles Slade, *Made to Break: Technology and Obsolescence in America* (Cambridge, MA, 2006), 30, 32 (quotation).

7. Ibid., 36, 40.

8. Michael A. Bernstein, "Why the Great Depression Was Great: Toward a New Understanding of the Interwar Economic Crisis in the United States," in *The Rise and Fall of the New Deal Order, 1930–1980*, ed. Steve Fraser and Gary Gerstle (Princeton, NJ, 1989), 39–40.

9. Slade, *Made to Break*, 74–75 (quotations), 81.

10. Lizabeth Cohen, *A Consumers' Republic: The Politics of Mass Consumption in Postwar America* (New York, 2003), 294 (quotation); Rogers, *Gone Tomorrow*, 114.

11. Quoted in Cohen, *Consumers' Republic*, 126.

12. John H. Fenton, "Vermont's Session Has Budget Clash," *New York Times*, February 1, 1953.

13. Susan Strasser, *Waste and Want: A Social History of Trash* (New York, 1999), 171–172.

14. Thomas Hine, *The Total Package: The Evolution and Secret Meaning of Boxes, Bottles, Cans, and Tubes* (Boston, 1995), 154; Busch, "Throwaway Ethic in America," 138 (quotation).

15. Rogers, *Gone Tomorrow*, 134, 141–143.

16. Jeffrey L. Meikle, "Material Doubts: The Consequences of Plastic," *Environmental History* 2 (July 1997): 279 (1st quotation); Malcolm W. Browne, "World Threat of Plastic Trash Defies Technological Solution," *New York Times*, September 6, 1987; Rogers, *Gone Tomorrow*, 148 (2d quotation).

17. Quoted in Rogers, *Gone Tomorrow*, 150–151.

18. Melosi, *Sanitary City*, 340 (table 17.1), 398 (table 20.1); Meikle, "Material Doubts," 290.

19. William Rathje and Cullen Murphy, *Rubbish: The Archeology of Garbage* (New York, 1992), 101–102, 166 (quotations).

20. Browne, "World Threat of Plastic Trash."

21. U.S. Congress, House Committee on Small Business, *Scrap Tire Management and Recycling Opportunities*, 101st Cong., 2d sess., 1990, 131, 133–134; U.S. Congress, Office of Technology Assessment, *Facing America's Trash: What Next for Municipal Solid Waste?*, OTA-O-424 (1989), 118.

22. U.S. Congress, Office of Technology Assessment, *Facing America's Trash*, 339.

23. U.S. Congress, House Committee on Small Business, *Scrap Tire Management*, 71; Jane Holtz Kay, *Asphalt Nation: How the Automobile Took over America and How We Can Take It Back* (New York, 1998), 87.

24. Donald Kennedy and Marjorie Lucks, "Rubber, Blight, and Mosquitoes: Biogeography Meets the Global Economy," *Environmental History* 4 (July 1999): 369, 376–377; Chester G. Moore and Carl J. Mitchell, "Aedes Albopictus in the United States: Ten-Year Presence and Public Health Implication," *Emerging Infectious Diseases* 3 (July/September 1997), http://www.cdc.gov/ncidod/EID/vol3no3/moore.htm (accessed October 13, 2000).

25. Quoted in Chip Brown, "Blazing Tires: Virginia's Own Volcano," *Washington Post*, November 6, 1983.

26. Quoted in Reed Tucker, "What Will Happen to All Those Recalled Tires?," *Fortune*, October 16, 2000, 60.

27. Benjamin Miller, *Fat of the Land: Garbage of New York the Last Two Hundred Years* (New York, 2000), 233; Rathje and Murphy, *Rubbish*, 85–86.

28. Rathje and Murphy, *Rubbish*, 4, 119–120.

29. Rogers, *Gone Tomorrow*, 155–156, 185; William L. Rathje, "Rubbish!," *Atlantic Monthly*, December 1989, 101–102.

30. Miller, *Fat of the Land*, 296.

31. Kirsten Engel, "Reconsidering the National Market in Sold Waste: Trade-Offs in Equity, Efficiency, Environmental Protection, and State Autonomy," *North Carolina Law Review* 73 (April 1995): 1495–1496.

32. Melosi, *Sanitary City*, 401–402.

33. Miller, *Fat of the Land*, 289–290.

34. Quoted in ibid., 290.

35. Engel, "Reconsidering the National Market," 1493–1495.

36. Elizabeth Royte, *Garbage Land: On the Secret Trail of Trash* (New York, 2005), 127–128; Melinda Beck, "Buried Alive," *Newsweek*, November 27, 1989, 68.

37. Rathje and Murphy, *Rubbish*, 206–207.

38. Royte, *Garbage Land*, 282.

39. Immanuel Wallerstein, *Historical Capitalism* (London, 1983), 40.

40. John Belamy Foster, "'Let Them Eat Pollution': Capitalism and the World Environment," *Monthly Review* 44 (January 1993): 10, 11 (1st and 2d quotations); Rogers, *Gone Tomorrow*, 201.

41. David Naguib Pellow and Lisa Sun-Hee Park, *The Silicon Valley of Dreams: Environmental Injustice, Immigrant Workers, and the High-Tech Global Economy* (New York, 2002), 81 (table 4.5); Slade, *Made to Break*, 261.

42. Slade, *Made to Break*, 196, 198; Jan Mazurek, *Making Microchips: Policy, Globalization, and Economic Restructuring in the Semiconductor Industry* (Cambridge, MA, 1999), 3; Rogers, *Gone Tomorrow*, 2.

43. Elizabeth Grossman, *High Tech Trash: Digital Devices, Hidden Toxics, and Human Health* (Washington, DC, 2006), 185.

44. Ibid., 200–201; Melosi, *Sanitary City*, 397 (figure 20.1).

45. Ian Urbina, "Unwanted Electronic Gear Rising in Toxic Piles," *New York Times*, March 18, 2013.

CHAPTER 15: SHADES OF GREEN

1. Quoted in "Oil Slick Fire Ruins Flats Shipyard," *Plain Dealer* (Cleveland, OH), November 2, 1952.
2. "Cuyahoga River on Fire," *Plain Dealer* (Cleveland, OH), January 1, 1900.
3. "Oil Slick Fire Damages 2 River Spans," *Plain Dealer* (Cleveland, OH), June 23, 1969; Roger Brown, "1969 River Blaze Scarred Image," *Plain Dealer* (Cleveland, OH), June 18, 1989 (Barry quotation); "A Letter from the Publisher" and "The Cities: The Price of Optimism," Time, August 1, 1969, 41.
4. Kirkpatrick Sale, *The Green Revolution: The American Environmental Movement, 1962–1992* (New York, 1993), 80.
5. Joseph Anthony Interrante, "A Moveable Feast: The Automobile and the Spatial Transformation of American Culture, 1890–1940" (Ph.D. diss., Harvard University, 1983), 94–97, 98 (quotation); Paul Shriver Sutter, "Driven Wild: The Intellectual and Cultural Origins of Wilderness Advocacy During the Interwar Years" (Ph.D. diss., University of Kansas, 1997), 39.
6. Aldo Leopold, *A Sand County Almanac* (New York, [1949] 1966), x, 240.
7. Sutter, "Driven Wild," 4, 9–10, 63, 66–67, 431, 448.
8. Paul W. Hirt, *A Conspiracy of Optimism: Management of the National Forests Since World War Two* (Lincoln, NE, 1994), xx, xxiii, xxv, 162–163; Richard N. L. Andrews, *Managing the Environment, Managing Ourselves: A History of American Environmental Policy* (New Haven, CT, 1999), 194.
9. Hirt, *Conspiracy of Optimism*, 164–165, 229–231; Andrews, *Managing the Environment*, 196; Sale, *Green Revolution*, 15.
10. Marc Reisner, *Cadillac Desert: The American West and Its Disappearing Water* (New York, 1986), 140, 294.
11. Hal K. Rothman, *The Greening of a Nation? Environmentalism in the United States Since 1945* (Fort Worth, TX, 1998), 41 (quotation); Russell Martin, *A Story That Stands Like a Dam: Glen Canyon and the Struggle for the Soul of the West* (New York, 1989), 64–65, 69; Reisner, *Cadillac Desert*, 295.
12. Quoted in John McPhee, *Encounters with the Archdruid* (New York, 1971), 166.
13. Martin, *Story That Stands*, 291; McPhee, *Encounters with the Archdruid*, 241 (Brower quotation).
14. Gregg Mitman, *Reel Nature: America's Romance with Wildlife on Film* (Cambridge, MA, 1999), 115 (quotation), 123.
15. Ibid., 126, 134.
16. Linda Lear, *Rachel Carson: Witness for Nature* (New York, 1997), 428; Andrews, *Managing the Environment*, 188; Rachel Carson, *Silent Spring* (Boston, [1962] 1987), 189.
17. Robert Gottlieb, *Forcing the Spring: The Transformation of the American Environmental Movement* (Washington, DC, 1993), 85 (quotation); Stephen Fox, *John Muir and His Legacy: The American Conservation Movement* (Boston, 1981), 292.
18. Adam Rome, "'Give Earth a Chance': The Environmental Movement and the Sixties," *Journal of American History* 90 (September 2003): 534.
19. Jerome Namias, "Nature and Possible Causes of the Northeastern United States Drought During 1962–65," *Monthly Weather Review* 94 (September 1966): 543–554.
20. William Ashworth, *The Late, Great Lakes: An Environmental History* (New York, 1986), 133, 142 (quotation); William McGucken, *Lake Erie Rehabilitated: Controlling Cultural Eutrophication, 1960s–1990s* (Akron, OH, 2000), 18–19.
21. Quoted in Ashworth, *Late, Great Lakes*, 143.
22. Rothman, *Greening of a Nation?*, 103.
23. Warren J. Belasco, *Appetite for Change: How the Counterculture Took on the Food Industry, 1966–1988* (New York, 1989), 21 (1st quotation), 36–37; Sale, *Green Revolution*, 23 (2d quotation).

24. Terry H. Anderson, *The Movement and the Sixties* (New York, 1995), 343 (quotation), 344–347.

25. J. Brooks Flippen, *Nixon and the Environment* (Albuquerque, NM, 2000), 227–228.

26. Andrews, *Managing the Environment*, 232–236.

27. Ibid., 236–237.

28. Adam Rome, *The Genius of Earth Day: How a 1970 Teach-In Unexpectedly Made the First Green Generation* (New York, 2013), 59, 116; Rome, "'Give Earth a Chance,'" 550 (quotation).

29. Sale, *Green Revolution*, 33 (table); Andrews, *Managing the Environment*, 238.

30. Christopher J. Bosso, *Environment Inc.: From Grassroots to Beltway* (Lawrence, KS, 2005), 89.

31. Ibid., 114 (quotation); Mark Dowie, *Losing Ground: American Environmentalism at the Close of the Twentieth Century* (Cambridge, MA, 1995), 56.

32. David Kirkpatrick, "Environmentalism: The New Crusade," *Fortune*, February 12, 1990, 47; Adam Shell, "Earth Day Spawns Corporate 'Feeding Frenzy,'" *Public Relations Journal*, February 1990 (quotation); Alecia Swasy, "Commercial Tie-ins Muddy Earth Day Observance," *Wall Street Journal*, April 15, 1991; Kirkpatrick Sale, "The Trouble with Earth Day," *Nation*, April 30, 1990, 595.

33. Quoted in Brian Tokar, *Earth for Sale: Reclaiming Ecology in the Age of Corporate Greenwash* (Boston, 1997), 35.

34. Samuel P. Hays, *Explorations in Environmental History: Essays* (Pittsburgh, PA, 1998), 258, 283; George A. Gonzalez, *Corporate Power and the Environment: The Political Economy of U.S. Environmental Policy* (Lanham, MD, 2001), 104; Philip Mirowski, *Never Let a Serious Crisis Go to Waste: How Neoliberalism Survived the Financial Meltdown* (London, 2013), 334.

35. U.S. Environmental Protection Agency, "Air Trends: Sulfur Dioxide," http://www.epa.gov/air/airtrends/sulfur.html (accessed May 13, 2007); Robert S. Devine, *Bush Versus the Environment* (New York, 2004), 36–37; Gonzalez, *Corporate Power*, 104. In 1993, the Tennessee Valley Authority bought 2.5 million dollars in pollution credits from Wisconsin Power and Light. Residents of Shelby County, Tennessee, which had a high rate of excess deaths from lung cancer, were subject to additional pollution emissions; citizens of Sheboygan County, Wisconsin, where lung cancer was much less of a problem, were spared. See Alexander Cockburn, "'Win-Win' with Bruce Babbitt: The Clinton Administration Meets the Environment," *New Left Review* 201 (September/ October): 49.

36. David C. Evers, Young-Ji Han, Charles T. Driscoll, Neil C. Kamman, M. Wing Goodale, Kathleen Fallon Lambert, Thomas M. Holsen, Celia Y. Chen, Thomas A. Clair, and Thomas Butler, "Biological Mercury Hotspots in the Northeastern United States and Southeastern Canada," *BioScience* 57 (January 2007): 29–43.

37. Philip Shabecoff, *A Fierce Green Fire: The American Environmental Movement* (New York, 1993), 235, 237.

38. Gottlieb, *Forcing the Spring*, 209; Dowie, *Losing Ground*, 172 (quotation).

39. Robert D. Bullard, ed., *Unequal Protection: Environmental Justice and Communities of Color* (San Francisco, 1994), 17.

40. Terence J. Centner, Warren Kriesel, and Andrew G. Keeler, "Environmental Justice and Toxic Releases: Establishing Evidence of Discriminatory Effect Based on Race and Not Income," *Wisconsin Environmental Law Journal* 3 (Summer 1996): 128–129, 143–146; Stephen Sandweiss, "The Social Construction of Environmental Justice," in *Environmental Injustices, Political Struggles: Race, Class, and the Environment*, ed. David E. Camacho (Durham, NC, 1998), 35.

41. Gottlieb, *Forcing the Spring*, 250–252; Harvey L. White, "Race, Class, and Environmental Hazards," in *Environmental Injustices, Political Struggles* (see note 40), 69; Judy Pasternak, "A Peril That Dwelt Among the Navajos," *Los Angeles Times*, November 19, 2006; idem, "Navajos' Desert Cleanup No More Than a Mirage," *Los Angeles Times*, November 21, 2006.

42. Dowie, *Losing Ground*, 134 (1st quotation); Sale, *Green Revolution*, 66 (2d quotation).

43. James D. Proctor, "Whose Nature? The Contested Moral Terrain of Ancient Forests," in *Uncommon Ground: Rethinking the Human Place in Nature*, ed. William Cronon (New York, 1996), 275–276.

44. William Dietrich, *The Final Forest: The Battle for the Last Great Trees of the Pacific Northwest* (New York, 1992), 74.

45. Quoted in Mark Hertsgaard, "Green Goes Grassroots: The Environmental Movement Today," *Nation*, July 31/August 7, 2006, 11.

46. Tom Athanasiou, *Divided Planet: The Ecology of Rich and Poor* (Boston, 1996), 233 (quotations); Donald Worster, *Under Western Skies: Nature and History in the American West* (New York, 1992), 213–217; Tokar, *Earth for Sale*, 19

47. Paul Hawken, Amory Lovins, and L. Hunter Lovins, *Natural Capitalism: Creating the Next Industrial Revolution* (Boston, 1999), 2, 11–14, 17, 29–32.

48. Deborah Solomon, "Calling Mr. Green," *New York Times Magazine*, May 20, 2007, 26; William McDonough and Michael Braungart, *Cradle to Cradle: Remaking the Way We Make Things* (New York, 2002), 15.

49. Ray C. Anderson, *Mid-Course Correction: Toward a Sustainable Enterprise: The Interface Model* (Atlanta, 1998), 5, 7; Hawken, Lovins, and Lovins, *Natural Capitalism*, 139–141; Bill McKibben, "Hype vs. Hope: Is Corporate Do-Goodery for Real?," *Mother Jones*, November/December 2006, 55.

50. Joel Bakan, *The Corporation: The Pathological Pursuit of Profit and Power* (New York, 2004), 34 (quotation), 60–84.

51. Hawken, Lovins, and Lovins, *Natural Capitalism*, 258.

52. "The Scotts Miracle-Gro Company Annual Shareholder Meeting," *Fair Disclosure Wire*, January 25, 2007.

53. Naomi Klein, *No Space, No Choice, No Jobs, No Logo* (New York, 2002), 327–329.

54. Heather Rogers, *Gone Tomorrow: The Hidden Life of Garbage* (New York, 2005), 225.

55. Elizabeth Royte, *Garbage Land: On the Secret Trail of Trash* (New York, 2005), 253–255; Rogers, *Gone Tomorrow*, 226–227.

56. GrassRoots Recycling Network, "Coca-Cola Campaign," May 2002, http://www.grrn.org/coke/cc-facts.html (accessed May 15, 2007); Jim Motavalli, "Zero Waste," E, March/April 2001, 28; Jeremiah A. Armstrong, "Environmental Groups Urge Coca-Cola to Recycle," *University Wire*, November 20, 1998; "New Pepsi-Coke Challenge Launched by GrassRoots Recycling Network," *PR Newswire*, July 2, 2002.

57. Elizabeth Grossman, *High Tech Trash: Digital Devices, Hidden Toxics, and Human Health* (Washington, DC, 2006), 156; David Wood and Robin Schneider, "ToxicDude.com: The Dell Campaign," in *Challenging the Chip: Labor Rights and Environmental Justice in the Global Electronics Industry*, ed. Ted Smith, David A. Sonnenfeld, and David Naguib Pellow (Philadelphia, 2006), 285.

58. Klein, *No Logo*, 3–5, 197 (quotation); Wood and Schneider, "ToxicDude.com," 287.

59. Wood and Schneider, "ToxicDude.com," 288–289, 290 (quotation).

60. Quoted in Scott Carlson, "Old Computers Never Die—They Just Cost Colleges Money in New Ways," *Chronicle of Higher Education*, February 14, 2003.

61. Wood and Schneider, "ToxicDude.com," 289, 292, 294; Grossman, *High Tech Trash*, 157 (quotation).

62. "Second International Conference on the Protection of the North Sea: Ministerial Declaration Calling for Reduction of Pollution," *International Legal Materials* 27 (May 1988): 835, 838; Ted Steinberg, *American Green: The Obsessive Quest for the Perfect Lawn* (New York, 2006), 204–205.

63. Alexander Cockburn, "Understanding the World with Paul Sweezy," *Nation*, March 22, 2004, 8.

CHAPTER 16: CAPITALISM VERSUS THE EARTH

1. Thomas K. McCraw, "Introduction," in *Creating Modern Capitalism: How Entrepreneurs, Companies, and Countries Triumphed in Three Industrial Revolutions*, ed. Thomas K. McCraw (Cambridge, MA, 1995), 3 (quotation); Justin Gillis and Nadja Popovich, "The U.S. Is the Biggest Carbon Polluter in History," *New York Times*, June 1, 2017.

2. David Graeber, *Debt: The First 5,000 Years* (Brooklyn, NY, 2011), 366.

3. Will Steffen, Wendy Broadgate, Lisa Deutsch, Owen Gaffney, and Cornelia Ludwig, "The Trajectory of the Anthropocene: The Great Acceleration," *Anthropocene Review* 2 (2015): 82.

4. J. R. McNeill and Peter Engelke, *The Great Acceleration: An Environmental History of the Anthropocene Since 1945* (Cambridge, MA, 2014), 4.

5. Daniel Yergin, *The Prize: The Epic Quest for Oil, Money, and Power* (New York, 1991), 208.

6. Lizabeth Cohen, *A Consumers' Republic: The Politics of Mass Consumption in Postwar America* (New York, 2003), 61 (quotations); Robert M. Collins, *More: The Politics of Economic Growth in Postwar America* (New York, 2000), 9–10; Matthew T. Huber, *Lifeblood: Oil, Freedom, and the Forces of Capital* (Minneapolis, MN, 2013), 41.

7. Cohen, *Consumers' Republic*, 118 (quotation); Collins, *More*, 33, 36; Alain Lipietz, *Towards a New Economic Order: Postfordism, Ecology, and Democracy*, trans. Malcolm Slater (New York, 1992), 12.

8. Ian Angus, *Facing the Anthropocene: Fossil Capitalism and the Crisis of the Earth System* (New York, 2016), 120–121; Timothy Mitchell, *Carbon Democracy: Political Power in the Age of Oil* (London, 2011), 37.

9. Matthew T. Huber, "Enforcing Scarcity: Oil, Violence, and the Making of the Market," *Annals of the Association of American Geographers* 101 (2011): 822–823; Michael T. Klare, *Rising Powers, Shrinking Planet: The New Geopolitics of Energy* (New York, 2008), 183.

10. Michael T. Klare, *Blood and Oil: The Dangers and Consequences of America's Growing Dependence on Imported Petroleum* (New York, 2004), 28; Huber, *Lifeblood*, 69–70.

11. Victoria de Grazia, *Irresistible Empire: America's Advance Through 20th-Century Europe* (Cambridge, MA, 2005), 339, 346–347; Leo Panitch and Sam Gindin, *The Making of Global Capitalism: The Political Economy of American Empire* (London, 2012), 97–98.

12. Mitchell, *Carbon Democracy*, 29–30; Panitch and Gindin, *Making of Global Capitalism*, 84–85, 98, 101.

13. De Grazia, *Irresistible Empire*, 422. In 2014, Proctor & Gamble eliminated phosphates from its laundry detergents. See Erica Gies, "Proctor & Gamble Touts 'Win-Win' of Cutting Phosphates in All Laundry Soaps," *Guardian*, January 27, 2014.

14. Chalmers Johnson, *The Sorrows of Empire: Militarism, Secrecy, and the End of the Republic* (New York, 2004), 167–168, 217–220; Panitch and Gindin, *Making of Global Capitalism*, 103–104.

15. Cohen, *Consumers' Republic*, 126–127; Huber, *Lifeblood*, 72.

16. Panitch and Gindin, *Making of Global Capitalism*, 10, 74; Cheryl Payer, *The Debt Trap: The International Monetary Fund and the Third World* (New York, 1974), 22–23; David M. Kotz, *The Rise and Fall of Neoliberal Capitalism* (Cambridge, MA, 2015), 12–13.

17. Quoted in Bruce Rich, *Mortgaging the Earth: The World Bank, Environmental Impoverishment, and the Crisis of Development* (Boston, 1994), 54–55.

18. Payer, *Debt Trap*, 75–76, 78; Chalmers Johnson, *Blowback: The Costs and Consequences of American Empire* (New York, 2000), 74; Sanjeev Khagram, *Dams and Development: Transnational Struggles for Water and Power* (Ithaca, NY, 2004), 161–162.

19. Payer, *Debt Trap*, 79, 83, 85–86.

20. Panitch and Gindin, *Making of Global Capitalism*, 75; Khagram, *Dams and Development*, 159–160, 164; Patrick McCully, *Silenced Rivers: The Ecology and Politics of Large Dams* (London, 2001), 31.

21. Rich, Mortgaging the Earth, 232–234; William U. Chandler, The Myth of the TVA: Conservation and Development in the Tennessee Valley, 1933–1983 (Cambridge, MA, 1984), 78.

22. Khagram, Dams and Development, 7, 143, 145; McCully, Silenced Rivers, 258. Some 1 million square kilometers of land were flooded, or 386,102 square miles. Texas is 268,596 square miles.

23. Rich, Mortgaging the Earth, 14–15, 17.

24. Richard Tucker, Insatiable Appetite: The United States and the Ecological Degradation of the Tropical World (Berkeley, 2000), 163, 168, 345.

25. Rich, Mortgaging the Earth, 19.

26. John H. Perkins, Geopolitics and the Green Revolution: Wheat, Genes, and the Cold War (New York, 1997), 117, 119–120, 258.

27. Jack Doyle, Altered Harvest: Agriculture, Genetics, and the Fate of the World's Food Supply (New York, 1985), 35–40; Ruth Schwartz Cowan, A Social History of American Technology (New York, 1997), 303–310.

28. J. R. McNeill, Something New Under the Sun: An Environmental History of the Twentieth-Century World (New York, 2000), 220–221; Nick Cullather, The Hungry World: America's Cold War Battle Against Poverty in Asia (Cambridge, MA, 2010), 49; Perkins, Geopolitics and the Green Revolution, 138–139; Doyle, Altered Harvest, 257.

29. Magdalena Barros Nock, "The Mexican Peasantry and the Ejido in the Neo-liberal Period," in Disappearing Peasantries? Rural Labour in Africa, Asia and Latin America, ed. Deborah Bryceson, Cristóbal Kay, and Jos Mooij (London, 2000), 161–163; Cullather, Hungry World, 68.

30. Richard Manning, Food's Frontier: The Next Green Revolution (New York, 2000), 4–5; Jan Breman, "Labour and Landlessness in South and South-East Asia," in Disappearing Peasantries? (see note 29), 240.

31. Vandana Shiva, The Violence of the Green Revolution: Third World Agriculture, Ecology and Politics (London, 1991), 63–64.

32. Ibid., 74–75, 118; Doyle, Altered Harvest, 261 (quotation), 262; McNeill, Something New Under the Sun, 224.

33. McNeill, Something New Under the Sun, 223–224; Vandana Shiva, Stolen Harvest: The Hijacking of the Global Food Supply (Cambridge, MA, 2000), 80.

34. Shiva, Violence of the Green Revolution, 91; David Weir and Mark Schapiro, Circle of Poison: Pesticides and People in a Hungry World (Oakland, CA, 1981), 37; Cullather, Hungry World, 251–252.

35. James C. Scott, Weapons of the Weak: Everyday Forms of Peasant Resistance (New Haven, CT, 1985), 56, 80, 148; Weir and Schapiro, Circle of Poison, 37–38; Cullather, Hungry World, 266.

36. Panitch and Gindin, Making of Global Capitalism, 144; Aaron Brenner, Robert Brenner, and Cal Winslow, eds., Rebel Rank and File: Labor Militancy and Revolt from Below During the Long 1970s (London, 2010), 3.

37. David Harvey, A Brief History of Neoliberalism (Oxford, UK, 2005), 10–15; Kotz, Rise and Fall, 66–67.

38. Harvey, Brief History of Neoliberalism, 20, 38, 42; Philip Mirowski, Never Let a Serious Crisis Go to Waste: How Neoliberalism Survived the Financial Meltdown (London, 2013), 54; Robert Pollin, Contours of Descent: U.S. Economic Fractures and the Landscape of Global Austerity (London, 2003), 8.

39. Harvey, Brief History of Neoliberalism, 7–9, 22, 175; Panitch and Gindin, Making of Global Capitalism, 216.

40. Lipietz, Towards a New Economic Order, 52.

41. Robert M. Solow, "The Economics of Resources or the Resources of Economics," American Economic Review 64 (May 1974): 12; Mitchell, Carbon Democracy, 196–197.

42. Panitch and Gindin, *Making of Global Capitalism*, 168; Joel Bakan, *The Corporation: The Pathological Pursuit of Profit and Power* (New York, 2004), 135; Kotz, *Rise and Fall*, 70 (quotation).

43. Mitchell, *Carbon Democracy*, 185; Graeber, *Debt*, 2.

44. Susan George, *The Debt Boomerang: How Third World Debt Harms Us All* (Boulder, CO, 1992), xv, xvi; Harvey, *Brief History of Neoliberalism*, 29; for pillaging of resources, see Rich, *Mortgaging the Earth*, 188.

45. David Pearce, Neil Adger, David Maddison, and Dominic Moran, "Debt and the Environment," *Scientific American* 272 (June 1995): 53; George, *Debt Boomerang*, 10, 13, 16; Susan George, *A Fate Worse Than Debt* (New York, 1988), 164–165; Rich, *Mortgaging the Earth*, 26–28.

46. Pearce et al., "Debt and the Environment," 53; McNeill, *Something New Under the Sun*, 236.

47. William I. Robinson, *Latin America and Global Capitalism: A Critical Globalization Perspective* (Baltimore, 2008), 60 (quotation), 62, 66–68, 71–72, 76.

48. Food and Agriculture Organization of the United Nations, *The State of World Fisheries and Aquaculture 2006* (Rome, 2007), 16; Derek Hall, "The International Political Ecology of Industrial Shrimp Aquaculture and Industrial Plantation Forestry in Southeast Asia," *Journal of Southeast Asian Studies* 34 (June 2003): 251–253, 254 (quotation), 255, 257, 259–260.

49. Hall, "International Political Ecology," 252, 258 (quotation).

50. *Diamond v. Chakrabarty* 447 U.S. 303 (1980).

51. Quoted in Shiva, *Stolen Harvest*, 11.

52. Marc Lappé and Britt Bailey, *Against the Grain: Biotechnology and the Corporate Takeover of Your Food* (Monroe, ME, 1998), 52–53; Rick Weiss, "Seeds of Discord: Monsanto's Gene Police Raise Alarm on Farmers' Rights, Rural Tradition," *Washington Post*, February 3, 1999.

53. Michael Parenti, *Against Empire* (San Francisco, 1995), 32–33; William I. Robinson, *Global Capitalism and the Crisis of Humanity* (New York, 2014), 87–88.

54. Keith Aoki, "Neocolonialism, Anticommons Property, and Biopiracy in the (Not-So-Brave) New World Order of International Intellectual Property Protection," *Indiana Journal of Global Legal Studies* 6 (Fall 1998): 51; Naomi Roht-Arriaza, "Of Seeds and Shamans: The Appropriation of the Scientific and Technical Knowledge of Indigenous and Local Communities," *Michigan Journal of International Law* 17 (Summer 1996): 922 (quotation).

55. Jack Ralph Kloppenburg, Jr., *First the Seed: The Political Economy of Plant Biotechnology, 1492–2000* (Cambridge, UK, 1988), 152 (1st quotation), 185–186; Roht-Arriaza, "Of Seeds and Shamans," 932–933; Jeremy Rifkin, *The Biotech Century: Harnessing the Gene and Remaking the World* (New York, 1998), 52 (2d quotation).

56. Doyle, *Altered Harvest*, 313 (quotation); Vandana Shiva, "War Against Nature and the People of the South," in *Views from the South: The Effects of Globalization and the WTO on Third World Countries*, ed. Sarah Anderson (np., 2000), 115; Laurie Anne Whitt, "Indigenous Peoples, Intellectual Property and the New Imperial Science," *Oklahoma City University Law Review* 23 (Spring/Summer 1998): 257.

57. Jeffrey Rothfeder, *Every Drop for Sale: Our Desperate Battle over Water in a World About to Run Out* (New York, 2004), 8, 101; Shawn Tully, "Water, Water Everywhere," *Fortune*, May 15, 2000, 344.

58. Maude Barlow and Tony Clarke, *Blue Gold: The Battle Against Corporate Theft of the World's Water* (Toronto, 2002), 156; Rothfeder, *Every Drop for Sale*, 87 (1st quotation), 53 (2d quotation), 115.

59. William Finnegan, "Leasing the Rain," *New Yorker*, April 8, 2002, 47 (1st quotation); Rothfeder, *Every Drop for Sale*, 108, 112 (2d quotation), 114.

60. David E. Nye, *Consuming Power: A Social History of American Energies* (Cambridge, MA, 1999), 6; Anthony Giddens, *The Politics of Climate Change* (Cambridge, 2009), 183–185; U.S. Environmental Protection Agency, "Global Greenhous Gas Emissions Data," https://www.epa.gov/ghgemissions/global-greenhouse-gas-emissions-data (accessed April 5, 2018); Gillis and Popovich, "Biggest Carbon Polluter" (quotation).

61. Nye, *Consuming Power*, 187, 202, 205, 238.

62. McNeill, *Something New Under the Sun*, 109; Elizabeth Kolbert, *Field Notes from a Catastrophe: Man, Nature, and Climate Change* (New York, 2006), 44; U.S. Department of Commerce, National Oceanic and Atmospheric Administration, "Trends in Atmospheric Carbon Dioxide," http://www.esrl.noaa.gov/gmd/ccgg/trends/#mlo (accessed April 4, 2018).

63. NASA, "NASA, NOAA Data Show 2016 Warmest Year on Record Globally," January 18, 2017, https://www.nasa.gov/press-release/nasa-noaa-data-show-2016-warmest-year-on-record-globally (accessed April 4, 2018).

64. Kolbert, *Field Notes from a Catastrophe*, 13, 26, 87; Elizabeth Kolbert, "The Darkening Sea: What Carbon Emissions Are Doing to the Ocean," *New Yorker*, November 20, 2006, 68, 72; Brian Fagan, *The Great Warming: Climate Change and the Rise and Fall of Civilizations* (New York, 2008), xvii; Ted Steinberg, *Gotham Unbound: The Ecological History of Greater New York* (New York, 2014), 334, 342, 350.

65. Tim P. Barnett et al., "Human-Induced Changes in the Hydrology of the Western United States," *Science* 319 (February 2008): 1080–1083.

66. Naomi Oreskes and Erik M. Conway, *Merchants of Doubt: How a Handful of Scientists Obscured the Truth on Issues from Tobacco Smoke to Global Warming* (New York, 2010), 170–171.

67. Intergovernmental Panel on Climate Change, *Climate Change 2013: The Physical Science Basis*, Summary for Policymakers, 17, https://www.ipcc.ch/pdf/assessment-report/ar5/wg1/WG1AR5_SPM_FINAL.pdf (accessed April 4, 2018).

68. Nicholas Stern, *Stern Review on the Economics of Climate Change*, executive summary, http://www.hm-treasury.gov.uk/media/8AC/F7/Executive_Summary.pdf (accessed May 16, 2007), i.

69. John L. Brooke, *Climate Change and the Course of Global History* (New York, 2014), 1; Will Steffen, Angelina Sanderson, Peter Tyson, Jill Jäger, Pamela Matson, Berrien Moore, Frank Oldfied, et al., *Global Change and the Earth System: A Planet Under Pressure* (Berlin, 2005), 6 (figure 1.7); Peter M. Vitousek, Harold A. Mooney, Jane Lubchenco, and Jerry M. Melillo, "Human Domination of Earth's Ecosystems," *Science* 277 (July 25, 1997): 495; Will Steffen, Paul J. Crutzen, and John R. McNeill, "The Anthropocene: Are Humans Now Overwhelming the Great Forces of Nature?," *Ambio* 36 (December 2007): 617; McNeill and Engelke, *Great Acceleration*, 4, 208.

70. McNeill and Engelke, *Great Acceleration*, 9, 11.

71. Andreas Malm, *Fossil Capital: The Rise of Steam Power and the Roots of Global Warming* (London, 2016), 328; Panitch and Gindin, *Making of Global Capitalism*, 189; U.S. General Accounting Office, *Automobile Fuel Economy: Potential Effects of Increasing the Corporate Average Fuel Economy Standards*, GAO/RCED-00-194 (Washington, DC, 2000), 6; Jack Doyle, *Taken for a Ride: Detroit's Big Three and the Politics of Pollution* (New York, 2000), 396, 401–402.

72. Harvey, *Brief History of Neoliberalism*, 129; Panitch and Gindin, *Making of Global Capitalism*, 293–294, 296; Malm, *Fossil Capital*, 331, 342–343; Andreas Malm, "China as Chimney of the World: The Fossil Capital Hypothesis," *Organization & Environment* 25 (June 2012): 146–177.

73. Mirowski, *Never Let a Serious Crisis*, 337; Oreskes and Conway, *Merchants of Doubt*, 34; Ross Gelbspan, *The Heat Is On: The High Stakes Battle over Earth's Threatened Climate* (Reading, MA, 1997), 34 (quotation).

74. McNeill and Engelke, *Great Acceleration*, 112, 114.

75. United Nations Human Settlements Programme, *The Challenge of Slums: Global Report on Human Settlements 2003* (London, 2003), xxv; Mike Davis, *Planet of Slums* (London, 2006), 153; Harvey, *Brief History of Neoliberalism*, 99–103.

76. Davis, *Planet of Slums*, 6–7, 126–127; Harvey, *Brief History of Neoliberalism*, 126–127, 150.

77. Fredric Jameson, "Future City," *New Left Review* 21 (May/June 2003): 76.

78. Harvard Public Opinion Project, *Survey of Young Americans' Attitudes Toward Politics and Public Service*, 29th ed. (2016), 7, accessed March 24, 2018, http://iop.harvard.edu/sites/default/files/content/160425_Harvard%20IOP%20Spring%20Report_update.pdf.

BIBLIOGRAPHY

Aduddell, Robert, and Louis Cain. "Location and Collusion in the Meat Packing Industry." In *Business Enterprise and Economic Change*, edited by Louis P. Cain and Paul J. Uselding. Kent, OH: Kent State Univ. Press, 1973.

Aiken, Charles S. *The Cotton Plantation South Since the Civil War*. Baltimore: Johns Hopkins Univ. Press, 1998.

Anderson, M. Kat, Michael G. Barbour, and Valerie Whitworth. "A World of Balance and Plenty: Land, Plants, Animals, and Humans in a Pre-European California." In *Contested Eden: California Before the Gold Rush*, edited by Ramón A. Gutiérrez and Richard J. Orsi. Berkeley: Univ. of California Press, 1998.

Anderson, Terry H. *The Movement and the Sixties*. New York: Oxford Univ. Press, 1995.

Andrews, Richard N. L. *Managing the Environment, Managing Ourselves: A History of American Environmental Policy*. New Haven, CT: Yale Univ. Press, 1999.

Andrews, Thomas G. *Killing for Coal: America's Deadliest Labor War*. Cambridge, MA: Harvard Univ. Press, 2008.

Angus, Ian. *Facing the Anthropocene: Fossil Capitalism and the Crisis of the Earth System*. New York: Monthly Review Press, 2016.

Aoki, Keith. "Neocolonialism, Anticommons Property, and Biopiracy in the (Not-So-Brave) New World Order of International Intellectual Property Protection." *Indiana Journal of Global Legal Studies* 6 (Fall 1998): 11–58.

Armstrong, Ellis L., Michael C. Robinson, and Suellen M. Hoy, eds. *History of Public Works in the United States, 1776–1976*. Chicago: American Public Works Association, 1976.

Arnould, Richard J. "Changing Patterns of Concentration in American Meat Packing, 1880–1963." *Business History Review* 45 (Spring 1971): 18–34.

Arsenault, Raymond. "The End of the Long Hot Summer: The Air Conditioner and Southern Culture." *Journal of Southern History* 50 (November 1984): 597–628.

Ashworth, William. *The Late, Great Lakes: An Environmental History*. New York: Alfred A. Knopf, 1986.

Athanasiou, Tom. *Divided Planet: The Ecology of Rich and Poor*. Boston: Little, Brown, 1996.

Bakan, Joel. *The Corporation: The Pathological Pursuit of Profit and Power*. New York: Free Press, 2004.

Ballon, Hilary, and Kenneth T. Jackson, eds. *Robert Moses and the Modern City: The Transformation of New York*. W. W. Norton, 2007.

Banner, Stuart. *How the Indians Lost Their Land: Law and Power on the Frontier*. Cambridge, MA: Belknap Press of Harvard Univ. Press, 2005.

Barger, Harold, and Hans H. Landsberg. *American Agriculture, 1899–1939: A Study of Output, Employment and Productivity*. New York: National Bureau of Economic Research, 1942.

Barlow, Maude, and Tony Clarke. *Blue Gold: The Battle Against Corporate Theft of the World's Water*. Toronto: Stoddart, 2002.

Baron, William R. "Eighteenth-Century New England Climate Variation and Its Suggested Impact on Society." *Maine Historical Society Quarterly* 21 (Spring 1982): 201–218.

Baron, William, and Anne F. Bridges. "Making Hay in Northern New England: Maine as a Case Study, 1800–1850." *Agricultural History* 57 (April 1983): 165–180.

Belasco, Warren J. *Appetite for Change: How the Counterculture Took on the Food Industry, 1966–1988.* New York: Pantheon, 1989.

Bello, Walden. *Dark Victory: The United States and Global Poverty.* 2d ed. London: Pluto, 1999.

Berlin, Ira. *Many Thousands Gone: The First Two Centuries of Slavery in North America.* Cambridge, MA: Belknap Press of Harvard Univ. Press, 1998.

Berman, Marshall. *All That Is Solid Melts into Air: The Experience of Modernity.* New York: Penguin, 1982.

Bianco, Martha Janet. "Private Profit Versus Public Service: Competing Demands in Urban Transportation History and Policy, Portland Oregon, 1872–1970." Ph.D. diss., Portland State Univ., 1994.

Blackmar, Elizabeth. "Accountability for Public Health: Regulating the Housing Market in Nineteenth-Century New York City." In *Hives of Sickness: Public Health and Epidemics in New York City,* edited by David Rosner. New Brunswick, NJ: Rutgers Univ. Press, 1995.

———. "Contemplating the Force of Nature." *Radical Historians Newsletter,* no. 70 (May 1994).

Block, Fred, and Margaret R. Somers. *The Power of Market Fundamentalism: Karl Polanyi's Critique.* Cambridge, MA: Harvard Univ. Press, 2014.

Blumberg, Louis, and Robert Gottlieb. *War on Waste: Can America Win Its Battle with Garbage?* Washington, DC: Island Press, 1989.

Bogue, Margaret Beattie. *Fishing the Great Lakes: An Environmental History, 1783–1933.* Madison: Univ. of Wisconsin Press, 2000.

Bolster, W. Jeffrey. *The Mortal Sea: Fishing the Atlantic in the Age of Sail.* Cambridge, MA: Belknap Press of Harvard Univ. Press, 2012.

Bormann, F. Herbert, Diana Balmori, and Gordon T. Geballe. *Redesigning the American Lawn: A Search for Environmental Harmony.* New Haven, CT: Yale Univ. Press, 1993.

Bosso, Christopher J. *Environment Inc.: From Grassroots to Beltway.* Lawrence: Univ. Press of Kansas, 2005.

Bouton, Terry. *Taming Democracy: "The People," the Founders, and the Troubled Ending of the American Revolution.* New York: Oxford Univ. Press, 2007.

Bowden, Martyn J., Robert W. Kates, Paul A. Kay, William E. Riebsame, Richard A. Warrick, Douglas L. Johnson, Harvey A. Gould, and Daniel Weiner. "The Effect of Climate Fluctuations on Human Populations: Two Hypotheses." In *Climate and History: Studies in Past Climates and Their Impact on Man,* edited by T. M. L. Wigley, M. J. Ingram, and G. Farmer. Cambridge: Cambridge Univ. Press, 1981.

Box, Thadis W. "Range Deterioration in West Texas." *Southwestern Historical Quarterly* 71 (July 1967): 37–45.

Brady, Lisa M. "The Wilderness of War: Nature and Strategy in the American Civil War." *Environmental History* 10 (July 2005): 421–447.

Braund, Kathryn Holland. "'Hog Wild' and 'Nuts': Billy Boll Weevil Comes to the Alabama Wiregrass." *Agricultural History* 63 (Summer 1989): 15–39.

Brechin, Gray. *Imperial San Francisco: Urban Power, Earthly Ruin.* Berkeley: Univ. of California Press, 1999.

Breen, T. H. *Tobacco Culture: The Mentality of the Great Tidewater Planters on the Eve of Revolution.* Princeton, NJ: Princeton Univ. Press, 1985.

Breman, Jan. "Labour and Landlessness in South and South-East Asia." In *Disappearing Peasantries? Rural Labour in Africa, Asia and Latin America,* edited by Deborah Bryceson, Cristóbal Kay, and Jos Mooij. London: Intermediate Technology Publications, 2000.

Brick, Philip. "Taking Back the Rural West." In *Let the People Judge: Wise Use and the Private Property Rights Movement,* edited by John Echeverria and Raymond Booth Eby. Washington, DC: Island Press, 1995.

Brooke, John L. *Climate Change and the Course of Global History*. New York: Cambridge Univ. Press, 2014.

Brown, Lester R., Michael Renner, and Brian Halweil. *Vital Signs 2000:The Environmental Trends That Are Shaping Our Future*. New York: W. W. Norton, 2000.

Brown, R. Ben. "Closing the Southern Range: A Chapter in the Decline of the Southern Yeomanry." American Bar Foundation, Working Paper #9020, 1990.

———. "The Southern Range: A Study in Nineteenth Century Law and Society." Ph.D. diss., Univ. of Michigan, 1993.

Buell, Lawrence. *The Environmental Imagination:Thoreau, Nature Writing, and the Formation of American Culture*. Cambridge, MA: Harvard Univ. Press, 1995.

Bugos, Glen E. "Intellectual Property Protection in the American Chicken-Breeding Industry." *Business History Review* 66 (Spring 1992): 127–168.

Bullard, Robert D., ed. *Unequal Protection: Environmental Justice and Communities of Color*. San Francisco: Sierra Club Books, 1994.

Burrows, Edwin G., and Mike Wallace. *Gotham: A History of New York City to 1898*. New York: Oxford Univ. Press, 1999.

Busch, Jane Celia. "The Throwaway Ethic in America." Ph.D. diss., Univ. of Pennsylvania, 1983.

Bushman, Richard Lyman. "Markets and Composite Farms in Early America." *William and Mary Quarterly* 55 (July 1998): 351–374.

Callicott, J. Baird, ed. *Companion to A Sand County Almanac: Interpretive and Critical Essays*. Madison: Univ. of Wisconsin Press, 1987.

Calloway, Colin G. *New Worlds for All: Indians, Europeans, and the Remaking of Early America*. Baltimore: Johns Hopkins Univ. Press, 1997.

———. *One Vast Winter Count: The Native American West Before Lewis and Clark*. Lincoln: Univ. of Nebraska Press, 2003.

Carney, Judith A. *Black Rice:The African Origins of Rice Cultivation in the Americas*. Cambridge, MA: Harvard Univ. Press, 2001.

Caro, Robert A. *The Power Broker: Robert Moses and the Fall of New York*. New York: Vintage, 1975.

Carroll, Charles F. *The Timber Economy of Puritan New England*. Providence, RI: Brown Univ. Press, 1973.

Carson, Rachel. *Silent Spring*. 1962. Reprint. Boston: Houghton Mifflin, 1987.

Caudill, Harry M. *My Land Is Dying*. New York: Dutton, 1971.

———. *Night Comes to the Cumberlands*. Boston: Atlantic Monthly, 1962.

Centner, Terence J., Warren Kriesel, and Andrew G. Keeler. "Environmental Justice and Toxic Releases: Establishing Evidence of Discriminatory Effect Based on Race and Not Income." *Wisconsin Environmental Law Journal* 3 (Summer 1996): 119–158.

Chadde, Steve W., and Charles E. Kay. "Tall-Willow Communities on Yellowstone's Northern Range: A Test of the 'Natural-Regulation' Paradigm." In *The Greater Yellowstone Ecosystem: Redefining America's Wilderness Heritage*, edited by Robert B. Keiter and Mark S. Boyce. New Haven, CT: Yale Univ. Press, 1991.

Chan, Sucheng. *This Bitter-Sweet Soil:The Chinese in California Agriculture, 1860–1910*. Berkeley: Univ. of California Press, 1986.

Chandler, William U. *The Myth of the TVA: Conservation and Development in the Tennessee Valley, 1933–1983*. Cambridge, MA: Ballinger, 1984.

Chaplin, Joyce E. *An Anxious Pursuit: Agricultural Innovation and Modernity in the Lower South, 1730–1815*. Chapel Hill: Univ. of North Carolina Press, 1993.

———. "Tidal Rice Cultivation and the Problem of Slavery in South Carolina and Georgia, 1760–1815." *William and Mary Quarterly* 49 (January 1992): 29–61.

Chase, Alston. *In a Dark Wood: The Fight over Forests and the Rising Tyranny of Ecology.* Boston: Houghton Mifflin, 1995.

—. *Playing God in Yellowstone: The Destruction of America's First National Park.* San Diego: Harcourt Brace, 1987.

Chesson, Michael B. "Harlots or Heroines? A New Look at the Richmond Bread Riot." *Virginia Magazine of History and Biography* 92 (April 1984): 131–175.

Clark, Christopher. *The Roots of Rural Capitalism: Western Massachusetts, 1780–1860.* Ithaca, NY: Cornell Univ. Press, 1990.

Clegg, John J. "Capitalism and Slavery." *Critical Historical Studies* 2 (Fall 2015): 281–304.

Clements, Kendrick A. *Hoover, Conservation, and Consumerism: Engineering the Good Life.* Lawrence: Univ. Press of Kansas, 2000.

Clover, Charles. *The End of the Line: How Overfishing Is Changing the World and What We Eat.* New York: New Press, 2006.

Cockburn, Alexander. "A Short, Meat-Oriented History of the World: From Eden to the Mattole." *New Left Review* 215 (January/February 1996): 16–42.

Cohen, Leah Hager. *Glass, Paper, Beans: Revelations on the Nature and Value of Ordinary Things.* New York: Doubleday, 1997.

Cohen, Lisabeth. *A Consumers' Republic: The Politics of Mass Consumption in Postwar America.* New York: Alfred A. Knopf, 2003.

Cohen, Michael P. *The Pathless Way: John Muir and American Wilderness.* Madison: Univ. of Wisconsin Press, 1984.

Colby, Charles C. "The California Raisin Industry—A Study in Geographic Interpretation." *Annals of the Association of American Geographers* 14 (June 1924): 49–108.

Collins, Robert M. *More: The Politics of Economic Growth in Postwar America.* New York: Oxford Univ. Press, 2000.

Colomina, Beatriz. "The Lawn at War: 1941–1961." In *The American Lawn,* edited by Georges Teyssot. New York: Princeton Architectural Press, 1999.

Commoner, Barry. *The Closing Circle: Nature, Man and Technology.* New York: Alfred A. Knopf, 1971.

—. *The Poverty of Power: Energy and the Economic Crisis.* New York: Bantam, 1977.

Conkin, Paul K. "Hot, Humid, and Sad." *Journal of Southern History* 64 (February 1998): 3–22.

Corbett, Katharine T. "Draining the Metropolis: The Politics of Sewers in Nineteenth Century St. Louis." In *Common Fields: An Environmental History of St. Louis,* edited by Andrew Hurley. St. Louis: Missouri Historical Society, 1997.

Coughenour, Michael B., and Francis J. Singer. "The Concept of Overgrazing and Its Application to Yellowstone's Northern Range." In *The Greater Yellowstone Ecosystem: Redefining America's Wilderness Heritage,* edited by Robert B. Keiter and Mark S. Boyce. New Haven, CT: Yale Univ. Press, 1991.

Cowan, Ruth Schwartz. *A Social History of American Technology.* New York: Oxford Univ. Press, 1997.

Cowdrey, Albert E. *This Land, This South: An Environmental History.* Rev. ed. Lexington: Univ. of Kentucky Press, 1996.

Cox, Thomas R., Robert S. Maxwell, Phillip Drennon Thomas, and Joseph J. Malone. *This Well-Wooded Land: Americans and Their Forests from Colonial Times to the Present.* Lincoln: Univ. of Nebraska Press, 1985.

Craighead, John J. "Yellowstone in Transition." In *The Greater Yellowstone Ecosystem: Redefining America's Wilderness Heritage,* edited by Robert B. Keiter and Mark S. Boyce. New Haven, CT: Yale Univ. Press, 1991.

Craven, Avery Odelle. *Soil Exhaustion as a Factor in the Agricultural History of Virginia and Maryland, 1607–1860.* Urbana: Univ. of Illinois Press, 1926.

Cronon, William. *Changes in the Land: Indians, Colonists, and the Ecology of New England.* New York: Hill and Wang, 1983.

———. "Modes of Prophecy and Production: Placing Nature in History." *Journal of American History* 76 (March 1990): 1122–1131.

———. *Nature's Metropolis: Chicago and the Great West.* New York: W. W. Norton, 1991.

———. "A Place for Stories: Nature, History, and Narrative." *Journal of American History* 78 (March 1992): 1347–1376.

———, ed. *Uncommon Ground: Rethinking the Human Place in Nature.* New York: W. W. Norton, 1996.

———. "The Uses of Environmental History." *Environmental History Review* 17 (Fall 1993): 1–22.

Cronon, William, and Richard White. "Indians in the Land." *American Heritage* 37 (August/September 1986): 18–25.

Crosby, Alfred W., Jr. *The Columbian Exchange: Biological and Cultural Consequences of 1492.* Westport, CT: Greenwood, 1972.

———. *Ecological Imperialism: The Biological Expansion of Europe, 900–1900.* New York: Cambridge Univ. Press, 1986.

Cuff, Timothy. "A Weighty Issue Revisited: New Evidence on Commercial Swine Weights and Pork Production in Mid-Nineteenth Century America." *Agricultural History* 66 (Fall 1992): 55–74.

Cullather, Nick. *The Hungry World: America's Cold War Battle Against Poverty in Asia.* Cambridge, MA: Harvard Univ. Press, 2010.

Cumbler, John T. "The Early Making of an Environmental Consciousness: Fish, Fisheries Commissions, and the Connecticut River." *Environmental History Review* 15 (Winter 1991): 73–91.

———. *Reasonable Use: The People, the Environment, and the State: New England, 1790–1930.* New York: Oxford Univ. Press, 2001.

Dale, Edward Everett. *The Range Cattle Industry: Ranching on the Great Plains from 1865 to 1925.* Norman: Univ. of Oklahoma Press, 1960.

Daniels, John D. "The Indian Population of North America in 1492." *William and Mary Quarterly* 49 (April 1992): 298–320.

D'Antonio, Michael. *Atomic Harvest: Hanford and the Lethal Toll of America's Nuclear Arsenal.* New York: Crown, 1993.

Dasmann, Raymond F. *The Destruction of California.* New York: Macmillan, 1965.

Davis, David Brion. *Inhuman Bondage: The Rise and Fall of Slavery in the New World.* New York: Oxford Univ. Press, 2006.

Davis, Donald Edward. *Where There Are Mountains: An Environmental History of the Southern Appalachians.* Athens: Univ. of Georgia Press, 2000.

Davis, John, and Dave Foreman, eds. *The Earth First! Reader: Ten Years of Radical Environmentalism.* Salt Lake City, UT: Peregrine Smith, 1991.

Davis, Mike. *Ecology of Fear: Los Angeles and the Imagination of Disaster.* New York: Metropolitan, 1998.

———. *Late Victorian Holocausts: El Niño Famines and the Making of the Third World.* London: Verso, 2001.

———. *Planet of Slums.* London: Verso, 2006.

Davis, Susan G. *Spectacular Nature: Corporate Culture and the Sea World Experience.* Berkeley: Univ. of California Press, 1997.

Dawson, Robert, and Gray Brechin. *Farewell, Promised Land: Waking from the California Dream.* Berkeley: Univ. of California Press, 1999.

Dean, Warren. *Brazil and the Struggle for Rubber: A Study in Environmental History.* New York: Cambridge Univ. Press, 1987.

DeBuys, William. *Salt Dreams: Land and Water in Low-Down California.* Albuquerque: Univ. of New Mexico Press, 1999.

Deffeyes, Kenneth S. *Beyond Oil: The View from Hubbert's Peak.* New York: Hill and Wang, 2006.

De Grazia, Victoria. *Irresistible Empire: America's Advance Through Twentieth-Century Europe.* Cambridge, MA: Belknap Press of Harvard Univ. Press, 2005.

Deloria, Vine, Jr. *Red Earth, White Lies: Native Americans and the Myth of Scientific Fact.* New York: Scribner, 1995.

Denevan, William M., ed. "Charles Mann and Humanized Landscapes." *Geographical Review* 96 (July 2006): 483–486.

———. *The Native Population of the Americas in 1492.* Madison: Univ. of Wisconsin Press, 1976.

Devine, Robert S. *Alien Invasion: America's Battle with Non-Native Animals and Plants.* Washington, DC: National Geographic Society, 1998.

———. *Bush Versus the Environment.* New York: Anchor Books, 2004.

Diamond, Jared. *Guns, Germs, and Steel: The Fates of Human Societies.* New York: W. W. Norton, 1997.

———. *The Third Chimpanzee: The Evolution and Future of the Human Animal.* New York: Harper Collins, 1992.

———. "Why Was Post-Pleistocene Development of Human Societies Slightly More Rapid in the Old World Than in the New World?" In *Americans Before Columbus: Ice Age Origins,* compiled and edited by Ronald C. Carlisle. Pittsburgh, PA: Univ. of Pittsburgh Press, 1988.

Di Chiro, Giovanna. "Nature as Community: The Convergence of Environment and Social Justice." In *Uncommon Ground: Rethinking the Human Place in Nature,* edited by William Cronon. New York: W. W. Norton, 1996.

Dietrich, William. *The Final Forest: The Battle for the Last Great Trees of the Pacific Northwest.* New York: Simon and Schuster, 1992.

Dobyns, Henry F. *Their Numbers Become Thinned: Native Population Dynamics in Eastern North America.* Knoxville: Univ. of Tennessee Press, 1983.

Donahue, Brian. "'Dammed at Both Ends and Cursed in the Middle': The 'Flowage' of the Concord River Meadows, 1798–1862." *Environmental Review* 13 (Fall/Winter 1989): 47–67.

———. "The Forests and Fields of Concord: An Ecological History, 1750–1850." *Chronos* 2 (Fall 1983): 15–63.

———. *The Great Meadow: Farmers and the Land in Colonial Concord.* New Haven, CT: Yale Univ. Press, 2004.

Dorman, Robert L. *A Word for Nature: Four Pioneering Environmental Advocates, 1845–1913.* Chapel Hill: Univ. of North Carolina Press, 1998.

Dowie, Mark. *Losing Ground: American Environmentalism at the Close of the Twentieth Century.* Cambridge, MA: MIT Press, 1995.

Doyle, Jack. *Altered Harvest: Agriculture, Genetics, and the Fate of the World's Food Supply.* New York: Viking, 1985.

———. *Taken for a Ride: Detroit's Big Three and the Politics of Pollution.* New York: Four Walls Eight Windows, 2000.

Dunaway, Wilma A. *The First American Frontier: Transition to Capitalism in Southern Appalachia, 1700–1860.* Chapel Hill: Univ. of North Carolina Press, 1996.

Duncan, Colin A. M. *The Centrality of Agriculture: Between Humankind and the Rest of Nature*. Montreal: McGill-Queen's Univ. Press, 1996.

Dunlap, Thomas R. *DDT: Scientists, Citizens, and Public Policy*. Princeton, NJ: Princeton Univ. Press, 1981.

———. "Values for Varmints: Predator Control and Environmental Ideas, 1920–1939." *Pacific Historical Review* 53 (May 1984): 141–161.

———. "Wildlife, Science, and the National Parks, 1920–1940." *Pacific Historical Review* 59 (May 1990): 187–202.

Durning, Alan B., and Holly B. Brough. "Taking Stock: Animal Farming and the Environment." Worldwatch Paper 103, July 1991.

Earle, Carville. *Geographical Inquiry and American Historical Problems*. Stanford, CA: Stanford Univ. Press, 1992.

Easterbrook, Gregg. *A Moment on the Earth: The Coming Age of Environmental Optimism*. New York: Viking Penguin, 1995.

Eckbo, Dean, Austin, and Williams. *Open Space: The Choices Before California; The Urban Metropolitan Open Space Study*. San Francisco, 1969.

Edelson, S. Max. "Planting the Lowcountry: Agricultural Enterprise and Economic Experience in the Lower South, 1695–1785." Ph.D. diss., Johns Hopkins Univ., 1998.

Elkind, Sarah S. *Bay Cities and Water Politics: The Battle for Resources in Boston and Oakland*. Lawrence: Univ. Press of Kansas, 1998.

Eller, Ronald D. *Miners, Millhands and Mountaineers: Industrialization of the Appalachian South, 1880–1930*. Knoxville: Univ. of Tennessee Press, 1982.

Engel, Kirsten. "Reconsidering the National Market in Solid Waste: Trade-Offs in Equity, Efficiency, Environmental Protection, and State Autonomy." *North Carolina Law Review* 73 (April 1995): 1481–1566.

Ewens, Lara E. "Seed Wars: Biotechnology, Intellectual Property, and the Quest for High Yield Seeds." *Boston College International and Comparative Law Review* 23 (Spring 2000): 285–310.

Fagan, Brian. *The Great Warming: Climate Change and the Rise and Fall of Civilizations*. New York: Bloomsbury Press, 2008.

———. *The Little Ice Age: How Climate Made History, 1300–1850*. New York: Basic Books, 2000.

Faust, Drew Gilpin. *The Creation of Confederate Nationalism*. Baton Rouge: Louisiana State Univ. Press, 1988.

Fenn, Elizabeth A. "Biological Warfare in Eighteenth-Century North America: Beyond Jeffrey Amherst." *Journal of American History* 86 (March 2000): 1552–1580.

Ferguson, Denzel, and Nancy Ferguson. *Sacred Cows at the Public Trough*. Bend, OR: Maverick Publications, 1983.

Fiege, Mark. "Gettysburg and the Organic Nature of the American Civil War." In *Natural Enemy, Natural Ally: Toward an Environmental History of Warfare*, edited by Richard P. Tucker and Edmund Russell. Corvallis: Oregon State Univ. Press, 2004.

———. *Irrigated Eden: The Making of an Agricultural Landscape in the American West*. Seattle: Univ. of Washington Press, 1999.

Field, Barry. "The Evolution of Individual Property Rights in Massachusetts Agriculture, 17th–19th Centuries." *Northeastern Journal of Agricultural and Resource Economics* 14 (October 1985): 97–109.

Fischer, David Hackett. *Albion's Seed: Four British Folkways in America*. New York: Oxford Univ. Press, 1989.

Fite, Gilbert C. *Cotton Fields No More: Southern Agriculture, 1865–1980*. Lexington: Univ. of Kentucky Press, 1984.

Flader, Susan L. *Thinking Like a Mountain: Aldo Leopold and the Evolution of an Ecological Attitude Toward Deer, Wolves, and Forests*. Columbia: Univ. of Missouri Press, 1974.

Flannery, Tim. *The Eternal Frontier: An Ecological History of North America and Its Peoples*. New York: Atlantic Monthly Press, 2001.

Flippen, J. Brooks. *Nixon and the Environment*. Albuquerque: Univ. of New Mexico Press, 2000.

Foner, Eric. *The Story of American Freedom*. New York: W. W. Norton, 1998.

Foster, David R. *Thoreau's Country: Journey Through a Transformed Landscape*. Cambridge, MA: Harvard Univ. Press, 1999.

Foster, John Bellamy. "Capitalism and the Ancient Forest: Battle over Old Growth Forest in the Pacific Northwest." *Monthly Review* 43 (October 1991): 1–16.

———. "'Let Them Eat Pollution': Capitalism and the World Environment." *Monthly Review* 44 (January 1993): 10–20.

Foster, John Bellamy, and Fred Magdoff. "Liebig, Marx, and the Depletion of Soil Fertility: Relevance for Today's Agriculture." In *Hungry for Profit: The Agribusiness Threat to Farmers, Food, and the Environment*, edited by Fred Magdoff, John Bellamy Foster, and Frederick H. Buttel. New York: Monthly Review Press, 2000.

Fox, Stephen. *John Muir and His Legacy: The American Conservation Movement*. Boston: Little, Brown and Company, 1981.

Frazier, Ian. *Great Plains*. New York: Farrar, Straus and Giroux, 1989.

Freeman, Douglas Southall. *R. E. Lee: A Biography*. 4 vols. New York: Charles Scribner's Sons, 1934–1935.

Freese, Barbara. *Coal: A Human History*. New York: Perseus, 2003.

Freeze, R. Allan. *The Environmental Pendulum: A Quest for the Truth About Toxic Chemicals, Human Health, and Environmental Protection*. Berkeley: Univ. of California Press, 2000.

Freund, Peter, and George Martin. *The Ecology of the Automobile*. Montreal: Black Rose, 1993.

Friedberger, Mark. "Cattlemen, Consumers, and Beef." *Environmental History Review* 18 (Fall 1994): 37–57.

Fromartz, Samuel. *Organic Inc.: Natural Foods and How They Grew*. Orlando, FL: Harcourt, 2006.

Gallagher, Carole. *American Ground Zero: The Secret Nuclear War*. Cambridge, MA: MIT Press, 1993.

Gates, Paul Wallace. *Agriculture and the Civil War*. New York: Alfred A. Knopf, 1965.

———. "Federal Land Policy in the South, 1866–1888." *Journal of Southern History* 6 (August 1940): 303–330.

Gelbspan, Ross. *The Heat Is On: The High Stakes Battle over Earth's Threatened Climate*. Reading, MA: Addison-Wesley, 1997.

Genovese, Eugene D. *The Political Economy of Slavery: Studies in the Economy and Society of the Slave South*. New York: Vintage, 1967.

———. *Roll, Jordan, Roll: The World the Slaves Made*. New York: Vintage, 1974.

George, Susan. *The Debt Boomerang: How Third World Debt Harms Us All*. Boulder, CO: Westview, 1992.

———. *A Fate Worse Than Debt*. New York: Grove Press, 1988.

Gilman, Carolyn, and Mary Jane Schneider. *The Way to Independence: Memories of a Hidatsa Indian Family, 1840–1920*. St. Paul: Minnesota Historical Society Press, 1987.

Goddard, Stephen B. *Getting There: The Epic Struggle Between Road and Rail in the American Century*. New York: Basic Books, 1994.

Gonzalez, George A. *Corporate Power and the Environment: The Political Economy of U.S. Environmental Policy*. Lanham, MD: Rowman and Littlefield, 2001.

Goodell, Jeff. *Big Coal: The Dirty Secret Behind America's Energy Future*. Boston: Houghton Mifflin, 2006.

Goodstein, David. *Out of Gas: The End of the Age of Oil*. New York: W. W. Norton, 2005.

Gordon, Deborah. *Steering a New Course: Transportation, Energy, and the Environment.* Washington, DC: Island Press, 1991.

Gottlieb, Robert. *Forcing the Spring: The Transformation of the American Environmental Movement.* Washington, DC: Island Press, 1993.

Graeber, David. *Debt: The First 5,000 Years.* Brooklyn, NY: Melville House, 2011.

Graham, Otis L. "Again the Backward Region? Environmental History in and of the American South." *Southern Cultures* 6 (Summer 2000): 50–72.

Gray, Lewis Cecil. *History of Agriculture in the Southern United States to 1860.* 2 vols. Reprint ed. Gloucester, MA: Peter Smith, 1958.

Greider, William. *One World, Ready or Not: The Manic Logic of Global Capitalism.* New York: Simon and Schuster, 1998.

Griffen, Keith. *The Political Economy of Agrarian Change: An Essay on the Green Revolution.* London: Macmillan, 1974.

Gross, Robert A. "Culture and Cultivation: Agriculture and Society in Thoreau's Concord." *Journal of American History* 69 (June 1982): 42–61.

———. *The Minutemen and Their World.* New York: Hill and Wang, 1976.

Grossman, Elizabeth. *High Tech Trash: Digital Devices, Hidden Toxics, and Human Health.* Washington, DC: Island Press, 2006.

Grossman, James R. *Land of Hope: Chicago, Black Southerners, and the Great Migration.* Chicago: Univ. of Chicago Press, 1989.

Groves, R. H., and F. Di Castri, eds. *Biogeography of Mediterranean Invasions.* Cambridge: Cambridge Univ. Press, 1991.

Guthman, Julie. *Agrarian Dreams: The Paradox of Organic Farming in California.* Berkeley: Univ. of California Press, 2004.

Gutiérrez, Ramón A. *When Jesus Came, the Corn Mothers Went Away.* Stanford, CA: Stanford Univ. Press, 1991.

Hahn, Steven. *The Roots of Southern Populism: Yeoman Farmers and the Transformation of the Georgia Upcountry, 1850–1890.* New York: Oxford Univ. Press, 1983.

———. "Hunting, Fishing, and Foraging: Common Rights and Class Relations in the Postbellum South." *Radical History Review* 26 (October 1982): 37–64.

———. "A Response: Common Cents or Historical Sense?" *Journal of Southern History* 59 (May 1993): 243–258.

Hall, Derek. "The International Political Ecology of Industrial Shrimp Aquaculture and Industrial Plantation Forestry in Southeast Asia." *Journal of Southeast Asian Studies* 34 (June 2003): 251–264.

Handlin, Oscar. *This Was America: True Accounts of People and Places, Manners and Customs, as Recorded by European Travelers to the Western Shore in the Eighteenth, Nineteenth, and Twentieth Centuries.* Cambridge, MA: Harvard Univ. Press, 1949.

Hardy, Charles. "Fish or Foul: A History of the Delaware River Basin Through the Perspective of the American Shad, 1682 to the Present." *Pennsylvania History* 66 (Autumn 1999): 506–534.

Harris, Marvin. *Cannibals and Kings: The Origins of Cultures.* New York: Random House, 1977.

———. *Cultural Materialism: The Struggle for a Science of Culture.* New York: Random House, 1979.

———. *The Sacred Cow and the Abominable Pig: Riddles of Food and Culture.* New York: Simon and Schuster, 1987.

Harris, Marvin, and Eric B. Ross. "How Beef Became King." *Psychology Today,* October 1978, 88–94.

Hartog, Hendrik. "Pigs and Positivism." *Wisconsin Law Review* 4 (July/August 1985): 899–935.

Harvey, David. *A Brief History of Neoliberalism.* Oxford: Oxford Univ. Press, 2005.

————. *The New Imperialism*. New York: Oxford Univ. Press, 2003.

————. *Rebel Cities: From the Right to the City to the Urban Revolution*. London: Verso, 2012.

————. *Seventeen Contradictions and the End of Capitalism*. New York: Oxford Univ. Press, 2014.

————. *The Urban Experience*. Baltimore: Johns Hopkins Univ. Press, 1989.

Harvey, Mark W. T. *A Symbol of Wilderness: Echo Park and the American Conservation Movement*. Albuquerque: Univ. of New Mexico Press, 1994.

Hawken, Paul, Amory Lovins, and L. Hunter Lovins. *Natural Capitalism: Creating the Next Industrial Revolution*. Boston: Little, Brown, 1999.

Haygood, Tamara Miner. "Cows, Ticks, and Disease: A Medical Interpretation of the Southern Cattle Industry." *Journal of Southern History* 52 (November 1986): 551–564.

Hays, Samuel P. *Beauty, Health, and Permanence: Environmental Politics in the United States, 1955–1985*. New York: Cambridge Univ. Press, 1987.

————. *Conservation and the Gospel of Efficiency: The Progressive Conservation Movement, 1890–1920*. Cambridge, MA: Harvard Univ. Press, 1959.

————. *Explorations in Environmental History: Essays*. Pittsburgh, PA: Univ. of Pittsburgh Press, 1998.

————. *A History of Environmental Politics Since 1945*. Pittsburgh, PA: Univ. of Pittsburgh Press, 2000.

Helms, John Douglas. "Just Lookin' for a Home: The Cotton Boll Weevil and the South." Ph.D. diss., Florida State Univ., 1977.

Henige, David. *Numbers from Nowhere: The American Indian Contact Population Debate*. Norman: Univ. of Oklahoma Press, 1998.

Hill, Mary. *Gold: The California Story*. Berkeley: Univ. of California Press, 1999.

Hilliard, Sam Bowers. *Hog Meat and Hoecake: Food Supply in the Old South, 1840–1860*. Carbondale: Southern Illinois Univ. Press, 1972.

————. "The Tidewater Rice Plantation: An Ingenious Adaptation to Nature." *Geoscience and Man* 12 (June 1975): 57–66.

Hine, Thomas. *The Total Package: The Evolution and Secret Meanings of Boxes, Bottles, Cans, and Tubes*. Boston: Little, Brown and Company, 1995.

Hirt, Paul W. *A Conspiracy of Optimism: Management of the National Forests Since World War Two*. Lincoln: Univ. of Nebraska Press, 1994.

Hogan, David Gerard. *Selling 'em by the Sack: White Castle and the Creation of American Food*. New York: New York Univ. Press, 1997.

Hornaday, William T. *Our Vanishing Wild Life: Its Extermination and Preservation*. New York: Charles Scribner's Sons, 1913.

————. *Wild Life Conservation in Theory and Practice*. New Haven, CT: Yale Univ. Press, 1914.

Hoy, Suellen. *Chasing Dirt: The American Pursuit of Cleanliness*. New York: Oxford Univ. Press, 1995.

————. "The Garbage Disposer, the Public Health, and the Good Life." In *Technology and Choice: Readings from Technology and Culture*, edited by Marcel C. LaFollette and Jeffrey K. Stine. Chicago: Univ. of Chicago Press, 1991.

Huber, Matthew T. *Lifeblood: Oil, Freedom, and the Forces of Capital*. Minneapolis: Univ. of Minnesota Press, 2013.

————. "Enforcing Scarcity: Oil, Violence, and the Making of the Market." *Annals of the Association of American Geographers* 101 (April 2011): 816–826.

Humphrey, Thomas J. *Land and Liberty: Hudson Valley Riots in the Age of Revolution*. DeKalb: Northern Illinois Univ. Press, 2004.

Hundley, Norris, Jr. *The Great Thirst: Californians and Water, 1770s–1990s*. Berkeley: Univ. of California Press, 1992.

Hunt, Charles B. *Natural Regions of the United States and Canada*. San Francisco: Freeman, 1974.

Hurley, Andrew. *Class, Race, and Industrial Pollution in Gary, Indiana, 1945–1980.* Chapel Hill: Univ. of North Carolina Press, 1995.

Hurst, James Willard. *Law and Economic Growth: The Legal History of the Lumber Industry in Wisconsin, 1836–1915.* Rev. ed. Madison: Univ. of Wisconsin Press, 1984.

Igler, David. *Industrial Cowboys: Miller & Lux and the Transformation of the Far West, 1850–1920.* Berkeley: Univ. of California Press, 2001.

Interrante, Joseph. "A Moveable Feast: The Automobile and the Spatial Transformation of American Culture, 1890–1940." Ph.D. diss., Harvard Univ., 1983.

———. "The Road to Autopia: The Automobile and the Spatial Transformation of American Culture." In *The Automobile and American Culture,* edited by David L. Lewis and Laurence Goldstein. Ann Arbor: Univ. of Michigan Press, 1983.

———. "You Can't Go to Town in a Bathtub: Automobile Movement and the Reorganization of Rural American Space, 1900–1930." *Radical History Review* 21 (Fall 1979): 151–168.

Isenberg, Andrew C. *The Destruction of the Bison.* New York: Cambridge Univ. Press, 2000.

———. *Mining California: An Ecological History.* New York: Hill and Wang, 2005.

Iverson, Peter. *When Indians Became Cowboys: Native Peoples and Cattle Ranching in the American West.* Norman: Univ. of Oklahoma Press, 1994.

Jackle, John A., and Keith A. Sculle. *Fast Food: Roadside Restaurants in the Automobile Age.* Baltimore: Johns Hopkins Univ. Press, 1999.

Jackson, Kenneth T. *Crabgrass Frontier: The Suburbanization of the United States.* New York: Oxford Univ. Press, 1985.

Jacoby, Karl. *Crimes Against Nature: Squatters, Poachers, Thieves, and the Hidden History of American Conservation.* Berkeley: Univ. of California Press, 2001.

Jenkins, Virginia Scott. "'Fairway Living': Lawncare and Lifestyle from Croquet to the Golf Course." In *The American Lawn,* edited by Georges Teyssot. New York: Princeton Architectural Press, 1999.

———. *The Lawn: A History of an American Obsession.* Washington, DC: Smithsonian Institution Press, 1994.

Jennings, Francis. *The Invasion of America: Indians, Colonialism, and the Cant of Conquest.* Chapel Hill: Univ. of North Carolina Press, 1975.

Johnson, Chalmers. *Blowback: The Costs and Consequences of American Empire.* New York: Metropolitan, 2000.

———. *The Sorrows of Empire: Militarism, Secrecy, and the End of the Republic.* New York: Metropolitan, 2004.

Johnson, Hildegard Binder. *Order upon the Land: The U.S. Rectangular Land Survey and the Upper Mississippi Country.* New York: Oxford Univ. Press, 1976.

Johnson, Paul E. "The Modernization of Mayo Greenleaf Patch: Land, Family, and Marginality in New England, 1766–1818." *New England Quarterly* 55 (December 1982): 488–516.

Johnson, Stephen, Robert Dawson, and Gerald Haslam. *The Great Central Valley: California's Heartland.* Berkeley: Univ. of California Press, 1993.

Jones, Dorothy V. *License for Empire: Colonialism by Treaty in Early America.* Chicago: Univ. of Chicago Press, 1982.

Jones, E. L. *The European Miracle: Environments, Economics and Geopolitics in the History of Europe and Asia.* Cambridge: Cambridge Univ. Press, 1981.

———. "Creative Disruptions in American Agriculture, 1620–1820." *Agricultural History* 48 (October 1974): 510–528.

Jordan, Terry G. *North American Cattle-Ranching Frontiers: Origins, Diffusion, and Differentiation.* Albuquerque: Univ. of New Mexico Press, 1993.

Joyner, Charles. *Down by the Riverside: A South Carolina Slave Community.* Urbana: Univ. of Illinois Press, 1984.

Judd, Richard W. *Common Lands, Common People: The Origins of Conservation in Northern New England.* Cambridge, MA: Harvard Univ. Press, 1997.

Kantor, Shawn Everett, and J. Morgan Kousser. "Common Sense or Commonwealth? The Fence Law and Institutional Change in the Postbellum South." *Journal of Southern History* 59 (May 1993): 201–242.

Karliner, Joshua. *The Corporate Planet: Ecology and Politics in the Age of Globalization.* San Francisco: Sierra Club Books, 1997.

Kars, Marjoleine. *Breaking Loose Together: The Regulator Rebellion in Pre-Revolutionary North Carolina.* Chapel Hill: Univ. of North Carolina Press, 2002.

Kay, Charles E., and Randy T. Simmons, eds. *Wilderness and Political Ecology: Aboriginal Influences and the Original State of Nature.* Salt Lake City: Univ. of Utah Press, 2002.

Kay, Jane Holtz. *Asphalt Nation: How the Automobile Took over America and How We Can Take It Back.* Berkeley: Univ. of California Press, 1998.

Kelley, Robert. *Battling the Inland Sea: American Political Culture, Public Policy, and the Sacramento Valley, 1850–1986.* Berkeley: Univ. of California Press, 1989.

Kelton, Paul. *Epidemics and Enslavement: Biological Catastrophe in the Native Southeast, 1492–1715.* Lincoln: Univ. of Nebraska Press, 2007.

Kennedy, Donald, and Marjorie Lucks. "Rubber, Blight, and Mosquitoes: Biogeography Meets the Global Economy." *Environmental History* 4 (July 1999): 369–383.

Khagram, Sanjeev. *Dams and Development: Transnational Struggles for Water and Power.* Ithaca, NY: Cornell Univ. Press, 2004.

King, J. Crawford, Jr. "The Closing of the Southern Range: An Exploratory Study." *Journal of Southern History* 48 (February 1982): 53–70.

King, Margaret J. "Empires of Popular Culture: McDonald's and Disney." In *Ronald Revisited: The World of Ronald McDonald,* edited by Marshall William Fishwick. Bowling Green, OH: Bowling Green Univ. Popular Press, 1983.

Klare, Michael T. *Blood and Oil: The Dangers and Consequences of America's Growing Dependency on Imported Petroleum.* New York: Metropolitan, 2004.

———. *Rising Powers, Shrinking Planet: The New Geopolitics of Energy.* New York: Metropolitan, 2008.

Klein, Naomi. *No Space, No Choice, No Jobs, No Logo.* New York: Picador, 2002.

Klingle, Matthew W. *Emerald City: An Environmental History of Seattle.* New Haven, CT: Yale Univ. Press, 2007.

Kloppenburg, Jack Ralph, Jr. *First the Seed: The Political Economy of Plant Biotechnology, 1492–2000.* Cambridge: Cambridge Univ. Press, 1988.

Koeniger, A. Cash. "Climate and Southern Distinctiveness." *Journal of Southern History* 54 (February 1988): 21–44.

Kolbert, Elizabeth. *Field Notes from a Catastrophe: Man, Nature, and Climate Change.* New York: Bloomsbury, 2006.

Kottak, Conrad P. "Rituals at McDonald's." In *Ronald Revisited: The World of Ronald McDonald,* edited by Marshall William Fishwick. Bowling Green, OH: Bowling Green Univ. Popular Press, 1983.

Kotz, David M. *The Rise and Fall of Neoliberal Capitalism.* Cambridge, MA: Harvard Univ. Press, 2015.

Kovarik, William Joseph. "The Ethyl Controversy: The News Media and the Public Health Debate over Leaded Gasoline, 1924–1926." Ph.D. diss., Univ. of Maryland, College Park, 1993.

Krech, Shepard, III. *The Ecological Indian: Myth and History.* New York: W. W. Norton, 1999.

Kuletz, Valerie L. *The Tainted Desert: Environmental and Social Ruin in the American West*. New York: Routledge, 1998.

Kulik, Gary. "Dams, Fish, and Farmers: Defense of Public Rights in Eighteenth-Century Rhode Island." In *The Countryside in the Age of Capitalist Transformation*, edited by Steven Hahn and Jonathan Prude. Chapel Hill: Univ. of North Carolina Press, 1985.

Kulikoff, Alan. *Tobacco and Slaves: The Development of Southern Cultures in the Chesapeake, 1680–1800*. Chapel Hill: Univ. of North Carolina Press, 1986.

Kunstler, James Howard. *The Geography of Nowhere: The Rise and Decline of America's Man-Made Landscape*. New York: Simon and Schuster, 1993.

Kupperman, Karen Ordahl. "Climate and Mastery of the Wilderness in Seventeenth-Century New England." In *Seventeenth-Century New England*, edited by the Colonial Society of Massachusetts. Boston: Colonial Society of Massachusetts, 1984.

———. "Fear of Hot Climates in the Anglo-American Colonial Experience." *William and Mary Quarterly* 42 (April 1984): 213–240.

———. "The Puzzle of the American Climate in the Early Colonial Period." *American Historical Review* 87 (December 1982): 1262–1289.

Langston, Nancy. "Forest Dreams, Forest Nightmares: An Environmental History of a Forest Health Crisis." In *American Forests: Nature, Culture, and Politics*, edited by Char Miller. Lawrence: Univ. Press of Kansas, 1997.

———. *Forest Dreams, Forest Nightmares: The Paradox of Old Growth in the Inland West*. Seattle: Univ. of Washington Press, 1995.

———. *Toxic Bodies: Hormone Disruptors and the Legacy of DES*. New Haven, CT: Yale Univ. Press, 2010.

Laporte, Dominique. *History of Shit*. Translated by Nadia Benabid and Rodolphe el-Khoury. Cambridge, MA: MIT Press, 2000.

Lappé, Marc, and Britt Bailey. *Against the Grain: Biotechnology and the Corporate Takeover of Your Food*. Monroe, ME: Common Courage Press, 1998.

Lauck, Jon. *American Agriculture and the Problem of Monopoly: The Political Economy of Grain Belt Farming, 1953–1980*. Lincoln: Univ. of Nebraska Press, 2000.

Lear, Linda. *Rachel Carson: Witness for Nature*. New York: Henry Holt and Company, 1997.

Leavitt, Judith Walzer. *The Healthiest City: Milwaukee and the Politics of Health Reform*. Princeton, NJ: Princeton Univ. Press, 1982.

Leopold, Aldo. *A Sand County Almanac*. Reprint. New York: Oxford Univ. Press, 1966.

Levenstein, Harvey A. *Revolution at the Table: The Transformation of the American Diet*. New York: Oxford Univ. Press, 1988.

Lewis, Martin W. *Green Delusions: An Environmentalist Critique of Radical Environmentalism*. Durham, NC: Duke Univ. Press, 1992.

Lewis, Michael, ed. *American Wilderness: A New History*. New York: Oxford Univ. Press, 2007.

Lewis, Ronald L. *Transforming the Appalachian Countryside: Railroads, Deforestation, and Social Change in West Virginia, 1880–1920*. Chapel Hill: Univ. of North Carolina Press, 1998.

Lewis, Tom. *Divided Highways: Building the Interstate Highways, Transforming American Life*. New York: Viking, 1997.

Limerick, Patricia Nelson. *The Legacy of Conquest: The Unbroken Past of the American West*. New York: W. W. Norton, 1987.

Linder, Marc, and Lawrence S. Zacharias. *Of Cabbages and Kings County: Agriculture and the Formation of Modern Brooklyn*. Iowa City: Univ. of Iowa Press, 1999.

Linebaugh, Peter. "Enclosures from the Bottom Up." *Radical History Review* 108 (Fall 2010): 11–27.

Lipietz, Alain. *Towards a New Economic Order: Postfordism, Ecology, and Democracy*. Translated by Malcolm Slater. New York: Oxford Univ. Press, 1992.

Little, Charles E. *The Dying of the Trees: The Pandemic in America's Forests*. New York: Viking, 1995.

Lockridge, Kenneth. "Land, Population and the Evolution of New England Society, 1630–1790." *Past and Present* 39 (April 1968): 62–80.

Lockwood, Jeffrey C. *Locust: The Devastating Rise and Mysterious Disappearance of the Insect That Shaped the American Frontier*. New York: Basic Books, 2004.

Loeb, Alan P. "Birth of the Kettering Doctrine: Fordism, Sloanism and the Discovery of Tetraethyl Lead." *Business and Economic History* 24 (Fall 1995): 72–87.

Loewen, James W. *Lies My Teacher Told Me: Everything Your American History Textbook Got Wrong*. New York: Simon and Schuster, 1996.

Ludlum, David M. *Early American Winters, 1604–1820*. Boston: American Meteorological Society, 1966.

———. *Early American Winters, 1821–1870*. Boston: American Meteorological Society, 1968.

Luger, Stan. "Market Ideology and Administrative Fiat: The Rollback of Automotive Fuel Economy Standards." *Environmental History Review* 19 (Spring 1995): 76–93.

MacLeish, William H. *The Day Before America*. Boston: Houghton Mifflin, 1994.

MacLeitch, Gail D. "'Red' Labor: Iroquois Participation in the Atlantic Economy." *Labor Studies in Working-Class History of the Americas* 1 (Winter 2004): 69–90.

Madden, David, ed. *Beyond the Battlefield: The Ordinary Life and Extraordinary Times of the Civil War Soldier*. New York: Simon and Schuster, 2000.

Magoc, Chris J. *Yellowstone: The Creation and Selling of an American Landscape, 1870–1903*. Albuquerque: Univ. of New Mexico Press, 1999.

Malin, James C. *The Grasslands of North America: Prolegomena to Its History*. Gloucester, MA: Peter Smith, 1967.

———. *History and Ecology: Studies of the Grassland*. Edited by Robert P. Swierenga. Lincoln: Univ. of Nebraska Press, 1984.

Malm, Andreas. "China as Chimney of the World: The Fossil Capital Hypothesis." *Organization & Environment* 25 (June 2012): 146–177.

———. *Fossil Capital: The Rise of Steam Power and the Roots of Global Warming*. London: Verso, 2016.

Mann, Charles C. *1491: New Revelations of the Americas before Columbus*. 2d ed. New York: Vintage, 2011.

Manning, Richard. *Food's Frontier: The Next Green Revolution*. New York: North Point Press, 2000.

———. *Grassland: The History, Biology, Politics, and Promise of the American Prairie*. New York: Penguin, 1995.

Marden, Emily. "The Neem Tree Patent: International Conflict over the Commodification of Life." *Boston College International and Comparative Law Review* 22 (Spring 1999): 279–295.

Marks, Stuart A. *Southern Hunting in Black and White: Nature, History, and Ritual in a Carolina Community*. Princeton, NJ: Princeton Univ. Press, 1991.

Martin, Calvin. "The European Impact on the Culture of a Northeastern Algonquian Tribe: An Ecological Interpretation." *William and Mary Quarterly* 31 (January 1974): 3–26.

———. *Keepers of the Game: Indian-Animal Relationships and the Fur Trade*. Berkeley: Univ. of California Press, 1978.

———. *The Way of the Human Being*. New Haven, CT: Yale Univ. Press, 1999.

Martin, Russell. *A Story That Stands Like a Dam: Glen Canyon and the Struggle for the Soul of the West*. New York: Henry Holt and Company, 1989.

Matthiessen, Peter. *Wildlife in America*. Rev. ed. New York: Penguin, 1984.

McCarthy, Tom. *Auto Mania: Cars, Consumers, and the Environment*. New Haven, CT: Yale Univ. Press, 2007.

———. "The Coming Wonder? Foresight and Early Concerns About the Automobile." *Environmental History* 6 (January 2001): 46–74.

McCay, Bonnie J. *Oyster Wars and the Public Trust: Property, Law, and Ecology in New Jersey History.* Tucson: Univ. of Arizona Press, 1998.

McClelland, Peter D. *Sowing Modernity: America's First Agricultural Revolution.* Ithaca, NY: Cornell Univ. Press, 1997.

McCully, Patrick. *Silenced Rivers: The Ecology and Politics of Large Dams.* London: Zed Books, 2001.

McDonnell, Michael A. *Masters of Empire: Great Lakes Indians and the Making of America.* New York: Hill and Wang, 2015.

McDonough, William, and Michael Braungart. *Cradle to Cradle: Remaking the Way We Make Things.* New York: North Point Press, 2002.

McEvoy, Arthur F. *The Fisherman's Problem: Ecology and Law in the California Fisheries.* New York: Cambridge Univ. Press, 1986.

McGucken, William. *Lake Erie Rehabilitated: Controlling Cultural Eutrophication, 1960s–1990s.* Akron, OH: Univ. of Akron Press, 2000.

McKibben, Bill. *The End of Nature.* New York: Random House, 1989.

McMahon, Sarah F. "'All Things in Their Proper Season': Seasonal Rhythms of Diet in Nineteenth Century New England." *Agricultural History* 63 (Spring 1989): 130–151.

———. "A Comfortable Subsistence: The Changing Composition of Diet in Rural New England, 1620–1840." *William and Mary Quarterly* 42 (January 1985): 26–51.

McMath, Robert C., Jr. "Sandy Land and Hogs in the Timber: (Agri)cultural Origins of the Farmers' Alliance in Texas." In *The Countryside in the Age of Capitalist Transformation,* edited by Steven Hahn and Jonathan Prude. Chapel Hill: Univ. of North Carolina Press, 1985.

McNeill, J. R. *Mosquito Empires: Ecology and War in the Greater Caribbean, 1620–1914.* New York: Cambridge Univ. Press, 2010.

———. *Something New Under the Sun: An Environmental History of the Twentieth-Century World.* New York: W. W. Norton, 2000.

McNeill, J. R., and Peter Engelke. *The Great Acceleration: An Environmental History of the Anthropocene Since 1945.* Cambridge, MA: Belknap Press of Harvard Univ. Press, 2014.

McPhee, John. *The Control of Nature.* New York: Farrar Straus Giroux, 1989.

———. *Encounters with the Archdruid.* New York: Farrar Straus and Giroux, 1971.

McPherson, James M. *Battle Cry of Freedom: The Civil War Era.* New York: Oxford Univ. Press, 1988.

———. *Ordeal by Fire: The Civil War and Reconstruction.* New York: Alfred A. Knopf, 1982.

McShane, Clay. *Down the Asphalt Path: The Automobile and the American City.* New York: Columbia Univ. Press, 1994.

McShane, Clay, and Joel A. Tarr. "The Centrality of the Horse in the Nineteenth-Century American City." In *The Making of Urban America,* 2d ed., edited by Raymond A. Mohl. Wilmington, DE: Scholarly Resources, 1997.

McWilliams, Carey. *California: The Great Exception.* Reprint. Westport, CT: Greenwood, 1971.

———. *Factories in the Field: The Story of Migratory Farm Labor in California.* Reprint. Berkeley: Univ. of California Press, 1999.

Meagher, Mary, and Douglas B. Houston. *Yellowstone and the Biology of Time: Photographs Across a Century.* Norman: Univ. of Oklahoma Press, 1998.

Meikle, Jeffrey L. "Material Doubts: The Consequences of Plastic." *Environmental History* 2 (July 1997): 278–300.

Melosi, Martin V. *Coping with Abundance: Energy and Environment in Industrial America.* Philadelphia: Temple Univ. Press, 1985.

———. *Garbage in the Cities: Refuse, Reform, and the Environment, 1880–1980.* College Station: Texas A&M Univ. Press, 1981.

———, ed. *Pollution and Reform in American Cities, 1870–1930.* Austin: Univ. of Texas Press, 1980.

———. *The Sanitary City: Urban Infrastructure in America from Colonial Times to the Present.* Baltimore: Johns Hopkins Univ. Press, 2000.

Merchant, Carolyn. *Ecological Revolutions: Nature, Gender, and Science in New England.* Chapel Hill: Univ. of North Carolina Press, 1989.

———. "Gender and Environmental History." *Journal of American History* 76 (March 1990): 1117–1121.

Merrell, James H. *Into the American Woods: Negotiators on the Pennsylvania Frontier.* New York: W. W. Norton, 1999.

Merrens, H. Roy, and George D. Terry. "Dying in Paradise: Malaria, Mortality, and the Perceptual Environment in Colonial South Carolina." *Journal of Southern History* 50 (November 1984): 533–550.

Merrill, Michael. "Putting 'Capitalism' in Its Place: A Review of Recent Literature." *William and Mary Quarterly* 52 (April 1995): 315–326.

Miller, Benjamin. *Fat of the Land: Garbage of New York the Last Two Hundred Years.* New York: Four Walls Eight Windows, 2000.

Miller, Henry M. "Transforming a 'Splendid and Delightsome Land': Colonists and Ecological Change in the Chesapeake, 1607–1820." *Journal of the Washington Academy of Sciences* 76 (September 1986): 173–187.

Mintz, Sidney W. *Sweetness and Power: The Place of Sugar in Modern History.* New York: Penguin, 1985.

Mirowski, Philip. *Never Let a Serious Crisis Go to Waste: How Neoliberalism Survived the Financial Meltdown.* London: Verso, 2013.

Mitchell, Don. *The Lie of the Land: Migrant Workers and the California Landscape.* Minneapolis: Univ. of Minnesota Press, 1996.

Mitchell, Timothy. *Carbon Democracy: Political Power in the Age of Oil.* London: Verso, 2011.

Mitman, Gregg. *Reel Nature: America's Romance with Wildlife on Film.* Cambridge, MA: Harvard Univ. Press, 1999.

Morgan, Philip D. "The Ownership of Property by Slaves in the Mid-Nineteenth-Century Low Country." *Journal of Southern History* 49 (August 1983): 399–420.

———. "Work and Culture: The Task System and the World of Lowcountry Blacks, 1700 to 1880." *William and Mary Quarterly* 39 (October 1982): 563–599.

Morris, Edmund. *The Rise of Theodore Roosevelt.* New York: Coward, McCann, and Geoghegan, 1979.

Morrison, Samuel Eliot. *The Great Explorers: The European Discovery of America.* New York: Oxford Univ. Press, 1978.

Morse, Kathryn. *The Nature of Gold: An Environmental History of the Klondike Gold Rush.* Seattle: Univ. of Washington Press, 2003.

Muir, Diana. *Reflections in Bullough's Pond: Economy and Ecosystem in New England.* Hanover, NH: Univ. Press of New England, 2000.

Mulholland, Mitchell T. "Territoriality and Horticulture: A Perspective for Prehistoric Southern New England." In *Holocene Human Ecology in Northeastern North America,* edited by George P. Nicholas. New York: Plenum, 1988.

Namias, Jerome. "Nature and Possible Causes of the Northeastern United States Drought During 1962–65." *Monthly Weather Review* 94 (September 1966): 543–554.

Nash, Linda. *Inescapable Ecologies: A History of Environment, Disease, and Knowledge.* Berkeley: Univ. of California Press, 2006.

Nash, Roderick. *Wilderness and the American Mind.* 3d ed. New Haven, CT: Yale Univ. Press, 1982.

Nesson, Fern L. *Great Waters: A History of Boston's Water Supply.* Hanover, NH: Univ. Press of New England, 1983.

Nestle, Marion. "Food Lobbies, the Food Pyramid, and U.S. Nutrition Policy." In *The Nation's Health*, 5th ed., edited by Philip R. Lee and Carroll L. Estes. Sudbury, MA: Jones and Bartlett, 1997.

Noble, David F. *America by Design: Science, Technology and the Rise of Corporate Capitalism.* New York: Oxford Univ. Press, 1977.

Nock, Magdalena Barros. "The Mexican Peasantry and the Ejido in the Neo-liberal Period." In *Disappearing Peasantries? Rural Labour in Africa, Asia and Latin America*, edited by Deborah Bryceson, Cristóbal Kay, and Jos Mooij. London: Intermediate Technology Publications, 2000.

Nye, David E. *Consuming Power: A Social History of American Energies.* Cambridge, MA: MIT Press, 1999.

O'Brien, Jean. *Dispossession by Degrees: Indian Land and Identity in Natick, Massachusetts, 1650–1790.* Lincoln: Univ. of Nebraska Press, 1997.

O'Brien, Jim. "Environmentalism as a Mass Movement: Historical Notes." *Radical America* 17 (March/June 1983): 7–27.

Ogle, Maureen. *All the Modern Conveniences: American Household Plumbing, 1840–1890.* Baltimore: Johns Hopkins Univ. Press, 1996.

————. "Water Supply, Waste Disposal, and the Culture of Privatism in the Mid-Nineteenth-Century American City." *Journal of Urban History* 25 (March 1999): 321–347.

O'Malley, Michael. *Keeping Watch: A History of American Time.* New York: Penguin, 1990.

Opie, John. *The Law of the Land: Two Hundred Years of American Farmland Policy.* Lincoln: Univ. of Nebraska Press, 1987.

————. *Nature's Nation: An Environmental History of the United States.* Fort Worth, TX: Harcourt Brace, 1998.

————. *Ogallala: Water for a Dry Land.* Lincoln: Univ. of Nebraska Press, 1993.

Oreskes, Naomi, and Erik M. Conway. *Merchants of Doubt: How a Handful of Scientists Obscured the Truth on Issues of Tobacco Smoke to Global Warming.* New York: Bloomsbury Press, 2010.

Orsi, Jared. *Hazardous Metropolis: Flooding and Urban Ecology in Los Angeles.* Berkeley: Univ. of California Press, 2004.

Osgood, Ernest Staples. *The Day of the Cattlemen.* Minneapolis: Univ. of Minnesota Press, 1929.

Otto, John Solomon. *Southern Agriculture During the Civil War Era, 1860–1880.* Westport, CT: Greenwood Press, 1994.

Paehlke, Robert C. *Environmentalism and the Future of Progressive Politics.* New Haven, CT: Yale Univ. Press, 1989.

Panitch, Leo, and Sam Gindin. *The Making of Global Capitalism: The Political Economy of American Empire.* London: Verso, 2012.

Parent, Anthony S., Jr. *Foul Means: The Formation of a Slave Society in Virginia, 1660–1740.* Chapel Hill: Omohundro Institute of Early American History and Culture by Univ. of North Carolina Press, 2003.

Parenti, Michael. *Against Empire.* San Francisco: City Lights Books, 1995.

Patterson, William A., III, and Kenneth E. Sassaman. "Indian Fires in the Prehistory of New England." In *Holocene Human Ecology in Northeastern North America*, edited by George P. Nicholas. New York: Plenum, 1988.

Payer, Cheryl. *The Debt Trap: The International Monetary Fund and the Third World.* New York: Monthly Review Press, 1974.

Pearce, David, Neil Adger, David Maddison, and Dominic Moran. "Debt and the Environment." *Scientific American* 272 (June 1995): 52–56.

Pearce, Margaret Wickens. "Native Mapping in Southern New England Indian Deeds." In *Cartographic Encounters: Perspectives on Native American Mapmaking and Map Use*, edited by G. Malcolm Lewis. Chicago: Univ. of Chicago Press, 1998.

Perkins, John H. *Geopolitics and the Green Revolution: Wheat, Genes, and the Cold War.* New York: Oxford Univ. Press, 1997.

Petersen, Shannon C. "The Modern Ark: A History of the Endangered Species Act." Ph.D. diss., Univ. of Wisconsin, Madison, 2000.

Pimentel, David, L. E. Hurd, A. C. Bellotti, M. J. Forster, I. N. Oka, O. D. Sholes, and R. J. Whitman. "Food Production and the Energy Crisis." In *Food: Politics, Economics, Nutrition, and Research,* edited by Philip H. Abelson. Washington, DC: American Association for the Advancement of Science, 1975.

Pimentel, David, P. A. Oltenacu, M. C. Nesheim, John Krummel, M. S. Allen, and Sterling Chick. "The Potential for Grass-Fed Livestock: Resource Constraints." *Science* 207 (February 22, 1980): 843–848.

Pinchot, Gifford. *The Fight for Conservation.* New York: Doubleday, Page and Company, 1910.

Pisani, Donald J. *From Family Farm to Agribusiness: The Irrigation Crusade in California and the West, 1850–1931.* Berkeley: Univ. of California Press, 1984.

Polanyi, Karl. *The Great Transformation: The Political and Economic Origins of Our Time.* Boston: Beacon, 1944.

Pollan, Michael. *The Omnivore's Dilemma: A Natural History of Four Meals.* New York: Penguin, 2006.
———. *Second Nature: A Gardener's Education.* New York: Atlantic Monthly, 1991.

Pollin, Robert. *Contours of Descent: U.S. Economic Fractures and the Landscape of Global Austerity.* London: Verso, 2003.

Post, John D. *The Last Great Subsistence Crisis in the Western World.* Baltimore: Johns Hopkins Univ. Press, 1977.

Press, Frank, and Raymond Siever. *Understanding Earth.* New York: Freeman, 1994.

Preston, William. "Serpent in the Garden: Environmental Change in Colonial California." In *Contested Eden: California Before the Gold Rush,* edited by Ramón A. Gutiérrez and Richard J. Orsi. Berkeley: Univ. of California Press, 1998.

Price, Jennifer. *Flight Maps: Adventures with Nature in Modern America.* New York: Basic Books, 1999.

Proctor, James D. "Whose Nature? The Contested Moral Terrain of Ancient Forests." In *Uncommon Ground: Rethinking the Human Place in Nature,* edited by William Cronon. New York: W. W. Norton, 1996.

Pruitt, Bettye Hobbs. "Self-Sufficiency and the Agricultural Economy of Eighteenth-Century Massachusetts." *William and Mary Quarterly* 41 (July 1984): 333–364.

Pulido, Laura. *Environmental and Economic Justice: Two Chicano Struggles in the Southwest.* Tucson: Univ. of Arizona Press, 1996.

Pyne, Stephen J. *Fire in America: A Cultural History of Wildland and Rural Fire.* Rev. ed. Seattle: Univ. of Washington Press, 1997.
———. *Year of the Fires: The Story of the Great Fires of 1910.* New York: Viking, 2001.

Raitz, Karl B., and Richard Ulack. *Appalachia: A Regional Geography: Land, People, and Development.* Boulder, CO: Westview, 1984.

Rakestraw, Lawrence. "Conservation Historiography: An Assessment." *Pacific Historical Review* 41 (August 1972): 271–288.

Ramos, Tarso. "Wise Use in the West: The Case of the Northwest Timber Industry." In *Let the People Judge: Wise Use and the Private Property Rights Movement,* edited by John Echeverria and Raymond Booth Eby. Washington, DC: Island Press, 1995.

Ransom, Roger L., and Richard Sutch. *One Kind of Freedom: The Economic Consequences of Emancipation.* Cambridge: Cambridge Univ. Press, 1977.

Rappaport, Roy A. *Ecology, Meaning, and Religion.* Berkeley, CA: North Atlantic Books, 1979.
———. "The Flow of Energy in an Agricultural Society." *Scientific American* 225 (September 1971): 116–133.

————. "Nature, Culture, and Ecological Anthropology." In *Man, Culture, and Society*, edited by Harry L. Shapiro. London: Oxford Univ. Press, 1956.

————. *Pigs for the Ancestors: Ritual in the Ecology of a New Guinea People*. Rev. ed. New Haven, CT: Yale Univ. Press, 1984.

Rathje, William, and Cullen Murphy. *Rubbish: The Archeology of Garbage*. New York: Harper Collins, 1992.

Rawson, Michael. *Eden on the Charles: The Making of Boston*. Cambridge, MA: Harvard Univ. Press, 2010.

Redfern, Ron. *The Making of a Continent*. New York: Times Books, 1983.

Reece, Erik. *Lost Mountain: A Year in the Vanishing Wilderness: Radical Strip Mining and the Devastation of Appalachia*. New York: Riverhead, 2006.

Reed, David, ed. *Structural Adjustment, the Environment, and Sustainable Development*. London: Earthscan, 1996.

Reidy, Joseph P. *From Slavery to Agrarian Capitalism in the Cotton Plantation South: Central Georgia, 1800–1880*. Chapel Hill: Univ. of North Carolina Press, 1992.

Reiger, John F. *American Sportsmen and the Origins of Conservation*. New York: Winchester, 1975.

Reisner, Marc. *Cadillac Desert: The American West and Its Disappearing Water*. New York: Penguin, 1986.

Rice, James D. *Nature and History in the Potomac Country: From Hunter-Gatherers to the Age of Jefferson*. Baltimore: Johns Hopkins Univ. Press, 2009.

Rich, Bruce. *Mortgaging the Earth: The World Bank, Environmental Impoverishment, and the Crisis of Development*. Boston: Beacon, 1994.

Richter, Daniel K. *Facing East from Indian Country: A Native History of Early America*. Cambridge, MA: Harvard Univ. Press, 2001.

Rifkin, Jeremy. *Beyond Beef: The Rise and Fall of the Cattle Culture*. New York: Plume, 1993.

————. *The Biotech Century: Harnessing the Gene and Remaking the World*. New York: Tarcher/Putnam, 1998.

Ritvoe, Harriet. *The Animal Estate: The English and Other Creatures in the Victorian Age*. Cambridge, MA: Harvard Univ. Press, 1987.

Robbins, Paul. *Lawn People: How Grasses, Weeds, and Chemicals Make Us Who We Are*. Philadelphia: Temple Univ. Press, 2007.

Robbins, William G. *Hard Times in Paradise: Coos Bay, Oregon, 1850–1986*. Seattle: Univ. of Washington Press, 1988.

Roberts, Neil. *The Holocene: An Environmental History*. Oxford: Basil Blackwell, 1989.

Robinson, William I. *Global Capitalism and the Crisis of Humanity*. New York: Cambridge Univ. Press, 2014.

————. *Latin America and Global Capitalism: A Critical Globalization Perspective*. Baltimore: Johns Hopkins Univ. Press, 2008.

Rogers, Heather. *Gone Tomorrow: The Hidden Life of Garbage*. New York: New Press, 2005.

Rogin, Michael Paul. *Fathers and Children: Andrew Jackson and the Subjugation of the American Indian*. New York: Vintage, 1975.

Rohrbough, Malcolm J. *Days of Gold: The California Gold Rush and the American Nation*. Berkeley: Univ. of California Press, 1997.

Roht-Arriaza, Naomi. "Of Seeds and Shamans: The Appropriation of the Scientific and Technical Knowledge of Indigenous and Local Communities." *Michigan Journal of International Law* 17 (Summer 1996): 919–965.

Rome, Adam. *The Bulldozer in the Countryside: Suburban Sprawl and the Rise of American Environmentalism*. New York: Cambridge Univ. Press, 2001.

————. "Coming to Terms with Pollution: The Language of Environmental Reform, 1865–1915." *Environmental History* 3 (July 1996): 6–28.

————. *The Genius of Earth Day: How a 1970 Teach-In Unexpectedly Made the First Green Generation.* New York: Hill and Wang, 2013.

————. "William Whyte, Open Space, and Environmental Activism." *Geographical Review* 88 (April 1998): 259–274.

Rose, Mark. *Interstate: Express Highway Politics, 1939–1989.* Rev. ed. Knoxville: Univ. of Tennessee Press, 1990.

Rosenberg, Charles E. *The Cholera Years: The United States in 1832, 1849 and 1866.* Chicago: Univ. of Chicago Press, 1962.

Rosenkrantz, Barbara Gutmann. *Public Health and the State: Changing Views in Massachusetts, 1842–1936.* Cambridge, MA: Harvard Univ. Press, 1972.

Rosner, David, and Gerald Markowitz. "A 'Gift of God'? The Public Health Controversy over Leaded Gasoline During the 1920s." *American Journal of Public Health* 75 (April 1985): 344–352.

Ross, Andrew. *Strange Weather: Culture, Science and Technology in the Age of Limits.* London: Verso, 1991.

Rothenberg, Winifred B. "The Productivity Consequences of Market Integration: Agriculture in Massachusetts, 1771–1801." In *American Economic Growth and Standards of Living Before the Civil War*, edited by Robert E. Gallman and John Joseph Wallis. Chicago: Univ. of Chicago Press, 1992.

Rothfeder, Jeffrey. *Every Drop for Sale: Our Desperate Battle over Water in a World About to Run Out.* New York: Jeremy P. Tarcher/Penguin, 2004.

Rothman, Hal K. *Devil's Bargains: Tourism in the Twentieth-Century American West.* Lawrence: Univ. Press of Kansas, 1998.

————. *The Greening of a Nation? Environmentalism in the United States Since 1945.* Fort Worth, TX: Harcourt Brace, 1998.

Rowell, Andrew. *Green Backlash: Global Subversion of the Environmental Movement.* London: Routledge, 1996.

Royte, Elizabeth. *Garbage Land: On the Secret Trail of Trash.* New York: Little, Brown, 2005.

Rubin, Julius. "The Limits of Agricultural Progress in the Nineteenth-Century South." *Agricultural History* 49 (April 1975): 362–373.

Runte, Alfred. *National Parks: The American Experience.* Rev. ed. Lincoln: Univ. of Nebraska Press, 1987.

Russell, Edmund. "'Speaking of Annihilation': Mobilizing for War Against Human and Insect Enemies." *Journal of American History* 82 (March 1996): 1505–1529.

————. *War and Nature: Fighting Humans and Insects with Chemicals from World War I to Silent Spring.* New York: Cambridge Univ. Press, 2001.

Sabin, Paul. *Crude Politics: The California Oil Market, 1900–1940.* Berkeley: Univ. of California Press, 2005.

Sackman, Douglas C. *Orange Empire: California and the Fruits of Eden.* Berkeley: Univ. of California Press, 2005.

Sahlins, Marshall. *Stone Age Economics.* New York: Aldine de Gruyter, 1972.

Sale, Kirkpatrick. *The Green Revolution: The American Environmental Movement, 1962–1992.* New York: Hill and Wang, 1993.

Salstrom, Paul. *Appalachia's Path to Dependency: Rethinking a Region's Economic History, 1730–1940.* Lexington: Univ. of Kentucky Press, 1994.

Sandweiss, Stephen. "The Social Construction of Environmental Justice." In *Environmental Injustices, Political Struggles: Race, Class, and the Environment*, edited by David E. Camacho. Durham, NC: Duke Univ. Press, 1998.

Sauer, Carl Ortwin. *Sixteenth Century North America: The Land and the People as Seen by the Europeans.* Berkeley: Univ. of California Press, 1971.

Sawyer, Richard C. *To Make a Spotless Orange: Biological Control in California.* Ames: Iowa State Univ. Press, 1996.

Schell, Orville. *Modern Meat*. New York: Random House, 1984.

Schlosser, Eric. *Fast Food Nation: The Dark Side of the All-American Meal*. Boston: Houghton Mifflin, 2001.

Schrepfer, Susan R. *The Fight to Save the Redwoods: A History of Environmental Reform, 1917–1978*. Madison: Univ. of Wisconsin Press, 1983.

Schrepfer, Susan R., and Philip Scranton, eds. *Industrializing Organisms: Introducing Evolutionary History*. New York: Routledge, 2004.

Scott, James C. *Weapons of the Weak: Everyday Forms of Peasant Resistance*. New Haven, CT: Yale Univ. Press, 1985.

Seftel, Howard. "Government Regulation and the Rise of the California Fruit Industry: The Entrepreneurial Attack on Fruit Pests, 1880–1920." *Business History Review* 59 (Autumn 1985): 369–402.

Sellars, Richard West. *Preserving Nature in the National Parks: A History*. New Haven, CT: Yale Univ. Press, 1997.

Sellers, Christopher C. *Hazards of the Job: From Industrial Disease to Environmental Health Science*. Chapel Hill: Univ. of North Carolina Press, 1997.

Shabecoff, Philip. *A Fierce Green Fire: The American Environmental Movement*. New York: Hill and Wang, 1993.

Shah, Sonia. *Crude: The Story of Oil*. New York: Seven Stories Press, 2004.

Sherow, James Earl. *Watering the Valley: Development Along the High Plains Arkansas River, 1870–1950*. Lawrence: Univ. Press of Kansas, 1990.

Shiva, Vandana. *Stolen Harvest: The Hijacking of the Global Food Supply*. Cambridge, MA: South End, 2000.

———. *The Violence of the Green Revolution: Third World Agriculture, Ecology and Politics*. London: Zed, 1991.

———. "War Against Nature and the People of the South." In *Views from the South: The Effects of Globalization and the WTO on Third World Countries*, edited by Sarah Anderson. N.p.: Food First Books and the International Forum on Globalization, 2000.

Shoemaker, Nancy. *A Strange Likeness: Becoming Red and White in Eighteenth-Century North America*. New York: Oxford Univ. Press, 2004.

Silver, Timothy. *A New Face on the Countryside: Indians, Colonists, and Slaves in South Atlantic Forests, 1500–1800*. New York: Cambridge Univ. Press, 1990.

Sinclair, Upton. *The Jungle*. Reprint. New York: Bantam, 1981.

Skaggs, Jimmy M. *The Great Guano Rush: Entrepreneurs and American Overseas Expansion*. New York: St. Martin's Press, 1994.

———. *Prime Cut: Livestock Raising and Meatpacking in the United States, 1607–1983*. College Station: Texas A&M Press, 1986.

Slade, Giles. *Made to Break: Technology and Obsolescence in America*. Cambridge, MA: Harvard Univ. Press, 2006.

Smalley, Andrea L. *Wild by Nature: North American Animals Confront Colonization*. Baltimore: Johns Hopkins Univ. Press, 2017.

Smil, Vaclav. *Enriching the Earth: Fritz Haber, Carl Bosch, and the Transformation of World Food Production*. Cambridge, MA: MIT Press, 2001.

Smith, Barbara Clark. *The Freedoms We Lost: Consent and Resistance in Revolutionary America*. New York: New Press, 2010.

Smith, David C., Harold W. Borns, W. R. Baron, and Anne E. Bridges. "Climatic Stress and Maine Agriculture, 1785–1885." In *Climate and History: Studies in Past Climates and Their Impact on Man*, edited by T. M. L. Wigley, M. J. Ingram, and G. Farmer. Cambridge: Cambridge Univ. Press, 1981.

Smith, David C., and Anne E. Bridges. "The Brighton Market: Feeding Nineteenth-Century Boston." *Agricultural History* 56 (January 1982): 3–21.

Smith, Henry Nash. *Virgin Land: The American West as Symbol and Myth.* Cambridge, MA: Harvard Univ. Press, 1950.

Smith, Ted, David A. Sonnenfeld, and David Naguib Pellow. *Challenging the Chip: Labor Rights and Environmental Justice in the Global Electronics Industry.* Philadelphia: Temple Univ. Press, 2006.

Smits, David D. "The Frontier Army and the Destruction of the Buffalo: 1865–1883." *Western Historical Quarterly* 25 (Autumn 1994): 313–338.

Spann, Edward K. *The New Metropolis: New York City, 1840–1857.* New York: Columbia Univ. Press, 1981.

Spence, Clark C. *The Rainmakers: American "Pluviculture" to World War II.* Lincoln: Univ. of Nebraska Press, 1980.

Spence, Mark David. *Dispossessing the Wilderness: Indian Removal and the Making of the National Parks.* New York: Oxford Univ. Press, 1999.

Stahle, David W., Malcolm K. Cleaveland, Dennis B. Blanton, Matthew D. Therrell, and David A. Gray. "The Lost Colony and Jamestown Droughts." *Science* 280 (April 24, 1998): 564–567.

Starr, Kevin. *Inventing the Dream: California Through the Progressive Era.* New York: Oxford Univ. Press, 1985.

Steffen, Will, Wendy Broadgate, Lisa Deutsch, Owen Gaffney, and Cornelia Ludwig. "The Trajectory of the Anthropocene: The Great Acceleration." *Anthropocene Review* 2 (January 2015): 81–98.

Steffen, Will, Paul J. Crutzen, and John R. McNeill. "The Anthropocene: Are Humans Now Overwhelming the Great Forces of Nature?" *Ambio* 36 (December 2007): 614–621.

Steffen, Will, Angelina Sanderson, Peter Tyson, Jill Jäger, Pamela Matson, Berrien Moore, Frank Oldfied, et al. *Global Change and the Earth System: A Planet Under Pressure.* Berlin: Springer, 2005.

Stegner, Wallace. *Beyond the Hundredth Meridian: John Wesley Powell and the Second Opening of the West.* Boston: Houghton Mifflin, 1954.

Steinberg, Ted. *Acts of God: The Unnatural History of Natural Disaster in America.* 2d ed. New York: Oxford Univ. Press, 2006.

———. *American Green: The Obsessive Quest for the Perfect Lawn.* New York: W. W. Norton, 2006.

———. "Can Capitalism Save the Planet? On the Origins of Green Liberalism." *Radical History Review* 107 (Spring 2010): 7–24.

———. "Down to Earth: Nature, Agency, and Power in History." *American Historical Review* 107 (June 2002): 798–820.

———. "An Ecological Perspective on the Origins of Industrialization." *Environmental Review* 10 (Winter 1986): 261–276.

———. *Gotham Unbound: The Ecological History of Greater New York.* New York: Simon & Schuster, 2014.

———. *Nature Incorporated: Industrialization and the Waters of New England.* New York: Cambridge Univ. Press, 1991.

———. *Slide Mountain, or the Folly of Owning Nature.* Berkeley: Univ. of California Press, 1995.

Steinhart, Peter. *The Company of Wolves.* New York: Vintage, 1995.

Stewart, Mart A. *"What Nature Suffers to Groe": Life, Labor, and Landscape on the Georgia Coast, 1680–1920.* Athens: Univ. of Georgia Press, 1996.

———. "'Whether Wast, Deodand, or Stray': Cattle, Culture, and the Environment in Early Georgia." *Agricultural History* 65 (Summer 1991): 1–28.

Stiffarm, Lenore A., and Phil Lane, Jr. "The Demography of Native North America: A Question of American Indian Survival." In *The State of Native America: Genocide, Colonization, and Resistance,* edited by M. Annette Jaimes. Boston: South End, 1992.

Stilgoe, John R. *Common Landscape of America, 1580–1845.* New Haven, CT: Yale Univ. Press, 1982.

Stoll, Steven. *The Fruits of Natural Advantage: Making the Industrial Countryside in California.* Berkeley: Univ. of California Press, 1998.

——. *Larding the Lean Earth: Soil and Society in Nineteenth-Century America.* New York: Hill and Wang, 2002.

Stradling, David. *Making Mountains: New York City and the Catskills.* Seattle: Univ. of Washington Press, 2007.

——. *Smokestacks and Progressives: Environmentalists, Engineers, and Air Quality in America, 1881–1951.* Baltimore: Johns Hopkins Univ. Press, 1999.

Strasser, Susan. "'The Convenience Is Out of This World': The Garbage Disposer and American Consumer Culture." In *Getting and Spending: European and American Consumer Societies in the Twentieth Century,* edited by Susan Strasser, Charles McGovern, and Matthias Judt. New York: Cambridge Univ. Press, 1998.

——. *Satisfaction Guaranteed: The Making of the American Mass Market.* New York: Pantheon, 1989.

——. *Waste and Want: A Social History of Trash.* New York: Metropolitan, 1999.

Strickland, Arvarh E. "The Strange Affair of the Boll Weevil: The Pest as Liberator." *Agricultural History* 68 (Spring 1994): 157–168.

Strickland, John Scott. "Traditional Culture and Moral Economy: Social and Economic Change in the South Carolina Low Country, 1865–1910." In *The Countryside in the Age of Capitalist Transformation,* edited by Steven Hahn and Jonathan Prude. Chapel Hill: Univ. of North Carolina Press, 1985.

Strom, Claire. "Texas Fever and the Dispossession of the Southern Yeoman Farmer." *Journal of Southern History* 66 (February 2000): 49–74.

Sullivan, Robert. *The Meadowlands: Wilderness Adventures at the Edge of a City.* New York: Scribner, 1998.

Sutter, Paul. *Driven Wild: How the Fight Against Automobiles Launched the Modern Wilderness Movement.* Seattle: Univ. of Washington Press, 2002.

——. "Driven Wild: The Intellectual and Cultural Origins of Wilderness Advocacy During the Interwar Years." Ph.D. diss., Univ. of Kansas, 1997.

Tarr, Joel A. "A Note on the Horse as an Urban Power Source." *Journal of Urban History* 25 (March 1999): 434–448.

——. *The Search for the Ultimate Sink: Urban Pollution in Historical Perspective.* Akron, OH: Univ. of Akron Press, 1996.

Taylor, Alan. *American Colonies: The Settling of North America.* New York: Penguin, 2001.

——. "'The Hungry Year': 1789 on the Northern Border of Revolutionary America." In *Dreadful Visitations: Confronting Natural Catastrophe in the Age of Enlightenment,* edited by Alessa Johns. New York: Routledge, 1999.

——. *Liberty Men and Great Proprietors: The Revolutionary Settlement on the Maine Frontier.* Chapel Hill: Univ. of North Carolina Press, 1990.

——. "Unnatural Inequalities: Social and Environmental Histories." *Environmental History* 1 (October 1996): 6–19.

——. "'Wasty Ways': Stories of American Settlement." *Environmental History* 3 (July 1998): 291–310.

Taylor, Joseph E., III. *Making Salmon: An Environmental History of the Northwest Fisheries Crisis.* Seattle: Univ. of Washington Press, 1999.

Terrie, Philip G. "Recent Work in Environmental History." *American Studies International* 27 (October 1989): 42–65.

Teyssot, Georges, ed. *The American Lawn.* New York: Princeton Architectural Press, 1999.

Thompson, E. P. *Customs in Common: Studies in Traditional Popular Culture.* New York: New Press, 1991.

Tober, James A. *Who Owns the Wildlife? The Political Economy of Conservation in Nineteenth Century America.* Westport, CT: Greenwood, 1981.

Tokar, Brian. *Earth for Sale: Reclaiming Ecology in the Age of Corporate Greenwash.* Boston: South End Press, 1997.

Trimble, Stanley Wayne. *Man-Induced Soil Erosion on the Southern Piedmont, 1700–1970.* Ankeny, IA: Soil Conservation Society of America, 1974.

————. "Perspectives on the History of Soil Erosion Control in the Eastern United States." *Agricultural History* 59 (April 1985): 162–180.

Tucker, Richard P. *Insatiable Appetite: The United States and the Ecological Degradation of the Tropical World.* Berkeley: Univ. of California Press, 2000.

Tucker, Richard P., and Edmund Russell. *Natural Enemy, Natural Ally: Toward an Environmental History of Warfare.* Corvallis: Oregon State Univ. Press, 2004.

Tyrrell, Ian. *True Gardens of the Gods: Californian-Australian Environmental Reform, 1860–1930.* Berkeley: Univ. of California Press, 1999.

Vaught, David. *Cultivating California: Growers, Specialty Crops, and Labor, 1875–1920.* Baltimore: Johns Hopkins Univ. Press, 1999.

Verchick, Robert R. M. "The Commerce Clause, Environmental Justice, and the Interstate Garbage Wars." *Southern California Law Review* 70 (July 1997): 1239–1310.

————. "In a Greener Voice: Feminist Theory and Environmental Justice." *Harvard Women's Law Journal* 19 (Spring 1996): 23–88.

Vickers, Daniel. "Competency and Competition: Economic Culture in Early America." *William and Mary Quarterly* 47 (January 1990): 3–29.

Vidal, John. *McLibel: Burger Culture on Trial.* New York: New Press, 1997.

Vileisis, Ann. *Discovering the Unknown Landscape: A History of America's Wetlands.* Washington, DC: Island Press, 1997.

Vitousek, Peter M., Harold A. Mooney, Jane Lubchenco, and Jerry M. Melillo. "Human Domination of Earth's Ecosystems." *Science* 277 (July 25, 1997): 494–499.

Wallerstein, Immanuel. *Historical Capitalism.* New York: Verso, 1983.

Wallock, Leonard. "The Myth of the Master Builder: Robert Moses, New York, and the Dynamics of Metropolitan Development Since World War II." *Journal of Urban History* 17 (August 1991): 339–362.

Ward, G. M, P. L. Knox, and B. W. Hobson. "Beef Production Options and Requirements for Fossil Fuel." *Science* 198 (October 21, 1977): 265–271.

Ward, Geoffrey C. *The Civil War.* New York: Vintage, 1990.

Warren, Louis S. *The Hunter's Game: Poachers and Conservationists in Twentieth-Century America.* New Haven, CT: Yale Univ. Press, 1997.

Warrick, Richard A. "Drought in the US Great Plains: Shifting Social Consequences?" In *Interpretations of Calamity,* edited by K. Hewitt. Boston: Allen and Unwin, 1983.

Watkins, James L. *King Cotton: A Historical and Statistical Review, 1790 to 1908.* Reprint ed. New York: Negro Universities Press, 1969.

Watson, Harry L. "'The Common Rights of Mankind': Subsistence, Shad, and Commerce in the Early Republican South." *Journal of American History* 83 (June 1996): 13–43.

Weart, Spencer R. *The Discovery of Global Warming.* Cambridge, MA: Harvard Univ. Press, 2003.

Webb, Walter Prescott. *The Great Plains.* Boston: Ginn, 1931.

Weiman, David F. "The Economic Emancipation of the Non-Slaveholding Class: Up-country Farmers in the Georgia Cotton Economy." *Journal of Economic History* 45 (March 1985): 71–93.

Weir, David, and Mark Schapiro. *Circle of Poison: Pesticides and People in a Hungry World.* Oakland, CA: Institute for Food and Development Policy, 1981.

West, Elliott. *The Contested Plains: Indians, Goldseekers, and the Rush to Colorado.* Lawrence: Univ. Press of Kansas, 1998.

————. *The Way to the West: Essays on the Central Plains.* Albuquerque: Univ. of New Mexico Press, 1995.

Wheeler, David L. "The Blizzard of 1886 and Its Effect on the Range Cattle Industry in the Southern Plains." *Southwestern Historical Quarterly* 94 (January 1991): 415–432.

White, Harvey L. "Race, Class, and Environmental Hazards." In *Environmental Injustices, Political Struggles: Race, Class, and the Environment,* edited by David E. Camacho. Durham, NC: Duke Univ. Press, 1998.

White, Richard. "American Environmental History: The Development of a New Historical Field." *Pacific Historical Review* 54 (August 1985): 297–335.

————. "Animals and Enterprise." In *The Oxford History of the American West,* edited by Clyde A. Milner II, Carol A. O'Connor, and Martha A. Sandweiss. New York: Oxford Univ. Press, 1994.

————. "'Are You an Environmentalist or Do You Work for a Living?' Work and Nature." In *Uncommon Ground: Rethinking the Human Place in Nature,* edited by William Cronon. New York: W. W. Norton, 1996.

————. "Environmental History, Ecology, and Meaning." *Journal of American History* 76 (March 1990): 1111–1116.

————. *"It's Your Misfortune and None of My Own": A New History of the American West.* Norman: Univ. of Oklahoma Press, 1991.

————. *Land Use, Environment, and Social Change: The Shaping of Island County, Washington.* Seattle: Univ. of Washington Press, 1980.

————. *The Organic Machine: The Remaking of the Columbia River.* New York: Hill and Wang, 1995.

————. *The Roots of Dependency: Subsistence, Environment, and Social Change Among the Choctaws, Pawnees, and Navajos.* Lincoln: Univ. of Nebraska Press, 1983.

White, Richard, and William Cronon. "Ecological Change and Indian-White Relations." In *Handbook of North American Indians,* edited by William C. Sturtevant. Washington, DC: Smithsonian Institution Press, 1988.

Whitt, Laurie Anne. "Indigenous Peoples, Intellectual Property and the New Imperial Science." *Oklahoma City Univ. Law Review* 23 (Spring/Summer 1998): 211–259.

Whyte, William H. *The Last Landscape.* Garden City, NY: Doubleday, 1968.

Wicander, Reed, and James S. Monroe. *Historical Geology: Evolution of the Earth and Life Through Time.* 2d ed. Minneapolis, MN: West, 1993.

Wigley, Mark. "The Electric Lawn." In *The American Lawn,* edited by Georges Teyssot. New York: Princeton Architectural Press, 1999.

Wilcove, David S. *The Condor's Shadow: The Loss and Recovery of Wildlife in America.* New York: Freeman, 1999.

Wilkins, David E. *American Indian Sovereignty and the U.S. Supreme Court: The Masking of Justice.* Austin: Univ. of Texas Press, 1997.

Williams, Michael. *Americans and Their Forests: A Historical Geography.* New York: Cambridge Univ. Press, 1989.

Willis, Susan. *A Primer for Daily Life.* London: Routledge, 1991.

Wilson, Alexander. *The Culture of Nature: North American Landscape from Disney to the Exxon Valdez.* Cambridge, MA: Blackwell, 1992.

Wines, Richard A. *Fertilizer in America: From Waste Recycling to Resource Exploitation.* Philadelphia: Temple Univ. Press, 1985.

Wirth, John D. *Smelter Smoke in North America: The Politics of Transborder Pollution*. Lawrence: Univ. Press of Kansas, 2000.

Woeste, Victoria Saker. *The Farmer's Benevolent Trust: Law and Agricultural Cooperation in Industrial America, 1865–1945*. Chapel Hill: Univ. of North Carolina Press, 1998.

Wolf, Eric R. *Europe and the People Without History*. Berkeley: Univ. of California Press, 1982.

Wood, Ellen Meiksins. *The Origins of Capitalism: A Longer View*. London: Verso, 2002.

Wood, Peter H. *Black Majority: Negroes in Colonial South Carolina from 1670 Through the Stono Rebellion*. New York: Alfred A. Knopf, 1974.

Woodward, C. Vann. *Origins of the New South, 1877–1913*. Baton Rouge: Louisiana State Univ. Press, 1951.

Worster, Donald. *Dust Bowl: The Southern Plains in the 1930s*. New York: Oxford Univ. Press, 1979.

———, ed. *The Ends of the Earth: Perspectives on Modern Environmental History*. New York: Cambridge Univ. Press, 1988.

———. "History as Natural History: An Essay on Theory and Method." *Pacific Historical Review* 53 (February 1984): 1–19.

———. *Nature's Economy: A History of Ecological Ideas*. Reprint. New York: Cambridge Univ. Press, 1985.

———. *A River Running West: The Life of John Wesley Powell*. New York: Oxford Univ. Press, 2001.

———. *Rivers of Empire: Water, Aridity, and the Growth of the American West*. New York: Pantheon, 1985.

———. "Seeing Beyond Culture." *Journal of American History* 76 (March 1990): 1142–1147.

———. *Shrinking the Earth: The Rise and Decline of American Abundance*. New York: Oxford Univ. Press, 2016.

———. "A Tapestry of Change: Nature and Culture on the Prairie." In *The Inhabited Prairie*, photographed and compiled by Terry Evans. Lawrence: Univ. Press of Kansas, 1998.

———. "Transformations of the Earth: Toward an Agroecological Perspective in History." *Journal of American History* 76 (March 1990): 1087–1106.

———. *Under Western Skies: Nature and History in the American West*. New York: Oxford Univ. Press, 1992.

———. *An Unsettled Country: Changing Landscapes of the American West*. Albuquerque: Univ. of New Mexico Press, 1994.

———. *The Wealth of Nature: Environmental History and the Ecological Imagination*. New York: Oxford Univ. Press, 1993.

Wright, Gavin. *Old South, New South: Revolutions in the Southern Economy Since the Civil War*. New York: Basic Books, 1986.

———. *The Political Economy of the Cotton South: Households, Markets, and Wealth in the Nineteenth Century*. New York: W. W. Norton, 1978.

Wright, Susan. *Molecular Politics: Developing American and British Regulatory Policy for Genetic Engineering, 1972–1982*. Chicago: Univ. of Chicago Press, 1994.

Yago, Glenn. *The Decline of Transit: Urban Transportation in German and U.S. Cities, 1900–1970*. Cambridge: Cambridge Univ. Press, 1984.

Yeomans, Matthew. *Oil: Anatomy of an Industry*. New York: New Press, 2004.

Yergin, Daniel. *The Prize: The Epic Quest for Oil, Money and Power*. New York: Free Press, 1991.

Zimring, Carl A. *Cash for Your Trash: Scrap Recycling in America*. New Brunswick, NJ: Rutgers Univ. Press, 2005.

CREDITS

Figure 2.1:   Norman: University of Oklahoma Press
Figure 4.2:   The Grid (Hildegard Binder Johnson, Order upon the Land [New York: Oxford University Press, 1976]) By permission Oxford University Press.
Figure 4.4:   Wisconsin Historical Society Image ID #1784
Figure 4.5:   Minnesota Historical Society
Figure 5.1:   Clifton Waller Barrett Library of American Literature, University of Virginia Library
Figure 5.2:   Harvard University Press
Figure 5.3:   Georgia State University Library
Figure 6.2:   Forage Call (Lamont Buchanan, A Pictorial History of the Confederacy [New York: Crown, 1951]
Figure 7.3:   Great Smoky Mountains National Park
Figure 8.2:   Granger Collection
Figure 9.3:   USDA Forest Service
Figure 10.5:   Western Michigan University
Figure 12.2:   USDA Agricultural Division
Figure 13.3:   Getty Images
Figure 13.4:   Wisconsin Historical Society Image ID #1784
Figure 13.6:   University of Southern California
Figure 14.1:   Planned Obsolescence (General Motors Corp. Used with permission, GM Media Archives)
Figure 14.3:   Mary Chapman
Figure 14.4:   Basel Action Network
Figure 15.1:   Cuyahoga Fire, 1952 Special Collections, Cleveland State University Library
Figure 15.3:   National Park Service, Harpers Ferry, West Virginia
Figure 15.4:   Courtesy of the Library of Congress
Figure 15.5:   Special Collections, University of Buffalo
Figure 15.6:   Phil Howard, Michigan State University
Figure 15.7:   Silicon Valley Toxics Coalition, "Challenging the Chip"
Figure 16.2:   Paramount Vantage
Map P.1:   Map of North America (Adapted from Out of Many, vol. 2, Brief 3rd ed., A History of the American People, by Faragher, Buhle, Czitron, and Armitage, © 2001, by permission of Pearson Education, Inc., Upper Saddle River, NJ)
Graph 16.1:   Hockey Stick Graph (Climate Change 2001: The Scientific Basis. Contribution of Working Group I to the Third Assessment Report of the Intergovernmental Panel on Climate Change, Figure 1 of the Summary for Policymakers. Cambridge University Press.)

INDEX

Page numbers in **bold** refer to illustrations